AREA HANDBOOK

for

SOMALIA

Coauthors

Irving Kaplan

Margarita K. Dobert
James L. McLaughlin
Barbara Marvin
H. Mark Roth
Donald P. Whitaker

Research completed September 1976

Second Edition

Published 1977

(This handbook supersedes DA Pam 550-86, May 1969)

DA Pam 550-86

Library of Congress Cataloging in Publication Data

Kaplan, Irving, 1923-
   Area handbook for Somalia.

   "DA pam 550-86."
   "Prepared by Foreign Area Studies (FAS) of The American University."
   Bibliography: p. 351-372.
   Includes index.
   1. Somalia.   I. American University, Washington, D.C. Foreign Area Studies.   II. Title.
   DT401.K33   1977   309.1'67'73   77-5428

Second Edition, First Printing, 1977

For sale by the Superintendent of Documents, U.S. Government Printing Office
Washington, D.C. 20402

Stock No. 008-020-00646-7 / Catalog No. D 101.22:550-86/2

FOREWORD

This volume is one of a series of handbooks prepared by Foreign Area Studies (FAS) of The American University, designed to be useful to military and other personnel who need a convenient compilation of basic facts about the social, economic, political, and military institutions and practices of various countries. The emphasis is on objective description of the nation's present society and the kinds of possible or probable changes that might be expected in the future. The handbook seeks to present as full and as balanced an integrated exposition as limitations on space and research time permit. It was compiled from information available in openly published material. An extensive bibliography is provided to permit recourse to other published sources for more detailed information. There has been no attempt to express any specific point of view or to make policy recommendations. The contents of the handbook represent the work of the authors and FAS and do not represent the official view of the United States government.

An effort has been made to make the handbook as comprehensive as possible. It can be expected, however, that the material, interpretations, and conclusions are subject to modification in the light of new information and developments. Such corrections, additions, and suggestions for factual, interpretive, or other change as readers may have will be welcomed for use in future revisions. Comments may be addressed to:

The Director
Foreign Area Studies
The American University
5010 Wisconsin Avenue, N.W.
Washington, D.C. 20016

PREFACE

On October 21, 1969, some four months after research and writing on the first edition of the *Area Handbook for Somalia* were completed, a military coup overthrew the government in power. The leaders of the coup—senior military officers—established a regime under the Supreme Revolutionary Council (SRC) dedicated to revolutionary change not only in Somali political institutions but also in the society and economy, following a doctrine these leaders called scientific socialism. Although Somalia is a poor and sparsely settled country, its location òn the Horn of eastern Africa had always made it of some strategic importance. The area has also been of interest because of difficult relations with its immediate neighbors—Ethiopia, Kenya, and the French Territory of Afars and Issas (FTAI)—attributable to Somalia's stated ultimate goal of incorporating the Somali-populated portions of those territories into a greater Somalia. These factors alone may have warranted a revision of the first edition, but to them has been added the significant presence of the Soviet Union, which not only provides a good deal of material and technical aid and a large number of advisers but has established what appears to be a naval and missile base in the area, a situation that has excited much international controversy.

The *Area Handbook for Somalia* seeks to provide a compact and objective exposition of the dominant social, political, economic, and national security aspects of Somali society and to give the reader some idea of the forces at work at this time in Somalia's history. The authors have relied chiefly on published and unpublished documents and secondary sources, but knowledgeable individuals have been consulted on a number of points. Gaps in information occur, and sources differ in their interpretation of certain matters: such gaps and differences have been noted in the text. Where available books and articles provide amplification of detail and interpretation of the matter presented in a given chapter, the chapter's author has noted them in a final paragraph. Full references to these and other sources are to be found in the bibliography.

The handling of Somali names for places, persons, and other matters has proved to be a problem. Historically the spelling of such names and terms has varied with the extent of English or Italian influence, for example, Mogadishu and Mogadiscio for the country's capital.

There have also been variants within any one tradition since the Somali themselves and outsiders sought as best they could to approximate Somali sounds. There was also a tradition of rendering Somali in Arabic script. In 1973 the government decided that an existing Latin alphabet orthography (with minor modifications) was to be used to write Somali. Unfortunately no detailed list or dictionary using the new orthography was available as the handbook was being prepared. There are, moreover, indications that the new spelling is not always used consistently, particularly in the spelling of personal names. Where the new spelling is well established—as in the case of the names of administrative regions of Somalia—it has been used. Where an older spelling is well established for a well-known place, for example, Mogadishu (the new spelling is Muqdisho), it has been retained. Where the new spelling does not make the place name difficult to recognize, it has been used, for example, Hargeysa for the older Hargaysa (sometimes Hargeisa). In many other cases the decision has been arbitrary, but the spelling adopted has been consistently employed throughout the handbook.

An effort has been made to limit the use of foreign and technical terms. These have been briefly defined where they first appear in any chapter, or reference is made to the glossary, included in an appendix for the reader's convenience. Tons are metric unless otherwise specified.

The 1969 edition of the handbook was prepared by a team made up of Milena Choumenkovitch, Barbara Marvin, James L. McLaughlin, Harold D. Nelson, and Ernestine E. Rowland under the chairmanship of Irving Kaplan. Where appropriate, use has been made of materials from this earlier version.

The present study is a result of the joint efforts of a multidisciplinary team of researchers assisted by the support staff of Foreign Area Studies. The team was chaired by Irving Kaplan, who wrote chapter 1 and revised and updated chapter 2, prepared for the 1969 edition by James L. McLaughlin. Kaplan also coordinated the contributions of the other authors. Margarita K. Dobert wrote chapters 4, 5, and 6; James L. McLaughlin wrote chapters 8, 9, and 10; Barbara Marvin wrote chapters 12, 13, and 14; H. Mark Roth wrote chapters 15 and 16; and Donald P. Whitaker wrote chapters 3, 7, and 11.

COUNTRY PROFILE

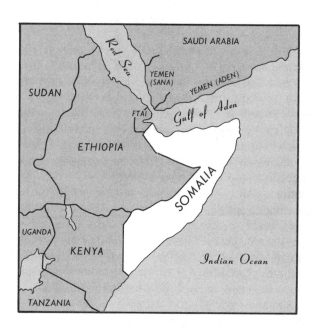

COUNTRY

Formal Name: Somali Democratic Republic.
Short Form: Somalia.
Term for Nationals: Somali.
Preindependence Political Status: British Somaliland attained independence June 26, 1960; Italian Somalia, from 1950 the Trust Territory of Somaliland under Italian Administration, attained independence July 1, 1960; two regions united on July 1, 1960, to form Republic of Somalia.
Capital: Mogadishu.

GEOGRAPHY

Size: Land area of 246,155 square miles (some Somali sources use total of about 262,000 square miles); sovereignty claimed over territorial waters up to 200 miles.

Topography: Generally flat plateau surfaces and plains predominate, the principal exception being rugged east-west ranges in far north that include Surud Ad, highest point at over 7,900 feet.

Climate: Continuously hot except at higher elevations in the north; two wet seasons bring erratic rainfall, largely from April to June and in October and November, averaging under twenty inches over most of country; droughts frequent; only two rivers in somewhat wetter southwest have permanent water flow.

SOCIETY

Population: Estimated at roughly 3.1 to 3.2 million within Somali territorial boundaries in 1975, growing at an estimated rate somewhere between 2.3 and 2.8 percent; predominantly rural; nomads and semi-nomads make up about three-fifths of total population.

Languages: Somali (for which a script was officially introduced in January 1973) spoken by all but a very few inhabitants. Several dialects, of which Common Somali is most widespread. English and Italian used in official documents and some newspapers. Arabic used by religious specialists and in some periodicals.

Ethnic Groups: All but a few nationals are ethnic Somali who are traditionally divided into Samaal (pastoral nomadic), about 75 percent, and Saab (sedentary or semisedentary in south on and between Juba and Shabelle rivers), about 20 percent. These in turn traditionally organized into descent groups of greater or lesser inclusiveness and size. Revolutionary government is trying to end significance of these descent groups in social and political matters and in law.

Religion: Somalia officially an Islamic state; most nationals are Sunni Muslims.

Education and Literacy: Modern education offered free at all levels; school attendance growing rapidly in mid-1970s; in settled areas shortage of places still remained a constraining factor at postprimary levels; mode of life greatly affected establishment of facilities and attendance among nomads. Introduction of new Somali script in early 1973 and massive literacy campaigns resulted in perhaps 60 percent of population possessing some degree of literacy by mid-1976.

Health: Weak modern medical infrastructure suffering from geographic imbalance, difficulty of caring for large mobile population, and shortage of medical personnel. Malaria, tuberculosis, parasitic and venereal infections, and childhood diseases are serious health problems, complicated by malnutrition and poor sanitary conditions.

GOVERNMENT AND POLITICS

Form: Until seizure of power by Marxist-influenced, Soviet-trained military leaders on October 21, 1969, Somalia was one of the developing world's few multiparty democracies. Takeover was fairly well received because of previous government's lack of progress in solving country's problems. After the coup, country governed by Supreme Revolutionary Council (SRC), composed of nineteen to twenty-five senior military officers. SRC, assisted by largely civilian cabinet, filled executive and legislative roles under presidency of former army commander Major General Mohamed Siad Barre. On July 1, 1976, SRC sponsored founding of Somali Socialist Revolutionary Party (SSRP): all SRC's functions passed to organs of the party, assisted by the government's new Council of Ministers. Government maintained total control over all means of public information, and public criticism of regime and its basic orientation was not tolerated.

Politics: Under the SSRP, as under the SRC, real control remained concentrated in the hands of President Siad and about ten other military and police officers. After formation of SSRP they held key posts in both the party executive and the Council of Ministers and were expected to continue to do so. Major change was that the new form opened the decisionmaking process to more civilian influences. Its founders saw the party primarily as a structure through which the ruling group's ideology could be effectively spread throughout the society. The ideology, labeled scientific socialism, was clearly indebted to but distinct from the Marxism-Leninism of the East European—particularly Soviet—and Asian communist states. Major political issues are hammered out within the leadership. Concerned primarily with conflicts over the speed of implementation of socialism and continuing rivalries among descent groups (clans and lineages), the significant elements in traditional sociopolitical order.

Administrative Divisions: Highly centralized government structure. Country divided into sixteen regions, each containing from three to seven districts—except for capital region, divided into fourteen quarters. Hierarchical structure of regional, district (or quarter), and village councils—most with members locally nominated but appointed by national government.

Legal System: Outwardly amalgam of British and Italian systems; Somali customary law has a small formal role, Islamic personal and family law a somewhat larger one. Four levels of courts honoring major guarantees of English law. However, those suspected or accused of often vague political offenses were subject to arbitrary arrest, detention, and trial by the separate National Security Court (NSC) system.

Major Features of International Relations: Significant issues: relations with immediate neighbors troubled greatly by Somalia's claims to major portions of their territories, based on the fact that these areas are inhabited principally by ethnic Somali. Strongly opposed to creation of United States military base in the eastern Africa-Indian Ocean area, despite the existence of Soviet military facilities on its own soil.

Membership and Treaties: Somali-Soviet civil and military cooperation carried out under joint treaty of July 1974. Only non-Arab member of the League of Arab States (Arab League). Member of the Organization of African Unity (OAU) and of its African Liberation Committee and the United Nations (UN) and most of its specialized agencies; associate member of the European Economic Community (EEC, also known as the Common Market) through the Lomé Convention.

ECONOMY

Salient Features: Among world's poorest countries; all data estimated: perhaps 70 percent of people at subsistence level in good years; 60 percent rely on stockraising, 15 to 20 percent on settled smallholder cultivation. Money income derived from exports of livestock and bananas from riverine plantations (once Italian, increasingly Somali owned).

Agriculture, Forestry, and Fishing: Stockraising and farming sustain population, export, and limited manufacturing. Sizable irrigation potential of two rivers hitherto exploited largely for bananas and sugar, henceforth also for food grain production on large state farms. Nomadic element, one of most predominant in sub-Saharan Africa, is subject of unplanned and some planned settlement. Stockraising increasingly exploited for cash income and government earnings. Fishing is basis of processing industry and export; fleet expanded mid-1970s. Forestry negligible.

Industry: Accounts for 6 percent of labor force, 8 percent of gross domestic product (GDP); yields development priority to rural sector. All large plants government operated; a number of small and medium-sized, Italian-owned plants also processing fish, meat, and crops.

Foreign Trade: Growing export earnings (from livestock, bananas, processed meat and fish, and hides and skins) outpaced by strong growth of import volume and prices. Resource gap amply filled by imports of development goods and food and other consumer imports; former and part of latter financed by net inflow of foreign grants and loans.

Electric Power: Installed capacity increased 96 percent from 1970 figure to 25,600 kilowatts in 1973, entirely dependent on imported fuel oil; hydroelectric capacity limited to five megawatts, to be produced by new Fanole power plant on Juba River by 1978.

Principal Aid Sources: Multilateral: European Development Fund (EDF), World Bank Group, and UN agencies. Bilateral: Arab members of Organization of Petroleum Exporting Countries (OPEC), People's Republic of China (PRC), Democratic People's Republic of Korea (North Korea), European members of Organization for Economic Cooperation and Development (OECD), and Soviet Union (not fully reported).

Currency: Somali shilling (see Glossary).

Fiscal Year: Corresponds to calendar year.

TRANSPORTATION AND COMMUNICATIONS

Roads: In 1975 there were 8,700 miles of dirt roads and tracks; 630 miles of gravel roads; 660 miles of asphalt-surfaced roads. The Development Program 1974-1978 called for an additional 1,000 miles of paved road. Much of the paved road is in the south. Most important projected segment is that from Belet Weyn in the south to Burao in the north.

Ports: Most important are Berbera on the northern coast and Mogadishu, Marka (Merca), and Kismayo on the southern coast. Others used for dhow trade and small boat fishing.

Airfields: Major (international standard) fields at Mogadishu and Hargeysa and a third being completed at Kismayo in 1976.

Telecommunications: Radio chief means of communication. Telephone linkage between major towns minimal but significant improvements projected.

NATIONAL SECURITY

Armed Forces: Army—20,000 air force—2,700; navy—300; active reserve—3,000; police—6,000. Voluntary service.

Major Tactical Units and Equipment: Army—six tank battalions, nine mechanized infantry battalions, five field artillery battalions; about 250 Soviet-built medium tanks. Air force—fifty-two combat aircraft; twenty-four MiG-21s, twenty-five earlier model MiGs; three short-range bombers. Navy—ten to twelve combat ships, mainly patrol craft; two with surface-to-surface missiles.

Military Budget: Sh100 million (US$15 million) in 1974. Approximately 5 percent of estimated 1972 gross national product (GNP).

Foreign Military Treaties: Twenty-year treaty with Soviet Union since 1974. Soviet Union provides matériel and financial and training support. Under separate arrangements Soviets construct and operate naval, missile, air, and communications facilities in Somalia.

SOMALIA
TABLE OF CONTENTS

xiii

LIST OF ILLUSTRATIONS

LIST OF TABLES

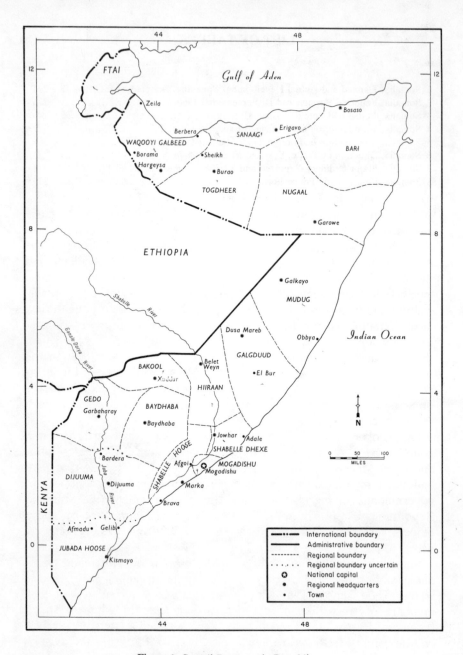

Figure 1. Somali Democratic Republic

SECTION I. SOCIAL

CHAPTER 1

GENERAL CHARACTER OF THE SOCIETY

When Somalia achieved independence in 1960, a parliamentary government—democratic in form and, in most respects, in substance and function—was established in a culturally, religiously, and linguistically homogeneous society of a little more than 2 million people. The new state incorporated two colonial territories, British Somaliland and the Trust Territory of Somaliland under Italian Administration (formerly Italian Somalia). The land was poor, and significant commercially exploitable resources were limited. As they had for centuries, most Somali relied for their livelihood exclusively or primarily on pastoral nomadism (or seminomadism) in a hard, arid land. A minority on the Juba and Shabelle rivers and on the plain between them in the south and a still smaller number in the northwest depended for all or part of their subsistence on cultivation, irrigated or rain fed. Numbers of Somali had some cash income from sale of livestock and from a few cash crops.

On October 21, 1969, the parliamentary regime was overthrown in a coup led by a group of senior military officers, apparently much influenced by Marxist notions. Initially, however, they argued that they had been motivated by the increasing corruption and nepotism in government. Having changed the form of government, the Supreme Revolutionary Council (SRC) established and dominated by these officers set about to revolutionize the society and the economy as well.

Somalia's homogeneity and the people's sense of nationhood eliminated one of the obstacles to unity so common among new African states. Their sense of unity was heightened by an awareness that numbers of their Somali brethren were located in adjacent states (Ethiopia, Kenya, and French Somaliland—later the French Territory of Afars and Issas; Issas are Somali (see fig. 1). All Somali strongly supported unification in a greater Somalia, but they were divided with respect to how to go about it. A good deal of political energy and time went into attempts to deal with the question in the first seven years of independence and led to rather difficult relations and at times to direct conflict with Ethiopia and Kenya.

Although they shared a common culture, the Somali were divided into kin-based groups of greater or lesser inclusiveness and size. The

1

characteristic relationship between any two of these groups (even if they were included by virtue of real or putative common ancestry in a descent group of larger scale) was one of competition or, at best, temporary alliance vis-à-vis other groups. Other principles, above all that of contract (*heer*—see Glossary), modified or reinforced but rarely overrode that of descent.

Within each unit decisionmaking and the interpersonal relations of Somali adult males were characterized by democracy and equality. Those who had greater wealth in livestock or had shown themselves to be better warriors, wiser dispute-settlers, or convincing speakers (in a society that valued skill in the use of language in ordinary intercourse, oratory, and poetry) might carry greater weight; but every man was entitled to a voice in the clan or lineage council (*shir*). In any case every man had to earn his prestige. One might inherit a few more animals than another, but in this hard land he needed both good luck and ability to keep them.

Beginning in the colonial period sources of wealth, power, and prestige that had not been available in the traditional society emerged: a few Somali became full-time entrepreneurs in agriculture or trade on a larger scale than had once been common (there had always been Somali traders, but they had retained their base in subsistence agriculture or herding); others became politicians or bureaucrats. Often access to jobs in the bureaucracy or in the higher reaches of the political hierarchy was associated with, if not dependent on, a level of education uncommon among the Somali.

There were exceptions to the traditional ideology and practice of equality and democracy. The pastoral nomadic Somali looked down on the sedentary Somali, and both looked down on a few very small groups engaged in despised (and sometimes feared) occupations. Among the Saab in the Juba and Shabelle river areas lived small groups whose ancestors had preceded the Somali and had been conquered by or had submitted to them and become their clients, but even these groups participated to a greater or lesser degree in the political and religious life of the locally dominant Somali clan or lineage. In the late eighteenth and particularly in the nineteenth century Somali, of both Saab and Samaal origin, acquired slaves from the area south and west of present-day Somalia who cultivated the land for them. The descendants of these occupational castelike groups, of clients, and of slaves constituted a very small portion of the total population, and their status in law and in practice had improved during the colonial period (when the slaves were freed) and at independence. In any case the basic pattern of democracy and equality characteristic of the vast majority set the tone for Somali social and political life as the country approached independence.

Traditionally a distinction was made between most Somali males who, especially among the nomads, were conceived of as warriors

2

and a smaller number who devoted themselves to religion. All but a handful of Somali were Muslims and, beginning in the nineteenth century, almost all became at least nominal members of one of several religious orders (brotherhoods); but religious figures had a role that put them outside daily Somali life. The distinction between warriors and religious figures involved recognition of different functions but not inequality. In some cases religious figures, especially long-dead ones who figured in the genealogies of certain clans and founders of Somali branches of religious brotherhoods, came to be thought of as having great spiritual power and were revered as saints whose tombs became the sites of pilgrimages. In other cases religious figures became warriors as well or at least provided stimulation and ideological leadership for holy wars (jihads). Such was Sayyid Mohamed ibn Abdullah Hassan who, from the late nineteenth century to 1920 when he was killed, led sections of his people against the British (and the Ethiopians).

The significance of descent groups, the traditional patterns of competition for scarce resources and the shifting alliances among them, and the notions of equality and democracy—including the right to speak one's mind—were transferred with modifications to the national system. Among the modifications was an increasing emphasis on the descent group that is called by modern specialists the clan-family (and by older analysts, the tribe). The clan-family (of which there are six) is the largest named descent group in Somali society. Four—Darod, Isaq, Hawiya, and Dir—are said to be descended from Samaal and comprised the pastoral nomadic Somali, although small segments had come to rely in part on cultivation. Two—Digil and Rahanwein—are said to be descended from Saab and comprised the sedentary Somali on and between the Shabelle and Juba rivers. Each of these clan-families included a number of clans, and these in turn comprised lineages of descending size and genealogical depth.

The clan-families varied in size, but all were too large and dispersed to have social, political, and economic functions in the traditional order. Most of these functions were carried out at the clan or lineage level or by the groups based on contract, chiefly the dia-paying groups (the members of which specifically contracted among themselves to be responsible for paying and receiving compensation for homicide and sometimes for other wrongs) and the relatively short-lived confederations of clans or lineages (which sometimes cut across clan-family boundaries).

In the period leading to independence and in the first years after independence, however, the clan-families came to be the building blocks for political parties. Sometimes the parties were built of a single such block, sometimes of an alliance of two or more. To some extent these clan-families corresponded to more or less specific, regionally based interests (for example, those of the sedentary Somali),

3

but sometimes a clan-family was so large and widely dispersed that the interests of its component clans and lineages were quite diverse. In the context of clan-family competition, especially in the first years after independence, each unit sought to maintain a degree of cohesiveness; but as the diversity of interests within them became more apparent or was intensified by changes in the availability of resources —including opportunities in government—to clans and lineages within a clan-family, the significance of the largest of these units for politics diminished.

In the nine years between independence and the military coup of October 1969 Somali political life was marked by parliamentary government, multiparty competition for office at elections, and competition within the ruling party between elections. A large number of parties, most of them ephemeral and most of them representing a limited local or descent-group constituency, contested each election. A few, more widely or at least more strongly based, survived several elections. One, the Somali Youth League (SYL), came to be clearly dominant in the United Nations (UN) Trust Territory even before independence and remained so in Somalia as a whole until the coup of 1969.

It was quite common for many of those elected to parliament under other party labels to accede to the SYL after an election in the hope of gaining access to ministerial posts and other perquisites. Given the heterogeneity of SYL membership and the Somali assumption that government existed to provide citizens with resources and opportunities and given further that such resources and opportunities were scarce, intraparty competition for their allocation was continuous. Party leaders apparently found it necessary to see to it that members of parliament were given material compensation for their continued support. As time went on, the latter became increasingly accustomed to a range of personal perquisites in addition to whatever government help they could obtain for their constituents.

Although some of the leading figures in the SYL stressed Somali unity as opposed to clan-family and clan divisions, the party was careful to allocate important governmental posts on a descent-group basis; among other things the president and the prime minister were always of different clan-families. The Somali people expected this and interpreted intraparty and intragovernmental conflict in these rather than in ideological terms, a pattern that persisted into the revolutionary period despite the SRC's strong stand against what is called tribalism.

Its internal difficulties and conflicts notwithstanding, the parliamentary regime did make attempts to develop the country's economy—an extraordinarily difficult task given the low level at which it was forced to begin. Even in 1975, fifteen years after independence, Somalia was among the ten poorest countries on the UN's list of the twenty-five

4

poorest—its per capita gross domestic product (GDP) estimated at US$80. In the circumstances the prerevolutionary government sought foreign aid wherever it could get it.

A good deal of planning and a number of feasibility studies were undertaken with such foreign financial and technical aid, and some projects got under way. Progress was slow, however, in part because the parliamentary regime and its associated bureaucracy were inexperienced and inefficient and—as time went on—increasingly corrupt, in part because an adequate base in resources and skilled personnel was lacking. The parliamentary government was also reluctant to undertake strong steps that might lead to conflict it could not control. Nevertheless the planning and feasibility studies and the infrastructure and plant completed during this period provided a base on which the revolutionary regime was able to build, although that regime preferred to stress the shortcomings rather than the accomplishments of its predecessor.

Somalia's leaders at independence wanted foreign aid not only for economic development but also for military forces. Their aim of establishing a greater Somalia that would include Somali living in adjacent states had been incorporated in the constitution and put Somalia at odds with those states. Unable to obtain support for a projected 20,000-man army (much larger than those of other African states of comparable size) from the United States, to which it first applied, the parliamentary government turned to the Soviet Union, which was willing to provide matériel, advice, and training.

Prime Minister Mohamed Ibrahim Egal, who came to power in mid-1967, turned Somali relations with neighbors from confrontation and hostility to accommodation—without, however, abandoning the ultimate goal of a greater Somalia—but Soviet aid was retained, and the army continued to grow. Soviet influence was offset by the general pro-Western orientation of Egal and other Somali leaders and by United States and other Western aid for the national police force; but the army, its senior leaders much taken with Soviet political as well as military doctrine, had become the best organized and strongest institution in the state by 1969.

When the military took over, established the SRC, and abolished parties and parliament, it justified its actions on the grounds that the parliamentary government and the SYL were riddled with corruption and nepotism, had misused public funds, and had catered to tribal (descent-group) interests. These charges were given considerable support by the observations of detached foreign analysts. Although many ordinary Somali were aware of the corruption and nepotism, it is not clear that these facts alone turned them away from the prerevolutionary system. It was rather that system's failure to provide them with the resources and opportunities that they expected from it that led most Somali to accept the new regime without protest.

5

The SRC, consisting entirely of military officers led by Major General Mohamed Siad Barre as president of the republic, soon made it clear that it intended to establish a society and economy guided by what it called scientific socialism—the doctrine of Marx, Engels, and Lenin adapted to the exigencies of Somalia. In mid-1976 the SRC sponsored its own replacement, the Somali Socialist Revolutionary Party (SSRP), but the basic doctrine and the wielders of power remained the same.

Resistance and public criticism of the regime and its ultimate goals were not permitted, but Siad and his colleagues did allow some criticism of individuals and of specific policies. The SRC placed heavy emphasis on educating the people to accept socialist goals and specific programs. Indeed some programs were treated as educational ventures, intended to train the participants in a socialist way of life even if purely economic considerations had to be deemphasized to do so.

The SRC began in 1970 by nationalizing banking, insurance, electric power, oil distribution, and the already partly state-owned sugar estate and refinery at Jowhar. Most other large manufacturing establishments (for example, meat and tuna canneries and a textile plant) had been constructed with foreign aid under the parliamentary regime as state enterprises but had barely gotten under way when the coup took place. Not long afterward much wholesale and retail trade, including especially those enterprises concerned with export and import, was taken over by the state. Some foreign-owned (chiefly Italian) firms remained in mid-1976, but most foreign and many Somali industrial and commercial enterprises were in state hands.

The SRC also placed heavy emphasis on self-help and what it called crash programs to develop social and economic infrastructure: roads, irrigation facilities, schools, and the like. All government employees and, for a time, persons employed by private firms were urged to "volunteer" to help in these activities, and sanctions for failing to do so sometimes were severe. At the same time the SRC introduced a number of austerity measures, chief of which was a reduction in pay for the civil and military services and a development levy on the pay of employees of private firms and public entities. Restraint in current expenditure and a notable improvement in the mobilization of fiscal revenue resulted in a greatly increased internal contribution to development. These resources and the regime's emphasis on self-reliance notwithstanding, Somalia continued to require major foreign aid to finance all capital imports and a share of consumption imports. After 1973 current spending was less effectively restrained as the civil service and the army grew and as pensions and other social services required increased current maintenance.

Most of Somalia's industrial plant and commercial activity was based on the processing and distribution of crops and animal products. First priority was therefore to be given to crop farming—partic-

6

ularly on state farms—and stockraising. The development of cultivation was to be accomplished primarily by the expansion of acreage and employment on state farm and by intensive spending on irrigation but in part by developing services to the great majority of farmers who remained smallholders.

The government anticipated and planned for changes in the social organization of production. The first step was the establishment of multipurpose cooperatives: each family was to retain its own land and stock, but such other services and activities as marketing and control of machinery were to be carried out in common. This was to be followed by a kind of collective farming reminiscent of that prevailing in the Soviet Union: all acreage save relatively small plots granted to each family was to be pooled and farmed collectively.

The first stage was barely under way in the mid-1970s, and it was not clear how soon cooperatives would encompass the great majority of cultivators and be fully engaged in all of the planned activities. A 1974 law established the second stage as an ultimate goal to be realized once the earlier stages had been successfully completed, the values of collectivism ingrained, and mutual trust established.

The relationship of cooperatives to the traditional modes of social organization and tenure has been addressed by the government to some extent. In long-settled land in the area of the Juba and Shabelle rivers and in the northwest, a given lineage allocated land to its component families or to attached client lineages of non-Somali or to Somali who were not members of the dominant lineage. The parliamentary regime had, in principle at least, ended the status of clientship, and the revolutionary regime was attempting in a variety of ways to minimize the significance of descent and *dia*-paying groups in political and legal matters, but it is not clear how it views the economic functions of lineages and clans. In any case cooperatives are rare in these areas. On the settlement projects where nomads had agreed to turn to crop farming after the great 1974-75 drought, the government has made a point of mixing families of different clans and lineages in the same entity.

It has been estimated that at independence as much as 80 percent of the population was wholly dependent on livestock for subsistence. The attractions of the towns and, to a lesser extent, the unplanned permanent conversion of nomads or seminomads to sedentary cultivation (often in response to drought that depleted their herds) diminished the proportion by the early 1970s to an estimated 60 percent.

Drought has been endemic in Somalia and has always led to temporary abandonment of pastoralism by those who suffered greatest losses. (Conversely Somali who had come to rely in part on cultivation were sometimes forced by local conditions—lack of rain or lack of flooding—to forego crops and local forage for a time and take their livestock elsewhere.) In 1974 and early 1975, however, an extraordi-

7

nary drought led to an extensive loss of livestock and famine for large numbers of nomads. By the spring of 1975 an estimated 250,000 were settled and fed in relief camps, and another 500,000 were given food outside the camps. The food grain harvests also failed, and many cultivators required help. As the drought ended, many pastoralists trekked north to return to herding, but more than 100,000—probably those whose losses had been greatest—agreed to the government's offer to resettle on farms where they were to become cultivators; and more than 15,000 were settled on the coast in an effort to convert them to fishermen.

How permanent such changes would be is open to question as are the precise intentions of the regime with respect to settling the nomads. In one of its early development plans the parliamentary government had referred to the need to make them sedentary. Apparently it was hoped that such settlement would alleviate overgrazing, increase the cultivation and production of food crops, allow the provision of educational and other services to those who had been nomads, and tie greater numbers of Somali more closely to the national society. In any case no firm plans were made—in part because converting nomads to the idea of cultivation, which they looked down upon, or to fishing, which they despised, would have been difficult if not impossible without coercion; moreover, sedentarization would have required an input of material and technical aid that the government was unable to provide.

Like the parliamentary government, the revolutionary regime wished to increase the production of food crops and was perhaps more concerned with establishing firmer control over the nomadic population—always a difficult task. When the 1974-75 drought made large numbers of nomads dependent upon the government to the point that they could contemplate cultivation and even fishing as a mode of life, the SRC noted that the necessary settlement of nomads and their conversion to cultivation made possible the partial realization of the government's ultimate objective of settling them.

In fact neither of the revolutionary regime's two development plans, including that for the 1974-78 period, specifically referred to sedentarization. They were, however, deeply concerned with increasing food crop production, to be accomplished largely through the expansion of state farms. These farms were to be manned in good part by young nomads who were to be trained in farming skills. Plans for improving stockraising and for increased sale of stock to the expanding government processing and export programs assumed, however, that many Somali would remain exclusively dependent on herding. Even so, traditional wide-ranging nomadic itineraries would be increasingly constrained by controlled rotation and regeneration of range in specific areas and by government holding grounds and ranches. If, as international lenders recommend, further planning is oriented to mixed (crop and livestock) farming, the numbers of pastoral nomads will be further diminished.

As part of its effort to educate Somali for economic development and a socialist way of life, the SRC took a step in 1973 that had been contemplated by the parliamentary regime but put off, probably because it required a choice that would have generated political conflict: the government decided on a Latin orthography for Somali and instituted a crash program to make as many people as possible literate in it. Until that decision was made, a Somali had to learn another language—English, Italian, or Arabic—in order to be able to read and write. According to outside observers the results of the crash program were quite satisfactory, and the country's small printing industry was fully engaged in producing textbooks and other reading material in the new script. It remained to be seen, however, whether a still largely nomadic and seminomadic population would have the opportunity and the stimulus to retain this new literacy.

In addition to changes in economic institutions and social services, including education, that may in time generate changes in the social structure, the revolutionary government has also carried out direct assaults on that structure. As may be expected of a regime that professes a variant of Marxist-Leninist doctrine, there have been the usual attacks on the bourgeoisie—government officials, traders, some of the wealthier artisans, the few professionals and large landholders —but it was recognized that Somali were not substantially differentiated by virtue of their relations to the means of production. The significant cleavages were those among clan-families, clans, and lineages. Of lesser significance but with traditional roots were the differences between patrons and clients, outlawed in principle but still governing attitudes if not material relations, and the disdainful way in which certain low status groups were treated or looked upon. All Somali were now to call each other comrade (*jalle*).

One important status difference was that between men and women. Equality in traditional Somali society and in the first decade of independence was restricted to men. The SRC began by urging women to take part in a variety of activities and to speak up at meetings. Then in early January 1975 a law was promulgated (and announced by President Siad) that gave women equal rights in a number of respects, particularly that of inheritance. Islamic law granted daughters half the share given sons in the estate of their father; Somali customary law ignored even that requirement. Siad, in announcing the change, argued that Islamic law foresaw ultimate equality and that only a few reactionary religious leaders would oppose it. A few religious leaders did in fact oppose it and were met by the ultimate sanction: in late January 1975 ten of them were executed, the largest group to suffer death since the military takeover.

9

President Siad and others had stressed the compatibility of Islam with scientific socialism and had indeed suggested that Islam implied the goals that the application of scientific socialism would realize. The executions of the religious leaders may therefore be seen as a warning to this important category of persons who were potential nuclei of resistance to the regime.

Another attack on the traditional system was the outlawing of *dia* for homicide. The parliamentary regime had made homicide a crime against the state, but it had also permitted the *dia*-paying groups to collect compensation in addition to the punishment meted out by the state, and it permitted these groups to sue for compensation even if the state had acquitted the defendant. The SRC outlawed this and stressed that individuals alone were to be held responsible for the wrongs they committed. *Dia*-paying groups were sometimes involved (if their contracts called for it) in payments for assault and other wrongs. They had also adapted to modern developments by taking on responsibility for payments for such accidents as automobile deaths and injuries. It is not altogether clear that these activities have also been outlawed but, given the government's emphasis on individual responsibility and its concern to break up traditional structures, it is likely that they will be.

Descent groups were also involved in a wide range of religious rites and life-cycle ceremonies, particularly marriages and funerals. In 1973 the municipal council of Mogadishu forbade such ceremonies on the grounds that they stressed lineage and clan solidarity. As of mid-1976 this prohibition had not been extended to other areas, but Mogadishu is after all the one place where many clans and lineages are represented.

The rhetoric and behavior of the revolutionary government raises the question of the extent to which it is tied to or dependent upon other states professing a similar doctrine, particularly the Soviet Union. The Somali army, so important to the revolutionary government not only because it is the bulwark of that government but also because of its significance in the country's relations with its neighbors, is trained and supplied almost exclusively by the Soviet Union, which in the early and mid-1970s was the source of roughly a quarter of Somalia's foreign aid. In fact this was not significantly different from the proportion supplied by the Soviets in the prerevolutionary period, but the Soviet presence is much larger—several thousand in the mid-1970s as opposed to a few hundred before the revolution—and they have a greater role as advisers, particularly among the military.

A good deal of aid, material and technical, has been supplied by other states and by international agencies, however. Somalia has made a point of seeking and getting aid and advise from Asian communist states, notably the Democratic People's Republic of Korea

(North Korea) and the People's Republic of China (PRC). The PRC has a contingent in the country engaged in roadbuilding, and President Siad has made a point of lauding its aid. Except for Italy and the Federal Republic of Germany (West Germany), the Western states have made their contributions through various international agencies—the United Nations, the World Bank Group (see Glossary), the European Economic Community (EEC, also known as the Common Market), and others. The aid given by these agencies is substantial. Also substantial is the aid given or promised as of mid-1976 by a number of Arab states. Although Somalia is not ethnically or linguistically Arab, it is Muslim and has been otherwise influenced by Arabic culture. In 1974 it became a member of the League of Arab States (Arab League).

In addition to Soviet aid and the presence of large numbers of Soviet citizens—whether military or other—in Somalia, the Soviet Union has constructed a naval and missile base at Berbera on the Gulf of Aden and, by all accounts, controls the base and access to it. Somalia denies that what exists at Berbera is a Soviet base, although the presence of the Soviets and what they have built is well attested. The key to the Somali version may be their conception of what would constitute a foreign base on Somali soil. In any case the Soviet presence implies considerable Soviet influence.

Despite this presence and the frequent laudatory allusions by President Siad and other Somali leaders to Soviet aid and Soviet leadership, persons with intensive and extensive firsthand experience with the Somali doubt that their sense of independence and of their own worth would permit them to become vehicles of Soviet will. There are, moreover, a number of accounts indicating that the Somali people are not comfortable in their interactions with the Soviet citizens in Somalia. Further most observers consider President Siad pragmatic with Somali concerns at the heart of whatever he does and therefore unlikely to respond to Soviet demands that, in his view, would not be advantageous or at least neutral with respect to Somalia. There is no question, however, that he regarded Somalia's goals and those of the Soviet Union as compatible on nearly all international questions.

CHAPTER 2

HISTORICAL SETTING

In a continent of ethnically heterogeneous states, Somalia lays strong claim to a common ethnic heritage and an ancient historical tradition. The Somali people have inhabited parts of the Horn of Africa for at least 1,000 years, sharing a common language and culture, including a common religion. The emergence of the modern state, however, was stimulated by the imposition of colonial rule in the late nineteenth century; it placed the majority of the Somalis under the rule of two colonial powers—Great Britain and Italy—but left them with a sense of nationhood that they had had no occasion to develop in their previous history.

The Somali, who already inhabited at least a portion of their present-day territory by the tenth century A.D., came into contact with the Arab world across the Gulf of Aden and formed a strong attachment to Islam. Arab influence was strongest in the coastal port cities, which date at least to the ninth century and probably earlier. The colonial powers and their advanced material culture had less psychological effect on the Somali than on many other African peoples because of Somali ties with Islam and their long-standing contacts with the Middle Eastern world.

Between the eleventh and fifteenth centuries a division of the Somali known as the Saab drove out or subjugated the earlier populations of the interriver and riverine areas of southern Somalia. They gained control of this relatively fertile region and made cultivation the basis of their economy, often using the remaining pre-Somali elements as labor and sometimes resorting to slaves for this purpose. Their brothers, called Samaal, living in the surrounding, drier regions, continued to engage in nomadic pastoralism; and differences in social structure, culture, and language developed between them and the Saab (see ch. 4). Despite their differences the agricultural Saab and the more numerous pastoral Samaal consider themselves one people.

The colonial era added other sources of variation. The Somali were grouped into two major divisions—Italian Somalia and British Somaliland—and three minor ones—the Northern Frontier District of Kenya and those areas of Ethiopia and of French Somaliland populated predominantly by Somali. Although the Italian and British territories followed different patterns of development and education, they were successfully amalgamated on July 1, 1960, into the independent Republic of Somalia.

Somalia's political history before independence differed radically from that of most new African states in the importance of the role of the United Nations (UN). The Italian colony was placed under UN control after it had been captured and administered by the British from 1941 to 1950. Somalia's final development before independence and its early and relatively painless attainment of independence were the result of direction given by the UN General Assembly. The impact of the UN on British Somaliland was also decisive. Because of ties generated during the period of British control, as well as existing ties among the Somali peoples, changes instituted by the UN in the Italian colony in the south had gradual repercussions in the north, leading Great Britain to grant independence to its territory there.

The early postindependence era was dominated by two difficult problems: the political and administrative unification of the former colonial territories and the conflict with Ethiopia, and later with Kenya, over Somalia's demands for the unification of all Somali. Internal political conflicts revolved around methods of handling these difficulties. Party composition and leadership fluctuated as new parties were formed. At each national election a great many parties, some with only a single candidate, were formed, but important parties were relatively few. One, the Somali Youth League (SYL), had been clearly dominant since before independence. The important political parties were not divided by significant ideological differences, and all the leaders had at one time or another served together in the SYL.

Much more significant was the tendency for the parties, before and after independence, to be organized on the basis of clan-families (see Glossary) or their constituent descent groups. By the end of the prerevolutionary period (1969) there were alliances across clan-family boundaries, but the units that made up these alliances were clans or smaller descent groups. These patterns reflected the fundamental mode of organization of the Somali in which lineages (usually related) of varying range and size came together or disaggregated in response to particular situations.

From its inception the SYL had sought to include among its leaders members of all clan-families, but its greatest support came initially from the largest of the units, the Darod. After the election of March 1969, which the SYL once again dominated, all but one opposition member of the parliament joined it, making the now de facto single party a congeries of regional, personal and, above all, lineage interests.

The conflicts among these interests, the time and energy given over to aggrandizing them as opposed to dealing with the country's more general problems, and the extent to which corruption had come to pervade relations among members and the operation of the govern-

14

ment and the National Assembly led to further disillusionment of a variety of critics, a number of whom were senior officers in Somalia's army. On October 21, 1969, these officers and their supporters acted. After an essentially bloodless coup they established the Supreme Revolutionary Council (SRC) (see ch. 9).

THE PRECOLONIAL PERIOD

The ultimate origins of the Somali and their earliest movements were still matters of scholarly dispute in the mid-1970s, as were the characteristics of the peoples who preceded them in the area that they occupy, whom the Somali dominated, absorbed, or drove out. There is no doubt, however, that the Somali were already established in much of their present-day territory several hundred years before the first recorded use of the name in the fifteenth century.

By the ninth century A.D., and probably earlier, Arabs from the Yemen and elsewhere on the Arabian Peninsula and a few Persians had established a number of coastal towns from Zeila in the north-west to Brava in the south, which became links in an extensive trading network between northeast Africa and southwest Asia and beyond. Somali were not to dominate these towns until hundreds of years later. In the southern interior negroid peoples had settled as cultivators along the Juba and Shabelle rivers and in the areas adjacent to them. Also in the south were bands of hunters and gatherers who, like other such groups in eastern Africa, may have been racially akin to the remnant Bushmen of southern Africa's Kalahari Desert. According to some accounts much of southern and central Somalia and parts of northern Somalia were inhabited by the Galla, who call themselves Oromo, most of whom live in neighboring Ethiopia (and to a lesser extent in Kenya).

There are very few Galla in present-day Somalia, but earlier sources place them near the lower Juba from the first quarter of the seventeenth century until the 1860s, when a section of the Somali crossing the river from the east destroyed or drove them out. At issue is whether they had ever been farther north in earlier times and had been replaced by Somali moving southward, a question closely connected to that of Somali origins.

Until the mid-1960s it was commonly thought that the pre-Somali cultivating peoples of the Juba-Shabelle region were speakers of Bantu languages like those who have long inhabited much of Kenya and Tanzania to the south. The evidence for that hypothesis has been seriously questioned, however, and the issue remained open in the mid-1970s. There are Swahili (one of the Bantu languages) speakers in the southern coastal area and others in the interior, but in some cases their ancestors are known to have arrived, as slaves, after the Somali.

Somali social organization is based on actual or putative kinship, which provides the basis for a range of related sociopolitical units from the largest entities—the clan-families, of which there are six—to the smallest—the lineage segments, of which there are thousands (see ch. 4). Their traditional genealogies trace the ancestry of these units to Arabs, particularly to members of the Quraysh, the tribe of the Prophet Muhammad, and ultimately to a common ancestor. In these accounts the ancestors of specific clan-families arrived in the northern part of the Horn of Africa at various times, perhaps 800 to 1,000 years ago, and established lineages that in the course of several hundred years of expansion moved from the northeast to the south and west, displacing Galla by force of arms as they went.

The scholars who have accepted their traditional history as a framework for the actual history of the Somali and supported or modified it by reference to documentary and other evidence of varying reliability acknowledge, as do many educated Somali, that many of the traditional references to Arab ancestry will not stand careful scrutiny and are probably a function of the desire of the deeply Islamic Somali to link themselves to the people of the Prophet. Those who question the basic framework acknowledge that there has been substantial Arab influence and even, on occasion, an infusion of Arab blood. They do, however, question whether the point of origin of the Somali was in the north, as even the modified version of traditional history implies, and they have queried the pre-Somali presence of the Galla in much of present-day Somalia.

On the basis of linguistic evidence supported by a critical reading of documentary sources, anthropologist Herbert S. Lewis argued in the mid-1960s that the point of origin of speakers of Eastern Cushitic languages, of which Somali is one and Galla another, lay in southern Ethiopia. All other Eastern Cushitic speakers, save the Afar and Saho who preceded the Somali move to the north, are still to be found in southern Ethiopia and northern Kenya. Lewis suggested further that the Somali began their expansion to the north and east substantially before the Galla and that there were Somali groups in southern Somalia as early as the twelfth century, three to four centuries before there is any clear record of Galla presence in the area. (In this he is supported by the work of the historian E. R. Turton.) In Lewis' view Somali groups preceded the Galla in the north: sections of the Galla moved, respectively, north and east beginning in the fifteenth and sixteenth centuries, and their contact with the Somali, usually hostile, dates from the sixteenth and seventeenth centuries.

Whatever the ultimate resolution of the question of Somali origins, there is considerable agreement that Somali were in much of present-day Somalia and in the part of present-day Ethiopia known as Ogaden at least by the twelfth century and very likely earlier. The process of their conversion to Islam probably began at about that time in the north under Arab influence but was not completed until some centuries later, particularly in the south. Arab impact was not limited to the north or to the earliest period. Arabs continued to arrive on the coast, north and south, for hundreds of years, some of them moving into the hinterland. In some cases they intermarried with the Somali and stimulated a limited degree of hierarchical political organization among some of them. In other cases the Arabs established villages enclaved among the Somali that persisted in the latter half of the twentieth century. These Arabs, called *gibil'aad* (pale skins) by the Somali, became their clients.

By the twelfth century the ancestors of some clan-families were established where many or most of their present-day descendants live, but movements of specific clans or smaller segments (lineages) continued into the nineteenth century, both over long distances and as slight shifts within a given clan-family area or lands contiguous to it. For example, the Dir clan-family, located primarily in the extreme northwest of the Somali distribution, has one clan, the Bimal, who live in two segments some 700 miles away on the southern coast. They claim to have arrived there 350 to 400 years ago. The Darod, the largest of the clan-families (and estimated at well over 1 million in Somalia proper in the latter half of the twentieth century), ranges from the northeast to contiguous areas of Ethiopia. They are also located west of the Juba River and extend into Kenya, an area they occupied in part during the 1860s after they had been forced out of the region between the Juba and Shabelle rivers by the Rahanwein, another clan-family, already settled there. It has been suggested that one important reason for the conflict between the two groups was that the Rahanwein, cattle herders and cultivators or at least patrons of cultivators and therefore dependent on farming, could not tolerate the presence of the camel-, sheep-, and goat-herding Darod, whose animals would have destroyed crop and pasture land.

Somali movements were in good part functions of the expansion or contraction of specific clans or clan segments and of the conflict between groups of a largely pastoral, nomadic people seeking access to grazing and water in a harsh environment. Such conflicts probably took place at least as often between clans and lineages of the same clan-family as between segments of different clan-families. Indeed from time to time there were alliances, however temporary, between clans of one family and clans of another.

In some cases alliances, whatever their composition, and conflict led to the formation of confederacies in which one lineage came to dominate the others, and its head, sometimes referred to as sultan, acquired a great deal of prestige. If he was successful in war, he also exercised some real political power, particularly in time of war, but such confederacies rarely endured for very long periods, and they did not lead to the establishment of political or administrative hierarchies.

17

Population dynamics and scarce resources were not the sole causes of conflict, and control over scarce material sources and trade routes was not the sole basis for power and the formation of large, if temporary, politicomilitary groupings. At various times numbers of Somali came together in support of a leader who was seen to have special religious powers and who demonstrated those powers in warfare, which to some extent had religious significance.

By the early fifteenth century the Muslim emirate of Adal, which had its capital in Zeila and some of its territory in what is present-day eastern Ethiopia, was ready to do battle over territory and religion with expanding Christian Abyssinia. Adal was part of the state of Ifat, whose ruling dynasty claimed Arab ancestry, however mixed they may have been with local peoples. The northern Somali were at least nominally under its control and fought in its armies. After initial successes these armies were defeated in 1415, and Ifat's sultan was killed. Abyssinian songs of victory dating from this period make the first known reference to the Somali.

By the second quarter of the next century Adal had again attempted the conquest of Abyssinia, this time under the leadership of Ahmad Gran (the left-handed), a leader of the opposition to a dynasty by this time more concerned with commerce than with jihad (holy war). Gran killed the sultan and assumed the religious title of imam. His refusal to pay tribute to the Abyssinian ruler led to war. In less than ten years, leading armies of Somali and Afar warriors, he conquered most of Ethiopia and forcibly converted thousands of Abyssinian Christians. The Abyssinians then sought the help of the Portuguese, who had already made themselves felt along the coast, and Gran appealed to the Ottoman Turks. With the help of Turkish mercenaries Gran held off the Portuguese but, after he had sent the mercenaries away, the newly crowned Ethiopian king and the Portuguese destroyed Gran's armies and killed Gran in 1542. The conflict continued into the 1570s, ending only when both Somali and Abyssinians had to face the invasion of the pagan Galla who, moving northeastward, drove a wedge between the antagonists.

Gran's campaigns had few lasting effects. Even during the time of his military successes he was unable to establish an administrative system encompassing the land and people he controlled or conquered. The pastoral nomadic Somali were willing to fight in his, and the Islamic, cause; they were not ready to be administered. Gran did become a folk hero to the Somali, who tend to think of him as one of themselves, although there is no clear evidence as to his origins. In a speech in the early 1970s the president of the country, Mohamed Siad Barre, referred to Gran and his campaigns as the first of the significant persons and events in Somali history.

The turmoil created by the conflict between Gran's forces and the Abyssinians, and especially the former's defeat, was one of the fac-

18

tors that generated movements of additional Somali clans from the west and the north into the region dominated by the middle and lower Juba and Shabelle rivers. Of the two clan-families, together called Saab, living in that region, whose livelihood is based on cattle keeping and cultivation, the Digil, by far the smaller, have apparently been there since the first millennium A.D. The traditions of the much larger Rahanwein have them arriving in the late fifteenth century for the first time and continuing to move in until the early seventeenth. When they arrived, they found the Ajuran confederation, apparently dominated by the Arab-influenced Hawiya, a Samaal clan-family who had entered the region from Ogaden in the fourteenth century or earlier. Ajuran rule, based on military power, came to an end by the mid-seventeenth century. Political arrangements thereafter usually involved longer or shorter lived confederations in which one or another Rahanwein clan or lineage was dominant.

The nineteenth century saw an intensification of the significance of cultivation among the southern Somali, made possible in part by the availability of slaves. Slaves in turn constituted one element in a Somali trade network that brought ivory, rhinoceros horn, aromatic woods, gum, and myrrh to the coastal towns for export and took cloth (some imported, some locally made), iron, dates, sugar, and jewelry up-country. For the purposes of this trade the Somali engaged in transactions with the peoples of southern Ethiopia and northern Kenya including the Galla. Some trade goods from the interior never reached the coast; coffee, sodium nitrate and, above all, slaves were absorbed by the Somali themselves. Originally some slaves were brought to Somalia from southern East African ports as a small part of the slave trade to the Middle East. As the British navy became increasingly successful in cutting off the seaborne trade, however, slaves were walked in from the south.

Non-Somali clients of Digil and Rahanwein Somali for some time had cultivated the interriver and riverine area, particularly along the lower Shabelle River running parallel to the coast. Given the reluctance of Somali to engage directly in farming themselves, however, there were limits to the quantity of land cultivated. The arrival of slaves, usually Bantu-speaking farming peoples, permitted the extension and intensification of farming, and even some of the Hawiya in the area became partly reliant on cultivation. When slavery was abolished toward the end of the nineteenth century, these people reverted to nomadic pastoralism.

During this period Somali of one clan-family or another became increasingly powerful in the towns and eventually displaced or absorbed the ruling groups of Arab origin that had dominated most of the southern coastal towns for centuries. In theory, however, these towns remained under the suzerainty of the sultanate of Omani, which had its base in Zanzibar, until the coastal area was formally transferred to Italian rule through sale in 1905.

THE COLONIAL DIVISION OF SOMALI-OCCUPIED
TERRITORY

In the second half of the nineteenth century four countries engaged in a contest for control over parts of Somali-populated territories, encountering little or no opposition from the Somali. Two factors distinguished the colonial race for control over Somali territory from that over the rest of Africa during the same period. First, the division of the territory among the imperial powers was carried out not over negotiating tables in Europe but by local imperial representatives who dealt with each piece of the area on a case-by-case basis. Second, the four contending powers were not all European. One was the Kingdom of Ethiopia, the only state in black Africa capable of contesting the Europeans. These distinctions and the processes of delimiting boundaries among the contending powers contributed directly to Somalia's unique position in international affairs in the 1960s as the only new state in Africa in which irredentism was a significant political issue (see ch. 10).

In 1875 Egypt, then under Ottoman Turkish rule, made the first colonial efforts in the area. The khedive of Egypt attempted to strengthen Ottoman overlordship over the western coast of both the Red Sea and the Gulf of Aden. His forces successfully occupied the principal ports and organized an efficient civil administration. During ten years of Egyptian rule strong efforts were made to expand inland at Ethiopian expense, but in 1885 the Mahdi rebellion in the Sudan forced the Egyptians to recall their forces to Egypt. Their place was quickly taken by the European powers.

Early British interest in the Somali coast appears to have been solely economic. Somali supplied the cattle required to sustain the British garrison holding the base at Aden at the strategic mouth of the Red Sea on the Suez Canal route from Great Britain to India. Establishment of a British protectorate over the Somali tribes was undertaken only to ensure an uninterrupted supply of fresh meat.

Italian and French interests in the area were consistent with traditional reasons for colonial expansion. In 1859 France had obtained a treaty with the Afar people for control of the port of Obock, north of present-day Djibouti, but had used it only as a trading station. Anglo-French rivalry along the route to India in the 1880s led the British to close the port of Aden to French shipping. As a result in 1884 the French began to develop a coaling station, first at Obock but later at Djibouti, as a strategic counterbalance to Aden.

The Italians entered the colonial race quite late and became interested in the Horn of Africa as one of the few parts of the continent not already claimed by a major power. The port of Assab in Eritrea had been purchased in 1870 by an Italian shipping firm for a coaling station. Ownership passed to the Italian government in 1882, and in

1885, with the agreement of the British, the Italians took over Massawa from the departing Egyptians, simultaneously laying claim to the entire Eritrean coast. The Italian government took the position that the Ethiopian kingdom should lie in its sphere of influence. Italian forces advanced inland and, after a minor victory over the Ethiopian forces, signed the Treaty of Ucciali with the new emperor, Menelik II. According to the Italians, but not to Emperor Menelik II, the treaty made Ethiopia their protectorate. The Italians then purported to act on Ethiopia's behalf in dealing with France and Great Britain on border questions, particularly as they expanded their colonial territory into what is present-day Somalia.

The Italian entry into Somalia proper began in early 1889, when the Somali sultans of Obbya, on the Indian Ocean coast, and Alula, on the Gulf of Aden, accepted the protection of Italy in exchange for annual payments. The most important Italian gain occurred in the same year and was obtained by leasing the ports of the Benadir coast (the area from Adale to Brava) partly on a sublease from the Imperial British East Africa Company and partly on a direct twenty-five-year lease from the coast's theoretical owner, the sultan of Zanzibar. The leases covered the area from Uarsciech southward through Mogadishu, Marka (Merca), and Brava to the mouth of the Juba River. The Italian government appointed a commercial firm as its representative. This company continued to expand the area under Italian control. Explorers traveling the inland areas signed a number of treaties with local clans, in some cases in return for armed protection against Ethiopian invaders. Control along the coast was reinforced and expanded with the help of the Italian navy.

Great Britain and Italy signed treaties in 1891 and 1894 defining the boundaries marking off Italian Somalia from British Somaliland and the Kenyan territories. The boundaries were not, however, discussed with Ethiopia or with the Somali. The inland boundaries divided the territories claimed by both the Somali and the Ethiopians by placing the Ogaden region in the Italian sphere and the Haud region in the British sphere (see fig. 2).

In March 1896 Italian forces advancing from Eritrea into Ethiopia in support of Italian claims were resoundingly defeated by Menelik II's troops in a three-day battle at Adowa. The defeat did not weaken Italy's position in Somalia despite the resulting opposition in Italy to colonial ventures and the financial collapse of the administering company. But it did make necessary a delimitation of the interior boundaries between the colonial powers and Ethiopia.

Arrangements for delimitation began in 1897 when a British negotiator, Rennell Rodd, led a special mission to Menelik II. Its main purpose, to ensure Ethiopian neutrality in the British campaign against the Mahdi rebellion in the neighboring Sudan, combined with the colonial government's very limited support for the British defensive po-

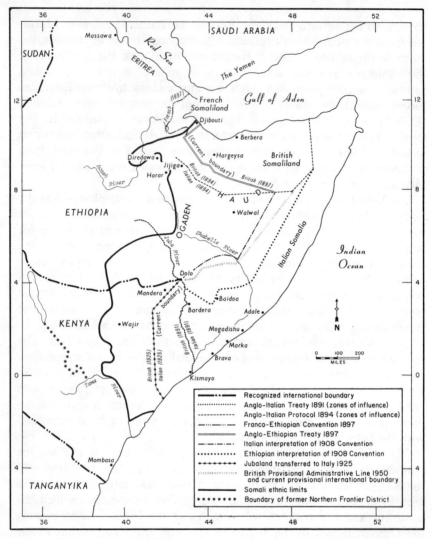

Figure 2. *Somalia, Frontiers and Colonial Boundaries, 1891-1960*

Source: Based on information from John Drysdale, *The Somali Dispute*, New York,
1964; and Somalia, Ministry of Foreign Affairs, *The Somali People's Quest for
Unity*, Mogadishu, 1965.

sition in Somalia, left the Rodd negotiators in a poor bargaining position.

The Ethiopian position was strengthened by the fact that Ethiopia
had already claimed historic suzerainty over the whole of Somalia and
had rapidly expanded its control over Somali-populated areas. Since
1887 a strong Ethiopian garrison had been established at Harar, just
beyond the territory claimed by the British. Ethiopia had finally obtained concessions of territory from Great Britain's colonial rivals,

the Italians in Eritrea and the French in Djibouti. The French had already voluntarily withdrawn their claimed boundaries by 100 kilometers (about sixty-two miles). All these factors combined to force the British hand.

Great Britain's only legal rights to Somalia were based on treaties signed with Somali clans, in which it had promised to serve as their protector. The primary motivation for the Somali signers was to obtain protection against the usurpation of their lands by the better armed Ethiopians. Nevertheless the British agreed to pull back their protectorate's boundaries by about eleven kilometers (about seven miles) opposite Harar and by nearly the full depth of the important Haud region to the south. The only reflection of Great Britain's promised protection of the Somali appeared in two clauses of the treaty with Ethiopia, one requiring the Ethiopian government to provide them with "good treatment" and orderly government, the other guaranteeing the nomads pasturage on either side of the new frontier.

Rodd and the few British administrators in British Somaliland expressed grave misgivings over the loss of territory, which included half of the comparatively fertile northern highlands and the vital seasonal grazing of the Haud. At this time, however, the Somali were little aware of the change. The treaty was not published, the boundary not immediately demarcated, and Ethiopian rule over the region only very lightly felt.

Immediately after the Rodd treaty, the Italian representative, Major Nerazzini, conducted negotiations to define the border between Italian Somalia and Ethiopia. The treaty arrangements, though definitive, were rather informal. Nerazzini and the emperor marked out the agreed on boundary on two copies of a German map but did not record the limits in the treaty itself. Both copies of the map promptly disappeared and have not been found. The only information on the location of the border was Nerazzini's report on his return that the agreed on line was parallel to the coast 180 miles inland and terminated at the cataracts of the Juba River. The Ethiopians claim that the decided boundary line was much closer to the coast. In 1908, eleven years after the Nerazzini treaty, an attempt was made to resolve the matter. The Italians paid an indemnity of 3 million lire to Ethiopia, but no agreement was reached except for the delimitation of the tripoint between Kenya, Somalia, and Ethiopia and the tracing of the border past Dolo on the Juba to Iet, 130 kilometers (about eighty miles) to the north.

Somalia's third boundary, that with Kenya, was the eventual outcome of a secret arrangement in 1915 between Great Britain and Italy as compensation for Italy's withdrawal of its support of the Central Powers in World War I. A treaty drawn up in 1920 and finally signed in 1924 provided that Italy take over the area west of the Juba River (Jubaland) up to the forty-first parallel, an act carried out in 1925. Although this boundary movement added a Somali-populated area roughly the size of Belgium to the country, it left a nearly equal portion within Kenya, providing further international problems after Somalia's independence.

MOHAMED ABDULLAH AND THE BIRTH OF SOMALI NATIONALISM

Until 1899 the only impediments to the expansion of colonial rule were the conflicting claims of the three European powers and the Ethiopians. The Somali succumbed to British, Italian and, to a limited extent, French overlordship through a series of treaties between the separate clans and the colonizers. The European powers limited their presence to the ports, which had historically been under non-Somali control, and were primarily interested in improving trade, which resulted in incidental benefits to the Somali. Initially, therefore, the European presence aroused only limited and local animosity.

In 1899, however, a remarkable figure, Sayyid Mohamed ibn Abdullah Hassan, came to the fore. An imam of the puritanic Salihiya *tariqa* (order or brotherhood—see Glossary) of Islam, Mohamed Abdullah had preached the order's stringent views in Berbera. He had been opposed there, however, by his coreligionists, who were largely members of the less severe Qadiriya order and who profited by the improved opportunities for trade under colonial rule. Mohamed Abdullah expressed shock at what he saw as foreign evils, brought by the colonial powers, that violated the precepts of Islam, particularly the drinking of alcohol and the propagation of Christianity, which he encountered at the French school and orphanage in Berbera.

Mohamed Abdullah returned to the interior, established a teaching center, and traveled widely to preach to the pastoralists, who were less impressed by the foreigners than were the coastal dwellers. He urged that the Europeans and missionaries be driven out, but he also preached against the Christian Ethiopians, ancient enemies. He sought to direct the interclan hostility of the warriors of his own Darod clan-family against the infidels and referred to his followers as *darwishes* (members of an order) rather than by the customary clan or lineage names. His ability as preacher, orator, and poet (the last a much-valued skill in Somali society) allowed him to gain a large following among the Darod and to a lesser extent among members of other clan-families in the north. Members of the Isaq clan-family, which by virtue of the group's location played a large role in commerce, opposed him, and some fought with the British against him. Mohammad Abdullah did not gain extensive support in Italian Somalia, but members of several clan-families declared themselves *darwishes* and acted as guerrillas in the interriver area, chiefly against Somali who were deemed too accommodating to the Italians.

Mohamad Abdullah's religious philosophy made him anathema to the larger Qadiriya order. In the end he was defeated as much by the efforts of his fellow Somali as by the British. They turned against him, tired of the chaos, disruption and, at times, famine that were consequences of the guerrilla campaign. For twenty years after his death the country remained quiescent under foreign domination and succumbed to many of the foreign influences, though not to Christianity, against which he had inveighed. Yet since nationalism in modern form began to appear in the mid-1940s, he has been lauded as the national hero and prime source of the Somali sense of national identity even by those who had been his enemies. Although his struggle was in vain, it served as the inspiration of the nationalism of the 1950s. President Siad included him among those who had been significant in Somali history.

COLONIAL ADMINISTRATION, 1920-41

The military campaign against Mohamed Abdullah stimulated the British to extend their control inland, for security reasons, to the borders with Ethiopia. The expansion of Italian control occurred during the same period but was largely the result of a desire to exploit the agricultural potential of the region between the Shabelle and Juba rivers and to provide economic opportunities for Italian settlers. By 1920 all of the British and Italian territories had accepted colonial sovereignty. Not until 1927, however, did the last of the segments of Italian Somalia come under direct administration, after the transfer to Italy in 1925 of the Trans-Juba area and the 1925-27 military campaign to end the semiautonomous status claimed by the sultans of Obbya and Mijerteyn.

Completion of the railroad from Djibouti to Addis Ababa ended the value of Great Britain's control of the historic trade routes from Zeila, but the Italians were able to reopen the ancient trade routes in the south from Ogaden to Mogadishu and thus to gain control of the import and export trade of portions of Ethiopia. This economic control helped to facilitate the gradual Italian infiltration of the underadministered areas of Ethiopia adjoining Somalia.

Within the Italian colony early hopes for using the territory to resettle farmers from Italy's poorer regions foundered, and other agricultural schemes, such as the large commercial plantations of the duke of Abruzzi, were slowed by the unforeseen difficulty involved in recruiting local labor. The potential labor market was composed largely of the sedentary peoples who had formerly been slaves or clients of the dominant Somali. These people, however, preferred work on their own lands to salaried labor, whereas the pastoralists, more interested in cash, were uninterested in agriculture. The colonial government at an early date began compulsory labor recruitment. The use of force to recruit workers continued even after new labor laws providing for higher wages and more attractive benefits were put into effect. Despite the difficulties agricultural production increased at a good rate. The duke of Abruzzi's company, the Italo-Somali Agricultural Society (Societa Agricola Italo-Somala-SAIS), held more than 75,000 acres, most of them close to the rivers. Export crops included bananas, sugarcane, and cotton. The colony's only other significant products were livestock, hides, and skins and salt from an Italian plant begun at Ras Hafun in 1920.

Widely felt changes began in the colony with the appointment of the first governor by the Italian fascist regime in 1922. The Fascists brought with them their propensity for construction. By 1928 about 3,800 miles of roads had been built, and a light railroad, later destroyed in World War II, connected plantations at Villagio Abruzzi (present-day Jowhar) and Afgoi to Mogadishu.

The fascist administration was highly centralized, and all posts of any importance were held by Italians. Limited educational facilities were created at the primary level, but the fascist government adopted racial legislation intended to ensure, in theory as well as in fact, the superior status of the colonists and the subject status of the Somali. The society was more open than would appear, however. Individual Italians often bent the rules to accommodate the Somali. The government itself recognized the authority of amenable indigenous leaders and appointed Somali judges to administer Islamic and customary law. Somali staffed the lower ranks of the police force, and more than 40,000 served in the Italian military campaign against Ethiopia in 1935.

Developments in British Somaliland between World War I and World War II were extremely limited. Twenty years of military campaigning had devastated much of the countryside. After 1920 the colonial administration was required by the home government to finance all its operations in the country from its own resources, but attempts to impose direct taxation proved impossible to implement because of Somali intransigence. Most revenues were derived from import and export duties, but the important trade route to Ethiopia, initially broken by the disturbances of the war years, was permanently closed by the completion of the Djibouti railroad. Government expenditure was only the equivalent of US$1.2 million in 1937, and as a consequence the very limited number of administrators were unable to implement any significant development programs. Efforts were restricted to the provision of veterinary and well-drilling services and to attempts to assist the agricultural improvements carried out by the Somali on their own initiative in the better watered areas of the northwestern highlands.

Other British efforts were aimed at the expansion of the extremely limited educational facilities. The first effort to increase the number of schools, however, was linked to the imposition of direct taxation, and opposition to taxation became popularly linked with opposition to the schools. This opposition was reinforced by the conservative religious feelings of the population, who saw Western education as a threat to Islam (see ch. 7).

SOMALIA AND THE ITALO-ETHIOPIAN WAR

The Italian government had begun a political and military infiltration of the Ogaden area before 1930. They were assisted in their intrusions by three factors. First, the boundary between Ethiopia and Italian Somalia was unmarked and not agreed on; second, because of staff shortages the Ethiopian government had never been able to expand its administration into the eastern half of the area; and third, the Italians had come to dominate the limited economy through their control of the external trade routes. In addition even at that time there were demands among the Somali for national unification or at least for European colonial protection for their fellows who lived under Christian rule in Ethiopia.

The Italians posed as the champions of Somali irredentism and attempted, with some success, to win the support of the Somali of Ogaden, who populated the area to a depth of 400 miles inside Ethiopia. From at least 1930 to 1935 Somali troops under Italian officers permanently occupied the territory to a depth of 100 miles, a fact that was evidently known but tacitly ignored by the Ethiopian government. On November 23, 1934, a military confrontation with these occupying forces occurred at Wal Wal, an area indisputably within Ethiopia.

Despite feeble attempts at mediation by the League of Nations, the Italian fascist government used the incident as an excuse to open a war of conquest against Ethiopia. Italian forces invaded Ethiopia, and the Somali-populated areas of southern Ethiopia were annexed to Italian Somalia.

After the outbreak of World War II the Italian army invaded British Somaliland to the north on August 11, 1940, and overran the territory. The Italian victory both there and in Ethiopia was, however, short lived. British forces, largely East African colonial troops, retook all of Ethiopia and both Somali territories by May 1941, capturing 170,000 Italian prisoners. The British resumed control of its territory and established temporary administration over Somalia and the eastern portions of Ethiopia. For the first time all the Somali, except the small segment in French Somaliland, came under a single colonial government. No common administration was set up, however, and the British agreed to an eventual return to Ethiopia of the areas formerly under its control.

THE BEGINNING OF NATIONAL DEVELOPMENT

The British military administrators who controlled the two Somali colonies from 1941 through 1949 accomplished more social and political change than their Italian and British predecessors had since colonial rule was first imposed. In the north the home government's change in attitude regarding the necessity for the protectorate to be self-supporting allowed the first real efforts at development to be undertaken. The capital was moved from the port of Berbera to Hargeysa in the religious and geographic center of the country in order to indicate the new government's planned involvement in Somali problems. Although the civil service remained inadequate in numbers, efforts were undertaken to improve agricultural and health services and to influence Somali opinion in favor of development. The military administration succeeded in opening a number of secular schools where there had only been subsidized Quranic schools before 1939 (see ch. 7).

The local court system was also revamped, and local advisory and planning committees were set up in the towns. In mid-1946 the Protectorate Advisory Council was set up, in which the districts were represented by appointed Somali of both modern and traditional opinion. The one politically motivated organization formed in the prewar years, the Somaliland National Society (SNS), was revitalized by the new currents.

The first British efforts in the south provided better pay and working conditions for the agricultural labor force. A new British-led police force, the Somalia Gendarmerie, was created and a police school founded. By 1947 the number of pupils in the elementary schools had increased to twice the prewar figure, and a center for training elementary-school teachers was opened. The British also provided for Somali to become junior officials in the civil and police services; the best training and positions were in the gendarmerie. In addition the first opportunities for the Somali to enter modern politics were provided during this period as Italian-appointed clan chiefs were gradually superseded by elected advisory assemblies at the clan level. District and provincial councils were also created in 1946 to advise the British district and provincial administrators.

The British continued to depend on the large number of Italian civilians in the colony to operate the industrial and technical services. Only those civilians who were regarded as Fascists and security risks were interned. In early 1943 those Italians who remained were allowed to form political associations. New Italian organizations of all political persuasions immediately sprang up and began to agitate for an eventual return to Italian rule. In the face of such pressure the British and Somali saw each other as allies. The British accordingly encouraged the formation of the first modern Somali political organization, the Somali Youth Club (SYC), founded in the south in May 1943.

The SYC was strengthened from the beginning by the inclusion of the more educated civil and police officers in its membership and leadership. These civil servants, who under any other British jurisdiction would have been prevented from engaging in politics by civil service rules, were allowed to join the SYC because it served as a counterweight to the Italian interests.

The SYC grew rapidly in popularity and had gained an estimated membership of 25,000 by 1946. Its name was changed to the Somali Youth League (SYL) in 1947, at which time branches operated not only in what had been Italian Somalia but also in British Somaliland and in the Somali-populated areas of Ethiopia and Kenya. The SYL had announced as its aims the unification of all Somali over and above clan and tribal differences, widespread opportunity for modern education, the development of the Somali language through the adoption of a written form, and finally the general protection of Somali interests, including opposition to colonial fragmentation and to the reimposition of Italian colonial rule. The SYC's thirteen founding members represented five of Somalia's six clan-family divisions, and its members made strong efforts to promote the concept of the Somali nation over clan divisions, going so far as to refuse to use their clan names. A second political body, initially called the Patriotic Benefit Union, was created in the same period. In 1947 it became the Somali Digil Clan Party (Hizbia Digil-Mirifle Somali—HDMS or HDM). The HDMS represented the agricultural clan-families of the region between the Juba and Shabelle rivers against what its supporters saw as the dominance of the SYL by pastoral interests. The HDMS received considerable financial support from the Italians and was accordingly less interested in preventing a return of Italian rule than was the SYL.

Although the SYL had some northern supporters, the chief parties in British Somaliland were the Somaliland National League (SNL), which represented the Isaq clan-family and had its roots in part in the earlier SNS, and the United Somali Party (USP), which represented the Dir and northern Darod.

At the end of World War II responsibility for deciding the future disposition of the Italian colonies fell to the Allied Powers' Council of Foreign Ministers, which appointed the Four Power Commission, composed of representatives from the United States, Great Britain, France, and the Soviet Union, to study the matter. In January 1948 the commission arrived in Mogadishu to compile evidence. The SYL obtained permission to stage a rally to demonstrate the strength of its supporters. Italian interests attempted to disrupt and discredit the rally by an armed attack. Riots were precipitated in which fifty-one Italians and seventeen Somali lost their lives. The commission continued its hearings, however, and was impressed by the program presented by the SYL's spokesmen, Abdillahi Issa and Haji Mohamed Hussein. In addition to the unification of all Somali territories, the SYL requested a trusteeship under an international commission for a ten-year period, followed by full independence.

The HDMS presented a similar program but requested a thirty-year trusteeship. It did, however, break with its former view that Italy should be the administering power. Also presenting their view were other Somali groups and Italian interests who favored an Italian trusteeship or even a return to Italian rule. Although the Four Power Commission was most impressed by the SYL's arguments, the Council of Foreign Ministers found itself unable to agree on an arrangement. The British government had initially supported SYL demands for a united Somali nation but, after being accused by both the Soviet Union and the United States of attempting to expand its colonial empire by controlling the proposed Greater Somalia, the British withdrew their support.

The unresolved issue was passed to the UN General Assembly for a decision. In November 1949 the territory was entrusted by the Assembly to the Italian government for a period of ten years under continuing strong UN supervision, with the clear proviso that the Italian administration was to prepare it for independence before the end of 1960. Although the SYL had continually opposed any return to Italian control, the UN decision was accepted without protest because of the guarantee that independence would be obtained in so short a period.

THE CREATION OF THE SOMALI STATE

The Trust Territory of Somaliland under Italian Administration entered the 1950s with a political advantage not held by other colonial territories; it had a set date for independence and the resulting opportunity to prepare more purposefully for self-government. The northern portion of the future state had no such advantage. Accordingly its development, although greatly accelerated by the British colonial government, proceeded haphazardly. The marked disparity between the two areas continued until their independence.

In view of expressed opposition to the return of Italian colonialism to the southern area, Italian rule over the trust was carefully circumscribed. The UN Trusteeship Agreement placed the administration of the territory not in the hands of the Italian government itself but rather under the control of a special Italian agency, the Italian Trusteeship Administration (Amministrazione Fiduciaria Italiana della Somalia—AFIS). The agreement also created the UN Advisory Council, based in Mogadishu, with an international membership. The council was empowered to examine AFIS programs and to recommend further actions to ensure the carrying out of the agreement's objectives.

In addition missions of the UN Trusteeship Council were to visit Somalia on a periodic basis, and the missions, as well as the Advisory Council, were to report directly to the Trusteeship Council. The agreement provided for the establishment of political institutions, expansion of the educational system, social and economic advancement for the Somali, and guarantees of complete freedom of speech, press, and petition.

Despite these protections initial relations between the new Italian administrators and the Somali nationalists were difficult. The Italians, fearing a violent display of opposition to their return, arrived with a show of military force and immediately attempted to suppress the SYL, which was seen as the center of anti-Italian feeling. Some SYL leaders were jailed, and others were dropped from the high civil service positions they had obtained under the British. The Somali reacted with riots, which were forcibly suppressed. This period of antagonism lasted for three years, until the launching of the first of the development programs began to provide an outlet for the energies of both the nationalists and the Italians. Political energies began to be absorbed at the same time by the implementation of the UN's stipulations for political development.

Major development planning was carried out in a series of seven-year development programs inaugurated in 1954. These were based on plans drawn up by the UN and by the United States International Cooperation Administration. They concentrated on efforts to stimulate indigenous agriculture and to improve the infrastructure. Exports tripled during the seven years of the program, but a severe balance-of-payments deficit persisted, and government revenues, largely dependent on import and export duties, continued to be wholly inadequate. As independence approached, the economic picture remained essentially the same.

The development plans for education were more successfully implemented. The number of children in school in 1957 had risen to double the 1952 figure. At that time nearly 2,000 students were enrolled in secondary, technical, and university-level programs in Somalia, Italy, and Egypt. In addition strong efforts were under way in the adult literacy field and in the training of civil servants and political leaders.

The development of governmental institutions to serve as a training ground and basis for the country's future self-government were far more encouraging than the economic picture. In line with the UN resolution the AFIS established a consultative national body, the Territorial Council, in 1950. The council immediately became an active body, engaging in full-scale debate of proposed AFIS legislation. The thirty-five-member body, which AFIS was required to consult on all important issues, included representatives of both traditional interests and the political parties—the latter gradually gaining dominance during the five years the council sat. The Territorial Council provided the

Somali with their first taste of the problems of national government. Those who participated in its deliberation gained experience in legislative and committee procedure, as well as a firsthand view of the political, social, and economic problems the newly created state would have to face. In addition its support for legislation gave legitimacy to the AFIS operation in Somali eyes.

A large number of other Somali were able to gain executive and legislative experience through participation in local government bodies. Municipal councils had been created in forty-eight population centers between 1950 and 1956. Although the members of the councils had at first been appointed, nationwide municipal elections were held in 1954. Aided by secretaries trained in municipal administration, who were appointed to each of the bodies, the members handled town planning, public services and, after 1956, fiscal and budgetary matters. The central government retained the power to overrule council decisions and to dismiss mayors and councillors.

The position of the district councils, which were responsible for rural areas, was considerably weaker that that of their urban counterparts. The councils were concerned with matters of customary law and with settling disputes over grazing and water rights. Efforts to give the councils wider powers were largely limited by the nature of the nomadic economy. The nomads' search for pasture required nearly constant movement, which made any identification with political boundaries, even interstate boundaries, all but impossible. The Advisory Council's hope that the district councils could be used as channels for development proved impossible to fulfill, and the reins of government in nomadic areas remained largely in the hands of district commissioners.

The 1954 municipal elections provided the first opportunity for widespread political activity and were conducted in a spirited but orderly fashion. Fifteen parties contested the 281 local seats; some 37,000 votes were cast, and eleven of the parties won seats. Only the SYL, however, which gained approximately 45 percent of the vote and 141 seats, and the HDMS with almost 25 percent of the vote and fifty-seven seats, were able to demonstrate control of significant portions of the electorate.

The first national elections were held in 1956 on the occasion of the Territorial Council's replacement by the new Legislative Assembly, which had sixty seats. These elections were contested by ten parties, but again only the SYL, with forty-three seats, and the HDMS, with thirteen seats, made significant showings. The remaining four Somali seats were won by the Somali Democratic Party (three) and a clan party, the Merehan Union (one). Ten other places in the assembly were reserved for elected representatives of the Italian, Arab, and Indian minorities.

The leader of the SYL in the assembly, Abdillahi Issa, was called on to become the first premier; the government was to have five other ministers, all Somali. The new assembly possessed full legislative power in all domestic matters, although the senior official of AFIS, the administrator, retained the power of absolute veto as well as the right to issue emergency regulations without prior assembly approval. The AFIS retained control over external relations, including the sensitive issue of resolving the frontier dispute with Ethiopia. Foreign financial affairs also remained under Italian control until February 1957, and defense and public order did not pass entirely into Somali hands until 1958.

The 1956 election was conducted in the settled areas by secret ballot and universal male suffrage. In the interior the nomadic nature of the society made registration much more difficult, and for this reason a clan voting system was established. The nomads of each clan met in a *shir* (traditional clan assembly) and decided jointly on the candidate for whom all their votes would be cast. There were 600 such assemblies. Clan leaders then informed the authorities of this decision and of the number of individual votes cast in the *shir*. Unfortunately the total number of votes cast in the territory far outnumbered the estimated size of the actual electorate. This incident marred the Somali political image and left a residue of interparty distrust for a number of years; because the SYL was the strongest party in the nomadic areas, it was said by its opponents to have gained the most from the alleged irregularities.

At the time of the 1956 election the clan-family distribution of the SYL's strength was estimated as 50 percent Darod, 30 percent Hawiya, 10 percent Digil and Rahanwein, and 10 percent other. These figures may be compared with the estimated division of the territorial population: 18 percent Darod, 38 percent Hawiya, and 29 percent Digil and Rahanwein. The HDMS found nearly all of its support among the cultivators of the Digil and Rahanwein, although the party's strength was primarily along lines of common economic interest rather than clan ties.

One of the first acts of the new SYL-dominated assembly was to make it illegal for political parties to bear the name of clans or tribes (clan-families). The HDMS immediately changed its full title to Somali Independent Constitutional Party (Hizbia Dustur Mustaquil Somali).

The Issa government remained in power for the four years until independence and thus was able to oversee the terms under which the new state was created. Its attitudes were modernist, pan-Somali, and nationalist, although it became and remained strongly pro-Italian once Italy was no longer seen as a threat to Somali independence. The government's first concerns were to improve the future state's economic stability so as to ensure foreign assistance to replace the support Italy would continue to provide until independence. It also pledged itself to grant voting rights to women, which it did in time for municipal elections in 1958. It strongly supported the promotion of Somali into all important government positions, but this did not constitute a major political issue because somalization was well under way before 1956. For example, all the sensitive posts of district commissioner had been turned over to Somali in 1955. All other posts were being somalized as fast as men could receive the required minimum educational background. Other efforts at modernization included attempts to weaken clan ties, particularly by limiting the use of the traditional collective punishment exacted from an entire group for the crimes of one of its members, and to further the breakup of the traditionally low status of persons in certain occupations (see ch. 4).

The government's second major concern was to draft a constitution that would become effective with independence. The most difficult provisions of the constitutional drafts were those concerning the concept of Greater Somalia, that is, for the ultimate inclusion of Somali-populated areas in Kenya, Ethiopia, French Somaliland, and British Somaliland into the Somali state. Such draft provisions became embroiled in the controversy over the choice of having either a unitary structure of government or a federal one, which would allow the other parts of Greater Somalia to be incorporated into the state more easily. This choice was complicated by HDMS support for federalism on a lower level, which might lessen the dominance of the numerically superior nomads over the cultivators of the interriver region, who were largely members of the HDMS. The SYL supported the concept of a unitary state, fearing that federalism would stimulate divisive clan interests. The SYL's political strength allowed its unitary view to prevail without difficulty.

Because of the SYL's near dominance of the political scene, the main political conflicts in the country gradually began to take place within the SYL rather than between the SYL and other groups. Internal divisions took form when forces within the SYL strove to dominate the party in order to make their own views or their own clans dominant. Individual politicians made efforts to stimulate the cleavage between the party's Hawiya and Darod supporters. Others accused the Issa government of being too friendly to the Italians and of doing nothing to achieve the goal of a Greater Somalia. In July 1957 Hussein, who had been president of the SYL in its early years, was again elected to lead the party. His own views conflicted strongly with those of the Issa government and with the party's leader in the legislature, assembly president Aden Abdulla Osman. Hussein led the party wing that favored a loosening of ties with the West and stronger relations with the Arab world, particularly with the United Arab Republic. His faction's policy led it to support the adoption of an Arabic script for writing Somali, another sensitive issue.

In April 1958, with the assistance of Osman, later to become the country's first president, Hussein and his supporters were expelled from the SYL without causing a major split in the party. Hussein then formed a new party, the Greater Somali League (GSL), sometimes referred to simply as "the Great"; it had a militant platform incorporating his philosophies of pan-Arabism and pan-Somalism. Although Hussein remained an important political figure, the GSL was unable to draw significant support away from the SYL, as was clearly demonstrated by the October 1958 municipal elections in which the SYL won 416 seats to the GSL's thirty-six. The HDMS won 175 seats in the contest, and the Liberal Party won twenty-seven.

The SYL further strengthened its position on the national level after the municipal elections, partially at the expense of the HDMS, because some Rahanwein politicians switched their allegiance to what was clearly the country's real power center. These changes came in time to assist the SYL in the final preindependence election for the newly expanded National Assembly, which was to have ninety seats. The GSL and the major portion of the HDMS alleged interference in their election campaigns and boycotted the election in protest. As a result sixty-one seats were uncontested and went to the SYL candidates by default. The party also won twenty-two of the contested seats, the Liberal Party won two seats, and the portion of the HDMS that did contest the election won five seats. Thus as independence approached, the SYL held all but seven of the ninety votes in the assembly.

The government formed in June 1959 consisted of fifteen ministerial and subministerial positions, again under the direction of Issa. The great expansion of the party allowed nearly all clans to be represented in it. Accordingly attempts were made to divide the cabinet positions among the representatives of all clan-families, but conflicts continued within the party and cabinet between conservative elements and modernists led by Abderashid Ali Shermarke.

The most interesting development of the preindependence period was the change in British Somaliland that allowed it to merge at independence with the Trust Territory to become a united nation. Between 1950 and 1960 development proceeded at a much accelerated pace in nearly all fields in comparison with earlier periods, although it did not match the efforts being made in the Trust Territory. The British colonial authorities were interested primarily in expanding educational opportunities. The first secondary school was opened in 1953. By 1960 additional schools were opened, and over 100 students were studying abroad. The number of Somali in important positions, however, remained very limited until just before independence.

Economic development was also restricted. Exports remained limited to hides and skins. Geological surveys were intensified, but no significant mineral resources were revealed. Strong efforts were made to expand agricultural and veterinary services and to improve the watering facilities for both farming and herding.

Until 1955 political changes did not go beyond the extension of limited authority to local government units. The SYL had opened branches in British Somaliland, but neither it nor the older SNL was able to stimulate any widespread interest. In late 1954, however, the return of the last British-administered sections of the Haud to Ethiopian authority provided a potent, popular political issue. Neither the Somali who lived in the Haud nor those who resided in British Somaliland but grazed their herds in the Haud were consulted or even alerted to the imminence of the Ethiopian takeover.

The protest was immediate and massive. The revitalized SNL and SYL jointly supported the National United Front (NUF), which had been formed under the leadership of Michael Mariano, a Christian Somali civil servant who had been active in the formative years of the SYL in the Italian territory. The NUF voiced demands for the return of the Haud to, and independence for, British Somaliland. It sent missions to London and to the UN in New York in an attempt to gain support for its position and to have the matter brought before the International Court of Justice. The British, feeling the pressure, sought unsuccessfully to purchase the disputed area from Ethiopia. The Ethiopians refused and in fact filed counterclaims of Ethiopian historical sovereignty over both the Somali territories, which served to stimulate Somali nationalism further.

In 1956 the British agreed to the gradual introduction of representative government in the protectorate and agreed not to oppose an eventual union between British Somaliland and an independent Somalia. In 1957 the Legislative Council was created; it had six members, all selected by the governor, to represent clan-families. Demands that the council's members be elected were ignored until 1958, when the body was expanded to include a total of twelve elected members, two appointed members, and fifteen ex officio members. As in the Trust Territory this first national election was by secret ballot in the urban centers but by acclamation by the *shir* of each clan in the rural areas.

New elections were held in February 1960 for the Legislative Assembly, with thirty-three elected members. This was the first election contested along party lines. Thirty-two of the seats were won by the SNL and its affiliate, the United Somali Party (USP); the one remaining seat went to a joint SYL-NUF candidate. Mohamed Ibrahim Egal became the leader of the four-member cabinet.

Ties between the political leaders in both Somali territories had been strengthened by the attitude of the 1959 Issa government in the Trust Territory, which had adopted the unification of the Somali as its primary program, and by the creation in July 1959 of the National

Pan-Somali Movement. Although the leadership of the SNL would have preferred to postpone unification until the north might be closer to the south in development, popular opinion in the north, as well as the position taken by the USP and SYL-NUF, was too strongly in favor of unity for a delay to be countenanced.

In April 1960 the British government agreed in principle to the ending of its rule in time for British Somaliland to unite with the Trust Territory on the July independence date that had already been set by the UN. Leaders of the two territories met in Mogadishu in mid-April and agreed to an amalgamation resulting in a unitary state under an elected president as head of state and a ministerial form of government responsible to an amalgamated national legislature composed of the 123 members of the two territorial assemblies. British Somaliland received its independence on June 26, 1960, and merged with the Trust Territory to form the independent Republic of Somalia on July 1, 1960.

FROM INDEPENDENCE TO THE REVOLUTION

At the time of independence the north (that is, British Somaliland) had two functioning political parties: the SNL, dominated by the Isaq clan-family, who constituted a numerical majority in that region, and the USP, composed largely of Dir and Darod. In a unified Somalia, however, the Isaq were a small minority, and the northern Darod were able to combine in the SYL with members of the same clan-family from the south. The Dir, with few representatives in the south, were drawn by weak traditional ties to the Hawiya on the one hand and by common regional feeling and problems to the Isaq on the other hand.

The southern opposition party, the GSL, pro-Arab in outlook and militantly pan-Somali in attitude, attracted the support of the SNL and the USP against the SYL, which had adopted a moderate stand before independence and had been responsible for a constitutional provision calling for unification of all Somali territories by peaceful means.

The problem of integrating disparate colonial legacies also contributed to the cleavage between north and south. Northern disenchantment was underlined by the voting pattern in the first national election, the June 1961 referendum to ratify the constitution. Although the draft was overwhelmingly approved in the south, it was supported by less than 50 percent of the northern electorate. Those who voted against it evidently did so in order to register their displeasure rather than because they were actually opposed to the constitution's provisions.

Northern dissatisfaction continued to grow and reached a crisis in December 1961 when a group of British-trained junior army officers in the north rebelled because less well trained but higher ranking southerners were assigned as senior officers over their units. The junior officers urged a separation of north and south. The basic strength of Somali unity was displayed, however, in the reaction of the northern noncommissioned officers who, incensed by this attempt at secession, arrested the rebels.

Thereafter, in order to placate the north, the government made strong efforts to ensure that north-south disputes were conducted on the level of interparty politics. In early 1962 the GSL leader, Hussein, attempted to form an amalgamated party, the Somali Democratic Union (SDU), to serve as an organized opposition to the SYL. The attempt was unsuccessful as the northern SNL remained linked to the SYL in the coalition government.

In May 1962, however, two northern SNL cabinet ministers resigned, including Egal, who later became prime minister. They took the SNL followers into a new party, the Somali National Congress (SNC), which received widespread support in the north. It also gained support in the south when a portion of the SYL (predominantly composed of Hawiya) joined it. The move gave the country three major political parties with national appeal, further blurring north-south lines.

Countrywide municipal elections, in which the SYL won 74 percent of the seats, were held in November 1963. These were followed in March 1964 by the country's first postindependence national elections. Again the SYL triumphed, winning sixty-nine of 123 seats. Their true margin of victory was even greater, as the fifty-four seats won by the opposition were divided among a number of small parties.

After the 1964 election for the National Assembly a governmental crisis occurred that left Somalia ungoverned until the beginning of September. Empowered to select the candidate for prime minister after an election or a fall of government, President Osman chose Abdirazak Haji Hussein as his nominee instead of the incumbent, Shermarke, who had the endorsement of the SYL party leadership. Shermarke had been prime minister for the four previous years, and Osman decided that a new leader might be able to present new ideas for solving national problems.

Before being presented to the National Assembly for approval, the newly nominated prime minister had to draw up a cabinet. His choices further strained intraparty harmony and broke the unwritten rules of clan and regional balance, as he picked the ministers for their abilities without regard to their origins. Only two members from the Shermarke cabinet were retained, and the number of posts in northern hands was increased from two to five, a third of the seats in the new cabinet.

The SYL's governing Central Committee and its parliamentary groups were split. Hussein had been a member of the party since 1944 and had also been a member of two previous Shermarke cabinets. His primary appeal was to younger and better educated members of the party. A number of the political leaders who had been left out of the cabinet joined Shermarke's supporters to form an opposition group within the party. As a result the Hussein faction found it necessary to seek support among the non-SYL members of the National Assembly.

Although the disagreements primarily involved personal or group political ambitions, the debate leading to the initial vote of confidence centered on the unification of all Somali-populated territories, the issue that continued to dominate Somali politics. Hussein was portrayed as willing to recognize the legitimacy of continued Kenyan and Ethiopian sovereignty over Somali areas. Both Osman and the prime minister-designate were indeed interested in giving priority to solving the country's internal economic and social problems, but Hussein made clear his support for militant pan-Somalism.

The nominated cabinet failed to obtain a vote of confidence by two ballots (fifty-nine to fifty-seven); seven National Assembly members, including Shermarke, abstained; forty-eight members of the SYL voted for Hussein, thirty-three against him. Despite the apparent split in the SYL it continued to attract members of other parties. In the first three months after the election seventeen members of the parliamentary opposition resigned from their parties to join the SYL.

President Osman chose to ignore the results of the vote and again nominated Hussein as prime minister. After extensive intraparty negotiation, which included the reinstatement of four party officials expelled for voting against him, Hussein presented a second cabinet list that included all but one of his earlier nominees. The new cabinet, however, contained three other ministerial positions filled by men chosen to mollify opposition factions. The new cabinet was approved on September 27 with the support of eighty-three of the eighty-nine SYL members in the assembly. The new prime minister remained in office until the presidential elections of June 1967.

The presidential elections, conducted by secret polling of the members of the National Assembly, pitted the former prime minister, Shermarke, against the incumbent, Osman. Again the apparent issue for those casting ballots was moderation versus militancy on the pan-Somali question. President Osman, through Hussein, had stressed the need to give first priority to internal improvements; Shermarke, as prime minister, had led the country during the period when pan-Somalism reached its most militant position. This distinction, as well as personal differences, led to Shermarke's election as president of the republic.

The new president nominated Mohamed Ibrahim Egal as prime minister the next month. Egal raised the membership of the cabinet from thirteen to fifteen members and included representatives of every major clan-family, as well as some members of the rival SNC. His appointment was confirmed by the National Assembly in August without grave conflict. Although Egal was an important political supporter of Shermarke in the presidential election, he was a northerner and had led the 1962 defection of the northern SNL assembly members from the government. He had also been closely involved in the founding of the SNC but, along with many other northern members of that group, had rejoined the SYL after the 1964 elections.

A more important difference between Shermarke and Egal, other than their past affiliations, was the prime minister's moderate position on pan-Somali issues and his desire for improved relations with the rest of Africa, as well as his apparent wish to redirect the nation's energies from combat with its neighbors to the battle against internal economic and social ills. Although his blunting of the militant tones of pan-Somali claims would earlier have been considered political suicide and many of his policies seemed more in line with those of former President Osman, Egal continued to hold the confidence of both President Shermarke and the National Assembly for the eighteen months preceding the March 1969 national elections.

One result of his policies was a great improvement in relations with Kenya and Ethiopia. This improvement led to a lowering of tensions in the country's border regions, a resumption of free access for the herds of the nomads to the vital transfrontier grazing areas, and a reopening of profitable trade routes, including the direct road between Mogadishu and Hargeysa. In addition the energies of national political leaders and the resources of the meager national economy were no longer fully occupied with international issues, and greater efforts to plan internal improvements could be undertaken. The diminution of tensions had another effect, however. To some extent the level of Somali cohesion depended on conflicts between Somalia on the one hand and Ethiopia and Kenya on the other. As these were reduced, clans and lineages within clan-families tended to revert to internal conflict.

The March 1969 elections were the first to combine voting for municipal and National Assembly posts. A total of sixty-four parties contested the elections. Only the SYL, however, presented candidates in every election district, and they were unopposed for twelve seats in five districts. Eight other parties presented lists of candidates for national offices in twelve or more districts. Of the remaining fifty-five parties, only twenty-four gained representation in the assembly, and all of these were disbanded almost immediately when their fifty members joined the SYL.

Both the plethora of parties and the defection to the majority party were typical of Somali parliamentary elections. The majority of the minor parties represented individual candidates. In order to register, a candidate needed the support either of 500 voters or of his clan, expressed through a vote of its *shir*. After registering he then attempted to become the official candidate of some major grouping but, failing this, was left as an individual contestant on the ballot. Balloting was by party list, making the individual candidate in effect a party. This explains not only the proliferation of small parties but also the transience of party support; many candidates affiliated with a major party only long enough to use its symbol in the election campaign and, if elected, abandoned it for the winning side as soon as the National Assembly met. Thus by the end of May 1969 the SYL parliamentary group had swelled from seventy-three to 109 members.

In addition the eleven members of the SNC had formed with the SYL a coalition, which held 120 of the 123 seats in the assembly. A few of these 120 left the SYL after the composition of Prime Minister Egal's cabinet became clear and after the announcement of his future policies, both of which were bound to displease some of those who had joined to be on the winning side after the election.

In the enormous listing of candidates the almost 900,000 voters in 1969 had the opportunity to defeat incumbents and evidently took delight in doing so. Of the former deputies seventy-seven were not returned. The defeated members included eight of the eighteen members of the previous cabinet. These figures did not unequivocally demonstrate dissatisfaction with the previous government, however. Statistically they were nearly identical with the results of the 1964 election and, given the profusion of parties and the system of proportional representation, a clear conclusion cannot be reached solely on the basis of the election results.

The fact that a single party, the SYL, dominated the field implied neither stability nor solidarity. As anthropologist I.M. Lewis, a leading authority on the Somali, has noted: "the SYL Government . . . could not be other than an extremely heterogeneous assemblage of competing personal, family and lineage interests. The maintenance of any semblance of unity with such an ill-assorted crew would clearly prove a most costly business."

At the same time the many who had lost seats in the assembly and those who had supported the losers (some of whom had run for the first time) were frustrated and angry. A number of charges were made of election rigging by the government, at least some firmly founded, and discontent was exacerbated when the Supreme Court, under its newly appointed president, denied that it had jurisdiction over election petitions, although it had accepted such jurisdiction on an earlier occasion.

The Egal government's increasingly friendly relations with Ethiopia and Kenya were also a source of dissatisfaction for some. Moreover these ties could always be used rhetorically against the government by those whose primary discontents lay elsewhere.

"Finally," as I.M. Lewis puts it, "official corruption and nepotism seemed to be flourishing on a scale hitherto unknown in the Republic

. . . . but there was little sign that either the [Prime Minister] or the President were unduly disturbed by their persistence." It may be argued that, in a society based on kinship and one in which kin groups perceived each other as either enemies or allies in competition for scarce resources, nepotism and corruption might be seen as normal. Nevertheless there were some who were embittered by it and by the ineptitude of the National Assembly. "It had," says Lewis, "been turned into a sordid marketplace where deputies traded their votes for personal rewards with scant regard for the interests of their constituents."

Among the dissatisfied were intellectuals and many of the military and the police. (General Mohammad Abshir Musa, the chief of police, had resigned just before the elections on the grounds that the politicians had interfered with police work.) Of these the most significant element was the military, which had hitherto remained outside politics; this was partly because the previous governments had not called upon it for support and partly because, unlike most other African forces, it had a genuine external mission supported by all Somali—that of protecting the borders with Kenya and Ethiopia.

The stage was set for a coup, but the event that precipitated it was apparently accidental. On October 15, 1969, President Shermarke was killed by a policeman while Prime Minister Egal was out of the country. The assassin was apparently a member of a lineage said to have been badly treated by the president, and he was subsequently tried and executed by the revolutionary government. Egal returned to Mogadishu to arrange for the naming of a new president by the National Assembly; his choice was, like Shermarke, a member of the Darod clan-family (Egal was an Isaq.) Critics of the government, particularly a group of army officers, apparently saw no hope for improvement. In the early morning of October 21, 1969, when the results of the assembly's deliberations were apparent, the army under its commander, Major General Mohamed Siad Barre, took over important points in Mogadishu and rounded up government officials and other important political figures. In this enterprise the police cooperated with the army, but according to some accounts its collaboration was initially somewhat reluctant.

The new governing body was announced as the Supreme Revolutionary Council (SRC). Political parties were made illegal, and the National Assembly was abolished. The goals of the new regime were said to be an end to corruption and tribalism and a return to true democracy and justice. Existing treaties were to be honored, but national liberation movements and Somali unification were to be supported. The country was renamed the Somali Democratic Republic.

* * *

The basic argument for the modified traditional view of Somali origins and migrations is given by I.M. Lewis in "The Somali Conquest

42

of the Horn of Africa." The revisionist view is presented by Herbert S. Lewis in "The Origins of the Galla and Somali," which is supported and amplified by E.R. Turton's "Bantu, Galla, and Somali Migrations in the Horn of Africa: A Reassessment of the Juba-Tana Area." I.M. Lewis provides a general, easily accessible historical account in *The Modern History of Somaliland.* Lee Vincent Cassanelli's doctoral dissertation, *The Benaadir Past: Essays in Southern Somali History,* gives an interesting and complex view of developments in the Juba-Shabelle region and adjacent areas from early times to the onset of Italian control. I.M. Lewis calls on his thorough knowledge of Somali society and politics to analyze the background and initial consequences of the military coup of October 1969 in "The Politics of the 1969 Somali Coup." (For further information see Bibliography.)

CHAPTER 3

GEOGRAPHY AND POPULATION

Situated in northeast Africa and the easternmost country of that continent, the Somali Democratic Republic (Somalia) has a land area of 246,155 square miles, according to standard reference authorities, roughly comparable to that of the state of Texas. Some Somali sources put the total at about 262,000 square miles, which seems to be related to territorial claims (see ch. 10). The country has the shape of the number 7 and is the cap of the geographic region commonly referred to as the Horn of Africa, which includes Ethiopia and the political unit known in 1976 as the French Territory of Afars and Issas (FTAI). Somalia's northern limits, which face the Gulf of Aden, lie about 12° north of the equator. Its eastern and southern bounds face the Indian Ocean; the southernmost point of the country reaches about 1½° below the equator. Landward it shares borders on the northwest with the FTAI, on the west with Ethiopia, and on the southwest with Kenya (see fig. 1).

The terrain is in general relatively flat, consisting of plateau surfaces and plains except in the north, where rugged, west-east mountain ranges lie at varying distances from the Gulf of Aden coast. Climatically the country is in the tropics, and throughout the year temperatures are hot, although there are exceptions at higher elevations in the north. Because rainfall is sparse, most of Somalia has a harsh, semiarid-to-arid environment that has enforced on much of the population a largely nomadic life-style based on livestock husbandry. Only in limited areas of moderate rainfall in the northwest and particularly in the southwest, where the country's two perennial rivers are found, is cultivation practiced to any extent (see ch. 13).

The local geology suggests the presence of valuable mineral deposits. As of 1976, however, only a few significant sites had been located, and mineral production played a very minor role in the economy.

The population inhabiting this climatically rather forbidding land was estimated to total over 3 million in mid-1976. The lack of reliable census data to that time, however, for a population that includes a large proportion of uncounted nomad pastoralists, introduced the possibility of considerable error in the calculated figure. It was clearly apparent, nonetheless, that the population was largely rural, to a smaller extent nomadic, and generally youthful and had a high degree

45

of cultural and linquistic homogeneity (see ch. 4). Nomadism and the question of settling and redirecting the efforts of the pastoral population toward other productive economic activities posed perhaps the greatest problem faced by the government in the mid-1970s.

CLIMATE AND PHYSICAL GEOGRAPHY

Climate

Climate is the overriding factor influencing much of Somali life, the time of arrival and the sufficiency of rainfall being for the large nomadic population the major determinants of whether grazing will be adequate for their livestock and for the enjoyment of relative prosperity or whether pasturage and water will be in short supply, animals lost, and existence grim. Under conditions of severe drought, such as occurred during 1974 and early 1975, the situation can become disastrous.

Though less prominent in parts of the northern highlands and in the southwestern coastal area of the Juba and Shabelle (literally, leopard) rivers, four seasons are observable, two wet and two dry. These are determined by the northeast and southwest monsoonal winds and the transitional lulls between them that result in alternating periods of moisture and aridity. During the main periods of monsoonal airflow, winds blow parallel to the coast and deposit little rainfall. In the first of these periods—from late December or early January until about March, when the northeast monsoon is dominant—hot, dry, and dusty winds are prevalent. This season, known locally as *jilal*, is the harshest time of year for the nomadic groups.

Beginning in March and extending into May and sometimes June, a transitional period known as *gu*, during which the monsoonal winds change direction, brings the country's heaviest, though still comparatively meager, rains. The third and longest season, *hagaa*, begins in June as the southwest monsoon becomes ascendant. By July pastures and vegetation begin to dry up, and dust, blown by the strong winds, is everywhere. The *hagaa* season continues through August and is the hottest period of the year in the north; along the Gulf of Aden temperatures may soar to 120°F. Along the southwest coast, however, cooling sea breezes from the Indian Ocean make this period comparatively pleasant; showers also occur during this time in this coastal area. The second wet season, called *dayr* by the Somali, is the shorter of the two, but its intermittent rains during the lull between the southwest and northeast monsoons—mostly in October and November—account in some areas for about 30 percent of the annual rainfall.

Most of the country receives less than twenty inches of rain annually; a large area, encompassing the northeastern and much of the northern parts, receives as little as two to six inches. Certain higher areas in the north, however, record over twenty inches annually. The southwest receives an average of thirteen to twenty inches, and some coastal spots average more than twenty inches (see fig. 3). Rainfall is

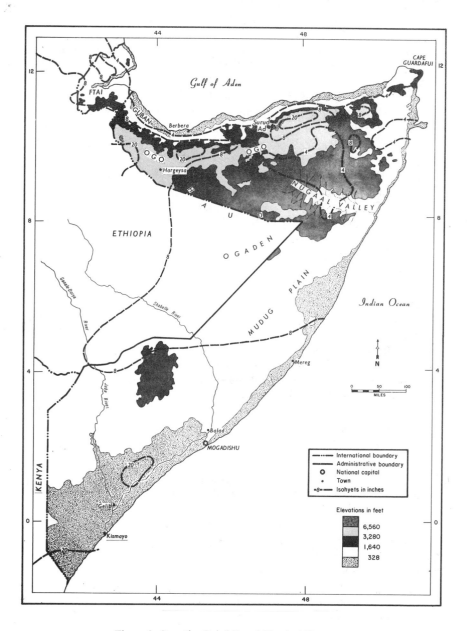

Figure 3. Somalia, Rainfall and Physical Features

largely in the form of showers or localized rains and is characterized by an extreme degree of variability that cannot be ignored in any program for the development of rain-fed agriculture.

Mean daily maximum temperatures range from 85°F to 105°F, although they are lower at the higher elevations and along the Indian Ocean coast. Mean daily minimum temperatures usually vary from the mid-60°s to the higher 80°s.

The northern part of the country has the greatest temperature extremes; readings range from below freezing in the highlands in December to more than 120°F in the coastal plain skirting the Gulf of Aden in July. The region's relative humidity ranges from approximately 40 percent in midafternoon to 85 percent at night, varying somewhat with the season. During the colder months at the higher elevations, from December to February, visibility is often restricted by fog.

The southern part of the country exhibits less extreme temperatures, ranging from about 65°F to 105°F; the hottest season is from February through April. Coastal temperatures are usually from 10°F to 15°F degrees cooler than those inland. There is little variation in the coastal zone's relative humidity, which usually remains above 70 percent even during the dry seasons.

Physical Geography

Physiographically Somalia is a land of limited contrast. In the north, paralleling the Gulf of Aden coast, is a maritime plain that varies in width from about thirty-five miles in the west to as little as one or two miles in the east. Scrub-covered, semiarid, and generally drab in appearance, this plain, known as the Guban (burnt land) because of its heat and dryness during much of the year, is crossed by broad, shallow watercourses that are beds of dry sand except in the rainy seasons. When the rains arrive, however, the vegetation is quickly renewed, and for a time the Guban provides some grazing for nomad livestock.

Away from the gulf the plain rises to the precipitous north-facing cliffs of dissected highlands, which form rugged mountain ranges that extend from the northwestern border with Ethiopia eastward to the tip of the horn, where they end in sheer cliffs at Cape Guardafui. The elevation along the crest of these mountains averages about 6,000 feet above sea level in the area about thirty miles south of Berbera and eastward from that area continues at between 6,000 and 7,000 feet almost to Cape Guardafui. The country's high point, Surud Ad, which rises to over 7,900 feet, is located near the town of Erigavo.

To the south the mountains descend, often in scarped ledges, through a region of broken mountain terrain, shallow plateau valleys, and usually dry watercourses, known to the Somali as the Ogo. This region merges into an elevated plateau devoid of perennial rivers that, in its especially arid eastern part, which is interspersed with a number of isolated mountain ranges, gradually slopes toward the Indian Ocean; in central Somalia it constitutes the Mudug Plain. A major feature of the eastern section is the long and broad Nugaal Valley, which has an extensive net of intermittent seasonal watercourses. The entire eastern area, whose population consists mainly of pastoral nomads, is in a zone of low and erratic rainfall. It was a major disaster area during the great drought of 1974 and early 1975.

The western part of the plateau is characterized by shallow valleys and dry watercourses. Annual rainfall is greater, however, and in the west are flat areas of arable land that provide a home for dryland farming cultivators. Most important, it is an area of permanent wells to which the predominantly nomadic population returns during the dry seasons. The western plateau slopes gently southward and merges imperceptibly into a zone known as the Haud, a broad, undulating area that constitutes some of the best grazing lands for the Somali nomad despite the lack of appreciable rainfall for over half the year. Enhancing the value of the Haud are the natural depressions that flood during periods of rain to become temporary lakes and ponds.

The Haud, continuing for 100 miles or more into the Ogaden region of Ethiopia, is part of the vast Somali Plateau, which lies between the northern Somalian mountains and the highlands of southeast Ethiopia and extends southward and eastward through Ethiopia into central and southwest Somalia. An Anglo-Ethiopian agreement during the colonial era provided for access to the Ethiopian part of the plateau by British-protected Somali herdsmen from the north. Somalia has laid claim to part of this area, and the newly independent Somali government in 1960 refused to acknowledge the agreement. A major dispute erupted in 1964, and a territorial delimitation with Ethiopia had still not been reached by mid-1976 (see ch. 2; ch. 10). In the mid-1970s Somali nomads continued to move back and forth with the seasons throughout the Haud in the constant search for forage for their animals (see International Boundaries and Political Subdivisions, this ch.).

The physiography of southwestern Somalia is dominated by the country's only two permanent rivers, the Juba and Shabelle. These rivers, which originate in the Ethiopian highlands, flow generally southward, cutting wide valleys in the Somali Plateau as it descends toward the sea; the plateau's elevation falls off rapidly in this area. A succeeding large coastal zone, which includes the lower reaches of the rivers and extends from the Mudug Plain to the Kenya border, averages 600 feet or less above sea level.

The Juba enters the Indian Ocean at Kismayo. Although the Shabelle at one time apparently reached the sea near Marka (Merca), its course changed in prehistoric times; in its present-day course it turns south-

southwestward near Balad, about twenty miles north of Mogadishu, and follows a path parallel to the coast for about 140 miles. The river is perennial only to a point southwest of Mogadishu; thereafter it consists of swampy areas and dry reaches and is finally lost in the sand east of Gelib, not far from the Juba River. During flood seasons in about April to May (the *gu* rainy period) and October to November (*dayr* rains), the river may be full to near Gelib and occasionally may even break through to the Juba farther south. Favorable rainfall and soil conditions make this entire river region a fertile agricultural area and the center of the country's largest sedentary population (see ch. 4; ch. 13).

SOILS AND VEGETATION

Except in a few areas where irrigation or adequate and sufficiently reliable rainfall permits the cultivation of crops, the structure of the country's soils is of little direct present-day economic concern. Most of the northern, northeastern, and north-central parts of Somalia have calcareous, gypseous, or saline soils. Where rainfall is low, these soils support scattered low trees, including various acacias, and widely interspersed patches of grass. This vegetation deteriorates into a sub-desert association of low bushes and grass clumps in the highly arid areas of the northeast and along the Gulf of Aden.

As elevations and rainfall increase in the maritime ranges of the north, the vegetation becomes denser. Aloes are common, and on the higher plateau areas of the Ogo there is some open woodland. At a few spots above 5,000 feet the remnants of juniper forests—protected by the state—and areas of the candelabra euphorbia occur. In the more arid highlands of the northeast *Boswellia* and *Commiphora* trees are sources respectively of the frankincense and myrrh for which Somalia has been known since ancient times.

A broad plateau area encompassing the northern city of Hargeysa, which receives a comparatively high rainfall, has calcareous, sandy, well-drained soils with a moderate organic content. This area is covered naturally by open woodland, much of which has been degraded by overgrazing, and occasionally extensive grassland. Parts of this area have been under cultivation to grow sorghum and maize (corn) since the 1930s; in 1976 it constituted the only significant region of sedentary cultivation outside the southwestern part of the country (see ch. 13).

The semiarid Haud south of the Hargeysa area contains red calcareous soils that continue into the Ogaden region of Ethiopia. The Haud is covered mostly by an open, semiarid woodland of scattered trees, mainly acacias, underlain by grasses that include species especially favored by livestock as forage. As the Haud merges into the Mudug Plain in central Somalia, the aridity increases, and soils take on a reddish-brown hue. The vegetation here displays a subdesert character but farther southward gradually changes to semiarid woodland and grass as the annual precipitation increases.

In comparison with these areas, the region encompassing the Shabelle and Juba rivers is relatively well watered and constitutes the most promising arable zone in the country. Soils vary from reddish to dark clays in the lowland between the rivers and support a rich pasturage. Fine-textured black alluvium occurs near the rivers, and farther inland lie fertile black soils. The semiarid climate, the alternating cycle of wet and dry seasons, and the high evaporation rates, however, have had adverse effects on the soil. Soils along the Shabelle have an inadequate water-holding capacity and tend to be saline because of the alkaline river water. Moreover they are deficient in organic matter and plant nutrients. The soils along the Juba are less saline and, although their organic content is low, they have a fairly high level of nitrates. The zone around and between the two rivers contains the country's most productive agricultural activities, and it is here that the government has concentrated much of its land development effort (see ch. 13).

The region's natural vegetation is arid to subarid savanna, open woodland, and thickets and underlying grasses that frequently are abundant. In places there are areas of grassland, and in the far southwestern part near the Kenya border some dry evergreen forest is found.

Along the Indian Ocean from Mereg southwestward to near Kismayo lies a stretch of fixed coastal sand dunes. Their reddish to yellowish soils contain small amounts of organic matter and some plant nutrients that, where rainfall is sufficient, have permitted growth of scattered scrub and grass clumps. Overgrazing, particularly in the area between Mogadishu and Kismayo, has resulted in the destruction of the protective vegetation cover and the gradual movement of the dunes inland, threatening agricultural areas and human installations. New efforts to stabilize these dunes by replanting have been made since the early 1970s, reportedly with some success (see ch. 13).

Minor vegetation includes that found in the swamps into which the Shabelle River empties most of the year and in other large swamp areas in the lower course of the Juba River. Mangrove forests are also found at points along the coast, particularly from Kismayo to near the Kenya border. Uncontrolled exploitation appears to have caused some damage to forests in that area. Other mangrove forests are located near Mogadishu and at a number of spots along the northeastern and northern coasts.

MINERALS

The country's proven mineral resources were few, and the importance of mining to the national economy remained minimal in the mid-

1970s (see ch. 14). Extensive explorations for mineral wealth have been made since World War II by foreign firms, the United Nations, and the Somali government. A number of deposits of varying potential have been located, including relatively low-grade iron ore and uranium and several other radioactive minerals. Large deposits of good-quality sepiolite (meerschaum) exist near El Bur in Galgduud Region, and in the area of Berbera in the northern part of the country there are major deposits of gypsum and anhydrite. Limestone and sandstone also exist around Berbera. Tin deposits were mined near Bosaso during the period of Italian colonization, and additional deposits have been located in that general vicinity. Potentially important finds of piezoquartz have been made in several areas of northwestern Somalia.

Other mineral occurrences, mostly in the northern part of the country, include ores of copper, chromium, lead, manganese, molybdenum, nickel, and zinc. In the mid-1970s further exploration was required to determine their economic value.

Somalia's location and geology suggest the possibility of oil and gas deposits. Exploration has been carried out since about 1950, but to mid-1976 no significant finds had been made. Both terrestrial and offshore exploration were continuing, however.

WILDLIFE

Somalia has a large variety of big game and smaller wild animals, but comparisons of accounts of the situation around the beginning of the twentieth century and that existing in the 1960s indicate that numbers and ranges have been greatly reduced. Although both authorized hunting and poaching have been factors, studies have shown that the primary causes for the disappearance of certain large game animals in some areas have been their crowding out by the steadily growing numbers of livestock, their exclusion from the country's scarce watering spots as the result of human preemption, and the widespread cutting of trees and other vegetation that has destroyed the natural cover and the grazing capacity of the land.

Surveys in 1964 and 1968 showed that the destruction of large wildlife had been particularly severe in the north. Various antelope, as well as elephant, rhinoceros, and giraffe, which had been reported in large numbers in that area in the early 1900s, were completely gone; other formerly abundant species, including several gazelles, dik-dik, kudu, lion, and wild donkey, were greatly reduced in number.

In early 1969 the existing game laws were consolidated and strengthened, and a number of reserve areas were designated in which hunting was controlled or completely prohibited; several other areas were also placed under partial restrictions. In 1974 there were twenty-one protective reserves of all kinds, including one area in the southwestern corner of the country that was to be developed into a national game park. Expansion of management and policing staffs was planned during the Development Program 1974-1978.

For various reasons, including natural habitat, the ranges of some larger mammals are restricted to certain parts of the country. Herbivores found in the southwestern part of Somalia are elephant, giraffe, black rhinoceros (in the mid-1970s classified as an endangered species), buffalo, and zebra; some zebra are also found in the far north. Inhabiting areas along the Juba and Shabelle rivers is the hippopotamus, and in waters along the coast is the endangered dugong. The Somali wild donkey, also considered endangered, is found only in the northeast. The larger herbivores most prevalent throughout the country, however, are the antelopes and gazelles; some species, such as the gerenuk, lesser kudu, and oryx, are widespread; others are more limited in range, such as the bush and red dik-diks and waterbuck found in the southwest and the hartebeest that inhabits the Haud.

Large predators include the leopard, cheetah, lion, serval, and lynx; common smaller forms are the fox and jackal. There are also hyenas and wild dogs. Reduction in numbers of the larger predators, especially the leopard and cheetah, through excessive hunting and poaching for skins (Somali leopard skins are of high quality and have been in demand in world markets), has upset the natural balance and has had the undesirable side effect of substantial increases in monkeys and warthogs, both of which are considered pests because of the destruction and damage they cause. Other common small mammals are the mongoose, badger, and squirrel.

Snakes are common in a considerable variety, including such dangerous forms as puff adders, spitting cobras, and a black snake that is apparently a mamba. Pythons are common in the southwestern part of the country. Other large reptiles are crocodiles, which infest the Juba and Shabelle rivers, monitor lizards, and large sea turtles, which frequent coastal waters.

Houseflies, ants, mosquitoes, and cockroaches are numerous, especially during the rainy seasons. Mosquitoes are prevalent throughout the year in areas where there is permanent water; they include the vector of malaria (see ch. 6). Other insects of note are scorpions, ticks, sand flies and, at certain times of the year, locusts.

A striking feature of the wildlife is the great variety of birds—about 450 species and subspecies. About half of these are migratory forms from eastern Europe, eastern Mediterranean countries, and Asia Minor that have winter quarters in Somalia. Water birds are particularly numerous and include ducks, geese, pelicans, herons, flamingos, cormorants, ospreys, and many others. Among birds of prey are eagles, hawks, vultures, owls, and ravens. The wide variety of game birds in different parts of the country includes guinea fowl, grouse, bustard, dove, and partridge. Probably the country's most notable bird is the ostrich, which is common on the open plains.

Although freshwater fish occur in the Juba and Shabelle rivers, information was unavailable on their kinds. Rockfish and snapper are found along the coast, as are rock lobster and shrimp. Pelagic fish include mackerel, shark, tuna, and such game fish as barracuda, dolphin, marlin, and sailfish.

INTERNATIONAL BOUNDARIES AND POLITICAL SUBDIVISIONS

The country's frontiers in 1976 with the adjacent states of Kenya and Ethiopia and the French Territory of Afars and Issas (FTAI) were established while present-day Somalia was occupied by Great Britain and Italy before Somalian independence in 1960. The several boundaries were fixed with little or no consideration for the territorial distribution of the Somali people or for the traditional livestock grazing patterns dictated by climatic factors that result in the pastoral nomads' regular seasonal migrations through most of the border areas. Independent Somalia's reluctance to accept these arrangements has led to several major disputes; in 1976 border issues continued to plague relations with neighboring territories (see ch. 2; ch. 10).

The northwest boundary between Somalia and the FTAI (thirty-four miles in length) was established by an Anglo-French agreement in 1888. Although the boundary is an arbitrarily drawn straight line that separates the Issa Somali from kinsmen in Somalia, the Somali government has recognized the line's legality.

On the west the boundary with Kenya (424 miles in length) resulted from a 1925 agreement between Great Britain and Italy that moved the border, which was then along the Juba River, westward to its present-day position, generally along 41° east longitude. The adjustment—made in considerable part as compensation for Italy's having thrown in its lot with the Allied powers in World War I—brought a large number of Somali nomads, who had been extending their grazing ranges into Kenya since the early 1900s, back into Italian Somalia. Large numbers remained in Kenya, however, and after independence in 1960 Somalia laid claim to Somali-inhabited lands west of the boundary. Unrest and sporadic violence resulted in growing tensions that were eased only in 1967 through the mediation of Zambian President Kenneth Kaunda, which led to the issuance of a joint Somalian-Kenyan statement implying at least de facto recognition of the existing border by Somalia.

Agreements among Great Britain, Italy, and Ethiopia in 1897 and 1908 established the basis for the disputed present-day border between Somalia and Ethiopia (about 994 miles in length). The border consists of three sectors, including a demarcated twenty-two-mile stretch running northeast from the Kenya-Somalia-Ethiopia tripoint to the town of Dolo, where the Dewa and Ganale-Dorya rivers join to form the Juba River. From that point eastward to the intersection of 8° north latitude and 48° east longitude, a distance of 509 miles, only a provisional administrative line existed in 1976. The third sector, initially agreed to by Great Britain and Ethiopia in 1897, is demarcated from this intersection westward for 463 miles to the Somalia-Ethiopia-FTAI tripoint.

The provisional administrative line resulted from the inability of Somalian and Ethiopian representatives to reach agreement in 1959 on a definite boundary in this area, a section of which had originally been part of Italian Somalia and a larger portion of which had been annexed to Italian Somalia during the occupation of Ethiopia by Italy in the mid-1930s (see ch. 2). At independence, moreover, the Somali government accorded only de facto recognition to the entire boundary with Ethiopia, a situation that continued to exist in mid-1976.

Somalia also has a coastline on the Gulf of Aden and the Indian Ocean totaling almost 1,840 statute miles. By Law Number 37 of September 10, 1972 (Law on the Somali Territorial Sea and Ports), territorial waters were declared to be under Somali sovereignty up to 200 miles from the country's continental and insular coasts. Along parts of the coast where there are deep indentations or fringing islands, straight base lines were used to connect appropriate points. The waters on the landward side of these base lines were declared to be inland waters. Certain restrictions on the use of, and passage through, the territorial waters were also stipulated by the law (see ch. 15; ch. 16).

In early 1976 the country had sixteen first-order administrative divisions, known as regions, which were subdivided into seventy-eight districts. Both regions and districts were headed by officials appointed by the central government (see ch. 8).

SETTLEMENT PATTERNS AND MAN-MADE FEATURES

Perhaps three-fifths of the population is nomadic or seminomadic—pure nomads are estimated to constitute two-fifths—and engages in mass cyclical migrations related to the alternation of wet and dry seasons. Such movements result in periodic changes in settlement patterns, particularly in the largely nomadic northern and northeastern parts of the country. During the dry season the nomads of the Ogo highlands and plateau areas in the north and the Nugaal Valley in the northeast are generally concentrated in villages or large encampments at permanent wells or other reliable sources of water. With the coming of the rains, however, they scatter with their herds throughout the vast expanse of the Haud, where they form a pattern of dispersed small encampments during the wet season or as long as animal forage and water hold out. During this time the women, children, and most of the adult men generally remain with the sheep, goats, burden camels, and occasionally cattle. The grazing camels are herded at some distance by boys and young, unmarried men. Then, as the dry season progresses, the area becomes relatively empty again as reconcentration in the home villages or settlements occurs.

A nomadic population also inhabits the southwestern part of the country between the Juba River and the Kenya border. In mid-1976 little information was available on their migratory patterns or dispersal.

The southwest is the location of the country's best arable lands, which lie along the Juba and Shabelle rivers and in the interriver area, and of the major portion of the sedentary population, who reside in fixed agricultural villages and settlements. Nomads are found in this area, but many pastoralists also engage part time in farming; and although some migration occurs with the seasons, the overriding pattern is established by the sedentary population. In the mid-1970s this pattern was being further reinforced because well over 100,000 nomads from the drought-stricken north and northeast were being settled in sedentary agricultural occupations in the southwest (see ch. 13).

The location of many towns appears to have been determined largely by trade factors. The major ports, extending from Kismayo and Mogadishu in the southwest to Berbera and Zeila in the far northwest, were founded between the eighth and tenth centuries A.D. by Arab and Persian immigrants as points for conducting trade with the interior, a function they continued to perform in the 1970s. Unlike many other coastal areas of the continent, however, this area failed to develop important fishing ports despite the rather substantial fish resources of the Indian Ocean and the Gulf of Aden. This appears to reflect to a great extent the centuries-old Somali aversion to eating fish and the lack of any sizable inland market. The fisheries potential and the need to expand food production, coupled with the problem of finding occupations for nomads ruined by the 1974-75 drought, have resulted in the government's encouraging and assisting nomad families to settle permanently in fishing villages; some 10,000 nomads were reported established in such villages in late 1975.

Present-day inland towns in sparsely populated areas owe their location to their development as trading centers at caravan crossing points or regular stopping places along caravan routes. In some cases the ready availability of water throughout the year led to the growth of substantial settlements that provided market and service facilities for nomadic populations. Such was the case with Galkayo, an oasis in the Mudug Plain having permanent wells.

Town and village distribution in the agricultural areas of the Juba and Shabelle rivers is related in part to the development of market centers among the sedentary population. But a considerable number of such towns and villages originated with the founding of *jamahayo* (agricultural religious communities) by various Islamic brotherhoods during the nineteenth century; an example is the large town of Bardera, which evolved from a *jamaha* founded in 1819 (see ch. 5). Hargeysa, the largest town in northern Somalia, was also started as a religious community in the nineteenth century. Its growth into the country's second largest city was mainly stimulated, however, by it selection in 1942 as the administrative center for British Somaliland.

Perhaps the most salient man-made features in the mid-1970s were the ports of Mogadishu and Kismayo in the southwest and Berbera in the north. The road network of about 10,000 miles was still in a developmental stage; close to 90 percent consisted of dirt roads. Major airports existed at Mogadishu and Hargeysa, and completion of a third at Kismayo was anticipated in 1976. A network of about fifteen smaller domestic airports completed the principal features of the transportation system. The hub of this system and of communications, government administration, and cultural activity is the capital city of Mogadishu, which was estimated to have possibly 400,000 inhabitants in the mid-1970s (see ch. 14).

POPULATION

The first nationwide population census was taken during February 1975. It included a complete enumeration in all urban and settled rural areas and a sample enumeration of the nomadic population. The sample enumeration used water points as the chief sampling units. To mid-1976 no information had been issued on the total count or on other data secured in the census.

After independence, in 1962 and 1963, national manpower surveys were carried out in towns and settled rural areas under the supervision of demographers from the International Labor Organization (ILO). The information, combined with reevaluated data from Italian-sponsored surveys in 1953, formed the basis for the population estimate of slightly over 2.3 million in 1963. Surveys were not made of the nomadic population, however, and estimates of the number included in the total were of necessity quite speculative. Although further manpower surveys were made in the late 1960s and early 1970s, they were confined to the settled rural population and the towns until a pilot survey of nomadic households was made in Burao District in Togdheer Region in 1973.

In the mid-1970s reliable sources placed the estimated population at more than 3 million, including a United Nations estimate of 3.09 million in mid-1974 and a United States Bureau of the Census estimate of 3.16 million in mid-1975. Somali estimates have ranged as high as 4.5 million, but this figure apparently included substantial numbers of

Somali who lived in adjoining regions of Kenya, Ethiopia. and the FTAI. In light of the lack of reliable quantitative information on the large nomadic population, all population estimates for the country as a whole should be viewed with considerable circumspection.

Structure and Density

About 95 percent of the population was estimated to consist of ethnic Somali in 1968. The balance included people of other African origin, Arabs, and small numbers of Europeans and Asians, a term applied principally to Indians and Pakistanis (see ch. 4). Estimates made in the mid-1960s—based on the 1962 and 1963 manpower surveys, earlier Italian surveys, and assumptions that some nomads were included in the town surveys—placed 37 percent of the total population in the age-group below fifteen years, 58 percent in the group between fifteen and fifty-nine years, and 5 percent in the group sixty years of age and over, The ratio of males to females was estimated at the time to be about 108 to 100.

In the late 1960s surveys in towns in southern Somalia found more than 40 percent in the group under fifteen years of age. A manpower survey made in 1971 estimated that 45 percent of the total population was in the age bracket under fifteen years, another 53 percent between fifteen and sixty-five years, and 2 percent sixty-five and older. Improved living conditions leading to declining infant mortality presumably were a factor in the increase of the young population. They probably accounted also in considerable part for the large proportion (slightly over 50 percent) in the under-fifteen-year age-group found in the first survey aimed specifically at nomadic households, which was carried out in 1973 in the northern part of the country. This survey also found that males in the surveyed nomadic households outnumbered females by an estimated ratio of 106 to 100.

On the basis of the population estimate of 3.16 million the population density per square mile was close to thirteen in mid-1975. This figure is rather meaningless, however, since climatic conditions largely dictate a major concentration of population in the wetter southwest. A second, though variable, concentration is found in the northwest on the plateau around Hargeysa, in part because of the greater rainfall in the area (see Settlement Patterns and Man-Made Features, this ch.). Elsewhere in the country the population is generally sparse; in the particularly arid semidesert parts of the northeast it averages less than two people per square mile.

The extent of urbanization was unclear in mid-1976 pending the results of the 1975 census. In the mid-1960s some sixty populated places had been designated municipal centers, but fewer than twenty-five had 5,000 or more inhabitants; only nine had populations over 10,000, including Mogadishu, which was estimated to have almost

173,000 inhabitants in 1967. Mogadishu's population was estimated to have risen to nearly 250,000 by 1970 and as many as 400,000 by 1975. Urbanization has continued elsewhere, but information on the growth of other towns was negligible in mid-1976.

Among the reasons for the migration to Mogadishu, especially after 1960, was the hope of many that they could secure financial or political assistance from kinsmen who had obtained positions in the government during the somalization that occurred in the Italian trusteeship period. In the early 1970s the attractions of city life, including the possibility of wage employment, appeared to be the main drawing cards. Movement to the city has also been a result of the country's recurrent droughts.

In the mid-1970s the city's population was about 98 percent Somali. Although concentrations of Europeans and Asians were found in some places, none of the city's residential areas was dominated by non-Somali. Noteworthy was the general intermingling of clan groups, although occasional and sometimes violent altercations indicated that clan identities had not entirely disappeared.

Population Dynamics

On the basis of the government surveys of the late 1960s the average annual growth rate at the time was estimated to be about 2.9 percent. Subsequent estimates have placed the rate somewhat lower; for the 1970-74 period it was estimated by the United Nations at about 2.6 percent. The United States Bureau of the Census estimated a birthrate in 1974 of between forty-seven and forty-nine per 1,000 population and a death rate of between twenty-one and twenty-four per 1,000 resulting in an annual rate of natural increase between 2.3 and 2.8 percent. The population would double in twenty-five to thirty years at the indicated rates. Growth rates could be affected, however, if nomadic Somali were to move permanently across present-day borders.

* * *

A detailed description of present-day Mogadishu is included in William Daniel Puzo's doctoral dissertation, *Mogadishu, Somalia: Geographic Aspects of Its Evolution, Population, Functions, and Morphology*, which also contains an extended account of the historical development of the city. The country's land and marine mammals are described in Ugo Funaioli's *Guida Breve dei Mammiferi della Somalia* (Brief Guide to the Mammals of Somalia), which also contains maps that provide a ready picture of the geographic distribution of the principal major forms; a chart also shows the range of habitat of different species. Although the guide is in Italian, the English name and Somali name or names are given for each species. Of particular interest to the specialist, the four-volume ornithological work of Geoffrey Archer and Eva M. Godman, *The Birds of British Somaliland and the Gulf of Aden*, also contains lengthy introductions in volumes one and three that include depictions from firsthand experience of natural and human features of broader interest from the early decades of the twentieth century. (For further information see Bibliography.)

CHAPTER 4

SOCIAL SYSTEM

The Somali, who constitute 95 percent or more of the country's population, are united by language, culture, devotion to Islam, and putative genealogical ties to a common ancestor. Genealogical ties, however, also provide the terms in which divisions among the Somali have occurred, and divisions have historically been more common than unity.

All Somali trace their origin to two brothers, Samaal and Saab, said to have been members of Muhammad's tribe, the Quraysh of Arabia, a notion based in part on the Somali devotion to Islam and in part on actual Arab influence (see ch. 2). The brothers are the ancestors of the largest kin-based units in Somali society, the clan-families (also referred to as tribes), of which six important ones exist in the present day. Four of these, the Dir, the Darod, the Isaq, and the Hawiya, constituting together an estimated 75 percent of the population, trace their descent from Samaal. Of these groups the majority, widely distributed, are nomadic and seminomadic pastoralists, but an increasing proportion are settled cultivators. The Digil and Rahanwein, who trace their descent from Saab, constitute about 20 percent of the population. They are settled in the river regions of southern Somalia and rely on a mixed economy of cattle husbandry and cultivation (see fig. 4).

Clan-families, too large and scattered for practical cooperation, never had any real political or economic functions. The clan-families served to some extent for a time before and after independence as rallying points in the formation of political parties, but their importance in this respect has considerably diminished (see ch. 9). The important units in the traditional system are the subdivisions of clan-families: the clans, the larger ones of which are subdivided into subclans, and the lineages, many of which are divided into secondary and even tertiary lineages. The Somali have no specific terms for these segments. Most commonly they used the word *rer*, which means "descendants of" and may refer to agnatic groups of differing genealogical depth.

Kinship as the basis for group formation and loyalty was modified but not overridden by the principle of contract. Membership in the same clan or lineage did not automatically confer certain rights or ob-

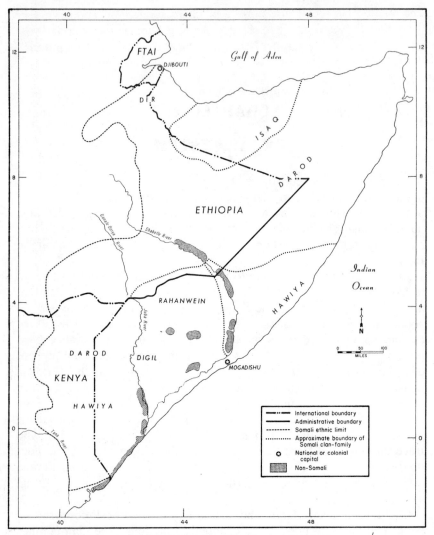

Figure 4. Somalia, Distribution of Clan-Families and Ethnic Groups

Source: Based on information from I.M. Lewis, *The Modern History of Somaliland*, New York, 1965, p. 206.

ligations. These were explicitly made the subject of treaties or contracts. Thus some but not all of the clans in a clan-family might unite for political and military purposes, and some but not all lineages within a clan might be associated for corporate responsibility, as in the paying and receiving of *dia* (Arabic for blood compensation; the Somali word is *mag*). Some of these alignments had a kinship base in that those who joined were or assumed they were descended from a particular wife of a common ancestor, but units formed by a contract or treaty could be broken up and new ones, based on a combination of different elements, formed.

62

The traditional social structure was characterized by competition and conflict between descent groups. Among Samaal the search for pasture and water drove clans and lineages physically apart or pitted them against each other. The Saab were less likely to engage in frequent physical conflict once they had settled, but they had a history of warfare over religious matters and of fighting the encroachments of camel-herding nomads.

There was a major distinction between Samaal and Saab. The Samaal tended to look down on the Saab for their practice of agriculture, and both groups considered themselves superior to non-Somali; they particularly disdained certain specialized occupational groups, such as metalworkers and leatherworkers.

By 1961 traditional patterns had begun to break down, and a new cleavage had emerged between the countryside and the towns, where most of the educated elite were concentrated. This elite had adopted a nationalist ideology and sought, theoretically at least, to transcend partisanship based on clan and clan-family ties, although they had little success and catered to those divisions themselves. The first two regimes after independence tackled—also without success—some of the divisive forces in Somali society. The rural population remained largely outside the national ambit.

The Supreme Revolutionary Council (SRC), which came to power in October 1969, undertook to involve all the people and to reshape and transform the economic and social structure under the banner of scientific socialism. The leaders tried to close the gap between nomads and cultivators, and the severe drought of the 1974-75 period, which led to the settlement of large numbers of pastoralists in the riverine region, indirectly helped these efforts. The SRC also tried through education and indoctrination to shift loyalties from the narrow kinship group to the nation. Apparently the leaders were able to engender genuine enthusiasm and cooperation among the population.

TRADITIONAL SOCIAL STRUCTURES

Despite their common background Samaal and Saab evolved differently as they adapted to different ecological conditions. Large numbers of Samaal live in areas that support only a pastoralism based mainly on camels, sheep, and goats (including the area west of the Juba River). The Saab live in the area between the Shabelle and Juba rivers, where they raise cattle. Because cows, unlike camels, do not give enough milk during the hot dry season, the Saab had either to cultivate or to exchange goods with cultivators and in the process mixed with them. This had social consequences. Whereas the Samaal have remained fiercely egalitarian and homogeneous, the Saab have developed a heterogeneous society that accorded higher or lower status to different groups depending on their origin and occupation.

The lineage remained the focal point of loyalty for roaming pastoralists. Group cohesion assumed a territorial dimension among the settled agriculturists.

Samaal

Descent Groups

The Samaal keep a careful count of their ancestors and are relatively cautious about adopting strangers or affiliating with them, whether singly or in groups. The greater the number of generations between a person and the ancestor, the greater the prestige. This is especially true when there are many collateral branches, because generational depth usually implies a large number of members and, consequently, greater power. Some ancient clans, however, have dwindled in size and have had to attach themselves to segments of other clan-families. Also, small groups that were detached from the main body of their clan often made alliances with the clan in whose territory they were living. Such a protective alliance was called a "pile of shields" (fashanbur) because it added to the collective fighting strength. If the detached group was in serious trouble, however, the parent group might send help, as the northern Darod occasionally did for their kin in the Trans-Juba area.

Clans are the largest political units, and most have heads known as soldaan (sultan) who have largely honorary and ceremonial functions. The title is of Arabic origin and may be used interchangeably with such Somali terms as bokor (belt—to bind people together). The number of clans within a clan-family varies, and there is a good deal of difference among them as to size, but the average is roughly 100,-000 people. Clans are associated with a given territory, essentially defined by the circuit of nomadic migration and not by specific boundaries, so that the territories of neighboring clans tend to overlap.

Some clans associated with contiguous territories have joined in confederations with internal subgroupings. The important Mijerteyn subconfederacy, for example, was part of the Kombe-Harti confederacy within the Kaballa, one of the two major divisions of the Darod clan-family. These confederations were constituted, usually for military purposes, by means of contracts or treaties but were described in kinship terms. A confederation's clans could presumably be genealogically traced to a specific wife of the common ancestor. Customarily the treaties or contracts were set down in writing by the presiding religious leader.

Internally clans are segmented into primary lineages whose genealogical depth ranges from twelve to fourteen generations. The lineage is the important economic unit. Because of the nomadic life-style lineages are widely distributed. Segments of lineages split off to create secondary or even tertiary lineages in continuous fission because they

64

have grown too unwieldy or because of quarrels (see fig. 5). Sometimes, however, segments that have become too small fuse with other segments.

The political and economic business of any functioning segment in Samaal society has traditionally been managed by an informally constituted council, the *shir*, which would include all the adult males in the group. Each of the males might speak and take part in deliberation, but age and seniority of lineage took precedence. An older man or one from an older lineage would customarily be asked to speak before the others. The term elder *(oday)* could be applied to any adult male, but those with more prestige and experience might be asked to judge disputes over a wide area and act as leaders of political activity.

Samaal men follow either a secular or a religious life, both considered of equal dignity. Most religious Samaal retain their secular ties to clan, lineage, and contractual groups, although they should in principle avoid partisanship. A few have settled in religious communities (see ch. 5).

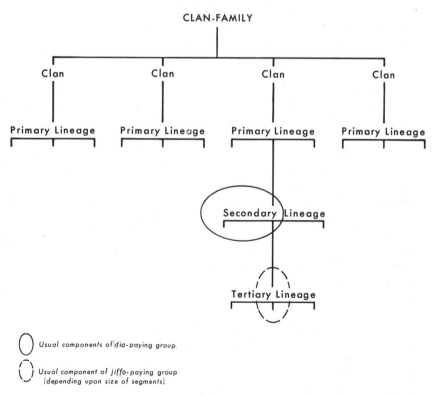

Figure 5. Somalia, Model of Samaal (Nomadic) Descent-Group Segmentation

Samaal consider their status as herders and warriors to be nobler than any other with the exception of a life devoted to religion. Cultivating Samaal groups exist, however, in various places, mainly in the Hargeysa and Borama areas. These cultivating groups, which also keep livestock, continue to be accepted as fellow Samaal by the pastoralists but traditionally have been considered to have lost prestige, even if they have gained economically. Some Samaal even attached themselves as cultivating clients *(arifa)* to stockraising Saab in the riverine region but often ended this relationship either when they were able to resume their former pastoral activities or when the economic advantages of cultivation diminished. The lineage pattern remains intact among Samaal cultivators, and they define themselves in terms of their lineage affiliation, although the community also commands loyalty.

Dia-Paying Groups

Although clans are identified with specific territories, pastureland is thought of as God's gift to all. Wells, however, are considered to belong to the man who was responsible for having them dug and to his lineage. This ownership is not always recognized by other groups. Since more than one clan migrates over a given territory and lineages mingle with each other in the pastures, there is a good deal of disagreement over the possession of the water sources, which are essential to the survival of the flocks. It has always been necessary for a lineage to be able to support its claims with real or potential force.

Relations between groups and individuals are therefore suffused with the notion of relative power, defined largely in martial terms. Typically the term *warrior* is used for adult men. Aggressiveness and a capacity for intense partisanship are considered desirable characteristics; distrust of strangers marks the Samaal view of others. Armed conflict would probably have been constant if it had not been for the existence of *dia*-paying groups, which made peaceful settling of disputes possible in a competitive environment. *Dia*-paying groups are alliances that lineages within a clan form with each other by means of a *heer* (written contract) primarily for the purpose of distributing the burden of paying compensation for homicide. As in the case of clan associations, the lineages align themselves on a theoretical basis of maternal kinship. Since *dia*-paying groups are established by contract, individual lineages may withdraw and form or join another one. During the colonial period the *heer* was filed with district commissioners or residents.

Dia was customarily fixed at 100 camels for a man and fifty for a women (less if the deed was done within the *dia*-paying group). The lineages in the group share in making payments and in receiving payments for the loss of one of their own members. The part of the compensation given to the immediate kin of a murdered man or paid by the immediate kin of the man responsible is known as *jiffo* (small-

66

er portion). The term *immediate kin* in this context refers to an agnatic group descended from a common ancestor three or four generations back. The immediate kin band together by contract within the *dia*-paying group to carry the financial burden of the *jiffo*, often a third of the total *dia* payment.

Both *dia*-paying and *jiffo*-paying groups are important units of social and economic organization aside from their stated purpose. They function as mutual-aid groups in time of emergency. Both groups establish regulations and are able to apply sanctions to enforce them; if a man refuses to pay his share of the camels for a fine, the elders may order him bound to a tree while his livestock are killed one by one in front of him until he agrees to cooperate. When a lineage belongs to a *dia*-paying group, the camels carry the group's brand rather than that of the lineage, implying the transfer of ownership rights. In 1964 it was estimated that more than 1,000 *dia*-paying groups existed in the republic. Among the nomadic people they ranged in membership from 200 to more than 5,000 men, among the sedentary from 5,000 to 100,000.

Dia-paying groups were ruled by the elders in council, who settled disputes, sometimes forcibly. When conciliation between *dia*-paying groups was impossible, the only resort was to fighting. A man's primary loyalty was therefore to his *dia*-paying group, which guaranteed his security and protected his property.

Family and Marriage

Marriage is a secular contract having both economic and political importance. The immediate parties to the contract are regarded as representatives of their lineages, and the marriage is seen as a political bond between lineages or *dia*-paying groups. To validate the marriage a standard series of payments is negotiated by elders representing the bride and the groom.

The family is an economic unit and has a division of labor on the basis of age and sex. It may have economic interests in more than one geographical region if territorial location and number of family members permit.

Samaal marriages are exogamous. Solidarity is assumed within the lineage or clan, and goodwill is promoted by marrying outside. A *dia*-paying group contract often specifies that marriage is not desirable within it and that a fine must be paid to the girl's father if marriage occurs. If a couple is separated by six or more generations within the lineage, however, marriage is not considered unlawful. It may nevertheless be disapproved of because it does not create a potentially advantageous new relationship. Even at the level of clan-families, the Darod and Isaq consider themselves linked to the Dir by virtue of the marriage of their respective ancestors to daughters of Dir chieftains. Clans and lineages have become linked in a similar manner.

67

A wife retains strong ties with her natal group, however, and never becomes legally a member of her husband's lineage. It is her father's and not her husband's *dia*-paying and *jiffo*-paying group that pays or receives fines on her behalf. Her children belong to her husband's lineage, but her own lineage has recognized bonds of affection with them and may even help in her sons' marital payments.

Saab

The Saab are Somali who between the eleventh and fourteenth centuries began settling in the area between the Juba and Shabelle rivers. In doing so they mixed by intermarriage or by a system of adoption with non-Somali. They also intermixed with groups of Samaal.

The Saab are composed of the Digil and Rahanwein clan-families. Genealogically the Digil are believed to be the descendants of the ancestor Saab, and the Rahanwein are an offshoot of the Digil. The name Saab is falling into disuse because it is also used by the Samaal as a pejorative designation (*sab*, low) for people who follow certain disdained occupations. Although this view is changing, Samaal have tended to feel that the Saab lowered themselves by their practice of agriculture and by their readiness to assimilate foreign elements into their lineages.

Formally the social structure of the Saab resembles that of the Samaal in that it is based on a putative descent-group pattern. Actually significant differences exist. Saab clans—roughly equal in size to Samaal clans—are confederations of lineages and probably contain representatives of all Somali clan-families and assimilated non-Somali. The Saab clans came into being through a pack or promise (*balan*) between the original founding segments. The clans and their subdivisions, although assumed to be true descent groups, tend to have only a very small core of the original group that bore the name and a larger proportion of inmarried, adopted, and assimilated members and descendants of former clients. All speak the Somali dialect of the founding group, and all tend to have very shallow genealogies as compared with the Samaal. Because of their heterogeneity cohesion is weak, and Saab typically marry within their descent group, often following the Arab practice of preferential marriage with a father's brother's daughter.

Another important contrast with peripatetic Samaal society is the importance of territoriality. Saab clans live within clearly marked borders. The entire clan (or large subclan) constitutes the *dia*-paying group. The term *rer*, which the Samaal use in connection with descent, is often used by the Saab with a place name, such as *rer barawa* (children of Brava).

Most Saab clans are subdivided into three subclans, each called a *gember* (stool), although some, like the Jiddu clans of the Digil clan-family, are divided into only two. Clans and subclans usually have single heads. In some cases, however, as among the Helai clans of the Rahanwein, there are no clan heads. Clan affairs are handled by leading elders called *gobwein*, who have assistants called *gobyar*.

Clans or subclans are subdivided into lineages that reckon three to five generations from ancestor to youngest member. The lineage is the important economic unit. It traditionally owns land and water rights, which the headmen distribute to individuals.

The manner of formation of Saab clans has led to the development of recognized social inequalities. Members may be physically indistinguishable to outsiders, but insiders know each one's place on the social scale. At the top are the putative descendants of the original clan treatymakers, although they usually cannot prove descent. They are called *urad* (firstborn) or *mindihay* (knife bearer). Traditionally they initiate all joint clan activities, such as the rainmaking ceremony *(roobdoon)*, and they ritually slaughter animals for sacrifice.

Socially somewhat lower are former clients. They were often from small, weak, or newly immigrated lineages that were allocated land for cultivation by the patron group in return for protection. Clients had to give up their former associations and promise to follow the customs of the adopted clan. At first they were not permitted to participate in major decisions, dig a well on their own, or build a permanent house. Only after they had been assimilated were they allowed to take part in political councils and become members of *dia*-paying groups. The older the client group, the higher its social rank.

Specialized Occupational Groups

Certain occupational groups, such as hunters, leather dressers, smiths, and medicine men, are known as *sab* among the Samaal and as *bon* (low caste, as opposed to *gob*, noble) among the Saab. The most numerous group is the Midgaan, who act as barbers and circumcisers. They are also hunters, although this activity has been restricted by the government since 1970.

The Yibir (called Yahhar in the south) make amulets for newborn Somali babies and protective charms for the newly married. The Tumal are blacksmiths, the Dardown weavers, and the Madarrala and the Gaggab are tanners and shoemakers; there are several other groups.

Physically members of these occupational groups are like the Somali; culturally they have many customs of their own. They are of unknown ethnic origin, although some authorities suggest and the groups believe that they may be derived from the original population. They speak Somali but also use what are usually referred to as secret languages, which might better be compared to localized slang or occupational jargon.

The occupational groups lack clans but have lineages that are usually considered to belong to the lineages of the Samaal or Saab, whom they serve economically and ceremonially but with whom they do not intermarry. The patrons claim damages on their behalf in case of death or injury but are not responsible in the same degree as for a kinsman. The occupational groups tend to live in settlements not far from their patrons or contiguous with them. Some, such as the Yibir medicine men, have no fixed residence but wander among the settlements. Altogether these occupational groups are very roughly estimated to make up about 1 percent of the population.

Riverine People of Non-Somali Origin

Along the Indian Ocean coast and in the valleys of the Juba and Shabelle rivers there are small groups of people—most of them cultivators—that differ culturally and physically from the Somali. Originally they spoke their own languages (experts disagree whether these were Bantu languages or not), but most of them eventually became Somali-speakers (see ch.2).

Somali refer to some of the non-Somali riverine people as *habasho* (sing., *habash*). Italians referred to them as *liberti* because they considered them to be liberated slaves. And in fact some were descendants of slaves who arrived in the early and middle nineteenth century, especially at the time when British ships patrolled the waters to suppress the slave trade and slaves from countries to the south of Somalia were transported overland. Some were shipped from the Somali coast to Arabia, but some were sold locally and tended to adopt the genealogy of their Somali owners. Others ran away and founded communities along the rivers.

Most of the *habasho*, however, are descendants of the people who originally lived on the rich black land along the riverbanks and were often able to defend their land successfully against Somali and other intruders, helped probably by the prevailing malaria and the abundance of tsetse flies. Somali nomads maintained treaties with the *habasho* so that they could pass through the area to water their livestock. The nomads regarded the *habasho* as equals largely because of their ability to take care of themselves economically and militarily. The *habasho* were said to possess special skills in magic, but after conversion to Islam they often became members and even heads of religious communities.

Some riverine people remained independent. Others became cultivators for cattle-raising Saab in client-patron relationships. They did not intermarry or eat with Saab; but they could not be driven from the land, which was regarded as theirs. They received part of *dia* payments, and they participated in rainmaking and other religious ceremonies of the patron clan. For example, the Gobawein near Lugh Ganana on the Juba River acted as cultivators for the Gasar Gudda (a Rahanwein clan). Often clients had the name of the lineage to which they were bound. The Helai of Baydhaba (Baidoa) were under the patronage of the Helai of the Bur Acaba (the largest of the Rahanwein clans); the Tunni Torre were under the patronage of the Tunni (a Digil clan) of Brava. Still others federated with Saab clans or lineages on a nearly equal footing. The Shidle were accepted as a branch of the Mobilen (a Trans-Juba Hawiya clan) but acknowledged the authority of the hereditary Mobilen chief.

Other groups are the Shabelle, Rer Issa, Kabole, and Makanne along the Shabelle River. On the Juba River live the Gosha (forest people), supposedly of slave origin, who were freed at the time of the suppression of the slave trade in the nineteenth century and still follow some of their old customs, such as using animal masks in their rituals.

Along the coast live the Bajun and Amarani, derived from a mixture of coastal populations. They are fishermen, sailors, and merchants who may be related to Arab and Persian settlers and who display a number of Indonesian elements in their culture. The Amarani, estimated to number fewer than 1,000 in the 1960s, inhabit small fishing communities in and near Brava, Mogadishu, Marka (Merca), and the inland town of Afgoi on the Shabelle River. The Bajun live along the east African coast and the coastal islands from Kismayo southward into Kenya as far as Lamu and in scattered communities as far away as Mozambique.

The Amarani and the Bajun have little contact with outsiders except in towns. Partial geographic isolation and an active ethnic consciousness separate them from the Somali since they speak their own languages. The Amarani speak Bravanese (also called Chimbalazi or Chimini), a Swahili dialect for which a traditional form of Arabic transcription has been used, increasing its practical importance in the area. The Bajun speak a Swahili dialect known as Ki-Bajun (also called Ki-Tukuu or Faza Swahili) with numerous subdialects. Their language is rich in nautical terms.

The Boni and the Eile belong to those scattered groups of hunters found throughout eastern Africa believed to derive from the original prehistoric population. There are perhaps between 1,000 and 2,000 Boni in Somalia, but no reliable figures are available. They live near and south of the Juba River, continuing into Kenya. They have preserved their own Cushitic language and religion to some extent but also speak Somali or neighboring languages when necessary. Some practice cultivation; others have gone to work as laborers in the towns.

The Eile specialize in hunting with dogs, which Muslims consider unclean. They live in the Bur Acaba District. The Somali consider all hunting groups socially inferior.

SOMALI LANGUAGE AND COMMUNICATION

According to one generally accepted view Somali is a member of the eastern subdivision of the Cushitic branch of the Afro-Asiatic phylum of languages. Eastern Cushitic languages are also spoken by the Galla (Oromo) of Ethiopia and Kenya, the Afar and Saho of northeastern Ethiopia and the French Territory of Afars and Issas (FTAI), and a number of groups in southern Ethiopia and northern Kenya (see ch. 2).

Most speakers of Somali dialects are ethnic Somali, but some are of non-Somali origin. Of the several Somali dialects, the most widely used is Common Somali, a term applied to a group of mutually intelligible subdialects. Common Somali is spoken in most of Somalia and by Somali in adjacent territories (Ethiopia, Kenya, and the FTAI) and is used by broadcasting stations in Somalia and in Somali-language broadcasts originating outside the country. It has also been the lingua franca of traders, religious students, and pilgrims to the tombs of Somali saints. Coastal Somali is spoken in the region formerly called Benadir (the coast and its immediate hinterland from north of Adale to south of Brave); Central Somali is spoken in the Bakool, Gedo, and Baydhaba regions, chiefly by members of the Rahanwein clan-family. Speakers of Common and Coastal Somali are able to understand each other after a few weeks of close contact, speakers of Common and Central Somali only after a few months.

Verbal facility is highly valued in a society where until the early 1970s comparatively few people could read and write. Children are early trained with riddles and tongue twisters to attain good diction, and intelligence is judged by alertness and skill in the use of words. A potential father-in-law questioning a suitor will judge his capability by the alertness and appropriateness of his responses to seemingly innocent catch-questions.

The art of negotiation, involving careful use of language, is exercised in interpersonal as well as in political and diplomatic relations: because pride is very important in Somali society, a blunt request or a blunt refusal that might lead to a loss of face by either party is avoided. For example, a man wishing for another's cooperation in a project and not desiring to make an issue of it that might cause ill feelings will approach the subject indirectly to discover the other's probable attitude. If it is unfavorable, he may refrain from asking the favor in order to avoid a direct rejection. The other, in trying to sound out the first man's object, will attempt to reply in such a way as to give the correct impression. All serious negotiation is carried on in this manner, including marriage proposals. The art of negotiation has developed into a form of etiquette; Europeans, accustomed to speaking more directly, are often considered crude. Negotiating skillfully has to some extent developed into an art form.

Humor is important as a conscious means of softening criticism or unpalatable advice or of extricating oneself from embarrassing situation. Most jokes are based on puns and shades of meaning.

Verbal expression is related to role; religious devotees, for instance, must refrain from complaining about hardships. Speechmakers in political or religious assemblies, litigants, and preachers are expected to possess a reserve a poetry and poetic proverbs for appropriate use. Even everyday speech tends to be ornamented in the same way; the poetic style is terse and vivid with condensed meanings and carefully chosen words and alliterations. Political administrators have been judged for their capability on the basis of their use of this poetic style; those unwilling or unable to master it have been unpopular, but those with an impressive oratorical style have been highly esteemed and compared with "the excellent men of old times."

SOCIAL CHANGE AFTER WORLD WAR II

In the period between the end of World War II and independence factors promoting social change were limited. Except for the development of banana and sugarcane plantations in the south there was no significant wage employment and no large-scale permanent displacement of persons.

Somali who were well educated in the Islamic tradition deplored the divisions along clan lines within the society and demanded that the universality of Islamic religious thought be implemented in the relations between groups. The Somali Youth League (SYL), which was formed in the 1940s and which was deeply influenced by the religious elite, attempted to do away with clan and clan-family barriers, and its members considered it a point of honor to refuse to identify themselves by such hereditary affiliation. One of the first acts of the SYL-dominated assembly in 1956 was to make it illegal for political parties to bear the names of clans and clan-families.

Somali leaders tackled other social divisions. They made conscious efforts to eliminate the traditional disabilities of lower status groups and to bring members of ethnic minorities into political life. On March 2, 1960, just before independence, the Legislative Assembly of the Trust Territory of Somaliland under Italian Administration passed a law that abolished the status of client. The law stated that every Somali citizen had the right to live and farm where he chose, regardless of hereditary affiliation. Subsequently, however, many patron clans in the riverine area, when their clients tried to assert their independence, retaliated by withholding customary farming and watering rights. They no longer included clients in dia-paying arrangements and in some cases tried to oust them from the land that had been theirs to work on under the former client-patron agreement. Some cases were brought before the courts, but more often the old arrangements were quietly continued.

Social change was more pronounced in the towns. Somali towns are of two sorts: those with a history extending back to the tenth century A.D. or earlier and those that grew around administrative centers and markets. In the older coastal towns there may be one or two dominant lineages, but these have in most cases no direct kin-based relationship with the surrounding area. In the newer towns one or two lineages connected with clans in the surrounding area are usually dominant, and occasional hostilities may break out.

Mogadishu, the nation's cultural, political, and economic center, is the major forum for exchange between different parts of the country. Here live not only independent local clans who have been urbanized for generations but also members of all clan-families, although Samaal greatly outnumber Saab.

The growing importance of certain skills gave some occupational groups social and economic advantages. Many Tumal, for example, became mechanics and settled in town, usually in less desirable quarters but no longer as Somali bondsmen. In southern port towns carpenters, weavers, and other artisans formed guilds to protect their common interests. As technical occupations became more acceptable, Samaal and Saab found this kind of modern work suitable for themselves and, as members of traditional occupational groups achieved relatively higher status, social acceptance proceeded to the point of intermarriage. The appellation Midgaan came to be considered pejorative and was forbidden by law.

City dwellers included government officials, independently working traders and artisans, and large numbers of unskilled laborers and unemployed persons. Newcomers settled wherever they could, regardless of their neighbors' affiliations. Many had come to the city to escape the rigors and often the social pressures of rural living. Others were temporary migrants in search of work who intended to return to the countryside eventually.

Contacts between town and countryside remained close and were mutually influential. Most town dwellers, although their life-style had changed, retained or at least continued to understand the attitude of their rural relatives. Nomadic families frequently had one member living in town who kept in constant touch with them and played an active part in building up the family herd by sending money. Religious and political leaders and owners of large herds customarily spend part of their time in towns to take care of family and lineage interests. Nomads frequently went into town to trade.

The institution of *dia* compensation for homicide, which had originated in the nomadic environment, has been extended to cover death in traffic accidents. The underlying notion of group responsibility for serious crimes, however, was no longer acceptable to the new leaders. This was expressed in three precedent-setting judgments by the Supreme Court, one in 1962 and two in 1964. Collective payment for murder was no longer considered acceptable. Payments for unpremeditated homicide or serious injury, however, was defined as compensation for a tort rather than as a crime. Most far reaching was the last of the three decisions; it allowed an individual to leave his *dia*-paying group, which henceforth would no longer be liable for him. Formerly only an entire lineage could decide to abrogate the contract that had bound it to other lineages in a *dia*-paying group. The Supreme Court decision undermined an important aspect of the traditional social system that had been based on the indissolubility of the blood bond.

EFFECTS OF THE REVOLUTION

The military leadership that came into power in October 1969 continued in a more forceful fashion some of the changes initiated under the previous regime. It also introduced elements that constituted a total break with the past.

Scientific socialism was declared the new regime's guide and frame of reference by the so-called Second Charter of the Revolution, made public in January 1971. It was based on a pragmatic version of the leaders' understanding of Marxism adapted to local social and economic conditions (see ch. 9).

Marxist ideas were brought to Somalia by young men who had studied in communist countries or had been influenced by contact with communist parties in France and Italy. They were inspired by the example of Cuba and the People's Republic of China and on their return were repelled by the widespread corruption and ineptness of the government. They joined the ranks of the frustrated intelligentsia who sided with the military when it took power.

In trying to introduce scientific socialism the regime was faced with the problem that no class struggle in the Marxist sense had existed in Somalia. There was no proletariat and no class of entrepreneurs. There was a small bourgeoisie composed of government officials, traders, artisans, and a few professionals. The new leaders focused instead on the divisions in the society: the cleavages between clans, between the sedentary and the nomadic, between rich and poor herdsmen, between strong and weak pastoral lineages that competed by force for pastures and wells, between patrons and clients in the cultivating regions, and between urban and rural people, and the continuing disdain for certain low-status groups. Members of religious brotherhoods and of political parties had called each other brother. Now all

Somali, regardless of hereditary affiliation, were asked to call each other comrade *(jalle)*. Scientific socialism was regarded by the revolutionary leaders as the only means to ensure the economic development of the country without creating new social inequalities.

The campaign to win people over to the new ideology began immediately. Government employees, army and police officers, students, doctors, teachers, and other professionals were forced to attend three-month indoctrination courses. Members of the Supreme Revolutionary Council (SRC) traveled all over the country to explain the role of a socialist government at hundreds of meetings and before newly formed local revolutionary committees. In 1970 the central Public Relations Office was set up in Mogadishu to provide political education and liaison between the people and the leadership. Permanent guidance centers were eventually opened in each of the fourteen quarters of Mogadishu and in other towns and villages, where discussion groups met and lectures were given not only on the new ideology but also on health and on agricultural techniques. Literacy classes were held at the centers, and actors, poets, and dancers from the capital gave performances that conveyed the new message.

In 1974 about 25,000 secondary-level students went off into the rural areas to take a nationwide census of people and resources, to teach literacy skills, and to spread the ideas of scientific socialism. Schools were closed for seven months, and only students who were under fifteen or were pursuing technical courses were excused. The campaign aimed at reaching Somali who had been only peripherally involved with the national state. Using young people to teach adults, however, went counter to the values of a society in which authority traditionally rested with the elders. To prepare the ground psychologically, radio messages asked rural people to extend a warm welcome to the young visitors from the town, who would bring new ideas but would in turn learn from the elders. A side effect of the campaign was to bring rural and urban people together. Many parents who had never been outside Mogadishu or Kismayo—and had been reluctant to let their children go—visited them in their rural surroundings and presumably acquired a new understanding.

The regime tried to involve the people not only through teaching and explaining but through active participation as well. It called for an end to corruption and lethargy and for the use of self-help *(iska wa uqabso)* schemes. It also hoped to reduce urban unemployment through such projects and to inspire young people to return to the rural areas. As a result guidance centers, roads, schools, health centers, and storage silos for grain were built by free labor with material supplied by the government. In Mogadishu government employees gave up to seven hours of free labor a week to build roads and housing estates. About seventy miles from the capital thousands worked on Fridays (a Muslim holiday) to the sound of drums and singing.

76

They fought the encroaching sand dunes by spreading dirt over sand and planting shrubs and other plants. Such projects were undertaken with the active support of uniformed girls and boys—the Victory Pioneers—a wing of the army organized by the SRC.

The Development Program 1971-1973 called for the establishment of hundreds of cooperatives. Most of these were to be in the cultivating areas, but for the first time some were also to be established among nomads for selling animals. In the mid-1970s, however, animals were still sold to individual traders, who received most of the profits.

A seminar for workers dealing with the establishment of labor unions and workers' councils began in December 1970 in Mogadishu and lasted forty-five days. Within a year a trade union with nationwide branches was founded, and workers' councils were set up in various enterprises. By the mid-1970s, however, neither labor unions nor workers' councils seemed very effective.

In connection with the new councils of local government various committees were set up under the supervision of the local branch of the Public Relations Office (see ch. 8). The committees dealt with different subjects—self-help projects, cooperatives, and others—and various segments of the population were represented on them, including young people and women.

The revolutionary regime continued a trend begun earlier regarding women. Under customary Somali law, reinforced by Islamic practices, a woman was always under the legal protection of her father, her husband or, in case of his death, her husband's father or brother. In blood compensation her injury or death was valued at half that of a man's. Daughters inherited half or a third as much as sons, and in some parts of Somalia they could inherit neither camels nor land. After World War II all political parties established women's committees. In the Italian south women voted for the first time in the municipal election in 1958; in the formerly British north they voted first in the 1961 national referendum on the constitution. Their role in public affairs, however, remained minimal.

This changed with the revolution. Women were urged to take an active part in government, in sports, in self-help projects, and in committee and council discussions. Special committees were set up to deal strictly with women's affairs. On January 12, 1975, President Mohamed Siad Barre announced the decision by the SRC and the Council of the Secretaries of state to give equal rights to women in several respects, including equal inheritance rights. This led to protests by some conservative Islamic leaders (see ch. 5). Later in the month the president announced that the government would introduce a law governing polygamy and divorce. Polygamy would no longer be permitted unless men were able to support several wives as required by Islam, and men would no longer be able to divorce their wives at will.

The role of the traditional leaders was also altered to fit the new ideology. After the 1969 coup the title of elder was abolished and replaced by that of peacekeeper *(nabaddon)*. These were the appointed spokesmen of what were officially regarded as social groups composed of individual pastoralists or cultivators. They had become official representatives of all local people, irrespective of kinship ties. Among other duties the peacekeepers had to defend and support the poor peasant or herdsman, a function formerly fulfilled by the lineage.

By thus changing the role of the elders the regime attacked the authority and solidarity of the tribal system that they were condemning as one of the divisive forces in the country. It had led, the SRC claimed, to nepotism in government and warfare among pastoralists. Tribalism, which was defined as giving one's primary loyalty to lineage or clan instead of to the nation, was banned by law and attacked in plays, posters, speeches, and circulars and symbolically destroyed in burials and burnings.

Drought as much as the spread of revolutionary ideas helped to lessen another deep division in Somali society—that between cultivators and nomads. The severe drought that began in 1974 drove more than 500,000 pastoralists to accept government help, and by 1975 about 125,000 had been resettled and turned into cultivators and even fishermen in the largest such enterprise ever undertaken in Africa. Members of different clans were purposely mixed in the populations of the new settlements. The settlers dealt as individuals with local councils, committees, and courts whose composition was also heterogeneous. *Dia* payments for major crimes had been declared illegal before the revolution. After 1969 people who ignored this law were imprisoned and charged with fostering tribalism.

A law passed by the local government in September 1973 at Mogadishu represented another attack on the traditional system. It banned weddings, burials, and religious rites held on a tribal basis. Wedding ceremonies were henceforth to be celebrated at guidance centers or other public places, such as hotels, and no longer could money be collected from lineage members for the burial of a dead member.

The purpose of all these actions was to transform society. The new leaders believed that the traditional structures, though adequate for a preindustrial society, were a hindrance to modernizing efforts. They went to great lengths to introduce changes slowly, by persuasion rather than by coercion. It was impossible for outsiders to determine in the mid-1970s how extensive these revolutionary changes were and how permanent they would prove to be. Somali had shown themselves adaptable to change in the past. A great deal will probably depend on whether economic and other tangible rewards flow from the social changes initiated by the government and therefore generate further change, particularly a loosening of the ties that bind an individual to his kinship group (see ch. 9).

* * *

For a more detailed description of traditional Samaal society see I.M. Lewis' *A Pastoral Democracy*; for a description of Saab society see I.M. Lewis' "From Nomadism to Cultivation," in *Man in Africa*, edited by Mary Douglas and Phyllis M. Kaberry; and for a slanted but informed view of postrevolutionary goals by an Italian Communist see Luigi Pestalozza's *The Somalian Revolution*. (For further information see Bibliography.)

CHAPTER 5

RELIGIOUS LIFE

The vast majority of Somali are Muslims. Loyalty to Islam reinforces the national distinctions that set the Somali off from their immediate neighbors on the African continent, most of whom either are Christians or adhere to indigenous African beliefs.

The ideal of Islam is a society organized for the implementation of Islamic precepts, which implies a lack of distinction between the secular and the religious spheres. In Somalia this ideal has only been approximated—and less fully in the north than in the settled regions of the south where religious leaders were an integral part of the social and political structure. Among nomads the exigencies of a pastoral life conferred great importance on the warrior's role, and religious leaders were expected to remain aloof from political matters (see ch. 4). Whatever the discrepancies between the requirements of Islam and Somali practice, the Somali see themselves as devout Muslims.

The role of religious functionaries began to shrink little by little in the 1950s and 1960s as some of their legal and political functions were transferred to secular authorities. Nevertheless Islam continued to be accepted as a complete guide to life.

This situation changed substantially with the revolution of 1969. In their efforts to mobilize popular support for the economic and social transformation of Somali society, the new leaders introduced a vigorously secular ideology that they called scientific socialism (see ch. 9). This was not at odds with Islam, they declared, but was actually compatible with Quranic principles. The new leaders utterly condemned atheism. Nevertheless they relegated religion to the moral sphere, and religious leaders were warned not to meddle in politics.

There has been opposition to the government's ideology by leaders whose social and political role has been curtailed and presumably among some of their faithful followers, especially in more remote areas. Very likely most Somali did not perceive scientific socialism's secular outlook as fundamentally alien to Islam. They judge the new ideology not on whether it is compatible with Islamic values but on its practical applications and whether it contradicts long-established practices. The regime has had a measure of success in urban areas and among some of the younger and less tradition-oriented members of society. But in the mid-1970s it was almost impossible for outsiders to judge the success of the government's attempt to win support for scientific socialism and to assess its impact on religious life.

ISLAM

History and Tenets

Islam, founded in A.D. 622 when the Prophet Muhammad left Mecca and marched with his followers to Medina, spread first in Arabia, then east and west across northern Africa and the Middle East under the successors of Muhammad. It was brought to Somalia around the tenth century or earlier by merchants and seamen from southern Arabia, who sailed their dhows from ports along the Red Sea and the Persian Gulf and founded settlements along the Somali coast, some of which eventually became large-scale trading ports.

According to Somali tradition a number of their clans stemmed from Arabs who married local women. Some of these clan ancestors are regarded as saints by their descendants, and their tombs have become places of pilgrimage. Until the advent of Somali nationalism, Arabian ancestry was highly valued as a concrete link with the Prophet. The putative national ancestors, Samaal and Saab, are traditionally believed to have been two brothers from the Prophet's tribe, the Quraysh (see ch. 2; ch. 4).

The word *Islam* means submission to God, and a Muslim is one who has submitted. The basic concept of Islam is stated in its creed: "There is no god but God, and Muhammad is his prophet." The greatest possible sin is to claim that any being shares God's power. (Muhammad himself never claimed divine origin or a relationship to Allah.) Recitation of this creed, performance of daily prayers according to prescribed rules, fasting during the lunar month of Ramadan, almsgiving, and making the pilgrimage to Mecca constitute the so-called Five Pillars of the Faith or basic duties of devout Muslims. Four of these duties may be modified in certain special circumstances. If the believer is ill, he may pray without prostrations and reduce the number of times he prays from the obligatory five to three. Fasting, which involves going without food, drink (including water), tobacco, and sexual relations from two hours before dawn until sunset, may be omitted during a journey but should be made up for at a later time. Almsgiving and the pilgrimage depend on one's ability to afford the expense.

The basic teaching of Islam is embodied in the Quran, which Muslims believe was given to Muhammad by God through the angel Gabriel. Muhammad regarded the provision of a scripture for his people as the most important part of his life's work. People of the Book—any religious community possessing a book of scriptures, thus including Christians and Jews—were elect. The Quran paralleled much of the Old and the New Testament, mentioning many of the prophets, especially Moses, as well as Jesus (called Issa) and Mary; but Muhammad declared that the Christian and Judaic scriptures had been corrupted by false teaching and that the Quran was the accurate version of revelation. Material related to Persian, Arabian, and other traditions is also included in the Quran.

After Muhammad's death his followers sought to regulate their lives scrupulously by his divinely inspired works. When they could not find a dictum in the Quran to cover a specific situation, they turned to the sayings, teachings, and precedents of his personal behavior that are collected in the hadith. Together the Quran and the hadith form the Sunna, a comprehensive guide to the spiritual, ethical, and social life of orthodox Muslims.

Quarrels over the succession to leadership led to a split of the Islamic community into Sunnites (traditionalists) and Shiites (from Shiat Ali or partisans of Ali). The Sunnites accept the legitimacy of the first four caliphs who succeeded Muhammad. The Shiites, however, believe that only the descendants of Ali, Muhammad's cousin who married the Prophet's daughter Fatima, are legitimate. Almost all Somali are Sunnites. Shiites are found mainly among the transient merchants in the ports, usually Indians and Pakistanis who have their own mosques.

Sharia, Islamic religious law, derives from the Quran, the hadith, *ijma* (consensus of believers), and from a large body of interpretive commentaries. Several schools of legal thought developed, among them the Shafii school, which is represented in Somalia. Sharia covers a number of categories of behavior: obligatory actions, desirable or recommended actions, indifferent actions, objectionable but not forbidden actions, and prohibited actions. The Five Pillars of the Faith would be in the first category, nightlong vigil and prayer in the second, and many ordinary secular activities in the third. Divorce is in the objectionable but permitted category ("the thing permitted but most hated by Allah"), whereas adultery and other sins are prohibited.

Certain commonly known rules are followed pertaining to ritual purity and cleanliness of the person and food. For example, washing is required after contact with unclean things and after specific activities. When water is not available, sand may be substituted. Food prohibitions follow the same general lines as the law of Moses: the consumption of blood is forbidden, as is the eating of pork and of the meat of animals that died of natural causes instead of being slaughtered. The Quran expressly notes, however, that some things forbidden to Jews are permitted to Muslims.

Circumcision is regarded in Islamic tradition as the seal of membership in the faith. Until this operation has been performed, a youth is not a true Muslim. Circumcision of girls (called clitoridectomy), widely practiced in Somalia, is not required by Islam because women are considered never to be as ritually clean as men. Traditionally circumcision of both girls and boys takes place by the time the child is eight; it should in any case precede puberty. Until this has been done, the child is considered *haram* (unlawful) and cannot, among other things, handle food for someone who maintains a state of ritual purity, for example, any man who is careful to perform the daily prayers. Circumcision renders the person fit for contact with ritually pure believers, for religious instruction, and especially for marriage. After circumcision a boy will have to pay attention to food taboos and ritual purity. A girl is not necessarily bound by food prohibitions because she is considered imperfect anyway by virtue of her sex.

All Somali tend to be fairly strict about Muslim regulations governing ritual purity. The settled Somali tend, however, to be strict regarding the general requirements of Islam, while the nomads have developed less rigid forms to meet their specific needs. For example, Muslims are permitted to omit certain duties while traveling, and nomads may take advantage of these exceptions, although in some instances their laxity in religious observance may arise from lack of instruction.

Devout nomadic Somali make the pilgrimage to Mecca when possible but more often go to the tomb of those clan ancestors who are considered to be saints. In settled areas such saints are usually associated with localities rather than with lineages.

Islam arose under conditions of life similar to those existing in much of Somalia, but it does not always agree with values and standards deriving from indigenous traditions. Somali stress pride in descent; but in Islam all Muslims, whatever their race, clan, or wealth, are considered equal before God. Through religious learning, sanctity, and zeal, even a slave may rise to be caliph. Muhammad himself demonstrated this principle by adopting a slave son as his own. For devout Somali, therefore, Islam broadens the traditional conception of equality of all clansmen to equality of all coreligionists.

Roles and Training

In Islam there are no priests to act as intermediaries between the believer and God, but there are religious teachers, preachers, and mosque officials. In Somalia religious training is most readily available in urban centers or wherever mosques exist, where children learn to memorize parts of the Quran. It is customary, however, for some teachers to travel on foot from place to place with their students. Such wandering groups, called *her*, depend for their living on the generosity of others. The hardships encountered during their migrations are considered valuable for the spiritual training of the students, who are not allowed to complain or to be aggressive when asking for alms.

84

The teachers serve the community by preaching, leading prayers, blessing the people and their livestock, counseling, arbitrating disputes, and performing marriages. They may be theologians, but they rarely stay with one lineage long enough to teach more than rudimentary religious principles.

In the absence of a wandering teacher nomads are more likely to depend on a local *wadad* (pl., *wadaddo*), a person associated with religious devotion, study, or leadership. The *wadaddo* may merely be students of the Quran on a fairly low level, or they may be notable religious leaders with the title sheikh (see Glossary). They carry out such ceremonies as sacrifices, blessings of the sick, marriages, and group prayers. During the digging of a well they are expected to pray for success and cheer the workers on rather than work themselves. They function as basic teachers and local notaries and, if properly educated, as judges and authorities of sharia. *Wadaddo* may be trained theologians, members of a religious brotherhood, or part of a lineage with a strong religious tradition. In the latter case they are not necessarily trained but are recognized as *wadaddo* merely by inheritance and thus entitled to lead prayers and to perform ritual sacrifices. Most of these are pastoral nomads and function within the regular clan pattern, participating in *dia*-paying groups (see Glossary; ch. 4). *Wadad* lineages are referred to as *Rer Au* and *Au*, traditional *wadad* titles.

Brotherhoods

Somali Islam is marked by the significance of brotherhoods (*tariqa*, plural of the Arabic word *tariq*, meaning way or path). The rise of these brotherhoods was connected with the development of sufism, a mystical current in Islam that began during the ninth and tenth centuries and reached its height during the twelfth and thirteenth. In Somalia Sufi orders appeared first in towns during the fifteenth century and rapidly became a revitalizing force. Sufism seeks a closer personal relationship with God through special spiritual disciplines. Escape from self is aided by poverty, seclusion, and other forms of self-denial. The term *Sufi* derives from the Arabic *suf*, meaning wool, from which the crude garment of the Muslim holy man was made.

Some members of Sufi brotherhoods tend to wander from place to place as religious beggars and teachers. They are best known for their often spectacular rituals (*dikr*, an Arabic word meaning testifying or remembrance), in which states of visionary ecstasy are brought on by group chanting of religious texts, by rythmic gestures, by dancing, and by deep breathing. The object is to free oneself from the body and to be lifted into the presence of God. Dervishes have been important as founders of *jamahayo* (agricultural communities; sing., *jamaha*). A few *jamahayo* contain only celibate men, but usually they are inhabited by families, specific regulations of behavior applying to women.

Three Sufi orders with various subdivisions are prominent in Somalia. In order of their introduction into the country they are the Qadiriya, the Ahmadiya-Idrisiya, and the Salihiya. A fourth, the Rifaiya, originally an offshoot from the Qadiriya, is represented mainly among Arabs residing in Mogadishu and Marka (Merca).

Qadiriya, the oldest and most orthodox order in Islam, was founded in Baghdad by Sayyid Abd al Kadir al Jilani in A.D. 1166 and introduced into Harar (Ethiopia) in the fifteenth century by Sherif Abubakr ibn Abdallah al Eidarus. It spread during the eighteenth century among the Galla and Somali of Ethiopia, often under the leadership of Somali sheikhs. Qadiriya was introduced into northern Somalia by Sheikh Abdarahman Zeilawi, who died in 1883. In an apparently separate development Qadiriya was brought into the southern Somalian port cities of Brava and Mogadishu at an uncertain date. Originally the Qadiriya congregations were established as monasterylike communities. In 1819 Sheikh Ibrahim Hassan Jebro acquired land on the Juba River and established a *jamaha* center of the kind that became common in southern Somalia, which attracted many marginal elements of the society.

Outstanding figures of the Qadiriya in Somalia include Sheikh Awes Muhammad Barawi (d. 1909), who spread the teaching of the order in the southern interior. He wrote a great deal of devotional poetry in Arabic and also attempted to translate traditional hymns from Arabic into Somali, working out his own phonetic system. Another is Sheikh Abd ar Rahman Abdallah of Mogadishu, who stressed mysticism rather than teaching. He was both a literary figure and an amateur astrologer and attempted a series of prohesies on the future of the city. His reputation for sanctity caused people to seek him out. His tomb at Mogadishu is a pilgrimage center for the Shabelle region, and his writings are still circulated by his followers.

The Ahmadiya-Idrisiya order, founded by Sayyid Ahmad Ibn Idris al Fasi (1760-1837) of Mecca, was brought to Somalia by Sheikh Ali Maye Durogba of Marka. He was a distinguished poet who joined the order during a pilgrimage to Mecca. His visions and reported miracles gained him a great reputation for sanctity, and his tomb became a place for pilgrimage. The Ahmadiya-Idrisiya, which has the smallest number of adherents of the three orders, has few ritual requirements beyond simple prayers and hymns. Its ceremonies, during which participants attain spectacular states of trance, attract converts mainly from the uneducated general public.

The Salihiya was established because of a conflict over the leadership of the Ahmadiya-Idrisiya. Ibrahim ar Rashid, who died at Mecca in 1874, claimed to be the true successor of the founder. His nephew and pupil, Muhammad ibn Salih, split off and created a separate order in 1887. Its seat was Mecca. The order spread first among the Somali of the Ogaden area of Ethiopia, entering Somalia from there about 1880. The most active proselytizer was Sheikh Muhammad Guled ar Rashidi, who became a regional leader. He settled among the Shidle (non-Somali cultivators occupying the middle reaches of the Shabelle River), where he obtained land and established a *jamaha*. Later he founded another *jamaha* among the Ajuran (a section of the Hawiya clan-family) and then returned to found still another among the Shidle before he died in 1918. He named his settlements after the holy centers of Islam—Mecca, Medina, and Misra, the Arabic name for Egypt, where Al-Azhar University is located.

Generally both Salihiya and Ahmadiya-Idrisiya leaders have been more interested in the establishment of *jamahayo* than in learning, since few had an advanced education. In the nomadic regions such leaders maintained their clan ties, and *jamaha* livestock was often herded with that of the lineage. In the agricultural regions of the south members of *jamahayo* often came from different lineages with whom they had severed connections.

The social importance of the brotherhoods' early work of establishing *jamahayo* cannot be emphasized enough. They not only cultivated and harvested cooperatively but developed effective agricultural methods as well. In Somalia's riverine region, for example, only *jamaha* members thought of stripping the brush from areas around their fields, thus reducing the breeding places of tsetse flies.

Customarily local leaders of brotherhoods go to the lineage heads in the areas where they wish to settle and ask for permission to build their community and mosque. A piece of land is usually given free, since the land is considered given to God and the donor thereby acquires merit and blessing. Often such land is an area lying between two clans or is one through which nomads have access to a river. The presence of a *jamaha* may act as a buffer between two hostile groups. Tenure is a matter of charity and may become precarious in case of disagreements. A great many *jamahayo* were established between 1880 and 1920. No statistics were available in the 1970s on the number of *jamahayo*, but in the 1950s there were more than ninety in the south with a total membership of about 35,000. Most were in the Bakool, Gedo and Baydhaba regions or along the middle and lower Shabelle River. There were fewer *jamahayo* in other regions, because climatic and soil conditions did not encourage agricultural settlements.

Leaders of brotherhoods are said to have *baraka*, a state of blessedness implying a spiritual power that is inherent in the religious office and that may later cling to the tomb of a revered leader. Leaders are called *caliph* as were the heads of Sunni Islam. The Qadiriya has caliphs in each large region but no overall head. The other orders have ties to motherhouses in Mecca. The customs of the different orders vary. The Qadiriya uses kat, a stimulant narcotic, as an aid to meditation and trance. The Salihiya expressly forbids the use of kat and of tobacco. Ahmadiya-Idrisiya members wear a turban and Salihiya women a veil. In contrast to most Somali, who are proud of their long bushy hair, Salihiya men shave their heads to shun vanity. The Rifaiya forbids the use of drums during ceremonies to avoid similarities with indigenous African rituals. Minor differences regarding the number of beads in the rosary and other ritual details also exist among the brotherhoods.

Membership in a brotherhood is theoretically a voluntary matter unrelated to kinship. Religious lineages, however, are often affiliated with a specific brotherhood, and generally a man will tend to join his father's order. Initiation is followed by the celebration of the brotherhood's particular rite. Novices swear to accept the caliph as their spiritual guide.

Each order has its own hierarchy, which is supposed to be a substitute for the kin group from which the members have separated themselves. Instead of ancestors previous heads of the order, known as the Chain of Blessing *(silsilad al baraka)*, are revered. This is especially true in the south, where residence tends to be more important than descent.

In Somalia there has been a great deal of devotional literature in connection with Sufism. The sophistication of the learned Sufi poets and theologians has been important in the development of Islamic education. It was also important in early attempts to provide a script for the Somali language.

Folk Islam

The Somali have interpreted or modified much of Islam in terms of their pre-Islamic heritage and their particular situation. In come cases pre-Islamic practices continue almost unchanged. The ancestors of clans, lineages, and lineage segments are commemorated in annual rites among the pastoralists. Among the settled cultivators where structured genealogies are absent such rites are replaced by rainmaking ceremonies celebrated by the entire clan.

The social significance of *baraka* exemplifies the process of modification. It is considered a gift from God to the founders and heads of Sufi brotherhoods, who also inherit *baraka* through their personal genealogies dating back to Muhammad. *Baraka* is similarly associated with secular leaders and their clan genealogies and is transmitted by having the retiring leader spit on the new one.

A leader has the power to bless and in some cases even to perform miracles and bring good luck to his people, but his *baraka* may have dangerous side effects. When the leader of a clan or a strong lineage visits that of another, it is customary for a relative to receive him first in order to draw off some of the power so that his own chief may not be injured. During a conference, chiefs of great power have been known to cover their face and expose only one eye in order not to cause injuries.

The traditional learning of a *wadad* includes a form of folk astronomy or astrology based on actual stellar movements and related to the changes of the seasons. Authorities differ as to whether it is lunar or solar. Its primary object is to signal the times for migration, although it may also be used for other predictions, such as determining the dates of rituals that are specifically Somali (and not Muslim). This folk astronomy is also used in connection with ritual and magical methods of healing and averting misfortune, as well as for divination.

Wadaddo help avert misfortune in other ways. For example, they make protective amulets and charms that transmit some of their own *baraka* to others, or they add the Quran's *baraka* to the amulet in the form of a written quotation. The *baraka* of a saint may be obtained from an object that has been touched to or laid near his tomb.

Wadaddo may use their power to curse as a sanction. Occasionally they are suspected of misusing this power against a rival, contrary to right religion. Generally, however, misfortune is not attributed to curses or witchcraft, nor is it considered a special punishment from God, since man's basic sinfulness would then make misfortune a permanent condition. Somali have accepted the orthodox Muslim view that a man's conduct will be judged in the afterlife. It is thought, however, that a person who behaves in a shockingly antisocial manner—a parricide, for example—is possessed of supernatural evil powers.

Despite formal Islam's uncompromising monotheism, Muslims everywhere believe in the existence of jinn, mortal spirits said to be descended from Iblis, a spirit fallen from heaven. Jinn own livestock, trade, live in houses, and get married. There are two kinds of spirits: those benevolent and believing, who carry out God's wishes, and those evil and unbelieving, who are a source of difficulties. Some spirits are learned in the Quran and are called *wadaddo* like their human counterparts. Somali have accepted the Arabic notion of jinn, but they lay greater practical and ceremonial stress on spirits of their own pre-Islamic traditions. Sometimes, however, they identify indigenous spirits with jinn.

Certain kinds of illness, including tuberculosis and pneumonia, and such symptoms as sneezing, coughing, vomiting, and loss of consciousness are believed to come from spirit possession. Involved are said to be the *wadaddo* of the spirit world, who attack without reason. According to legend they are the family spirits of Bokor Osman, a former sultan of the Usman Muhammad clan of the Mijerteyn area in northeast Somalia. It is said that when he died, his descendants refused to take the responsibility of controlling these spirits and merely sent them away, leaving them free to attack people. The condition is treated by a human *wadad*, preferably one who has recovered from the sickness himself. He reads portions of the Quran over the patient and bathes him with perfume, which in Somalia is associated with religious celebrations.

Although there is scriptural support for the existence of jinn and the spirit *wadaddo*, many Somali regard the belief in spirit possession as superstition. This is especially so in the case of possession by *zar* (derived from the name for god in certain Cushitic languages—also *saar*). This form of possession and the ceremony of exorcism used to treat it are sometimes referred to as the "cult of the *zar*." Legend has it that the *zar* was a spirit sent to the Somali by the Ethiopians as a revenge for some hostile act. The victims are said to be women with a grievance against their husbands. The symptoms are extreme forms of hysteria and fainting.

The exorcism ritual is conducted by a woman *(alaqa)* who has had the disease and is thus supposed to have some authority over the spirit—often a widow, a childless woman, or a divorcee. The ritual consists of a special kind of dance in which the victim and others participate. The victim tends to reproduce the symptoms and falls into a trance during the dance. The *alaqa* charges high fees and also pockets the offerings brought to appease the spirit, such as perfumes, fine clothing, dates, coffee, and similar items. Livestock, too, may be sacrificed. Some of these items must also be given to the victim "for the spirit." The illness enables a disgruntled wife to express her hostility without actually quarreling with her husband. If the illness recurs too often, the husband may suspect that the agent is an old woman whose malicious suggestions have brought on the condition. He may then consider a divorce. The religious authorities disapprove of *zar* dances and have banned them in many districts.

In a third kind of spirit possession, known as *gelid* (entering), the spirit of an injured person troubles the offender. A jilted girl, for example, cannot openly complain if a promise of marriage, arranged by the respective families, has been broken, since in traditional Somali society it is considered shameful to refer to love between a man and a woman. Only her spirit, entering the young man who was supposed to marry her and stating the grievance, brings the matter into the open. The exorcism consists of readings from the Quran and commands from a *wadad* that the spirit leave the afflicted person.

The same kind of possession is thought to be caused by the curse or evil power of a poor and helpless person who has been injured. The belief is that those who are weak in worldly matters are mystically endowed. Such persons are supposed to be under the special protection of God, and kind acts toward them bring religious merit, whereas unkind acts bring punishment. The evil eye, too, is associated with poor and unfortunate people, especially covetous women, in a way that suggests the European medieval idea of a witch.

It is consistent with this attitude that the Yibir, who are the least numerous and the weakest of the occupational castes and socially the least acceptable, are the most feared for their supernatural powers (see ch. 4). They make protective magic for their patrons on ritual occasions, and they bless newly married couples and newborn infants. The payments that they receive in return are said to be installments on the blood money for an ancestor, Muhammad Hanif, who was killed in a contest of magic with a Somali saint, Au Barkhadle (the Blessed One). Although the Yibir are nominally Muslims, their power is believed to be demonic, and they are said to be carried away by a wind spirit when they die.

ISLAM AND THE STATE

Islam seeks to control specific aspects of secular life in order to create an environment in which Muslims may lead a pious and virtuous life according to sharia. It does not require its followers to change their usual economic activities. It sets no limit on the legal accumulation of wealth and demands only specified contributions for charity. Since Islamic laws have their origin in prophecy and revelation, the past and present function of religious officials is to ascertain the precise will of God by interpreting the Quran and the hadith. Ingrained in Islam, therefore, is a certain inflexibility that has made it difficult to cope with the social, economic, and political changes resulting from the expansion of colonial rule in the late nineteenth century.

Reactions to these changes have varied within Islam. One response was totally to oppose westernization and to stress a return to orthodox Muslim traditions. The Sufi brotherhoods were in the forefront of such a movement. In Somalia the movement was led by Sayyid Mohamed ibn Abdullah Hassan, a noted early nationalist (see ch. 2). Most Sufi leaders, fearing a weakening of their authority, strongly opposed the spread of Western education.

Another response, originating in Egypt, was to reform Islam by reinterpreting it in modern terms. This was done by pointing out that early Islam had been partly a protest against abuse, corruption, and inequalities and by attempting to prove that traditional Muslim scriptures contained all the elements needed to deal with the forces of modernization. Islamic Socialism belongs to this school of thought, identified particularly with the late Gamal Abdul Nasser, who urged a just social order in accordance with Islamic principles. His ideas appealed to a number of Somali, especially those who had studied in Cairo in the 1950s and 1960s.

The Constitution of 1961 guaranteed freedom of religion but also declared the newly independent Republic of Somalia an Islamic state. The public course undertaken by the first two governments was vaguely defined as following the principles of Islamic Socialism. The coup of October 21, 1969, installed a radical regime committed to deep-rooted changes. Shortly after the coup *Stella d'Ottobre,* the official mouthpiece of the Supreme Revolutionary Council (SRC), published an editorial that dealt with the relations between Islam and socialism and the differences between scientific and Islamic socialism. Islamic Socialism, it said, had become a servant of capitalism and neocolonialism, a tool by which the rich and privileged manipulated society. In contrast scientific socialism and Islam were inspired by the same altruistic values. Religious leaders should therefore leave secular affairs to the new leaders, secure in the knowledge that they were striving for goals that conformed to Islamic principles. The editorial warned that those who attacked scientific socialism were actually opposing Islam itself. And in fact a number of protesting religious leaders were arrested and accused of counterrevolutionary propaganda and of conniving with reactionary elements in the Arabian Peninsula. Several members of religious tribunals were dismissed for corruption and incompetence.

The campaign for scientific socialism got properly under way on January 31, 1971. A new three-year development plan had been launched and workers' councils installed in rural plantations. The leaders felt compelled to win the active support of the deeply religious Somali people for the total transformation of the existing social structure of which the religious leaders were an integral part. In an interview in February Major Mohamed Yusuf Elmi Bashir, then a member of the SRC, said, "A good Muslim has to espouse Scientific Socialism because of its goals of justice, equality, and plenty for all." "Who is against Scientific Socialism is against the only system compatible with our religion," proclaimed *Stella d'Ottobre"* in March. In the same month the participants in a political plot were accused of wanting to reinstate Islamic Socialism, complete with the former power structures, thus opening the door to neocolonialism and capitalism (see ch. 9).

On September 4, 1971, about 100 religious teachers assembled in the capital and heard President Mohamed Siad Barre urge them to participate actively in the building of a new socialist society. He criticized their method of teaching in the Quranic schools and said that some of them used religion as a source of personal profit.

The campaign for scientific socialism and, paralleling it, the attack on what the regime referred to as the traditional upper classes, including the religious leaders, intensified in 1972. On January 26, on the occasion of Id al-Adha—the most important Islamic festival of the year—the president defined scientific socialism as half practical work and half ideological beliefs, but he declared it to be entirely compatible with Islam, since the Quran condemned exploitation and moneylending and urged compassion, unity, and cooperation among fellow

Muslims. He stressed the distinction between religion as an ideological instrument for the manipulation of power and religion as a moral force. President Siad condemned the antireligious attitude of confirmed Marxists who regard religion as the opium of the people. Religion, he said, was an integral part of the Somali world view, but it belonged in the private sphere, whereas scientific socialism dealt with such material concerns as poverty. Religious leaders should exercise their moral influence but refrain from interfering in political or economic matters. Scientific socialism was extolled in simple terms during the next nine months in the press, on the radio, in speeches, and at workers' meetings. Islamic and African socialism were branded as pseudosocialism, serving a reactionary and rapacious bourgeoisie.

In 1973 the National Adult Education Center in Mogadishu began a training program for Quranic teachers. After one session in July the press reported that the sixty participants had accepted the truth of scientific socialism and had promised to pray for its success. Whether they did this from conviction, from opportunism, or from a deep-seated feeling that scientific socialism represented only a short-lived threat to their ancient religion, no one can tell.

On January 11, 1975, President Siad, recalling the message of equality, justice, and social progress contained in the Quran, announced a new family law that gave women equal inheritance rights. The occasion was the twenty-seventh anniversary of the death of a national heroine, Hawa Othman Tako, who had been killed in 1948 during political demonstrations. Apparently the new law was seen as proof by some Somali that the SRC wanted to undermine the basic structure of Islamic society. In Mogadishu twenty-three religious leaders protested inside their mosques. They were arrested within hours and charged with acting at the instigation of a foreign power and with violating the security of the state. Ten of them were executed on January 23, 1975. Most religious leaders, however, remained silent despite the law's apparent attack on the traditionally subservient role of women under Islam (see ch. 4).

Although some religious leaders had opposed and others had supported the SRC's positions on the relationship between Islam and scientific socialism the extent to which the government's ideologies and laws (for example, the family law) were affecting the attitudes and practices of ordinary Somali was not known in the mid-1970s.

CHRISTIANITY

Exact figures on Christian affiliation were not available in the mid-1970s. A very small minority of Christian Somali exists, some of whom, notably the Mariano family, have been outstanding in the development of nationalism and independence (see ch. 2).

The first Christian missionaries, Swedish Lutherans, came to Somalia in 1809 and settled in the lower Juba area. They were evicted in 1934 by the Italians, who wanted to win support among the Muslim population of Somalia for their invasion of Christian Ethiopia. The Swedes were the only Protestants until the arrival in 1952 of the Pennsylvania-based Mennonites, who have their origin in the Anabaptist movement of the sixteenth-century Reformation. Mennonite schools, which introduced English education into southern Somalia, became popular in 1960 when English began replacing Italian as the official language. The Sudan Interior Mission, an independent fundamentalist evangelical missionary organization, represents the bulk of Protestant activity. In 1954 the mission established headquarters in Mogadishu and subsequently built two schools and a hospital in the interior.

During the colonial period the British did not allow proselytizing in their area. In former Italian Somalia the Roman Catholic Church established missions, charitable institutions, churches, and schools. The latter were used primarily by Europeans. Some Somali, however, attended, and a few went on to higher education.

Freedom of religion is guaranteed in Somalia, but in 1963 the constitution was amended to prohibit open propagation of Christianity. In October 1972 a law was passed under which the Ministry of Education would take over all private schools, including those run by the missions. In late 1970 most church activities were voluntarily suspended or greatly reduced.

* * *

For more detailed information on Somali Islam see I.M. Lewis' articles: "Sheiks and Warriors of Somaliland," "Conformity and Contrast in Somali Islam," and "Sufism in Somaliland: A Study in Tribal Islam." For a sympathetic perspective on the revolutionary regime's approach to Islam, see Luigi Pestalozza's *The Somalian Revolution.* (For further information see Bibliography.)

CHAPTER 6

LIVING CONDITIONS

In the mid-1970s Somalia's per capita income was one of the lowest in the world—estimates ranged from about US$50 to US$85 a year. Any average concealed wide differences between a small number of people—most of them in government service—who were comparatively well off and the large majority who participated only marginally in the money economy.

After taking power in 1969 the regime tried to diminish this gap by severely reducing government salaries, lowering rents, increasing taxes on real estate holdings, and curtailing the profits of merchants dealing in vital commodities. In 1974 the prevailing poverty was aggravated by the drought that, by the next year, had driven more than 250,000 pastoralists into emergency camps and forced 500,000 to 1 million to accept relief outside the camps. In mid-1975, in what was believed to be the biggest project of its kind ever undertaken in Africa, nearly half of those in the camps were relocated to take up settled farming on relatively productive land along the Juba and Shabelle rivers in the south or to become fishermen at settlements on the coast (see ch. 13).

The drought also accelerated the trend, begun after World War II, of rural people migrating to town in search of jobs and a better life. Because they usually lacked the skills needed in a modern economy, they were seldom able to find full-time urban employment.

Social welfare and community development services were still insufficient in 1976, but the government, by means of self-help projects and with aid from international organizations, was expanding both. It particularly tried to bring a modicum of medical care to all Somali, many of whom suffered from serious diseases, including tuberculosis and malaria. Medical problems were aggravated by inadequate diets.

LIVING PATTERNS

Rural

For the 80 percent or more of the people who are rural, living patterns are governed by the seasons, the level of rainfall, and other factors beyond human control. This probably explains the widespread intense interest in the movement of stars and the moon. Although the government and townspeople follow the Gregorian calendar, rural people depend on the astrologer and weather lore expert to prophesy the rains and winds, the time of foaling, and the best time to set out with the herds, and to set dates for feasts and other important events.

Camel Nomads

The long-distance travels of the camel nomads are dictated by the availability and distribution of water and grazing. During the rainy seasons they set out for their traditional pastures, many of which are across the border in Ethiopia in the Haud and Ogaden. During the dry seasons when the pastures dry up, they return to their home wells. Although no clan or lineage has special claim to any piece of land, there are traditionally established priority rights to the areas centered on these wells, which belong to the family of the person who dug them (see ch. 13).

These fully nomadic people raise not only camels that need to be watered infrequently but also sheep, goats, and cattle that have to be watered every few days; thus camels are herded separately from the other animals. The family camp (*gurgi*, or *rer* after the basic social unit that constitutes it) takes care of the sheep, goats, and one or two cows or milch camels, which provide the main item of the diet, as well as a few burden camels. The camp, which is always set up within easy reach of wells, comprises people related through paternal links—a man, his wife or wives, his unmarried children and, often, close relatives. Some camps contain several families. The camp moves when water and grazing become exhausted and a scout has found another suitable spot.

Young unmarried men and boys from the age of six take the camels on migrations to faraway pastures. Along the route the camels, which can survive two weeks or more without drinking, browse on the tough and thorny twigs of stunted scrub. The herds vary in size, but each herder needs five to ten camels because only a few of the animals produce milk at any one time, providing his only sustenance. Close kinsmen traditionally pool their herds and herd them in common, although each herd is fenced off within a separate corral.

In a single year a camel camp may travel over 1,000 miles. Moving with the camp is strenuous and exhausting work. Wherever the men and animals settle for a while, thorn fences must be built to protect the camels from thieves and wild animals. Watering the flocks, too, is tedious because wells are often very deep. Buckets made from skins or a camel's stomach are hauled out hand over hand and tipped into a trough from which two or three camels can drink at the same time.

During the rainy seasons the family camp and the camel camp move close to each other. This is the time of abundance and the time for feasting, courting, marriages, and social gatherings, and for council meetings and religious activities. Families split up again with the beginning of the next dry season.

Wherever there are permanent wells there are market centers consisting perhaps of only one shop. Traders and shopkeepers usually belong to the same lineage as the camel nomads. They may actually live in a larger town and only bring some of their goods—by camel or truck—to the marketplace as long as its well has water and attracts people.

Usually there is also a coffee shop—with an earthen floor and a fire in the corner—where people gather to drink spiced tea rather than coffee. There is also a mosque, often no more than an open area surrounded by a thorn fence (see ch. 5).

A well-established division of labor exists between the sexes. At a young age girls learn to cook, to care for younger siblings, and to look after the goats, sheep, and milch camels. Women set up the huts and take them down, pack the household goods on the transport camels, and lead them to the next location. Women also lead the camels to the wells to fetch water. They milk the goats (but not the camels), and they may take milk and ghee (clarified butter made from cow's or goat's milk but never from camel's milk) to the market to sell. Women also weave ropes and cords from bark fibers.

Boys, until they are six or seven years old, help their mothers in looking after the sheep and goats. Then they join the world of men, going with their older unmarried brothers on long migrations, learning early to withstand hunger, thirst, and physical strain. Once married, men spend less time with the camels unless they have no younger brothers or servants who can look after the animals. But they continue to manage the herds and to look after the wells, which must be maintained constantly. They also travel to market towns to buy provisions or to sell animals, milk, and skins.

Establishing and increasing the herds is the primary concern of nomadic people. At birth a son is usually given a milch camel or a cow or a few goats and sheep as the nucleus of his future herd. Over the years the herd will reproduce and grow through various gifts and perhaps purchases. There will be livestock payments at the time of marriage and eventually the inheritance of part of the paternal herd. Sheep and goats always carry the brand of an individual owner, but camels carry the brand of the lineage (or *dia*-paying group—see Glossary) and are counted as lineage assets, although they also have a private owner who uses them for his own benefit.

Cattle Raisers

Many cattle raisers in the center and south of Somalia are seminomadic or even sedentary, some never moving very far from their home village, which is always centered on a well. Cattle, unlike camels, cannot be without water for more than two or three days. The grazing areas ring the villages at a distance of about three or four hours' walk. Cattle raisers usually also own some camels, sheep, and goats.

Cattle owners, however, in contrast to camel herders, are not self-sufficient. Cows do not give enough milk for sustenance during the dry season, and their owner must therefore either exchange with cultivators or adopt cultivation himself. He must also protect the grazing grounds from camels that would eat them bare. This presumably is why the Digil and Rahanwein clan-families forced the Hawiya and Darod who came from the north to settle farther south in the Trans-Juba area.

Cultivators

Because of the presence of the tsetse fly in parts of the river valleys, the cultivators along the banks of the Juba and Shabelle rivers, who are partly or wholly of non-Somali origin, keep hardly any livestock. Their principal crop is maize (corn), which needs a fair amount of water. Some cultivators use small pumps to bring water from the river into channels among the crops. Most, however, use the floodwater that spills over the riverbanks, either to water crops already planted or to plant on the marshland after the flood has receded. Cultivators skillfully use the natural conditions in their area, but their methods, in comparison with controlled irrigation, are relatively inefficient and wasteful of scarce water resources.

In contrast to the riverine villagers, cultivators in the area between the rivers—mostly members of the Digil or Rahanwein clan-families by origin or adoption—practice dryland farming. Their principal crop is sorghum rather than maize. About two-thirds of the cultivators keep small herds of cattle and some camels and goats. Villages are situated near a water source, usually a well or man-made pond both of which are constructed and maintained by the villagers. Land for growing and grazing is permanently owned by a lineage, and the right to use it is acquired by virtue of lineage membership.

The south receives at least 60 percent of its annual rainfall during the rainy season (*gu*) that begins in March or April. This is the time to plant maize, millet, sorghum, cotton, groundnuts (peanuts), sesame, tobacco, and such vegetables as beans, cassava, onions and tomatoes. All except cassava can be planted again during the *dayr*, the rainy season that begins in October and is also the season of the first harvest. Cassava is planted only once but can be left in the ground and harvested at any time. Such fruits as bananas can be picked throughout the year. As with the nomads, the cohesive social unit among cultivators that collaborates in producing and consuming is the *rer*, a group of people related through paternal links.

Nomadic pastoralists, mostly from the Jubada Hoose Region (lower Juba), drive large herds of camels, goats, and sheep through the inter-river area. Where land is cultivated, the livestock graze on the crop stubble and cut stalks after the harvest or range over the much larger areas of nonarable pastureland.

Not all cultivators of the northwest, who are members of Samaal clan-families, are wholly settled. Many are transhumant pastoralists, or seminomads. Those who are settled usually keep cattle as well as plow oxen, and most have a more numerous flock of sheep and goats. Cultivating families often own one or two camels for prestige reasons and as a store of wealth, but relatively few individuals own camel herds. Sometimes a cultivator will send one wife and her children to the southern pastures in the spring and summer with the sheep and goats, or he may have brothers who can go farther afield with a small herd of camels. Some cultivating settlements may be deprived of half their population during the spring and summer months and expand again at harvesttime. The cattle are usually kept near the village. Cultivators of the northwest use a wooden oxplow for cultivation instead of the short-handled hoe characteristic of the southern area and of much of agriculture in Africa.

Among the sedentary people, too, certain jobs are performed only by men and others only by women. Generally men do such heavy and intermittent work as clearing and preparing the ground, and women do such tedious and routine tasks as weeding and hoeing. Men dig and clean the wells, but only women draw water. Men build the houses, but women do the plastering and thatching. Young children help their elders, learning early to do the jobs they will be expected to perform as adults.

Fishermen

Fishing is the main occupation of the scattered peoples who live along the coast and on the islands. The Bajun in the south use double outrigger canoes, which resemble those in use along the Malay Peninsula and among the Polynesian islands. The Bajun have developed a special technique to catch turtles with the aid of trained suckerfish. The fish, attached to a line, clamps onto the shell of the turtle. Both are reeled in, and the fish is used again.

In the north the fishermen on the eastern coast of the Bari Region net sharks and then kill them with harpoons. They salt the meat, sell it in local markets, and export the dried tails and fins to India.

North of Hafun the villagers collect ambergris, which is washed up on the beaches, and sell it to traders. Because of special conditions in the area, the coastal people south of Hafun are able to collect pelagic fish that the sea throws onto the shore. They dry the fish and sell them.

Urban

The Somali have no urban tradition; all the major towns were founded by Arabs or Europeans. Nevertheless migration to the towns became established after World War II. In 1976 almost all inhabitants of the capital were Somali. They had come from all parts of the country and tended to settle wherever they found an available spot, so that people from different regions and belonging to different clans live next to each other.

The vast majority are unemployed or underemployed. They manage to live on very little, subsisting partly on the animals they brought along with them to the city and partly on the help they get from relatives.

Most of those who are employed work for either the government or commercial and industrial enterprises. The self-employed are traders or artisans, or they perform a variety of services, such as carrying water. Generally government employees are better off than others. The socialist-minded government in power after 1969 sought to reduce the divisions between the people by restricting the growth of the income of the wealthier portion. It reduced the salaries of civil servants, restructuring the pay scales so that the highest apparently was more than six times the lowest, and—by a law passed in 1976—prohibited public employees from engaging in speculatory business enterprises, such as building houses. Small-scale businesses, unless they are involved with basic commodities, are not interfered with. In fact, in March 1972 construction of a commercial center was completed in Mogadishu, and its more than 100 shops were put at the disposition of small merchants and artisans at moderate rent.

The urban poor, despite the fact that they have escaped the rigors and uncertainty of a nomadic existence, often are worse off than rural people, particularly those living in the cultivating areas. A large proportion of their income is spent on food, fuel, and housing, items they were formerly able to procure largely by their own labor. They also develop new needs by being exposed to such hitherto unknown consumer goods as modern clothing, furniture, canned goods, and bottled drinks.

Many come to the towns for limited periods during droughts or other calamities and leave again when conditions improve or when they have saved enough money to start a herd, buy a particular coveted item, or get married. Large numbers arrive only during certain times of the year. The population of Hargeysa, for example, is said to increase by 25 to 30 percent during the dry season.

HOUSING

Somali live in a wide variety of houses, all of which are represented in Mogadishu. They range from Western-style villas to the collapsible dwellings of the nomads. The administrative and business buildings and the residential sections are in the center of town, laid out and largely built by the Italians. There, too, are the large square luxury houses of the well-to-do, set in the middle of spacious yards that are surrounded by high stone walls. Arab-style houses, one or two stories high and with crenellated roofs, are built of stucco and have pastel-colored or whitewashed walls. Metal shutters or iron bars protect windows and doors on the first floor, and inside a large staircase leads to a terrace on the flat roof. Although Europeans and Asians are concentrated in certain areas, Somali live in all sections.

Smaller and more densely populated city blocks planned by the Italians ring the center. Farther out are the housing estates built since independence by the Somali government for low-income groups. In that area the density is lower, and there are many open spaces and few commercial buildings. Still farther out on the circumference of the city are haphazardly built clusters, mostly nomad huts and mud houses. That is where newcomers to the city first settle.

Usually immigrants first build the kind of housing they were used to. Nomads set up elongated portable dwellings (*agal*), which can easily be mounted or dismantled and transported by camel. People from settled rural areas build a one-room *muudul* by making a cylindrical framework of slender posts and vines that they plaster with a mixture of mud, ashes, and dung. A nine-foot-high center pole supports a conical thatch roof.

Immigrants often stay in the place where they first settle but improve or replace their dwellings. Once they have decided to remain permanently, they build an *arish*, a rectangular house with a two-sided sloping roof, which is constructed in the same manner as the *muudul*. The *arish*, which is painted white or rose, is larger than the *muudul*, measuring from ten to twenty feet in width by twenty-five to fifty feet in length. In Mogadishu it is usually covered with a metal roof. As the owner's financial situation improves, he might replace this house with a more substantial one made of wood or even of stone that he quarries in his spare time.

Nearly 98 percent of the houses in Mogadishu had neither water nor electricity in the early 1970s. The Development Program 1974-1978 cited a need for 54,663 new houses, 48 percent of them in Mogadishu. Housing shortages were also severe in Hargeysa, Kismayo, and Berbera. The government has tried to cope with the mushrooming shantytowns by razing them and replacing them with planned housing. Lack of capital, qualified labor, and building materials, most of which must be imported at great cost, hamper these efforts.

In the countryside houses may not be adequate or particularly sanitary, but people are able to build them with readily available materials. Nomads use pliant branches or weeds to build the frames of their dwellings, elongated hemispheres that measure three to four yards across and two to three yards high. Mats made of rawhide or woven from grass, sisal, or other fibers are used to cover the outside, the floor, and the entrance.

The most important item of furnishing is the bed, made of wooden palm-leaf ribs supported by four wooden stakes, and covered with skins or furs. Household utensils include water bags made of leather, decorated wooden vessels and mats, stools, headrests, camel bells, spoons, and combs and boxes, some of them embellished with carved geometric design. All these belongings can easily be loaded onto camels and transported to another location.

Metal roofs are a sign of prosperity among the settled cultivators. Most houses, however, are covered with thatch. Household goods tend to be somewhat more numerous and heavier than those of the nomads. They include some rough wooden furniture, more substantial bedding, hollowed gourds to store food and water, woven bags, and earthenware utensils.

CLOTHING

The most common dress of Somali men and women is the *futa* (also called *maro* or *tob*), seven yards of cotton wrapped in sarong fashion around the body. This is in accord with the Islamic precept that the legs of both men and women must be covered. The *futa* is usually white but soon acquires an ocher color through repeated washing in muddy water. Herders wrap a second *futa* around their heads as protection against the hot sun. Women often wear two or three of different colors.

Islam also prescribes that women should veil their faces, but in Somalia this is not followed. Only the hair of older women is covered. Urbanites have increasingly adopted Western-style clothes, and the modern revolutionary emphasis of the regime has even made shorts acceptable for girls who engage in various sports. Both men and women wear necklaces and bracelets of gold, silver, and ivory. They also wear amulets—small leather bags with verses from the Quran inside—lions' claws, hairs from elephants' tails, and sharks' teeth.

Pastoralists always carry a double-edged dagger, a weapon that also serves as a handy all-around tool. The typical practice of herdsmen is to carry on their shoulders a stick on which they rest their arms.

DIET AND NUTRITION

The country's resources are limited and, despite efforts to develop agriculture and livestock breeding, food production is insufficient. Frequent shortages are caused by drought, flood, crop disease, or periodic locust infestation. Consequently the diets of most Somali are inadequate, unbalanced, or both. A marked drop in the population's food intake also occurs during the dry season when local supplies are sparse. This is particularly true among nomads, whose total caloric intake during such times barely amounts to 50 percent of daily requirements. The milch camels produce little, and their owners have to trade hides and animals for foodstuffs.

Among the northern pastoralists milk forms the basic diet of the young men who travel with the camel herds. During the rainy seasons men may drink from eight to ten quarts a day, supplemented with a little durra or other kinds of sorghum and perhaps meat once or twice a month when a sickly young camel or an old one has to be butchered. In the family camp, however, with its flocks of sheep and goats and a few cattle, food is more plentiful and includes sugar, sorghum, durra, rice, dates, and tea as well as milk.

The diet of the sedentary rural population is 25 percent deficient in protein. It consists mainly of locally cultivated maize, durra, sorghum, beans, and very limited amounts of vegetables and fruits. Fish consumption is restricted to the coastal population, although the government is attempting to popularize fish among the inland peoples.

Urban diets, according to a study by the Food and Agriculture Organization (FAO), proved to be sufficient in calories and only slightly deficient in protein. They were, however, short on vitamins and calcium and too high in fat and sugar. Rice was the main staple, although it had to be imported. A variety of other foodstuffs was usually available, diets being generally related to income and educational levels.

The stimulants most often used are coffee and tea. Coffee beans are browned in butter over a slow fire. Tea is steeped with cloves, cinnamon, and Indian seed called *el*, and lots of sugar. The leaves of the kat plant *(Catha edulis)*, which contain a stimulant related to the benzedrine family, are chewed by people during religious dances and often by truckdrivers or others who have to make prolonged physical efforts.

In times of scarcity prices have had a tendency to rise exorbitantly. Especially in the countryside traders have taken advantage of shortages to charge three to four times as much as in town. In November 1970 a decree was passed that set uniform prices for maize everywhere; another decree in July 1971 covered other grains. To provide a more even supply of foodstuffs, underground storage silos were built in villages, usually as part of self-help programs. In January 1975, because of the particularly grim situation caused by the prolonged drought, food rationing based on a nationwide system of identity cards was introduced, the first time it had ever been attempted in an African country. Security forces and police were ordered to wipe out the black market.

Diseases related to dietary deficiencies and undernourishment are found throughout the country. This is especially noticeable in children up to three years of age. Many are suckled until their fifth year. Studies have shown that protein, which is essential for growth, produces the opposite effect when it is almost the sole source of nutrition.

Improvement of the diet requires the expansion of agriculture and the introduction of such nutritionally rich foods as vegetables and fish, which are not eaten by most Somali even when available. Recognizing the fundamental importance of a proper diet to health, the government set up the National Nutrition Board in 1972. It was to design a nutritional policy for the country in collaboration with various ministries. Apparently it did not function properly and was to be revitalized under the Development Program 1974-1978. The students who participated in the 1974 literacy campaign and census taking also collected information on people's eating habits. Schools and radiobroadcasts spread knowledge of proper nutrition.

HEALTH

The high incidence of disease that persisted into the mid-1970s was a reflection of a difficult environment, inadequate diet, and insufficient medical care. Conditions varied, however, from region to region and from season to season. The lack of roads and the existence of a largely mobile population, which often spread disease and escaped medical controls, contributed to the enormous difficulty of supplying adequate and constant health care. The average life expectancy was estimated at forty-one years and infant mortality at 177 per 1,000 births. It was believed that about two-thirds of the morbidity and mortality rates were due to preventable causes and to disease in infancy and childhood that could be controlled by simple preventive measures.

In March 1972 the government took control of all medical services and permitted no further private practice. It attempted to provide a modicum of health care for the rural and nomadic areas. Beginning in October 1972 patients were admitted without cost to government hospitals and dispensaries. The import and distribution of pharmaceutical products was nationalized in the same year, and drugs were made available at reasonable cost.

Prevalent Diseases

Pulmonary tuberculosis, malaria, and infectious and parasitic diseases constitute the country's major health problems. In addition schistosomiasis (bilharzia), tetanus, venereal disease, leprosy, heart disease, poliomyelitis, and a variety of skin and eye diseases severely impair the population's health and productivity.

Ecological, economic, and social conditions favor a high and increasing incidence of tuberculosis. The disease, which is transmitted through contact with sick persons, is widespread among the mobile part of the population that is constantly regrouping. Tuberculosis also spreads easily among people who sleep in close proximity within the transportable huts of the nomads or in the poorly constructed, poorly ventilated houses of most sedentary people.

104

Limited data show that the incidence of tuberculosis is especially high among the lower age-groups and that nearly 80 percent of boys between the ages of ten and fourteen among the nomadic population are affected. It has been suggested that this is due to the custom of sending them out with the young men to graze camels under very severe physical conditions.

The World Health Organization (WHO) began a major tuberculosis control scheme in 1964, directed from the tuberculosis center in Mogadishu. The project aimed at preventing and controlling the disease by mass vaccination and sputum examination. Control measures have been carried out in urban centers but have been difficult to implement among the roughly two-thirds of the population who are nomadic or seminomadic.

Outbreaks of malaria occur in endemic and epidemic forms. During the rainy seasons the entire Somali population is exposed. In the south malaria persists throughout the year. In the north the incidence of malaria is high from November through May. During the dry seasons the larvae of the *Anopheles gambiae,* the main vector that has proved particularly tough and adaptable, are confined to a few wells. The larvae are transported in nomads' water skins, and the adult mosquitoes proliferate in the shallow basins of water that dot the landscape after the heavy semiannual rains. The building of water tanks that store the water collected during the rainy seasons has actually extended the time and surface area (in contrast to narrow deep wells) in which mosquitoes can breed. Vectors have also been discovered in the mats used in the construction of the nomads' portable huts. The mats that make up the walls may well be turned inside out at the next setting up so that any insecticide that might have been sprayed inside the hut will be swept away by the wind.

The number of people stricken by malaria varies between 100,000 and 200,000 annually, according to WHO reports. Somali government health statistics show that the worst affected regions are Shabelle Hoose (lower Shabelle) and Jubada Hoose (lower Juba). The situation is also serious in Shabelle Dhexe (central Shabelle) and Hiiraan. Together these four regions accounted for 68.6 percent of all recognized cases in 1973. The government, in cooperation with WHO and the United Nations Children's Fund (UNICEF), trains personnel and undertakes malaria eradication programs that have become part of the rural health services and will eventually cover the entire country. In the past such activities had been confined mainly to Mogadishu. In the mid-1970s it was reported that ongoing programs had considerably reduced the incidence of malaria.

Smallpox has never been widespread, and no serious outbreaks have been recorded since 1950. When ten cases originating in neighboring countries occurred in 1973, a major inoculation campaign was carried out in the lower river valley areas. Smallpox vaccination has been made compulsory for all schoolchildren.

Two million people were inoculated after a cholera outbreak in December 1970. Because not enough medical personnel were available, the government used student volunteers.

Leprosy, for which local health centers are always on the lookout, is found throughout the country. Complete diagnosis and treatment is given at such large medical establishments as the leprosarium at Alessandra near Gelib. The facility accommodates some 500 patients who have been settled as a self-sufficient farming community.

The incidence of poliomyelitis is relatively high. Beginning in 1967 antipolio campaigns, focusing on young children in urban areas, were mounted by the government.

Spot checks revealed that 75 percent of the population had one or more kinds of intestinal parasites. Schistosomiasis exists particularly in the marshy areas along the rivers in the south. It is estimated that in some parts of the riverine area almost 100 percent of the population is affected.

Venereal diseases are widespread in towns and among the nomads; so are skin and eye diseases. Tick-borne relapsing fever is found throughout the south. Communicable childhood diseases are partly responsible for the high mortality rate.

Malnutrition has made people more susceptible to disease. In the camps where refugees from the drought were housed in 1975 about 12,000 (mostly children) died, not only from the effects of prolonged hunger but also from diarrhea and bronchitis, which their weakened systems could no longer fight.

Medical Services

The organization and administration of health services is the responsibility of the Ministry of Health. It deals with general technical services, preventive and curative medicine, epidemiology, communicable disease control, and environmental sanitation. Medical directors, responsible to the ministry, head the regional public health services and are responsible for the administration of medical institutions and public health services in their area. Under them are the municipal health services, located in almost all regional capitals and the principal towns of districts.

In 1973 there were 5,387 beds available in sixty-three hospitals, of which the best and most modern was the Mogadishu General Hospital. It had been built in 1965 with funds supplied by the European Economic Community (EEC, also known as the Common Market). About a third of the beds were in tuberculosis hospitals.

Only the large hospitals had laboratory and diagnostic services. There were a few mobile X-ray units, but the shortage of trained technicians did not allow for efficient diagnostic services.

The Development Program 1974-1978 provided for building or upgrading hospitals at thirteen regional headquarters and for building or expanding fifteen hospitals at the district level. The plan also proposed building two mental hospitals, a 400-bed one at Mogadishu and a 200-bed one at Hargeysa. The new hospital at Mogadishu will replace the 250 beds for mental patients available at Forlainini Hospital.

The plan also called for a 1,000-patient tuberculosis sanitorium outside Mogadishu to be used as a teaching facility, four new regional tuberculosis sanitoriums, a communicable disease hospital to serve also as a field-training hospital for medical students, the 400-bed University Hospital, and a maternity and pediatric hospital. According to the plan 200 multipurpose mobile teams were to serve districts without health facilities. Quite a number of small new health facilities were built through self-help schemes. Some of these are no more than simple mud and thatch buildings staffed by volunteer nurses, but they provide rudimentary medical care to people who otherwise would have none.

The effectiveness of medical institutions has been considerably limited because of the acute shortage of medical and paramedical personnel. The number of physicians at regional and district facilities rarely exceeds two or three for up to 1,000 patients. At independence there were no Somali physicians, and during the early 1960s professional care was provided by foreign physicians who came under short-term contracts and were paid by international organizations or under bilateral foreign aid programs.

In 1973 there were 104 Somali and sixty-four expatriate physicians practicing. Other medical personnel included twenty-two dentists, 164 midwives, 868 medical assistants (including nurses), fifty-six technical assistants and twenty-two pharmacists. The majority of the population received medical care in small dispensaries manned by medical assistants who were trained to give first aid and to recognize and treat a limited number of diseases.

WHO, UNICEF, the World Food Program (WFP), and the International Labor Organization (ILO) have provided assistance in training, rehabilitation, and disease eradication programs. Medical teams from the Soviet Union and the People's Republic of China (PRC) have been providing health care. In 1976 it was reported that the PRC had started construction of a modern maternity and pediatric hospital of Mogadishu.

Medical Education

Somali doctors had to train abroad until the building of the Somali National University's Faculty of Medicine. It was completed in 1974, partly using voluntary labor. It is equipped with a large operating theater, a library, laboratories, and classrooms.

A small nursing school has been operating at Hargeysa since the early 1960s. It is located next to the Hargeysa Hospital, and its clinical facilities are available to students. A nursing school at Mogadishu, offering three-year courses and capable of training 290 nurses at one time, opened in November 1971.

Several training centers give courses to paramedical personnel in health administration, X-ray and laboratory techniques, pharmacy, midwifery, and other specific fields. The first such center was the Health Training Institute at Mogadishu, which was established in 1959 with assistance from WHO and UNICEF. In the mid-1970s, however, it appeared that the shortage of people knowledgeable in public health, administration, epidemiology, pediatrics, and other specialized fields would continue for some time.

Folk Medicine

In traditional Somali society medical care is provided by the Midgaan and by *waddado* (see ch. 5). Somali are skilled herbalists, and these traditional practitioners use herbs, myrrh, and other vegetable and animal products to cure or relieve a variety of ailments. Cauterization and bloodletting are used to treat headaches, pneumonia, tapeworm, rheumatism, and other ills.

Some traditional medical views anticipated modern developments. When Richard Burton traveled through northern Somaliland in 1854, he reported scornfully that the people associated the bite of the mosquito with fever. Somali traditionally vaccinated persons sick with smallpox on the wrist with lymph taken from a calf suffering from the disease. Patients were isolated and their huts and other belongings burned.

Although Somali generally tend toward rational explanations for sickness, they attribute some physical and mental illnesses to sorcery, cursing, and the evil eye. Madness and epilepsy are often associated with spirit possession. Afflicted persons seek relief through magic, wearing amulets, reciting special formulas, and other psychological means.

Sanitation

The lack of safe water and waste disposal facilities and the difficulty of protecting food against contamination and decay are major reasons for the spread of disease, particularly in rural areas. Municipal health services are responsible for disposal of refuse, inspection of public places, control of water supplies, and general sanitation.

Available water is often contaminated. Drinking water, which is transported in skins on the backs of donkeys, is available all year only along the Juba and Shabelle rivers. In the rest of the country water frequently is available only from wells, sometimes at a great distance. In dry riverbeds or along the flat beaches brackish water collects in holes that women have dug into the sand and is ladled out with a coconut shell at the end of a stick. The holes are dug each day because the wind fills them with sand during the night.

At Mogadishu a water project was completed with United States aid as part of the Development Program 1971-1973. It included the construction of twenty wells on the outskirts of the city, two reservoirs with a combined capacity of 6 million gallons, and a water distribution system consisting of about sixty miles of pipes, 122 public fountains, two public points where water was sold, and about 5,000 service connections. The plans are to extend the system until 9.6 million gallons can be supplied daily. Planners, estimating the city's growth, consider that amount sufficient until 1985.

Refuse and human waste disposal systems are rudimentary. In large urban areas refuse is burned, but few small towns have such facilities. Even where piped water is available, no public sewer system exists. Some septic tanks and cesspools exist, but few houses are provided even with latrines.

The 25,000 students who conducted a census and gave literacy classes in 1974 also taught elementary principles of hygiene and sanitation. Victory Pioneers, the youth wing of the army, also promote public health awareness in Mogadishu and elsewhere.

WELFARE

Social welfare and community development programs have been in force since independence. The need for such services grew markedly as migration to urban areas, unemployment, housing shortages, and related social problems became more prominent in Somali life, particularly in Mogadishu, Hargeysa, and the larger towns. At independence the government established a social welfare organization within the Ministry of Interior. Under this organization's supervision preventive social welfare programs dealt with juvenile delinquents, the physically handicapped, the aged, abandoned children, and prostitutes; and it trained personnel for various local cooperative bodies. Curative efforts included the reorganization of the government orphanage at Mogadishu, expansion of the children's homes at Hargeysa and Uarsciech, and the establishment of a boys's village for vagrant children.

Since 1969 the regime has been publicly stressing its obligation to provide social welfare, particularly for those too old or too sick to work. It also stresses the obligation of people to help themselves. School building, low-cost housing, land clearance and conservation, improvement of range resources, and other projects of public benefit have been executed by voluntary labor with or without direct government assistance. The Victory Pioneers assist in local self-help projects.

No comprehensive social security system existed in 1976, but a number of provisions dealt with various related issues. Civil servants receive generous pensions, which had been increased by a 1970 act. Female employees are entitled to fourteen weeks of maternity leave at half pay according to the 1972 Labor Code, and all employees, including agricultural workers and technical students, receive benefits in case of incapacity or death resulting from work injuries. No minimum qualifying period is required.

Work injury benefits include—aside from medical treatment, hospitalization, drugs, appliances, and transportation—60 percent of earnings for the first ninety days and 75 percent thereafter until recovery or certification of permanent disability, in which case a pension is paid based on past earnings and the degree of disability. A supplementary sum of Sh200 (for value of the Somali shilling—see Glossary) is paid to those who have a perfect record of work attendance. In case of death a survivor pension is paid—40 percent of earnings to the widow and 20 percent to each of the first two children—in addition to a funeral grant. Additional children get less. The pension is reduced if the survivors include neither widow nor children.

The entire cost of the program is borne by the employer through contributions that vary accordingly to risk and that average 5 to 7 percent of the payroll. Maximum earnings for benefit purposes are Sh5,000 a year. Contributions and benefits are administered by the Somali Insurance Fund, which operates its own clinic at Mogadishu and a few medical facilities in other parts of the country.

Despite these various efforts, the welfare of most Somali continues to rest primarily with the immediate family and relatives to whom a person turns in times of sickness, unemployment, and old age. This traditional system has become less adequate as the family ceases to be a self-sufficient economic unit, as in the city. It survives there too, however, in modified form. Relatives help new arrivals by providing accommodations and food and generally cushioning them against the effects of rapid change.

At the request of the Somali government, international organizations give assistance in the form of technical advisers, surveys, and recommendations. The ILO, for example, has conducted a study concerning welfare services. The Soviet Union's Red Star Organization undertook construction of new headquarters for the Somali Red Crescent Society, which gives aid to the handicapped and needy and organizes courses in home nursing, first aid, and personal hygiene. During the extraordinary circumstances occasioned by the prolonged drought in the mid-1970s, help was provided by the WFP and by the Soviet Union, various Arab nations, and other states (see ch. 10).

SPORTS

Wrestling, spear throwing, target shooting, jumping, and racing competitions have been traditional pastimes for young Somali. Such

Western sports as soccer, basketball, and tennis were introduced under the colonial regime. Soccer became the most popular, and soccer tournaments have been regularly held at Mogadishu's Cons Stadium.

After the October 1969 revolution government encouragement led to a rapid growth of sports activities. One of the first undertakings of the Ministry of Sports and Labor, which was set up in 1970, was to organize all Somali interregional games. In June 1971 300 sportsmen competed in soccer, basketball, and field and track events. The number of teams in the National Soccer Division rose from four to ten, and a second division of twenty-four teams was established. Matches were played three times a week at Cons Stadium, whose seating capacity was increased from 300 to 20,000. A new basketball stadium that could be flood-lit at night was constructed at Mogadishu, and next to it an Olympic-sized swimming pool was built.

Sports activities had in the past been largely confined to the capital. President Mohamed Siad Barre urged that sports become organized in every city, town, and village; that young sportsmen mingle with each other; and that such contacts would not only help end tribalism and regionalism but also prepare the young for participation in Olympic and other international competitions. Eventually all major towns established sports teams and built stadiums, largely through self-help schemes. In the newly developed communities where nomad victims of the drought were settled as cultivators in 1975, special areas were set aside for such sports as volleyball and soccer.

Plans were made under the supervision of the Ministry of Sports and Labor to form regional sports committees, which would provide financial help. The Development Program 1974-1978 provided for the establishment of the Physical Culture and Sports Institute where thirty intermediate-school graduates would enroll every year for three-year courses to be trained as physical education teachers and as coaches for regional and district sports teams.

Girls, too, were encouraged to take up sports, a departure from traditional Somali attitudes. In the mid-1970s in Mogadishu alone twenty-five teams played basketball for either their school or their city quarter. Girls also played tennis at the newly established National Tennis Club in Mogadishu. They have represented their country in the Afro-Asian ping pong championship held in Peking. Girls have become soccer fans and eagerly follow the activities of various teams and stars. There were many girls among the 1,000 participants in the fourth regional sports tournament held in March 1976. By that time Somalia had begun to produce champions; Abdulle Wasuge, for example, won three gold medals in the East African Games and then placed first in the high jump competition at the All Africa Games.

CHAPTER 7

EDUCATION, INTELLECTUAL EXPRESSION, AND THE ARTS

Quranic schools had long been providing a form of education when, in the late 1800s, Great Britain and Italy began acquisition of the territory in the Horn of Africa that constitutes the modern Somali state. For half a century colonial domination was unable, except in the urban milieu of Mogadishu, to make Western education acceptable to the highly devout Somali Muslim population, who looked upon such education as a tool of Christian proselytizing.

After World War II, however, and particularly during the decade before independence in 1960, the advantages of modern education became apparent to a growing number of Somali. Development of formal education along Western lines continued during the 1960s and was followed in the years after the coup d'etat of 1969 by strong government encouragement and radical new measures, including the use of the Somali language and orthography. By 1976 there were widely distributed facilities that provided—chiefly for the sedentary and semisedentary population—growing opportunities for acquiring a modern education from primary schooling through university studies. This education, moreover, was free and since 1972 had been furnished exclusively by a system of public schools.

Only among the purely nomadic groups were modern educational facilities lacking, a situation that stemmed no longer from the nomads' rejection of modern education but from their mode of life. Among these groups Quranic schools imparting little more than the elements of knowledge needed for the study of the Quran continued to be the sole source of formal schooling for many. In the mid-1970s, however, the revolutionary government, with the help of international funds and technical assistance, was in the process of trying to remedy this situation, although its resolution may take a long time.

Strong government pressures existed for making the content of education more consonant with Somali needs, in the course thereof replacing foreign elements and concepts that were a carryover from the former British and Italian educational systems with Somali ones. The government emphasis on Somali culture had a bearing on the educated elite, whose members were almost entirely the products of Western-oriented education. This was especially true for those in government service, since ability to use the new Somali orthography had been made a prerequisite for employment. Perhaps aiding this change was the generally broad background of all native Somali in the traditional oral poetry—still very much a part of life in the mid-1970s —in which their long history had been transmitted, political and other causes espoused, and the spirit of modern nationalism fostered.

LANGUAGE AND LITERACY

Somali National Script

Although Somalia is one of the few African states south of the Sahara in which most of the people speak dialects of the same mother tongue, the country failed—for political, religious, and to some extent technical reasons—to adopt a script for Somali until 1972 (see ch. 4). As early as the 1880s European scholars had begun to analyze the Somali language with a view to preparing textbooks. A few suggested the short-form Ethiopic syllabary, but no attempts were made to carry this idea further. Other approaches used systems based on Latin script.

There was an even earlier tradition for the use of Arabic script on a practical level. Those who had some knowledge of reading from attending religious schools tended to work out systems of their own for business purposes, for letter writing, for writing petitions, and for recording poetry. These systems were not standardized and were known as Wadad Writing, a *wadad* being a religious scholar or practitioner. Young people who learned classical (Quranic) Arabic in school were unable to read this kind of text, which tended to be a mixture of Arabic and Somali.

A basic reason for the difficulty in the use of Arabic orthography was the difference between the phonemic structures of the two languages. Arabic consonantal signs can be readily modified to represent Somali sounds, but Arabic has only six potential vowels, three long and three short, whereas Somali has five long and five short. The consonantal modifications have also never been standardized. Despite these difficulties several poets adapted systems for writing their own works, and by 1920 several independent attempts were under way to transcribe Somali in Arabic script. There was great opposition at the time, however, from religious conservatives, who sometimes even threatened the experimenters with bodily harm because they felt the writing of Somali literature would detract from the study of sharia (religious law). During the next forty years some thirty other attempts were made to derive a Somali alphabet from Arabic, but all failed.

In the early 1920s a poet named Osman Yusuf Kenadid, who was a leader in the Sultanate of Obbya in Italian Somalia, worked out a new alphabet, although the order of the letters was mainly that of Arabic.

This script, known as the Osmanya alphabet, was introduced into the schools but, because it appeared to the Italian colonial authorities as a manifestation of nationalism, it was suppressed, and Osman was jailed in Mogadishu. After World War II the Somali Youth League (SYL) showed an interest in the Osmanya script. Nationalism was a factor in the SYL support, but its intemperate rejection of valid criticisms, such as the fact that the script could not be applied to all the principal dialects, gave the impression that their regional pride overrode national interests.

A Latin-based script was also advocated, and in 1955 an Italian elementary-school teacher, Bruno Panza, wrote a primer based on the Latin script and obtained permission to use it in teaching. An Italian-language newspaper introduced a daily page of Somali written in this alphabet. This aroused opposition from Muslim conservatives, who held that a "Christian" script was unsuitable for the language of a Muslim country.

The next definite action occurred in 1960, a few months after independence, when the Somali Language Committee was appointed to investigate the best means of writing Somali. The committee considered three alternative scripts: Arabic, Osmanya, and Latin. Its report, issued in January 1962, favored the Latin, which the committee regarded as best suited to represent the phonemic structure of Somali and flexible enough to be adjusted for the dialiects. Osmanya was not sufficiently adaptable to bridge the gap. A Latin system, moreover, which was used by many countries and was employed internationally for telegraphy and mathematics, also offered certain advantages to those who would find it necessary to seek higher education outside the country. Modern printing equipment would be more easily and reasonably available for Latin type. Existing Somali grammars prepared by various foreign scholars, though outdated for modern teaching methods, would give some initial advantage in the preparation of teaching materials. The recommendation was accepted on these grounds, but little implementation occurred. In fact government factions arose that supported the adoption of a particular script. Disagreement was so intense among them that concern over possible widespread violence and bloodshed led to a failure to act at all, although successive governments continued to reiterate their intention to resolve the issue.

The revolutionary government that came to power in October 1969 also set as one of its principal objectives the adoption of a script for written Somali. The Somali Language Committee was revived in 1971 and instructed to prepare textbooks for schools and adult education programs, a national grammar, and a new Somali dictionary. No decision was made at the time, however, on the use of a particular script, and each member of the committee worked in the one with which he was familiar. The understanding was that on adoption of the national script all materials would be immediately transcribed, a task considered relatively easy since agreement existed generally in the several scripts on the language's phonemes.

On the third anniversary of the revolution the government announced that a Latin script had been adopted—despite some pressures from the Arab world to use an Arabic orthography—and was to be used throughout Somalia effective January 1, 1973. The orthography adopted was that used by Shire Jaamac Axmed (the form of his name in the new script) in his literacy journal, *Iftiinka-Aqoonta*. Some opposition was voiced, but the government was much stronger politically than its predecessors, and such opposition was short lived (see ch. 9). As a prerequisite for continued service with the government, officials at all levels were given three months (later extended to six months) to learn the new script and become proficient in reading and writing Somali. During 1973 Somali and the new orthography also became the mediums of instruction in elementary schools. In the mid-1970s their use in secondary and higher education had just begun.

Literacy

The use of Arabic, English, and Italian as languages of instruction until the adoption of the new Somali script in 1972 and the generally low priority given to education in the country until the early 1970s were primary factors in the low literacy rate, estimated at 5 percent in 1972. In March 1973 the government committed itself to using the new script in a massive campaign to make the entire population literate by 1975. The first part of the campaign was carried out in a series of three-month instructional sessions in urban and settled areas during 1973 and early 1974 and reportedly resulted in several hundred thousand people's learning to read and write. As many as 8,000 teachers were recruited from among government employees, members of the armed forces, and the civilian population.

The campaign in settled areas was followed by preparations from early 1974 for a major effort among the nomads. This got under way in August and was carried out by an estimated 22,000 teachers (some sources go as high as 30,000), including 11,000 or 12,000 students from the last two grades of intermediate school and the first two grades of secondary school whose classes were closed during the particular school year. The rural program, whose main effort lasted until February 1975, when the student teachers took on the job of conducting a population and livestock census, was affected to some extent by the severe drought of the 1974-75 period but appears to have achieved substantial results. Enthusiasm for learning to read and write Somali was reported to be widespread in both rural and urban areas, and in mid-1976 a reliable source estimated that as much as 60 percent of the overall population had attained some degree of literacy. It seemed

116

likely, moreover, that by the end of the 1970s a very large proportion of the young population would be literate.

WESTERN EDUCATION: THE EARLY PERIOD, 1885 TO 1941

In precolonial time Quranic schools were the sole source of formal instruction. They provided basic training in arithmetic and in the reading and, to a lesser extent, the writing of Arabic; they also sought to inculcate principles of religion and morality. These schools stressed memorization of the Quran. Classes were attended by boys and girls for two years, and the skills acquired were rudimentary and often ephemeral. Some boys, however, continued their studies and acquired functional literacy in Arabic and a knowledge of Islamic law.

After the Italians came into possession of the Somali coast in 1885, the introduction of Western educational services was made the responsibility of state-aided Roman Catholic missions. These, however, were few and inadequately staffed, and the Muslim Somali population viewed mission efforts with such deep suspicion that the scope of Western education continued to be very limited.

In the 1920s the Italian government increased subsidies to the missions with the understanding that more primary schools would be opened for both Somali and Italian children. The number of Somali children attending mission schools remained very low, however, partly because many Somali attended Quranic schools by preference and partly because of continued mistrust of Italian schools. Opposition to Western education was less in Italian Somalia than in British Somaliland, however, in part because of the smaller proportion of nomads and in part because of the generally cosmopolitan atmosphere of Mogadishu.

Initially Somali and Italian children attended the same classes, but after the establishment of Italy's fascist regime the colonial authorities came to consider this practice inconsistent with the official view that the Italians were masters and the Somali subjects (see ch. 2). By 1929, therefore, separate classes had been established for Somali and Italian children. Schools run by Roman Catholic missionaries but supported by the government were free, however, and the government also gave financial support to Islamic mosques, shrines, and educational institutions.

By 1935 ten government schools were in operation. Some Somali and Arab children attended the Western schools, but none could continue beyond primary school—about five years. Middle school was offered to Italian children only, although arrangements were made for selected Somali youngsters to continue their studies outside the country.

In British Somaliland the first school, a French Roman Catholic mission school, opened in 1891 but closed eventually as a result of pressure from Somali religious leaders. Opposition to Western education proved to be even stronger in the British than in the Italian sector, and all attempts made by the government to establish Western schools for Somali children between 1895 and 1908 failed.

Further efforts at the time failed largely because the British home government refused to appropriate funds for what was considered an unprofitable colony. By 1919, however, small grants were being given to a few Somali boys to enable them to pursue their studies in the Sudan. In 1929 the government also granted money to selected Islamic schools with the agreement that arithmetic and the reading and writing of Arabic be taught systematically.

In the 1935-36 period British colonial authorities renewed attempts to establish a comprehensive educational system. A new government school was built in Berbera, and an education department was created. Both failed when they encountered strong opposition and riots ignited by religious feelings.

EDUCATIONAL DEVELOPMENT FROM WORLD WAR II TO INDEPENDENCE

When the British took over Italian Somalia after defeating the Italian army in East Africa in 1941, there were thirteen state-aided Italian mission schools in operation, offering elementary education to Somali and Italian children. Within nine years twenty-nine public schools were opened, having about 1,800 pupils; about 1,000 more students were in mission schools. In British Somaliland three elementary schools opened in 1942, in Hargeysa, Berbera, and Burao, and by 1945 there were seven elementary schools in the region, with an enrollment of 400 pupils. In addition nineteen Quranic schools received assistance from the administration. These developments, in time, increased interest in educational opportunities, particularly among the non-nomadic population of the formerly Italian sector. In 1945 the military administration also initiated two intermediate schools in the northern region and opened the first school for Somali nurses. In 1949 it opened the first secondary school for boys and the first school for girls.

Also instrumental in the development of Somali education was the SYL, founded in Mogadishu in 1943. Under its initiative a number of classes were started in major towns, and the English language and a new attitude toward Western education were introduced. In 1950, when the former Italian sector became the Trust Territory of Somaliland under Italian Administration and civil rule was reestablished in British Somaliland, there existed for the first time the basis for development of a sound educational system.

Under the United Nations Trusteeship Agreement the Italian administration was required to establish a system of public elementary, secondary, and vocational education and to provide university training abroad for Somali students. It was, moreover, to train Somali for government positions and prepare them to administer the country, which was to receive its independence in 1960.

A five-year program for the development of education was launched during the 1952-53 period, with assistance from the United Nations Educational, Scientific and Cultural Organization (UNESCO), which envisaged the establishment of 140 primary schools with an annual enrollment of some 22,000 pupils, roughly 10 percent of the estimated school-age population. It also provided for the expansion of secondary schools, vocational and technical schools, teacher training courses, and institutions of higher education.

At the time a few more than 6,000 children attended primary school. By 1957 some 135 primary schools had been established, but the enrollment of about 12,500 pupils was far short of the original goal. Moreover only about 50 percent of those who entered school completed the full five-year course. Just before independence, although primary attendance continued to rise, enrollment was still fewer than 16,000.

The program included a plan to provide education for the nomadic population, which involved the training of teachers who upon completion of their courses were sent to work with nomadic groups in the interior. Two years of experimental work with the nomads in the area around Afmadu, west of the Juba River, revealed a number of obstacles to providing them with systematic formal education. Their constant movement, independent character, and resistance to change introduced by outsiders eventually led to the termination of the project. The UNESCO experts decided that a temporary solution was to give Quranic teachers living among nomads short courses in improved techniques in preparing hides and skins and making cheese and other foodstuffs, which they in turn would demonstrate to headmen and their sons. The project did not give satisfactory results; teachers were hard to recruit and often would not return to the nomads after their training.

A problem that had plagued the educational system for many years and continued to be a concern in the mid-1970s was the shortage of trained teachers. In 1953 the Teacher Training Institute was opened in Mogadishu; it offered three-year courses for primary-school teachers. It was unable to meet the demand, so the courses were accelerated and their length shortened from three to one and two years. Although by 1959 there were approximately 470 Somali teachers, of whom 290 had teaching diplomas—the others qualified as assistant teachers—an estimated 200 foreign teachers recruited from Great Britain, Italy, or the United Arab Republic were also working in the Trust Territory.

Secondary education expanded slowly in the Italian-administered territory. The first secondary school opened in Mogadishu in 1950, offering a three-year lower secondary course. In 1953 a four-year upper secondary course was begun, and in 1959 two additional secondary schools were opened, one at Galkayo, the other at Baydhaba (Baidoa); they offered both levels of secondary education. All secondary school curricula were designed to give graduates the prerequisites for entering foreign universities.

Vocational and technical schooling were encouraged, but not until about 1957 did vocational training attract a growing number of students. In 1958 about 220 students were enrolled in the Vocational Training School in Mogadishu, and by 1960 there were approximately 450 students enrolled in five vocational institutions that offered training in agriculture, fisheries, commerce, carpentry, electronics, and other subjects. The International Labor Office supplied equipment as well as experts who organized courses and curricula.

The most important professional school established in this period was the School of Islamic Studies, founded in 1952. Rated as a lower secondary school, its aim was to provide trained judges (qadis) to administer Islamic law in the religious courts, as well as religious leaders. During the 1959-60 school year there were 189 students enrolled at the institution.

To meet the Trusteeship Agreement's emphasis on somalization and administrative training, the Italian administration established the School of Politics and Administration in 1950. Courses were restricted to Somali who were eighteen years of age or older and had some experience in government, politics, or commerce. Students who successfully completed the three-year course were given scholarships to pursue their studies in an eighteen-month course in Italy. By 1958 many middle-level district and administrative positions in the government were filled by Somali graduates from the school. It was converted into the School of Public Finance and Commerce and classified as an upper secondary school in 1958.

The Higher Institute of Economics and Law, created in 1954, became the University Institute of Somalia in January 1960. Requirement for admission was a diploma from upper secondary school or the School of Politics and Administration. Students with certificates from vocational or teacher training schools were also admitted for further studies. The institute's high standards resulted in a small number of graduates. Of the 336 students enrolled from 1954 to 1960, only fifty-eight received diplomas. Each of the graduates was given a scholarship and a two-year credit toward a degree from the University of Rome.

At the restoration of civil rule in British Somaliland in 1950, there were few educational facilities in the area. The new British civil authorities seemingly tried to make up for lost time; in addition well-educated Somali were needed to fill government positions. By 1955 there were nineteen four-year primary schools attended by more than

1,000 boys, three intermediate schools for boys attended by about 370 pupils, two vocational schools, one secondary school for boys, and one primary school for girls (attended by sixty-four pupils).

In 1957 the authorities put into effect the Three-Year Educational Plan, which involved the expansion of educational facilities at all levels and the launching of an adult educational program. The plan, however, did not satisfy the small group of Somali political leaders who had been voicing their dissatisfaction with British rule and with what they considered an inadequate educational program. When the British government announced its decision to grant British Somaliland its independence in 1960, it also increased the budget for education and designed accelerated educational programs in a last-minute effort to give Somali some training for the responsibilities they were soon to undertake.

From 1955 until independence the number of primary schools for boys had doubled to thirty-eight and the number of students to over 2,000. There were three primary schools for girls, with 319 girls, and twelve intermediate schools for boys, with enrollment at nearly 1,040. A second secondary school for boys had been built, and the total enrollment had risen to seventy. Vocational and trade schools were training 100 pupils, and about 150 Somali were receiving degree and nondegree training in other British African dependencies or in Great Britain. There were forty-five trained Somali teachers compared with twenty-one in 1955 and eighty-five with little or no training in contrast to sixty-five in 1955. Although there was no institution of higher education in British Somaliland, Great Britain had agreed to support financially all scholarships for Somali students abroad through 1961.

EDUCATION IN THE 1960s

Soon after independence an administrative structure for education was established on the national level under the direction of the minister of education. The most pressing problem at the time was unification of the two educational systems. The British system in the north consisted of three years of primary school, four years of intermediate school, and four years of secondary education, a total of eleven years. The former Italian sector had a twelve-year program that included five years of primary work, three years of intermediate school, and four years of secondary school. Consolidation into three four-year cycles of primary, intermediate, and secondary education, which began in the 1964-65 school year, involved not only the reorganization of programs but also the preparation of common curricula. At the primary level curricular unification was attained in 1967; integrated syllabi for the intermediate schools were introduced in the same year. Preparation of curricula for secondary schools was then started, but they were not introduced until the 1970-71 school year. Problems were experienced in the changeover largely because teachers were not given adequate advanced preparation. Some teachers resisted the new curricula.

World War II had brought many Somali into contact with a wider world, and interest in education had begun to grow thereafter. With independence popular pressures for more educational opportunities increased. Enrollment in primary schools rose from almost 15,400 in the 1959-60 school year to more than 20,800 in the 1963-64 school year and almost 23,000 in the 1965-66 school year. At that point the government decided to restrict the intake into the primary system and to increase facilities at the intermediate level. The principal reasons appear to have been the desire to reduce the growing number of individuals who, completing only the four-year primary course, were insufficiently trained and the need to increase the number of better qualified persons to meet the need of the expanding economy.

The emphasis on intermediate education was accompanied by a substantial rise in the number of schools, from thirty-one in the 1963-64 school year to fifty-seven in the 1968-69 school year and an increase in enrollment from over 4,800 to over 10,600 in the same interval. An important aspect of the increase was the large number of girls who attended intermediate schools, rising from just over 700 in the 1963-64 school year to almost 2,200 in the 1968-69 school year. Religious objections to female education lessened during this time, although the change was greater in the southern part of the country where, in absolute numbers, considerably more females were in school than in the former British sector. The change also reflected the apparent belief of government leaders that women would have to participate more actively in the development of the new Somali nation-state (see ch. 4).

Enrollment in secondary education, which was limited to Mogadishu and a few large towns, also rose from over 1,100 in the 1963-64 school year to more than 3,100 in the 1968-69 school year. The expansion was due in considerable part to the provision of new facilities on the secondary level by various foreign countries, including the United States, which constructed the National Teachers Education Center at Afgoi; Italy; the Federal Republic of Germany (West Germany), which built a secondary technical institute at Burao; and the European Economic Community (EEC, also known as the Common Market). During this time the few vocational and technical schools, which were on the intermediate level, were phased out, in part to make additional facilities available for general intermediate education and in part because graduates had been found to be too young to get jobs; technical and vocational education were raised to the secondary level. Members of the educated elite disagreed on the emphasis to be given academic as against technical education in secondary schools; a considerable majority apparently favored academic training. In 1969 for every graduate from a technical school there were six who graduated from a school offering the general academic course.

As the 1960s began, higher education was available in Somalia only at the University Institute of Somalia in Mogadishu. Students took two- or three-year programs that could be credited toward a degree from an Italian university. Graduates of secondary schools in the north were encouraged to continue their studies at the institute, but the arrangement proved generally unsatisfactory because they usually could not speak Italian, the language of instruction at the institute. In 1968 the National Teachers Education Center initiated a four-year degree program in education. By 1969 plans were also under way to give the university institute higher status and legal authority to grant full degrees.

Throughout the decade the subject of the language of instruction for the school system remained unresolved as civilian governments were unable to make a decision on a national script for the Somali language. Quranic schools used Arabic, and the four-year consolidated primary program introduced throughout the country from the mid-1960s also used Arabic. In the former British sector English was the language of instruction in both intermediate and secondary schools. English also began to supplant Italian in areas other than Mogadishu. The use of foreign languages not only placed a strain on the Somali student but also resulted in a gradually developing dichotomy between the country's educated minority and the bulk of its population. Moreover almost all members of the country's educated elite at the end of the 1960s had received their higher education abroad. This point has been emphasized by the revolutionary government as a further factor that has caused undesirable alienation in many cases between the elite and other members of the society.

EDUCATION UNDER THE SUPREME REVOLUTIONARY COUNCIL (1969-76)

The relative lack of direction evident in educational policy during much of the period of civilian rule to October 1969 was replaced under the Supreme Revolutionary Council (SRC) by the enunciation of several positive goals reflecting the educational philosophy of the new revolutionary government. Among these goals were the expansion of the access to education to the largest possible number of students, including in the process a substantial increase in the number of girls enrolled in school; the introduction of syllabi that were geared to the country's particular social and economic requirements; the expansion of technical education—to the point where even the graduate from primary school would have learned some kind of skill; and the provision of higher education in Somalia so that with few exceptions students who went on to advanced studies would acquire their knowledge in the context of Somali surroundings. A strong effort to overcome illiteracy throughout the country was also announced.

Several decisions of major importance to the future of education in Somalia were made in the early 1970s. The adoption of an official Somali script in October 1972 in effect gave a genuinely Somali character to education for the first time (see Language and Literacy, this ch.). A second far-reaching decision was the nationalization of private schools also initiated at the time of adoption of the new script. In 1969 over 23 percent of student enrollment was in private institutions and, despite substantial rises in the number of students in public schools after 1970, more than 21 percent of the total enrollment in 1972 still was catered to by private schools. Most of the private schools, although under the Ministry of Education, were outside the national system and had different organizational structures and curricula. According to the government the nationalization was not aimed at the schools as such but was intended to establish a uniformity in the educational system and in studies throughout the country in order to promote the principles and purposes of Somalian scientific socialism among all students.

A third measure having important implications for education was the nationalization of the printing industry, also effected in 1972 (see ch. 11). Throughout the 1960s the educational system was plagued by a shortage of textbooks, attributed both to lack of funds—most textbooks were purchased abroad—and to administrative inefficiency. The overwhelming requirement for new texts in the Somali script for school use and also for proposed mass literacy campaigns was given as a major reason for the takeover of private printing establishments. Reportedly for a considerable time thereafter these, along with the government printing plant in Mogadishu, were utilized almost entirely for that work.

Preprimary Education

The preprimary training given by Quranic schools remained very much a part of the educational scene in the mid-1970s. Quranic teachers still traveled with nomadic groups, and many children have received no other education. Aside from these nomadic schools about thirteen or more fixed Quranic schools were found in urban areas. These schools were within the purview of the Ministry of Education, and in the mid-1970s efforts were under way to improve both their physical facilities and the quality of teaching through the provision of equipment and other materials and training courses for teachers.

Primary and Intermediate Education

In 1975 beginning education consisted of four years of primary school and four years that were designated intermediate school. Until

1972 the distinction between the cycles was emphasized by a requirement to pass a competitive examination upon completion of the first
four years. In that year, however, promotion to the intermediate level
was made automatic, and since then the two cycles have been treated
generally as a continuous eight-year program. A report was received
in mid-1976 that the two cycles had been consolidated into a six-year
program, but confirmation and further details of this move were not
available.

At the end of the 1960s primary and intermediate education facilities were largely concentrated in and around the larger urban centers.
The government's new policy stimulated a widespread self-help building program of classrooms and schools and a corresponding increase
in the number of students. Primary enrollment rose from under 25,000
in the 1968-69 school year to well over 72,000 in the 1973-74 school
year, including an increase in female students from about 23 to 30
percent, and skyrocketed to a reported 192,000 in the 1975-76 school
year. The government considered that by 1973 a reasonable regional
balance in educational opportunity at the primary level had been attained. Estimates of the percentage of children of primary school age
who were attending school varied, but by 1973 perhaps close to 16
percent of the total were in school. If planned annual increases of 10
percent in enrollment in first grade occur, about 50 percent of the age-
group will be in the four-year primary program in the early 1980s.

During this time the government was attempting to improve the distribution of intermediate school facilities, and through the 1972-73
school year eighteen new intermediate schools had been established in
smaller communities scattered in various parts of the country. Intermediate enrollment increased from over 10,600 in the 1968-69 school
year to more than 27,400 in the 1973-74 school year. The proportion
of females increased from about one in every five students to one in
every four.

Revisions in the curricula of primary and intermediate schools were
undertaken in the mid-1960s to make the subject matter more relevant
to Somali society. The languages of instruction, however, remained
non-Somali and, except perhaps for Arabic, still tended to divorce
even new course contents from the realities of the Somali surroundings. The 1972 decision to use Somali as the language of instruction in
primary school from January 1973 and the accompanying preparation
of new textbooks in Somali script radically altered this situation. At
the same time, according to the government, the new textbooks took
into consideration the aim of creating a society in which an individual
was trained to understand the world around him in the context of scientific socialism. Subjects included in the primary course were not
precisely known in early 1976, but an informed observer noted that
their basic goal apparently was to educated large numbers of the ris-

ing generation to be better farmers, herders, or workers at other oc-cupations.

Noteworthy in the mid-1970s in the primary-intermediate school program was the high rate of completion of schooling, reported to be about 90 percent for students in the primary cycle and only slightly less for those in the intermediate program. Moreover nine of every ten primary school students were going on to intermediate school. A combination of factors probably accounted for the apparent extremely low dropout rate. These included use of Somali as the language of instruction and the readily learned Somali script; automatic advance-ment between primary and secondary cycles from 1972; lack of tui-tion charges—the revolutionary government made education free at all levels; visible economic value of education in the form of job op-portunities; and individual student motivation, which one foreign source indicated was very high.

Secondary Education

During the 1960s secondary education facilities were limited largely to the areas of Mogadishu, Hargeysa, and Burao. The revolutionary government early decided that secondary education should be availa-ble to all qualified graduates of intermediate schools, although the Development Program 1974-1978 envisages about 60 percent of inter-mediate graduates actually entering the secondary system. At the same time passing grades for the general examination taken at the end of the intermediate course were liberalized, permitting a larger num-ber of students to continue to secondary studies. To meet growing requirements the number of schools, fifteen in the 1968-69 school year, had been increased to thirty-nine in 1976. The new schools, moreover, were spread throughout the country, and each region had at least one school.

In the mid-1970s most secondary schools offered courses that were basically academic. A project funded by the International Develop-ment Association (IDA) in the early 1970s provided assistance to ten general secondary schools and one specialized school in replacing some courses with subjects of a scientific and more practical nature. In 1975 a second IDA project was approved that will add buildings and equipment for prevocational training and training in agriculture, handicrafts, and domestic science at ten more schools. The schools selected include some in small towns where the added facilities are expected to tie in with local rural integrated development programs.

The increased enrollment that accompanied expansion of the sec-ondary educational system—10,500 students in the 1973-74 school year compared with 3,100 in the 1968-69 school year—was not expect-ed to result in unemployment problems, inasmuch as manpower de-mands for better trained individuals were growing steadily. The expansion of opportunities for higher education and for training as higher level technicians was also expected to add to the requirement for qualified secondary school graduates. Estimates of the number of graduates from the secondary system during the decade beginning in 1972 show an anticipated considerable shortfall (some 22,000 graduates compared with a requirement for about 29,000), but international economists have cautioned the government against any hasty further expansion of secondary schools until the picture becomes clearer.

Higher Education

In 1976 the principal institution providing postsecondary education was Somali National University. It had nine faculties—agriculture, chemistry, economics, education, engineering, geology, jurisprudence, medicine, and veterinary science—and a reported enrollment of over 2,000 students. The Development Program 1974-1978 projected an increase in enrollment to over 3,600 by 1978, but in mid-1976 expansion appeared to be slower than anticipated. More than 1,600 students were expected to graduate through 1978; little information was available on the situation in the mid-1970s. Italian and English were used as languages of instruction, depending to a considerable extent on the teaching personnel. Somalization of the staff was under way, but the stage of implementation was unknown; the Development Program 1974-1978 projected that Somali would fill all positions below the level of professor by 1978.

Only fragmentary information was available on other institutions of higher learning. In 1974 it was announced that the EEC would provide funds for the construction of another university, and work on that institution began sometime in 1975. In the early 1970s the degree program for teachers for secondary schools at the National Teachers Education Center became the College of Education of Somali National University.

Somali National University, founded in December 1970 from the University Institute in Mogadishu, was established by the SRC over the strong objections of many educated individuals who apparently felt that Somalia was not at the stage at which the high standards generally associated with Western university-level education could be attained. According to President Mohamed Siad Barre two principal reasons caused the objections to be overruled. First, higher education had to be available in Somalia if the majority of students were ever to have as a right the opportunity to receive it. Second, the social and cultural changes that occurred in many cases as the result of study abroad made it difficult or impossible for those who received a foreign education to administer the affairs of the Somali people and Somalia with any real understanding of local conditions and needs. It was believed, therefore, that it would be better for the educated elite to receive their training in Somalia, where the content of their education would be determined by the realities—the aspirations, needs, and surroundings—of their own country rather than by those associated with foreign academic life and economic conditions.

In early 1976 achievement of the SRC's goal appeared still to be some distance in the future. Foreign scholarships continued to be accepted, although information was scant on the donor countries and the number of students. Radio Mogadishu, for instance, reported in August 1975 that over 300 students were in the Soviet Union.

Technical and Vocational Education

Technical training facilities were limited as of early 1976. They consisted mainly of three technical institutes offering programs on the secondary level, one located in Mogadishu and the other two in the northwestern part of the country at Burao and Hargeysa. In addition there were two specialized facilities, a fisheries and marine institute in the Mogadishu area and an agricultural institute at Afgoi. A total of 950 students attended these schools in 1972. At the postsecondary level a technical college to accommodate 800 to 900 students was under construction in Mogadishu in late 1975 under a bilateral assistance agreement with the Democratic People's Republic of Korea (North Korea).

Teacher Training

The training of primary-school teachers was furnished in the mid-1960s by teachers colleges in Mogadishu and Hargeysa. The National Teachers Education Center, founded in 1963, also offered courses for teachers at the primary level. The slow increase in primary school enrollment during this time resulted in a surplus of teachers, and both training colleges were closed in 1968. In that year the National Teachers Education Center program was also converted into a degree course to train teachers for the secondary school system. Subsequently, until a primary teacher training course was reinstituted at the National Teachers Education Center in 1972, Somalia had neither a program nor facilities for the training of teachers for the primary level.

The upsurge in primary school enrollment in the early 1970s resulted in a shortage of teachers and at the same time pointed up the lack of qualifications of many teachers; more than three-fifths of all primary teachers did not meet government standards. In 1972 as a partial answer a two-year course for primary-school teachers, having an annual intake of 250 students, was begun at the National Teachers Education Center. The immediate demand was pressing, however, and was growing as more schools were completed under self-help projects. To help solve the problem the government in 1972 drafted about 750 national service volunteers (secondary school leavers who are required to complete a year of national service after completing the secondary course) and assigned them as primary-school teachers. In 1976 the number of volunteers reported to be serving as teachers was about 2,000.

An IDA education project for Somalia, announced in 1974, included the construction of a training college for primary-school teachers at Hargeysa. In the initial preparatory stages in mid-1976 the college was to have an enrollment of 800 students, and its graduates were expected to meet teacher needs at the primary level until the mid-1980s. In line with the revolutionary government's educational philosophy the students were also to be given training in civic leadership to equip them for wider roles in local community development activities and in the promotion of government policies along that line. Part of their training was also to include the practical aspects of simple agriculture, local handicraft manufacture, and home economics.

INTELLECTUAL EXPRESSION

In the mid-1970s the size of the Somali intellectual community resident within the country could only be surmised. President Siad has noted, however, that many Somali hold university degrees conferred in almost every field of knowledge. During the 1960s in particular, numbers of Somali studied abroad through foreign grants made under various international and bilateral aid programs and by nongovernmental organizations. In the mid-1960s over 1,200 students were studying abroad in degree and nondegree courses. By the early 1970s an estimated 1,500 students were taking higher education and postsecondary work in foreign countries, and Somalia was receiving offers of about 300 scholarships a year. In Somalia itself a degree program (in education) was begun in 1968, and in the following year Somali National University was authorized to grant degrees; the first degrees were awarded by the university in 1971.

The senior leadership in the revolutionary government appeared to have mixed feelings about intellectuals, distinguishing between a group that it considered to be carrying out research and other activities useful to Somalia and a group concerned with knowledge of little use to the advancement of the aims of the modern state. In this connection many of the intellectuals at Somali National University were reportedly viewed as functioning in an ivory tower. There was no evidence in early 1976, however, of governmental actions directly detrimental to the members of the intellectual community.

In contrast to the growing number of highly educated persons, facilities and opportunities for research were relatively limited. In particular there has long been a lack of outlets in print for intellectual expression. This situation was not improved by the nationalization of the printing industry in October 1972 or by the subsequent use of most of the industry's facilities to produce textbooks and other materials for the introduction of the new Somali orthography and of Somali as the language of instruction in the educational system (see Language and Literacy, this ch.).

The most active research area has been oral literature, in which Somali scholars were working even before independence. After independence these scholars worked in the Ministry of Education and as members of the Somali Language Committee. Their activities continued in the mid-1970s through the Academy of Somali Studies, which was set up in 1973 under the direction of the newly established Ministry of Culture and Higher Education. The academy also conducted research in other aspects of Somali culture and in the Somali language.

Members of the academy and some authors working in the same area of research whose work was approved by the academy were able to publish, but the opportunity did not exist in other social science fields in mid-1976. A few research articles in economics and finance were carried by the quarterly bulletin of the Somali National Bank. There was no domestic publication, however, that offered the opportunity for expressing views on internal politics. Reportedly, discussion of political matters by intellectuals was widespread, and such subjects as the handling by individuals of political situations and problems might be openly criticized. The weekly newspaper *Horseed* occasionally published special articles on international politics.

Foreign publications appeared to be available, at least in Mogadishu, without restriction. They included the major British and Italian newspapers and such magazines as *Time* and *Newsweek*. Reports indicated that government censorship of such publications was quite minor. Various foreign countries had cultural centers in Mogadishu that also made materials available to interested Somali. The government after the 1969 coup, however, generally discouraged Somali from attending these centers, although reportedly a somewhat more relaxed attitude prevailed by late 1975. Foreign radiobroadcasts were easily picked up, and there appeared to be no restrictions on listening.

POETRY AND OTHER LITERATURE

Somalia has a rich traditional oral literature of fables, legends, myths, riddles, and stories that have served to provide entertainment and to pass on from generation to generation customs, history, and general folklore. Much of this literature is narrated in prose, but over the centuries poetry came to be considered the supreme form of literary expression, and the good poet came to hold high status. Poetry became an effective medium to record history, advocate political change and political causes, glorify clan warfare, unify clan groups and, not least, express feelings of love.

Poetry was the vehicle of nationalism that was used to attack the colonial powers and, after independence, to call for the unification of Somali in Kenya and Ethiopia with the homeland. Notable poems of the colonial era are those of Somalia's national hero Sayyid Mohamed ibn Abdullah Hassan (1864-1920), who led a twenty-year struggle against the British in northern Somalia from the end of the nineteenth century (see ch. 2). In the early 1960s the power and vigor of nationalist poetic expression led to friction with neighboring Kenya, and the Somali government eventually restricted its use on radio. After 1969 the revolutionary government, in pursuit of its policy of antitribalism, excluded from radiobroadcasts poems that emphasized interclan strife and the glories of clan combat.

The composition and recitation of poetry have long been national pastimes, indulged in by such large numbers of people that students of Somali culture have labeled the country a nation of poets. Training in the art of expression begins early when young children are taught riddles and tongue twisters to improve their verbal skills. By young adulthood most Somali are well acquainted with the art of poetry. Thus the poet or reciter usually faces an informed and critical audience that will not hesitate to comment on his style or any significant deviation from recognized poems. Poems, regardless of length, are therefore memorized by the reciter and practiced until the presentation is letter-perfect. For the same reason, in contrast with situations in many other African societies where oral poetry often is extemporaneous, Somali usually compose and polish their poems in private until they are felt to be beyond criticism.

Classical Poetry

Long considered by Somali to be the best poetry were certain traditional styles of intricate and subtle verse that are defined by the expert as classical. In these styles symbolism and imagery are basic elements, and uncovering the real meaning of the allusions and metaphors is for Somali one of the main pleasures in listening to it. One of the chief characteristics of Somali classical poetry is alliteration. Its use follows strict rules and is based on the selection of a specific consonant or vowel with which at least one word in every poetic half-line must begin. The associated constraints of poetic form require a great deal of ingenuity, which is aided by the use of archaic words, to achieve the alliterative effect. At the same time, however, the poet must be careful that the search for alliterative language does not take him so far from the theme of the poem that listeners react unfavorably.

The highest literary form among classical styles is the *gabay*, which is sung or chanted by a man in solo performance. The *gabay* is usually concerned with serious matters, such as philosophical and political topics. It may, however, on occasion deal with love, in which case not only is superficial beauty described but a more penetrating analysis of the other features of the individual is also undertaken. The *gabay* is usually made up of thirty to 150 lines; the number of syllables in a line varies from fourteen to eighteen. The chant is slow and perhaps to the Western ear somewhat monotonous, never accompanied by music or handclapping, and the tempo shows little if any change during the recitation; the strength of the poem depends on the expressiveness of the words.

Another classical form is the *jiifto*, which in length resembles the *gabay*. The lines, however, tend to be somewhat shorter and are broken in the middle by a studied pause. Its tempo is quicker, but like the *gabay* it is chanted by a man alone and is never accompanied by music or audience participation. Themes are serious and often melancholy or philosophical in nature. This poetic form had also been used to convey warnings or to express reproach; it was ably used by Mohamed Abdullah in his attacks on colonialism.

A third classical form is the *geeraar*, varying considerably in length and having about six to eight syllables per line. The *geeraar* chant is more rapid and the tempo more lively than in the other two forms, but as in the case of the *gabay* and *jiifto* the recitation traditionally was always by a man in solo performance. Originally the *geeraar*, whose subject is usually conflict or war, was believed to have been recited on horseback and was used to lay down a challenge to another clan to fight. The *geeraar* was also used to insult an enemy before a battle began and to provide emotional encouragement to the reciter's own clan warriors. It was not known to what extent, if at all, this form were being used in mid-1976; its purpose certainly was at odds with the government's efforts to develop harmony among all Somali clans.

Although most composers of poetry have been men, the *buraambur*, a relatively short semiclassical composition, is in the particular purview of women. It is also chanted solo, but in contrast to the principal classical forms performed by men it may be accompanied by handclapping, drums, or tambourines. Men and women, however, are usually acquainted with the poetry of the other sex and frequently listen to it if the opportunity arises. A main difference between the poetry of men and women is that the male composer of a *gabay* or other classical form is usually known to the listener by name, whereas the identity of the female composer is rarely known.

How much classical poetry was being composed in the mid-1970s was not ascertainable. Concern has been expressed by various Somali scholars that it is dying out, and as a result considerable effort was apparently being expended in the mid-1970s to find and record existing poems. Poetic styles have presumably changed throughout Somali oral poetry history and, because poems were handed down only verbally, individual poems probably disappeared or survived depending on particular appeal or popularity. The art of composing poetry, however, continued vigorously, and there were no signs of a decline in interest in the 1970s; if anything, enthusiasm for composing poetry seems to have increased, especially in the modern poetic style known as *heello* that developed after the 1940s.

Modern Poetry

About 1943 a short lyric poem, which acquired the name *belwo*, was heard in the towns. Concerned almost invariably with love, it was frowned on by religious leaders as frivolous, but its popularity gradually spread with the expansion of radiobroadcasting. By the end of the decade longer poems in this style, called *heello*, were being sung. The earliest versions consisted of several successive *belwo*; frequently each had been composed by a different poet. By the mid-1950s, however, longer *heello* composed by one poet or perhaps several conjointly had appeared. These had their own melody and were accompanied routinely by musical instruments, including such Western ones as the flute and violin. Themes also expanded to include political topics, previously the exclusive domain of the classical poem.

From about the time of independence *heello* themes widened further to include additional areas of both domestic and international politics, Somali unification, the position and role of women in the new Somali state, and even such topics as sports. At the same time, however, the original theme of love continued to receive full attention in many of these poems. In the mid-1970s this poetic form was apparently enjoying great popularity among town inhabitants in particular, and some composers of the *heello* were as well known as those of *gabay* had been earlier. There were also indications that many pastoralists were familiar with *heello* through radiobroadcasts, although to what extent the *heello* had displaced the classical forms in rural areas was not known.

Somali Authors

The adoption of a single script for Somali in 1973 and efforts since then to spread literacy in the new orthography could be expected eventually to provide a reading public for prospective writers (see Language and Literacy, this ch.). In the mid-1970s, however, those who were known for their literary works were poets and playwrights whose poetry and dramas remained in oral form—although in some cases they were tape recorded.

Among the classical poets perhaps the most widely known is Mohamed Abdullah, a number of whose poems have been translated into English. Also famous is Raage Ugas (ca. early 1800s-1881), considered by the Somali one of their greatest poets. His work has also been translated into English and used as an example of classical Somali poetry. Ismaa'iil Mire (ca. 1880-1950) gained literary fame through his poetical history of Somalia. He is also well known as the leader of a major attack on the British in northern Somalia in 1913. Eminent also is Salaan Arrabey (ca. mid-1800s-1943), whose poetry is innovative in its introduction of many foreign terms and words, which he acquired during extensive travel abroad.

Modern poets of domestic repute include the originator of the *belwo*, Abdi Deegsi, who died in 1967. Another was Abdullahi Karshe, who was instrumental in the development of the later versions of the *heello* and was known in the early 1970s as the father of Somali music.

Playwrights were important producers of literature in the early 1970s. Much of their output, however, remained in oral form or was recorded only in notes, although some had been taped. Noted playwrights in the 1970s included Ali Hussein, Mohamed Ibrahim Hatrawi, and Hassan Sheikh Mumin. Mumin's *Shabeelnaagood* (Leopard among the Women) was published in translation by Oxford University Press in 1974. Nuruddin Farah, novelist, short story writer, and playwright, studied in India and has written works in English, among them *From a Crooked Rib,* a novel published abroad in 1970.

MUSIC AND DANCE

Traditional Somali music, though culturally distinctive, has features resulting from an intermingling with Arabic and oriental elements—visible in the harmonic aspects of the music—and the rhythms of black Africa (especially noticeable in the music of the sedentary peoples of the southwest, who have had a greater and more direct contact with black cultures). A particular feature of Somali music is the subordination of the rather limited variety of traditional musical instruments to the vocal component.

Instrumental music is especially limited among the nomadic population, a concomitant, presumably, of their migratory existence and the need to restrict the quantity of nonutilitarian possessions carried by a family's pack animals. Nomad songs are chanted and dances are performed chiefly to the accompaniment of handclapping, although a small drum or two wooden or metal blocks struck together may also be used to accentuate the rhythm. The traditional music of the sedentary cultivators of the southwest regularly uses a number of instruments, including skin-covered single-headed and two-headed drums, a wooden trumpet with palm-leaf reeds, and a twelve-string lute apparently of Arabic origin. The traditional music of the coastal towns employs a still wider range of instruments that includes flutes and tambourines.

Specific songs for almost all human activities are found throughout the population. For example, nomads have separate songs associated with watering camels, sheep, goats, cattle, and horses; and women sing special songs when they are erecting huts. Similarly cultivators have songs for reaping and threshing, gathering bananas, and many other activities. Although there are fixed patterns, a considerable amount of improvisation occurs. In group singing or chanting the antiphonal call-and-response pattern that is characteristic of much of black African singing is also found in Somalia. It can be heard in all parts of the country, but it is especially typical of the music of the sedentary population in the southwest.

Dancing occurs at both religious and civil festivals or on any auspicious occasion, but in general the dance is not as frequently performed as in other parts of Africa. Dancing is a part of such rituals as marriage or rainmaking ceremonies. Dances marking weddings are usually performed by members of the two lineages involved, young men from one group and young women from the other group. The rainmaking ritual dances are quite ancient and are performed at the beginning of the rainy seasons. They may last for a number of days and are accompanied by recitations and prayers from the Quran under the direction of holy men.

The government has encouraged the preservation of traditional dances and has established a folklore troupe that emphasizes such dances. It has at the same time discouraged the continuance of dances considered harmful, such as the ancient dance known as *saar*. This dance, apparently performed to a limited extent in the early 1970s, is essentially one of exorcism, intended to bring recovery from illness or madness resulting from the individual's believed possession by *saar* (or *zar*) (see ch. 5). The group carrying out the exorcism employs singing and handclapping, along with dancing, in the ceremony. Musical instruments used are the drum and wooden devices similar in their effect to castanets.

Modern Western dance music began to influence the development of Somali music after World War II. Western dance-band instruments were introduced in the early 1950s. In the mid-1970s bands in nightclubs played popular Western and Latin American music as well as similar music that was composed by Somali musicians. The young generation, especially in the towns, had considerable familiarity with Western popular music from foreign films. Moreover, although Western music as such did not appear to be broadcast over the radio network, Somali versions of jazz and other Western musical styles were played regularly by Somali dance bands on radio programs. Sudanese music also seemed to be popular.

DRAMA

Dramatic presentations in the mode of the Western play were among the most popular forms of entertainment in the mid-1970s.

They were also utilized as an important device for transmitting government political and social philosophy (see ch. 11). This art form appears to have been first used in the 1930s in skits in private homes in the Mogadishu area and was modeled on local Italian public performances. Its initial public appearance occurred during World War II when British teachers in northern Somalia, as part of the British military authorities' efforts to expand Western education in that part of the country, started making use of plays in school activities. Although many plays were in English, some were also in Arabic and based on dramatic highlights of early Islamic history. Parents appear to have been greatly impressed as well as entertained by this method of depicting such inspiring and familiar historical episodes and by the use of the language of the Quran, and the Western drama form was quickly accepted.

An important event in the evolution of the modern Somali drama occurred about 1944 when Somali was used in plays, making them understandable to everyone. The prose dialogue of succeeding plays (in many cases, simply skits) soon became interspersed with poetry that was patterned on the standard styles of oral literature, adding further to the aesthetic appeal of the play. Sometime after the end of the war a new embellishment, modern poetry, was added; it was sung to the accompaniment of Arab or Western musical instruments (see Poetry and Other Literature, this ch.). Such poetry was used to introduce the play and for the epilogue, and some was also sung in the body of the play. The result was the emergence by the mid-1950s of a distinctively Somali art form combining the traditional features of oral literature and Western stage drama. It was also about this time that conservative attitudes opposing stage roles for women were overcome; in the mid-1970s women were playing major parts.

In the course of its development the popularity of the modern Somali play was enhanced by a lack of strong competition from motion pictures. The latter were shown in urban areas but—with the exception of one or two films in the early 1970s—all feature productions screened were imported, and none used the Somali language. The absence until 1973 of a national script for Somali prevented the use of widely understandable subtitles, thereby further reducing motion picture appeal. Another factor making for the great popularity of stage plays has been that they permit the highly participatory nature of Somali audiences full rein.

In the mid-1970s stage performance were given in many parts of the country, some by traveling groups, others by local actors and actresses. Popularly known companies were that of Radio Hargeysa and especially the troupe at the National Theater (the center for contemporary dramatic performances, opened in Mogadishu in 1967). Dramatic shows were also presented by the Somali Broadcasting Service, but the limitations of time resulted in a somewhat changed format.

ARTS AND HANDICRAFTS

Traditional Arts and Handicrafts

The creation of objects primarily as art appears to have been, and continued to be in the mid-1970s, nonexistent among the nomadic and seminomadic population. In this these groups resembled other nomadic peoples, whose mode of life tends to discourage the acquisition of nonutilitarian possessions. Artistic expression does exist, but it is largely confined to ornamental work, including carving or incising such handicraft items as wooden spoons, ladles, combs, and hairpins; weaving colored patterns in mats and other straw products; and decorating items with cowrie shells. In line with the proscriptions of Islam against the depiction of human and animal forms, such traditional art is characterized generally by symmetrical patterns, geometrical designs, and other abstract forms.

Intricate carvings may also be found on such traditional handicraft items as wooden mortars, bowls, containers, boxes, stools, headrests, and canes. Milk containers in particular are often extensively decorated with incised designs or are encrusted with cowrie shells in symmetrical designs. Similarly, small vessels resembling Western flasks but larger—often three to four feet tall—may be finely decorated. These containers are usually in woven raffia cases, some of fine texture, and are carried by leather thongs that may be tooled with symmetrical designs. Simiarly, small vessels resembling Western flasks and carried by men to hold water for drinking and for ritual washing are often heavily carved.

Members of the Hawiya and Rahanwein clan-families make headrests, the supporting elements of which are usually decorated with carvings of geometrical designs. These graceful headrests are used by men, in part at least, to prevent the disarray of their elaborate hairstyles. Wooden stools, sometimes having carved designs, are also made but are not common among the nomads. Stools used by the Hawiya and Darod frequently have leather seat covers.

Although pottery is found throughout the country, ceramics are produced chiefly by the sedentary population in the southwest. Pottery styles along the coast are principally of Arabic origin, whereas those farther inland exhibit Bantu influences. In Bur Acaba District household items are carved from meerschaum, which occurs extensively in the area. Most ceramics are utilitarian; they include cooking pots, tea and coffee urns, incense and charcoal burners, and lamps for the interiors of Somali huts. Metal utensils and plastic ware were reported to have replaced some traditional pottery items among the nomads; among the seminomads and the sedentary population a much more extensive replacement has occurred.

137

At one time the weaving of cloth to make the *futa*, a sarong-like garment worn by men and women, was widespread. Domestic and imported commercial cloth has replaced much of the locally produced material, but the cotton Benadir cloth used for such garments continues to be handwoven by men in Mogadishu and the port towns of Brava and Marka (Merca). In the mid-1970s the government was encouraging the continued handloom production of this brightly colored cloth, which traditionally is woven either in solid colors or in stripes of red, blue, and yellow. Fezlike hats made locally are elaborately stitched or embroidered in traditional designs.

Baskets, other woven containers, and mats are widely produced from a variety of materials, including grass, palm leaves, reeds, sisal, and strips of wood. These materials are often separately dyed and then interwoven to produce pleasing shadings and designs. In another technique palm fibers are plaited into mats with a pattern on one side. Among the distinctive woven products are waterproof vessels and trays made from fine matting. Typical and widely distributed is the milk jug, coated inside with thickened tree sap (especially that of the acacia), which not only seals the matting but also appears to retard souring.

Leather handicraft articles include prayer mats, sandals, pouches, belts, straps, saddles, and shields. Some tooling of designs on leather apparently occurs, but the extent was unknown. Large leather pouches are sometimes decorated with cowrie shells in geometrical patterns, and shields may be embossed, incised, or occasionally painted.

Gold and silver jewelry is made in the large towns, chiefly by Indian and Pakistani craftsmen—their work often is in the traditional styles of the Asian subcontinent—but Somali also engage in this work. Ornaments include bracelets, necklaces, and earrings in numerous designs and of a great variety of materials. Silver was reportedly a favorite for bracelets, which are worn by women on arms and legs, but other metals, such as zinc, are also used.

Modern Plastic and Graphic Arts

Through the 1950s strong religious opposition to the depiction of animate beings discouraged the development of painting and sculpture using Western forms and styles. Changes in attitude emerged after independence in 1960 and, although some objections continued to be voiced in the mid-1970s, a small group of artists was producing works along Western lines. Paintings included oils and watercolors that had mostly traditional Somali themes, presumably influenced to some extent by the government's emphasis on the revival of Somali culture.

Sculptures were chiefly small objects that included such figures as camels or human beings, carved for the tourist trade. Most of the carvings were of wood, but some were of meerschaum. A few artists were reported to be very talented and to have the capacity to do large works. Facilities for casting bronzes were lacking, and the several large bronze figures found on monuments in Mogadishu in the mid-1970s were the works of foreign artists. Artwork, including instruction in drawing, was a regular part of school curricula in 1976. There were, however, no special art programs or schools specifically devoted to the teaching of art.

SECTION II. POLITICAL

CHAPTER 8

THE GOVERNMENTAL SYSTEM

Until 1969 Somalia was governed by a multiparty parliamentary system under a constitution written at independence in 1960 and ratified in 1961 (see ch. 2). On October 21, 1969, however, a group of army officers seized power and established the Supreme Revolutionary Council (SRC), then consisting of twenty-five military officers under the presidency of Major General Mohamed Siad Barre, until then commander of the armed forces. By its own initial declaration the SRC assumed the power to promulgate laws, to administer justice, and to govern the republic "in order to develop the country." Generally all powers and responsibilities provided for by the established laws were vested in the SRC, which suspended the constitution and revised those constitutional provisions "which were contrary to the spirit of the Revolution."

The stated objectives of the SRC in staging the revolution were to end widespread corruption and tribal nepotism, establish a written Somali language and end illiteracy, and bring about rapidly social, economic, and cultural development. These objectives were contained in the SRC's initial declaration, known as the First Charter of the Revolution. The later Second Charter of the Revolution emphasized the government's reorientation toward what it called scientific socialism and self-reliance. These two documents and Law Number 1 of October 21, 1969, form the basis for governing. The constitution itself was repealed by the SRC in February 1970.

Law Number 1 assigned to the SRC the functions previously performed by the president of the republic, the National Assembly, and the Council of Ministers (and individual ministers), as well as some of the duties of the Constitutional Court and the High Court of Justice. All existing legislation was to remain in force unless specifically abrogated by the SRC or unless "incompatible . . . with the spirit of the Revolution."

Under the SRC's direction the groundwork had been laid for the creation of a single socialist political party, the Somali Socialist Revolutionary Party (SSRP), whose formation was announced at the end of June 1976. The party's Supreme Council was to replace the SRC at the helm of government. Steps were simultaneously taken to bring civilians into major roles. Real executive power, however, remained in the hands of President Siad and three or four other senior military members of the former SRC.

PRE-1969 GOVERNMENT

The country obtained its independence in two stages. The colony of British Somaliland became independent on June 26, 1960, and united with the Trust Territory of Somaliland under Italian Administration on July 1, 1960, as an independent republic. A formal constitution was not ratified until June 20, 1961. In form and fact the newly created government was parliamentary, with executive power vested in the prime minister and in the Council of Ministers, which was responsible to the unicameral National Assembly. Throughout the first nine years of independence the National Assembly was a multiparty body. The president of the republic was the titular head of state, elected by a secret ballot of the members of the assembly. He selected the prime minister, who then had to obtain a vote of confidence from the assembly within thirty days.

It was the prime minister and his Council of Ministers, varying in number from eleven to twenty, who functioned as the country's executive. The ministers were usually chosen from among the members of the National Assembly and were collectively responsible to it. The popularly elected unicameral legislature was the real center of political power in the governmental system. Its 123 members were chosen in forty-seven electoral districts. Within each electoral district the seats were assigned by a complicated proportional representation, party-list system that further encouraged the tendency for a multiplicity of small, primarily local parties to appear. Thus sixty-four parties with a total of 1,000 candidates contested the 1969 election; only three of these parties operated nationwide.

The constitution provided for the complete independence of the judiciary. The highest court, the Supreme Court, with the addition of four extra members—two appointed by the Council of Ministers and two elected by the National Assembly—could function as the Constitutional Court.

Unlike the courts in many systems the Constitutional Court could decide on the conformity of legislation with the provisions of the constitution (and with the principles of Islam). The Supreme Court also adjudicated election disputes and served as the core of the High Court of Justice to hear impeachment cases.

Below the national level the country was divided administratively into eight regions and forty-seven districts, each headed by a regional governor or district commissioner appointed by the minister of interior. In the rural areas each recognizable local group, generally organized in terms of real or putative kinships, elected a representative who served as the channel through which directives were communicated downward and political and welfare demands of the people were passed upward (see ch. 4). Elected units of local government existed at the municipal level, and an elected council and mayor were in charge of the affairs of the city of Mogadishu and about sixty population centers.

After independence a major obstacle to the smooth operation of the country's administration was the vestiges of its division into British and Italian spheres. This was reflected most strikingly in the language situation. Somalia was one of the few countries in Africa whose people all spoke a common language. Nevertheless the mixed colonial tradition and the lack of agreement over a written language led to a situation in which civil servants were unable to communicate in writing with each other despite their common tongue. Other problems resulting from two different colonial traditions were largely bridged by the end of the 1960s.

The Somali approach to such problems was generally pragmatic; attempts were made to find working solutions unhindered by previous ties to one or the other of the colonial powers. This approach was facilitated by the fact that the numerically dominant southerners, although considerably influenced by the Italian colonial and trusteeship periods, had developed an admiration of the British style of administration during the almost nine years (1941 to 1950) that they were under British military government. In addition in this one respect the country's major governmental problem—underadministration—had worked to its benefit.

STRUCTURE OF THE NATIONAL GOVERNMENT

After the 1969 revolution the country's executive and legislative functions were centered in the SRC, but particular executive roles were filled by President Siad on the one hand and the subordinate Council of the Secretaries of State (CSS) on the other. President Siad held a number of formal roles: senior member of the armed forces, titular head of state, president of the SRC, and chairman of the CSS. His titles were of less importance than his personal authority, however. It was not clear how he functioned formally as head of state in relation to the SRC, but he appeared to serve as its chairman, the respected leader to whom all other members deferred (see ch. 9).

The SRC generally met once a week. Decisions within the SRC were said to be taken by majority vote, and conflicts within the group were rarely made public. The composition of the SRC has remained quite constant. Twenty-one of the twenty-five military officers who were members of the council in 1969 were members in 1976, and no new members were added during that time.

The only significant change occurred when three of the original members, including both vice presidents, were implicated in a coup attempt in May 1971. After their dismissal three other SRC officers were raised to positions as vice presidents. Later that year three less senior SRC members were appointed to serve as the president's advisory staff. They served as his personal assistants, whose assigned responsibility was jointly discussing matters with the president before they were submitted to the SRC or CSS. The advisory staff continued to function in early 1976.

Until late 1974 from three to seven SRC members also held posts within the CSS, generally heading the key ministries. In a major reform in December 1974 all but one of these withdrew. The exception was Brigadier General Mohamed Ali Samantar, one of the vice presidents, who continued to serve as secretary of state for defense.

In place of these cabinet roles the SRC members formed into four committees to oversee the operations of the government within general given areas. The committees were social and political affairs (which was briefly split into two separate committees and then rejoined), economic affairs, judicial affairs, and security affairs (chaired by Samantar).

In these roles and in their general duties as SRC members the officers conducted inspections of the national and local government agencies to ensure compliance with the SRC's policies and to encourage efficiency. They also served on or chaired other interministerial bodies or major governmental programs. For example, the members of the SRC's Economic Affairs Committee led the National Rehabilitation Committee, which directed efforts to ease the impact of the disastrous 1974-75 drought. They exercised direct supervision over the subordinate Settlement Development Agency, which conducted the effort to resettle large numbers of nomads, impoverished by the drought, in new farming projects (see ch. 3; ch. 13).

Other posts throughout the government were filled by SRC members or other senior army officers. For example, in 1973 one general was serving as extraordinary commissioner of the Port Authority and another as manager of the National Tourist Agency.

In addition to SRC military members, several civilians were permanently assigned as advisers to the four committees. In 1975 there were about seven in all, some of whom had previously served as cabinet secretaries.

Although only one SRC member continued to head a ministry after the 1974 reforms, two other senior officers who were not SRC members held key CSS posts throughout the 1974-76 period. One was a police general serving as secretary of state for interior; the other, an army officer, filled the post of secretary of state for agriculture. The other seventeen secretaries were civilians, chosen for their educational qualifications and technical competence. The CSS, like the SRC, held weekly general meetings, and not infrequently the two bodies met jointly to discuss major issues. By law both councils had to meet to approve the national budget. The SRC's role was clearly that of decisionmaker, and there were no public indications that the division of functions between the two was not working smoothly. Because it supervised the activities of the operating departments of the government, the role of the CSS overlapped to a degree the function of the SRC as the country's chief executive.

The number of ministries fluctuated from as few as eleven in 1965 to as many as twenty in 1975. The membership of the CSS, unlike that of the SRC, also fluctuated (major changes occurred about once a year), and in 1976 only three or four of the original secretaries were still in office (although others continued to hold high government posts).

The changes being carried out in mid-1976 were apparently motivated primarily by ideological considerations. As early as 1971 President Siad had announced that plans would be made for the creation of a political party to serve as the vehicle for inculcating the people with the SRC government's philosophy of scientific socialism. The formative congress of the party, the Somali Socialist Revolutionary Party (SSRP), was convened by the SRC leaders in late June 1976. The nineteen remaining SRC members and their six civilian advisers, the existing heads of eighteen government ministries, and thirty other figures were taken into the new party's Supreme Council. This body, it was announced, would henceforth set the direction of the country's policies.

Several governmental roles were altered with the creation of the party. At the national level the SSRP officially took over the administration of the country from the SRC on July 1, 1976. Real decisionmaking power, however, appeared to reside in the new party's Politburo and in the Council of Ministers, which replaced the CSS. The Politburo was composed solely of five military men: President Siad; Vice President Samantar, who also continued in the roles of head of the Ministry of Defense and army commander; the other two vice presidents; and a fifth member of the former SRC, who was also head of the National Security Service (NSS), the country's secret police. President Siad also became secretary general of the party as well as chairman of the Council of Ministers, and the SSRP congress attempted to elevate him to the rank of marshal, an honor that he declined. The military influence within the council was increased as five more former SRC members took over ministerial posts. The president and vice presidents were members, and the military thus held twelve of the twenty-three posts in the Council of Ministers. There were no changes in governmental structure at the regional and local levels, but the SRP was assigned the task of teaching and motivating the people (see ch. 9).

ADMINISTRATIVE STRUCTURE

Organization of Government Ministries

The ministers were charged with the operation of single ministries with one or more interrelated operating departments. Although described as technicians, the ministers filled the role of political heads of the ministries. The senior administrative official in each ministry was the director general, its ranking civil servant. His office was called the General Directorate and in larger ministries was divided into departments, each under a department head. The Ministry of Finance, for example, was divided into fiscal, accounting, and state domain departments. The divisions below departmental level were sections, services, and offices. Only the Office of the Magistrate of Accounts and the Office of the Judiciary do not come under any of the ministries.

Public Corporations

The public corporations were separate from but generally under the supervision of the ministries. They played a major role under the pre-1969 parliamentary government, which created twenty-one such bodies. The ideological commitment of the SRC to socialism, self-reliance, and state control greatly increased the importance of public corporations. Twenty-two more were created between 1969 and 1975. They ranged from corporations in the previously private sectors that had been nationalized, such as banking, consumer goods importing, manufacturing, and food processing, to those in new areas of development in which private capital had never been involved (such as the National Aid and Welfare Agency, the Port Authority, and the National University) (see ch. 12).

All but two of the thirty-nine public corporations still extant in the mid-1970s were under the supervision of a ministry. These two, the Crash Program Agency and the National Rehabilitation Committee, dealt with matters of an emergency nature and were under direct SRC control. In fact supervision of corporations was a major task of many of the ministries, perhaps a burden straining their limited resources of trained personnel in some cases. In 1974 the Ministry of Trade was responsible for eight corporations and the ministries of finance and industry for five each. The real relationship of ministry and public corporation was perhaps revealed by the government's public announcement at one point that the Ministry of Tourism was being abolished "because it had proved incapable of working in harmony with the State Hotel Agency."

The public corporations were staffed by members of the civil service who could be assigned to the corporations on the same basis as they were moved elsewhere in the government. The corporations were required to submit their annual financial statements to the parent ministry, and for some purposes they formed a part of the national budget (see ch. 12).

LEGAL SYSTEM

Since independence the primary problem faced by the Somali courts has been the existence of four disparate legal traditions, namely, English law, Italian law, the sharia (see Glossary), and Somali customary law, the last of which is related to but sometimes at variance with the sharia. Before independence the colonial court structures had attempted, as much as possible, to make use of the Islamic and customary systems. Somali sharia and customary courts were allowed to flourish and were given specific areas of jurisdiction by the colonial governments. At independence the former court divisions were rejected in favor of a unified, modern legal system.

The judicial organization and procedures that developed after independence were drawn primarily from the system of the Trust Territory but included important assurances found in British Somaliland's system. The sharia and customary court bodies were formally recognized as the courts of the qadis (traditional Islamic law specialists). They were at the bottom of the new structure, hearing most of the personal and minor civil cases. Many conflicts among the Somali were settled outside the court system by lineage councils, which privately exercised judicial authority and were able to arrange for compensation required by the *dia* system (see Glossary) (see ch. 4).

The bases for judicial decisions in the Italian system were the application and interpretation of a legal code, in contrast to the systematic use of case law (judicial precedent) in the English system. The need, however, to include elements of the English, sharia, and customary traditions in the decisionmaking process led Somalia to dependence on judicial precedents and the development of considerable case law. All judges were required to consider the sharia and customary law, particularly in civil disputes, although the important decisions merging the systems were generally made by the higher courts. In some instances rules of traditional systems that were in conflict with modern concepts were discarded, but others emerged from the scrutiny of the courts strengthened by formal approval. During the 1960s a unified penal code and a code of criminal court procedures were completed and put to use, but civil laws remained divided until the completion of a unified civil code in mid-1973.

Fundamental Human Rights

The constitution in force until the October 1969 revolution strongly protected the civil rights specified in the United Nations Declaration

147

of Human Rights. The country's record of honoring these rights was impressive not only by the standards of developing states but even by those of developed Western democracies.

These rights included the presumption of innocence before the courts; habeas corpus; the freedoms of political association, public expression, and personal liberty and movement; and the right to form labor unions and to strike. The ownership of all land was vested in the state—outright private ownership of land conflicts with Somali traditions; however, developed property and improved land could only be expropriated on the basis of equitable compensation. Perhaps most striking was the provision that allowed the Supreme Court, sitting with four additional members as the Constitutional Court, to review and overturn legislation incompatible with the country's constitution.

The revolution of 1969 brought to power a socialist-military government that attached considerably less importance to most of these rights. Habeas corpus was abolished in October 1970, although the presumption of innocence and provision of free legal assistance for indigent defendants in serious cases continued to be provided by the legal system. Even the right to form nonpolitical associations was to be closely controlled. It was made a crime for anyone to attempt to change the order established by the revolution. The SRC granted itself unlimited powers to detain anyone. It also delegated a similar power to the district and regional councils and to the NSS.

The Courts

The court system created in 1962 continued to function after the revolution, with some modifications. The provision for the Constitutional Court was abolished, however, and the High Court of Justice, designed to hear impeachment cases against major government leaders, was replaced by the National Security Court, which was outside the ordinary legal system and under the direct control of the SRC. The National Security Court was established in April 1970 to hear cases involving the assassination of President Abderashid Ali Shermarke and charges of corruption levied by the SRC against members of the old regime. The court also tried other serious cases with or without political connections. The court was composed of three members: a member of the SRC, sitting as president, and two other military judges. A special military attorney general served as the prosecutor. No other court could review its sentences; appeals from its decisions could be taken only to the SRC itself. In several cases sentences were apparently carried out within a week of their delivery.

In 1974 a new law on the organization of the judiciary was promulgated, which appeared to make only minor changes in the system. It did not deal with the National Security Court and the regular military courts of the armed forces. It apparently left no role for the subordinate or qadi courts of the old system. The SRC also announced the abolition of *dia*.

Four levels of courts continued to be provided. The number of district courts increased from forty-eight to seventy-eight with the increase in the number of districts (see Local Government, this ch.). These courts were divided into civil and criminal sections. Regional tribunals had three sections: an ordinary section dealing with penal and civil matters more serious than those allowed to be heard by the district courts; an assize section, which only considered major criminal cases (those punishable by more than ten years' imprisonment); and a labor law section. At the district and regional tribunals cases were heard by a single magistrate, assisted by two laymen, who with the judge decided questions of fact and voted on the guilt or innocence of the accused.

At the next level were the regional courts of appeal, comprising two sections. The ordinary section heard appeals from decisions of the district tribunals and from the ordinary sections of the regional tribunals. The second heard only appeals from the regional assize sections. In both sections a single judge presided, assisted in the ordinary sections by two laymen and in the other by four. The senior judge of the Court of Appeal (its president) served as the administrator of the courts in his region.

At the apex of the judicial system was the Supreme Court. The court was composed of a chief justice, whose title was president, a vice president, nine surrogate justices, and four laymen. In plenary session the court consisted of the president, two other judges, and four laymen. In ordinary session it had a presiding judge, two other judges, and two laymen. Whether the case was to be handled in plenary or ordinary session was decided by the court president on the basis of the importance of the matter being considered.

The Supreme Court was charged with ensuring the exact observance and the uniform interpretation of the law and exercising surveillance over the activities of the officers of the Public Ministry. It heard appeals against decisions and judgments made by the lower courts and against measures taken by public attorneys, and it settled questions of court jurisdiction.

Other Judicial Organs

The office that handled the prosecution of criminal matters was called the Public Ministry. It was headed by the procurator general (attorney general), who was assisted by ten deputies in Mogadishu and other deputies who served at the courts of appeal and the regional or district courts. The Public Ministry functioned under the direction of the secretary of state for justice. The procurator general supervised his own deputies and the judicial police.

Selection, appointment, and discipline of members of the judiciary were in the hands of the Higher Judicial Council. Before the 1969 revolution the council consisted of the president of the Supreme Court, two or three other justices, the minister of justice, and the minister of interior. In 1970 all positions on the council were taken over by SRC members. Entrance into the magistrature is by competitive written and oral examinations. To provide judicial and court reporting, the Ministry of Justice began publication of the quarterly *Law Review* in 1973.

LOCAL GOVERNMENT

The old constitution had placed considerable emphasis on decentralization of government. It provided for elected units in the towns and some representative features at the district level. One of the SRC's earliest acts was the abolition of the existing structure of local government. In the new order no municipal units existed. Instead the SRC increased the numer of regions from eight to sixteen and the number of districts from forty-eight to seventy-eight, stating that it was doing so in order to bring local government closer to the people (see fig. 1). Each of the regions contained from three to seven districts except the capital region, Mogadishu, which was subdivided in late 1973 into fourteen such units, referred to as quarters. A hierarchical structure of regional, district, and village councils was created, and its pattern was firmly set by the local government reform law of August 1972. At the regional and district levels these councils had both national government and local representation. The chairman was the regional or district commissioner (called the district development officer after 1972). All chairmen were army officers until 1973 or 1974, when a few civilian officials were appointed to both levels of leadership.

All heads of regional units of the government ministries also sat as members of regional councils together with chairmen of the subordinate district councils and a citizen from each district chosen by the regional council to represent his community's views. The district councils were similarly composed; community representatives were chosen from among local persons who actively supported the government. The districts were grouped into three categories by size: nine, thirteen, or seventeen community representatives were appointed for two-year renewable terms. The village councils, each with seven members, were chosen annually by the local residents and were the only elected bodies in the country. It was not clear which entities corresponded to village councils among the pastoral nomads who, in the mid-1970s, still constituted a great proportion of Somalia's people. The nomads' various kin-based groups traditionally had councils composed of all adult males, and it is likely that these functions continued in some capacity, but how they fit into the official structure was not described (see ch. 4).

In the towns village council-level units were elected at the ward level. Ward councils also existed in Mogadishu. The capital area constituted the country's sixteenth region and was the only place with separate municipal status. The region was governed by a mayor appointed by the SRC and a city council nominated to represent interest groups (youths, women, workers, and the revolutionary elite) in each of the quarters. The quarters had district council-level units called quarter committees. These were composed of six ex officio and twenty nominated representative members. In 1975 the post of mayor was still held by an army officer.

Supervision of the local government structure was one of the major duties of the Ministry of Interior, the only ministry always headed by a senior general. The regional council chairmen were responsible both to the ministry and to their councils for the operation of the local administration.

The staffs of the local government units were assigned to them by the unified national civil service. Planning for local projects was done by the local council. National government projects taking place within the local area must be done in consultation with the local council but, as most of the council were civil servants, the chances of conflict were reduced.

At least through 1974 the councils were in a relatively strong financial position; enough of the potential local tax revenues were left for their collection and use. In addition they were empowered, with prior ministerial approval, to borrow funds for development projects if these were of a productive kind.

Regional and district councils were required by statute to form six committees: economic development, social affairs, public security, finance, political orientation, and mediation and conciliation. The last two were charged respectively with running programs to inculcate into the people the SRC's ideology and with attempting to settle disputes between the various segments of the community (see ch. 4).

CIVIL SERVICE

The government operated a single civil service system that included nearly all the members of the national and local government staffs and the employees of the public corporations. Only day laborers were excluded. It had long been customary for many posts to be filled by temporary employees with short-term contracts and without civil service benefits and protections, but in March 1972 the SRC decreed that all such employees would immediately be accepted into the regular service.

There were over 77,500 government employees in May 1975—more than double the number in 1969, a fact in which the government took considerable pride. Most were civil servants, but about 10,000 were trainees of the Crash Program Agency, an organization set up to teach the rural people the "proper attitude" toward modern organized work (see ch. 13). More than half the civil servants were employed by the public corporations. Government employees were roughly equal in number to those in private enterprise (not including agricultural workers).

The unification and centralization of the civil service made it possible for the government to transfer personnel as needed from one sector of public employment to another. This ensured that well-qualified people could be stationed in less desirable areas in order to bolster the efficiency of local administration.

Centralization created problems, however. Frequent transfers seemed to be the rule, inhibiting the development of specialized skills and experience. For example, the men who served as ministerial directors general in 1974 had been moved every eighteen months on the average. In addition the degree of centralization was such that local units, corporations, and ministries had only weak disciplinary control over their employees. This did not aid the government's efforts to solve the problems of inefficiency and widespread corruption that, according to the president and other leaders, plagued the country.

In an effort to avoid the nepotism based on common kin-group affiliation that was so important a characteristic of the prerevolutionary system, the SRC created a national recruiting board that selected all new employees, not only for the civil service but also for private employment. In 1975 the functions of the existing State Employees Promotion Committee were transferred to an element of the SRC's Social and Political Committee.

Immediately after coming to power the SRC began a major effort to inculcate a new spirit into the civil service. The "morally corrupt" and the "antirevolutionaries" were barred from civil service benefits. Government employees were expected to be politically and ideologically committed to the SRC's scientific socialism. Promotions were dependent on receipt of favorable reports not only from employers but also from the security police in an employee's home district. Major reeducation projects were sponsored by the Somali Institute of Administration and Management (previously called the Institute of Public Administration). The institute also sponsored the professional training programs for the civil service. Both were conducted at the Halane Revolutionary Training School; other programs were conducted within the various ministries and at the National University. The Halane courses included a special program for persons returning from schooling abroad.

CHAPTER 9

POLITICAL DYNAMICS AND VALUES

Despite clan divisions the Somali, by virtue of their relative cultural, religious, and linguistic homogeneity, constitute a nation rather than an artificially united state, a fact that clearly distinguishes Somalia from most new African states. Independent since July 1, 1960, the country experienced nine years of rule by a multiparty parliament. Competition for parliamentary support served to divide the Somali rather than bring them closer together as politicians sought support from different regional and clan groups. Too much of the attention of government leaders was on political competition and the long-lasting threat of war with neighbors over territorial claims rather than on the development of the country—one of the world's ten poorest states.

The military men who seized power on October 21, 1969, explained that their behavior was motivated by the failures of the civilian rulers. The leaders of the new executive body, the Supreme Revolutionary Council (SRC), at first said that a return to constitutional order and civilian rule would be carried out quickly. No moves were made in that direction, however, and the power of the more radical members of the SRC was rapidly strengthened. Under the leadership of its president—Major General Mohamed Siad Barre, a former army commander—and three vice presidents, within two years the SRC had made clear that it intended to establish a new economic, social, and political order based on the ideology of scientific socialism. Steps were taken to create the base for a single ruling party dedicated to that ideology, to serve as what was termed the "vanguard of the proletariat."

The new leaders sought a social as well as a political revolution, including changes in the basic values long held by the Somali people —above all their tradition of democracy in which all were free to speak out on political issues and be equally heard. Freedom of speech and peaceful opposition to the new government's policies were not to be tolerated. At least for the first seven years under the SRC, all important decisions were made by the military-dominated leadership at the center, supported by the largely military structure at the regional and local levels (see ch. 8). Political disagreements that did occur were apparently ironed out within the ranks of the SRC. Major issues concerned the speed and degree of implementing socialist policies, the continuing demands of clan rivalry, foreign influences, and Somalia's irredentist claims. The formation of the Somali Socialist Revolutionary Party (SSRP) in 1976 appeared unlikely to alter this situation significantly in the near future. Although the SRC was abolished and all its authority legally transferred to the SSRP's executive organs, the members of the former SRC, including the president, took over the key posts in the party, particularly the posts in its Politburo, or inner executive. They also retained the key posts in the government. Therefore the changes appeared only to broaden, not to replace, the existing hierarchy.

POLITICAL VALUES

The objectives of the leaders of the governments after 1969 included a radical reorganization of Somalia's economic, political, and social systems. Regarding the economic system, the new government rapidly established state control over industry, imports, and wholesale trade (see ch. 12; ch. 14). Given the general disenchantment with the parliamentary government in 1969 because of its inefficiency and corruption, and the power available to the military leaders, the SRC's exercise of political control was only infrequently challenged.

Altering the political and social values of the Somali people, however, was an elusive and difficult objective because of the pervasive attachment of the Somali to their clan, lineage, and *dia*-paying group (see Glossary). The changes in the social order sought by the SRC were truly revolutionary, but they were considered a necessary first step toward ending the divisiveness that had plagued the parliamentary government and welding the Somali people into a truly cohesive national unit. Even greater changes were required if the sociopolitical order was to conform to the scientific socialism demanded by the government's ideology. By the mid-1970s some changes had been made in urban society, but the real impact on the traditional values of the agricultural and pastoral majority apparently was very limited.

Origins of Political Values

Modern Somali political values have their origins largely in traditional ones. Even under the impact of the modern world and changing internal political structures, the Somali have continued to value the freedom of the individual and to see it as limited only by personal abilities and the teachings of Islam.

Somali have historically lived in accordance with an egalitarian political tradition. In nomadic society—roughly 75 to 80 percent of the population in the colonial era—every man considered himself the equal of any other Somali and the superior of all outsiders. Only force of arms or of intellect could demonstrate superiority. Every

154

adult Somali male was either a warrior or an Islamic religious figure—roles of equal status. The nomad regarded his own way of life as the best; other groups and other ways of life were measured against it. Merchants (most of whom were town-dwelling Arabs) were considered social inferiors by the desert-dwelling nomads. The only socially inferior groups living among the nomadic Somali were the craftsmen *(sab)*, who served the nomadic society as wandering leatherworkers and metalworkers, but they constituted only about 1 percent of the population.

Roughly 20 percent of ethnic Somali were Saab (see Glossary), members of either the Digil or Rahanwein clan-families, whose economy was based on farming in the Juba-Shabelle interriver area. As they took up ownership of farmlands, a certain degree of social stratification developed, based on control of croplands and water rights. In addition the Saab gained control over the non-Somali groups who continued to inhabit the land along the rivers. Despite the growth of social stratification, the Saab did not develop strongly hierarchical values, in part because they continued to take in members of the nomadic clans who found the farming life easier but did not abandon their traditions. Thus the highest political ideals of the settled Saab were identical with those of the nomadic society.

Political activity before and during the colonial era took place within the kin-based groups that dominated Somali life. The largest of these, the clan-family, was too large and dispersed to have political significance in traditional society. Political activities and decisions usually took place in clans, in lineages, or in groups based in part on kinship but organized for specific purposes by contract (see ch. 4).

In each unit, whatever its level, political matters were handled by the *shir*, an informal council of adult males. Deference was given to age and experience, military prowess, and wealth; but any adult male was entitled to be heard in the *shir*. The office of sultan was hereditary but largely ceremonial; the sultan had to negotiate and cajole or persuade if his word was to be accepted, and in mediation his authority depended on mutual consent. The man's own capability and force of character affected his role directly. In no case was the role of the sacred or the political leader dramatized with formal deference. The Somali language makes no provision for honorific titles in its vocabulary.

The *shir* was also the decisionmaking body of the politically important *dia*-paying groups. Although such units often consisted of related lineages, the rights and obligations obtained within the group were based on a written contract. Similarly clans sometimes bound themselves into a military confederation by means of written contracts. In the *dia*-paying groups the contract provided for the establishment of legal regulations that took on the status of a local constitution. Constituent lineages of a *dia*-paying group could secede and realign themselves in order to improve their political or military position (see ch. 4).

These traditions were carried into modern political life. One condition of Somali life is the nearly universal feeling of personal equality. Another is the right to be heard on all issues in the *shir.* Rule by the *shir* provides a traditional basis for universal male involvement in the country's political system.

Within the *shir* opponents would usually seek to gain their ends by methods similar to those used in modern politics. For example, in order to win a contender had to work actively to line up a majority of those voting. Since the vote would bind the whole *shir,* including his opponents, he would seek to accommodate the opposition to avoid pressures that might later divide the group. Every effort would therefore be made to avoid a loss of face. In addition, since all could make themselves heard, any invitation to debate could lead to a virtually unending discussion. To turn this to his own advantage a contender could attempt to get his opponents to talk themselves and their listeners into exhaustion.

Because of the *dia*-paying group contract and traditional Islamic law, the Somali were familiar with the concept of the supremacy of binding written law. Within the *dia*-paying group rules were enforced by decisions of disinterested elders, often drawn from outside the community, who served as judges; this pattern served as a basis for acceptance of a modern judicial system. A political contract could be broken if it became in the interest of one of the units to do so. This was clearly mirrored in the fluid composition and lack of ideological orientation of the political parties during the parliamentary period after independence. The parties expanded and contracted and disappeared and reappeared as the groups composing them found it expedient to alter their allegiances.

The Character of Leadership

A Somali proverb states that three things bring about the downfall of a leader: bias (in judgment of cases), dry-handedness (stinginess), and indecisiveness. The Somali leader at any level is likely to be called upon for arbitration. In addition to being just, he should be skilled in negotiating, in conciliating, in persuading, and in the use of words; he should also be alert and intelligent and have a magnetic personality. These characteristics are needed to a greater or lesser degree by elders and religious practitioners who are called upon to arbitrate. They were superimposed on the character either of the warrior *(waranle),* the ideal secular man, or of the religious leader *(wadad).*

The Somali's conception of what a good man's character should be was conditioned by the role he played in society. The two most common roles were those of warrior and religious devotee. The warrior was expected to be physically fit, to fight well, and to have qualities of leadership. Aggressiveness, vanity for personal appearance, and a capacity for intense partisanship were not merely acceptable but desirable in his character. He was expected to choose his equipment with care and, if he was young enough to be looking for a wife, to be carefully groomed.

He was also expected to be alert and intelligent, characteristics that are judged by verbal skill and tested with riddles and subtle conversation. Leadership was a quality that he was expected to show as a member of the lineage or clan councils, where his verbal skills also were required. The body of Somali tradition and oral literature was to be memorized and ready for recall as a part of the cultural knowledge that a full member of the society needed; he was expected to use it in oratory, which was a skill of leadership.

A complimentary word describing a good warrior's character was *belayo*, literally meaning disaster or catastrophe, which implied that he could act decisively and brilliantly under emergency conditions so that disaster would be made to fall on the enemy. The concept implied both political skill and military force; for the younger man military force was more important, for the older skill.

Impact of the Colonial Era

The Somali emerged from more than sixty years of colonial rule with their political tradition not destroyed but rather revitalized and channeled into modern forms. Because the population was almost entirely Somali, the country was not confronted by the problem—often brought about by colonial rule—of welding heterogeneous groups into a single political unit. The common bond of Islam contributed strongly to homogeneity.

The image of the omnipotent colonial rule that, in the early colonial years at least, was found throughout Africa was weakened in Somalia by its division among four powers—Ethiopia, Great Britain, Italy, and France—which allowed the Somali to compare their rule and discover the weaknesses. The Italian image at the outset was weakened by Italy's disastrous military defeat by Ethiopia in 1893. Similarly the hero of latter-day Somali nationalism, Sayyid Mohamed ibn Abdullah Hassan, had held off British military forces for nearly twenty years. In addition Somalia's Islamic ties led it to look to Arab states as an alternative to European models.

More important than the weakness of the colonial image was the fact that there were never more than a few hundred Europeans in British Somaliland and the northern half of Italian Somalia. The colonizing powers had little or no economic interest in the country other than the limited colonial agricultural development of the interriver area.

Neither Western education, Western religion, nor Western commerce affected the majority of the Somali. The end of the colonial era, at least in the southern half of the country, could be foreseen at the end of World War II.

Thus those colonial burdens did comparatively little to destroy the traditional sociopolitical order. It was not strong enough to give credence to the modernizing yet essentially antidemocratic tradition inherent in paternalistic colonial rule. Instead the primary modernizing political influence came in the ten years of the United Nations (UN) trusteeship, under a rule designed to make the most of Somali tradition, to create democratic institutions, and to provide for independence without the need for an indigenous effort to force an end to colonial rule.

Islamic and Modern Egalitarianism

The basic tenets of Islam stress absolute egalitarianism: all Muslims, regardless of race, clan, wealth, or status, are equal before God. By definition, therefore, the Islamic faith runs counter to the idea of pride in descent or wealth. Esteem should ideally arise from religious learning and sanctity, and military activity is legitimate if undertaken against the enemies of Islam. Among the Somali, therefore, Islam has tended to broaden the traditional concept of equality of all clansmen to equality of all male coreligionists.

The national ideal held by all Somali is one of political and legal equality; more modern Somali also espouse equality for women and for minorities. In other respects the democratic ideal derived from Western political thought partly coincides with aspects of Somali culture. Conflict appeared in regard to equality of women, which is not in accord with traditional Somali or Islamic thought. Although the young nationalists attempted to implement their ideals in the 1960s, the world view necessary for implementation did not exist outside a small elite group.

Evolution of Values in the Modern System

During the period of parliamentary democracy (1960-69) the existence of freedom of press and speech was widely regarded as being derived from the traditional right of every man to be heard. In accord with both traditional and modern democratic values, modern politics was viewed as a realm not limited to one profession, clan, or class but open to all male members of society. Politics was at once the Somali's most practiced art and their favorite sport. A radio was the most desired possession of most nomads, not for its entertainment value but for news broadcasts. The level of political participation apparently often surpassed that in many developed Western democracies.

Clan Divisions and Politics

Divisions based on clan-families, clans, and similar kin groups continued to be one of the most powerful factors in political life. The majority of the people still regulated the structure of their political relations in terms of genealogical ties. Clan affiliations were extremely important in influencing group behavior, and clan divisions provided suggested lines of alliance and antagonism. As a rule efforts were made to maintain a clan balance, although in filling cabinet and civil service posts efforts might also be made to find the most qualified persons available; but the emphasis was on a choice that would not disturb clan sensitivities. The growth of crop farming and of urbanization had the greatest impact on the weakening of clan factions, particularly since the population, once estimated to be 80 percent nomadic, by the 1970s contained greatly increased urban and agricultural sections.

Pan-Somalism

The most important political issue in postindependence Somali politics has been the unification of all areas populated by Somali in the Horn of Africa into one country. From 1960 until 1968 it was presumed that this issue dominated popular opinion and that any government would fall if it did not demonstrate a militant attitude toward the neighboring nations that were seen as occupying Somali territory. However, the success of the government under Prime Minister Mohamed Ibrahim Egal after mid-1967 clearly demonstrated that a moderate stand was acceptable to the majority of the electorate and that demands that primacy be given to militancy and a resort to force no longer carried great weight. Egal's success apparently came about because he did not relinquish the controversial claims but merely ended the paramilitary confrontation over the issue so that they could be examined peacefully.

Popular support conceded this easing of tensions to the government in return for the prospects of an improved economic life in a state at peace. Support for improved relations with Kenya, Ethiopia, and France continued as détente brought easier conditions of trade, greater freedom of movement for nomads, and expectations of a rise in government expenditure on internal improvements rather than on war preparations (see ch. 10).

As one of its first acts the SRC denounced the border agreements that had been so painstakingly negotiated by the Egal government. In doing so, however, its only reason appeared to be a reluctance to give any credit to its predecessor. The SRC in fact adopted policies that did not conflict with the treaties' provisions; however, it felt compelled by popular opinion to reiterate the claims frequently. The compulsion reflected in part the divisions within the SRC that arose from the continuing importance of ethnic ties despite the anticlan policies of the government's ideology. SRC members who came from the border regions or whose clans had personal interests across the borders were particularly sensitive to irredentist questions. Notably troubled were members of the Issa clan (of the Dir clan-family) regarding the French Territory of Afars and Issas (FTAI), of the Isaq clan-family and portions of the northern Darod concerning the Ogaden region of Ethiopia, and of the southern Darod clans about the so-called Northern Frontier District of Kenya. Because of these sensitivities, in the mid-1970s the government's statements on the peaceful resolution of the irredentist claims often were ambiguous (see ch. 10).

View of the Government

The average Somali viewed the government in the context of traditional values: it was the replacement of the clan and contractual groups, which had drawn their support from their ability to provide members with protection from assault, a pooling of common resources during drought, a place in society for those too sick or too old to fend for themselves. and other social services. As the government created a modern state and weakened kin-based divisions—and particularly as urban centers grew and the basis of the national economy was modernized—it was expected to offer such social services. If the government was unable to do so, it would not satisfy the popular view of its reason for existence. Promising to find solutions to such problems and then proving unable to do so remained the greatest source of potential weakness for the government in the mid-1970s.

POLITICAL DYNAMICS

Somalia arrived at independence in 1960. During the previous ten years the UN trusteeship had a program for developing indigenous political leadership, and it was carried out with marked success. Because independence was guaranteed, anticolonialism was not a major issue, and political leaders were chiefly concerned with the country's own problems.

The early postindependence era was dominated by difficult problems: the political and administrative unification of the Trust Territory of Somaliland under Italian Administration with the smaller British Somaliland and the conflict with Ethiopia and later with Kenya over Somalia's demands for the unification of all Somali, Internal political conflicts revolved around methods of handling these difficulties. Party composition and leadership fluctuated as new parties were formed. At any national election a great many parties, some with only a single candidate, were formed; but important parties were relatively few, and one—the Somali Youth League (SYL)—had been clearly dominant since before independence. The leading political parties were not divided by significant ideological differences, however, and all the leaders had served together in the SYL. The modern political elite consisted of at most a few hundred men. Supported by the kin-

160

based groups with which they were affiliated, they competed for power and sought to limit access to real decisionmaking positions at the national level to their own ranks.

Between 1967 and 1969 there was a decisive turn in Somalia's approach toward its most difficult problem, that of pan-Somalism and international boundaries. Under the leadership of Prime Minister Egal relations with Ethiopia and Kenya improved greatly, reflecting the new attitude that a united Somali nation should be the result of peaceful negotiation rather than armed conflict. The electorate supported Egal, and political interest turned to the solution of internal social and economic problems.

Although democratic traditions were strong, observers of the Somali political scene recognized that the continuation of democracy depended on the ability of the political system to provide solutions to the country's social and economic problems. In 1969 the country was torn by a political contest, which for a long time diverted the government leaders' attention from the necessary efforts to solve these problems. This and concurrent charges of corruption, favoritism, and widespread election rigging increased popular disenchantment with the existing political order. In mid-October 1969, just as the political situation appeared to be settling down, President Abderashid Ali Shermarke was assassinated, apparently by a man motivated by personal hatred based on clashes between the president's clan and his own (see ch. 2). The assassination and the subsequent fight within the ruling SYL over the question of a replacement proved the final straws for those already disenchanted with the parliamentary system. On October 21, 1969, army leaders suspended the constitution and all organs of government.

Problems of Parliamentary Rule

The Somali had seemed to adapt their traditional democratic tendencies to the modern system after independence and to have national and cultural unity. By the late 1960s, however, it had become apparent that this picture was deceiving. In traditional society the six large clan-families into which the Somali divided themselves had played only a limited political role because most interaction took place on the level of the clans, lineages, and contractual groups (see ch. 4). In the first years after independence the importance of these divisions was partly masked by a common concern over the nearly constant threat of armed conflict with Ethiopia and Kenya. The leaders' political energies were also absorbed by the work required to solve the new country's administrative problems, particularly those resulting from the unification of the former Italian and British territories.

Inefficiency also presented a large problem and led to frequent squandering of the money the country was able to obtain. One major administrative burden resulted from the use of four official languages because no one was able to make the decision on what form written Somali should take.

As some of these problems became less acute, modern politics began to take shape on traditional foundations. Initial rivalry between northerners and southerners was replaced by competition among the clan-families, which were generally aligned in three groups, Saab (Digil and Rahanwein); Darod; and Isaq, Dir, and Hawiya. This was not a set pattern; the groups vied for the greatest share of power. The Darod, by far the largest and most widely dispersed clan-family, was open to greater internal political divisions among its clans and regional subunits.

Politicians, seeking support at the polls and knowing that the clans and lineages meeting in the *shir* decided as a whole how its members would vote, increasingly encouraged the strengthening of already deeply held clan allegiances. The major means of winning the support of a clan was to provide jobs and other favors for clan members. Certain ministries of the government became the reputed reserve of given clans. Great importance was placed on ensuring a clan balance in the Council of Ministers and lesser governmental posts.

The problem was worsened by the nature of the parliamentary rule. With scores of political parties, many of them very localized, a majority vote in the National Assembly could best be ensured by luring the members of the other parties into a coalition with the dominant SYL.

Not only Somali critics of the parliamentary government but also apparently detached foreign analysts observed that corruption (bribery, illegal hiring practices, and the misuse of public funds) was widespread, mostly by politicians attempting to strengthen their support among personal constituencies. Popular disenchantment with the existing government had apparently extended into the ranks of the armed forces and police. Disgusted with political interference, the highly respected chief of the national police resigned in early 1969; Siad, then army commander, and other military leaders had openly expressed dissatisfaction with parliamentary rule two or three years earlier, but these warnings had no effect.

Military in the Government

In 1976 the government in power was controlled by the leaders of the 1969 coup. From the coup until July 1976 the ruling SRC, an organ composed solely of senior military and police officers, led the country. During this period the only serious challenges to its power had come from conservative officers in its ranks who had attempted a countercoup in 1971 (see ch. 16). After their execution differences within the SRC seemed confined to those between exponents of more and less radical applications of what they conceived of as Marxism-Leninism or scientific socialism. Military involvement in the country's politics was very extensive: in 1973 at least 117 senior army officers held full-time positions in the administration, filling all local and regional government executive posts. The size and strength of the armed forces was doubled during this period despite a marked decline in the probability of external conflict and the enormous burden the increase placed on the country's fragile economy.

Major practical successes of the SRC were in reducing government inefficiency, corruption, and tribalism. Even with the power it had available, however, major problems continued to exist. It took the military leaders nearly three years to decide the vital question of a script for the Somali language. Important officials were still being arrested or publicly chastised for corrupt practices in 1976, and factors of ethnic balance were still considered by the government in making important appointments.

A major opportunity for civilian participation in this essentially military power structure was provided in 1970 by the creation of a cabinet (Council of the Secretaries of State) composed largely of civilians. It directed the operations of the government's ministries, and the authority of its members gradually grew; some members were co-opted in 1974 to serve as the advisory staff of the SRC. By the mid-1970s cabinet members and the civilian advisers apparently exerted significant influence in formulating government policy. The key decisions and the ideological direction of the country, however, clearly remained in the hands of the SRC and its most important member, President Siad. The continuing role of military leaders was in line with his statements in the mid-1970s that the army would not return to the barracks but would remain the vanguard of the revolution.

In late June and early July 1976 major changes to reduce the role of the military were instituted. The SRC dissolved itself, formally vesting its control over the country in the newly created political party, the SSRP. In lieu of creating representative bodies in the national government, a relatively important role was apparently intended for the new party's seventy-three-member, largely civilian, central committee.

Real power, however, continued to be held by the small group of military leaders who had been most influential in the SRC. First among these was the president, and closely associated with him were the three vice presidents, Major General Mohamed Ali Samantar, Major General Hussein Kulmi Afrah, and Colonel Ali Abokor. Of these Samantar filled the most conspicuous role: from about 1971 he served simultaneously as vice president, head of the defense ministry, and commander of the armed forces, positions he held in mid-1976. The president and the vice presidents automatically were members of the cabinet (called the Council of Ministers after the July 1976 changes). In addition the four—assisted by President Siad's son-in-law, Colonel Ahmed Suleiman Abdullah, an SRC member who continued to head the security police—also formed the Politburo of the ruling party.

The military continued to be closely involved in politics in other ways as well. The nineteen men of the SRC all became members of the central committee of the party, as did a number of other army and police officers. The SRC members held six out of nineteen ministerial posts, and two other ministries (interior and agriculture) were headed by general officers from outside the ranks of the SRC. Military involvement in politics at the lower levels continued: a number of officers still served as regional and district officials. Also named to the central committee—at times apparently referred to as the Supreme Council—were five of the six civilian advisers to the SRC and thirteen civilian members of the former cabinet, eleven of whom were named to the new Council of Ministers. Thus the key positions in the new structure went to the holders of such positions in the old structure and, although a few of the former SRC members seemed to slip on the scale, all were still within the two highest echelons of government.

Creation of the Somali Socialist Revolutionary Party

The existence of all political associations of any kind had been barred by one of the SRC's earliest acts. Yet although the Somali Socialist Revolutionary Party (SSRP) was not created until mid-1976, as early as 1971 the president had announced the SRC's intention to organize a single political party, and the SRC had begun working much earlier to form what it described as a "vanguard of the revolution" party. It was to be composed of members of the socialist elite from the entire nation. The early steps were aimed at creating organs at the local level. These were intended to spread the SRC ideology of scientific socialism among a major portion of the population. Directing this effort was a government unit immediately under the SRC. At first called the National Public Relations Office, indicating its duty of bringing the SRC's ideas to the people, it was retitled the National Political Office in 1973. Branch offices were opened in regional and district capitals and in some places at least down to the town or city ward level. Programs operated by the branch offices, supported by the Ministry of Information and National Guidance (whose public information duties seemed to overlap with the political officers' work), were extended throughout the country.

Gradually guidance centers (sometimes called orientation centers) were built throughout the country, generally by self-help programs. They served as focal points for government information activity, including informal educational programs and entertainment efforts, and as local meeting places for voluntary activites and for the district and local councils (see ch. 8). They also played an important role in or-

164

ganizing the mass literacy campaign (see ch. 7). The political officers at the local level were charged with both disseminating and gathering information; they reported to upper echelons on political, economic, social, and national security affairs in their areas. They were specifically charged with maintaining what was called an official register of justice, which listed both the staunch supporters of the revolution and those who, by their failure to participate actively in socialist programs or in other ways, appeared to be backsliders or opponents of the official ideology. According to the president, this and the guiding of the "masses to the . . . true meaning and application of scientific socialism" were the political officers' major responsibilities. They were to stimulate the formation of organizations of youth, local workers, and women, whose leading members would later form the basis for the political party.

Also under the political office were the Victory Pioneers (Gulwadayal), a uniformed group that officially was a special branch of the army. They actually performed police tasks under the local political officers' supervision. They were the element that conducted most surveillance work, looking for persons speaking out against government policy, preventing contacts with foreigners, and rounding up people for the prescribed voluntary labor programs (see ch. 16).

Presumably beyond the purview of the guidance centers, but also intended to stimulate the growth of a political elite, were the workers' committees. These were set up beginning in late 1972 in state-owned enterprises, private companies, and even government ministries. They were intended to participate fully in the management of the enterprise, but most apparently began with duties limited to assisting management on personnel questions. In 1976 it appeared that only a few of the committees were actively functioning.

With the establishment of the political party the national political office was abolished, its roles to be filled by the local party leadership. No information was available in late 1976 on the local structure of the party. According to press reports the membership of the party at its formation was 15,000. Some 3,000 people from the groups organized by the political office and from the ranks of the armed forces and police formed the party's constituent congress, which discussed and ratified, apparently with a few changes, the program recommended by the SRC. The key matters ratified were the party's program, its constitution, and the membership of the central committee (or Supreme Council) and of its Politburo. A number (variously reported as seven and seventeen) of party departments were also formed, such as foreign affairs, finance and commerce, security, and ideology. Among the men named as department chairmen were two additional former SRC members; they were put in charge of the departments for political institutes and defense affairs.

Information concerning opposition to the government was limited, reflecting the lack of significant organized opposition, the tight control of the army and police over the country, or both. President Siad, despite his purely military and police background, proved to be a skilled politician. He strongly preferred to win over the opposition or to find compromise solutions if those solutions would move the country in a direction compatible with his ideas. After 1971 no divisions within the SRC became public. On one or two occasions civilian cabinet members resigned from the government to protest specific policies of the SRC, but no reprisals were taken against them.

Within certain undefined limits criticism of personalities and of the specific directions being taken by the government was widespread and open, in line with Somali traditions. What was not tolerated was anything that seemed to indicate active support for the old order, opposition to the major lines of the government's ideology or anything that the authorities thought might serve as the basis on which significant opposition might build.

The Victory Pioneers and the National Security Service (NSS) attempted to ferret out and arrest those who verbally attacked the government, and jail sentences were imposed for "rumor mongering" against the revolution—for which the law provided heavy penalties. At village meetings people were told that they must destroy the old order by isolating hostile elements who were still heeded by the population. Political officers bragged that members of Muslim religious communities had been arrested by local authorities for counterrevolutionary activity and that local merchants had been jailed for "refusing to accept the new order." In the most notable case ten religious leaders were tried and executed for accusing the government of violating the teachings of the Quran by attempting to improve the position of women before the law (see ch. 16).

The general attitude of the government was that it should seek to win over its opponents by a mixture of coercion and blandishment, rather than simply suppress them. By 1975 even the most condemned leaders of the parliamentary regime had been amnestied, including former Prime Minister Egal and his minister of interior, long the chief villains in all SRC presentations. Surprisingly Egal was soon named to an ambassadorial post.

Major Challenges to the Supreme Revolutionary Council

The SRC announced on two occasions that it had discovered plotters initiating coup attempts against it. Both occurred before 1972 and were led by SRC members. In April 1970 the country's first vice president, Major General Jama Ali Korshel, head of the police force, was arrested and charged with treason. Korshel had not been among the military men who had plotted to bring the SRC to power and may have actually opposed them during their first few hours, so that he may have remained the odd figure in the SRC. The detailed allegations released as the reason for his arrest did not appear logical. It was apparent, however, that Korshel probably represented the more conservative elements within the police and army and thus was potentially if not actually in opposition to the socialist directions of the majority of the SRC members. Jailed after being tried by the newly created National Security Court, he was amnestied in 1974.

In May 1971 the second vice president, Major General Mohamed Ainanshe, and a fellow SRC member, Lieutenant Colonel Salah Gaveire Kedie, who had served as head of the Ministry of Defense in the first cabinet and later as secretary of state for communications, were arrested along with several other army officers in what was a much more serious attempt to oppose the SRC's majority. Gaveire reportedly was the mastermind, seeking to replace President Siad. The plotters sought the support of those whose families or clans had lost power in the 1969 overthrow of the government. Gaveire was rumored to have been a key figure in earlier confrontations within the SRC. Accused of plotting to assassinate the president, after a lengthy trial the two key figures were executed in July 1972.

SOMALIA'S SCIENTIFIC SOCIALISM

Somalia's apparently close alignment with the communist states and its proclaimed adherence to scientific socialism have led to frequent accusations by critics that the country has become a Soviet satellite. Several other factors have contributed to such a conclusion, particularly the military connection: the existence of major naval, air, and communication facilities at Berbera that were built and used by the Soviets; the exclusive dependence on the Soviet Union for arms and training for the large Somali army; the fact that the government is led by men trained in Soviet schools, who overthrew a Western-oriented, parliamentary democracy; almost constant Somali support for the positions in international affairs supported by the Soviet Union and the People's Republic of China (PRC); a proclaimed admiration for the ideology not only of Marx and Engels but also of Lenin; and the constant verbal rejection of the non-Marxist-Leninist forms of socialism that are current in most other African and Arab states. It would be a mistake, however, to conclude from these facts that Somalia must always be counted a member of the Soviet camp, for distinct and very important differences do exist.

Somalia's adherence to socialism officially began with President Siad's proclamation on the first anniversary of the SRC coup that the country was a socialist state, though without any history of Marxist class conflict. At that time the government proclaimed its ideology to be composed of three elements: the president's conception of community development, a form of socialism based on scientific principles, and Islam. Such a definition of socialism put the country clearly at variance with the Soviet model and, for that matter, with the PRC.

According to the president, socialism was the sharing of work and wealth to ensure justice, equality, and a life free of exploiters. The reasons for Somalia's adoption of socialism were, according to Siad, that it "gave dignity to man and his cherished values, and equality of rights and opportunities for property and happiness."

For Somalia the origins of socialism were to be found in the Muslim people and its roots in Islam. It is the social ideology inherent in the Quran reflected, for example, in the admonition that a vistor must be provided hospitality.

The government laid heavy emphasis on the argument that there was only one legitimate form of socialism, that is, scientific socialism; a debt is admitted not only to Marx and Engels but also to Lenin. But scientific socialism, though unified, must take different forms in different environments. The president and other important leaders frequently repeated that an adherence to scientific socialism is not demonstrated by copying the form of its implementation in other countries and that, according to Lenin, socialism must be applied according to the specific conditions of the country.

The leaders recognize that the three European sources of the ideology of scientific socialism were opposed to religion but say that it was because the religion they knew was a form of Christianity advantageous to the ruling classes. According to Vice President Abokor recognition of the true role of religion was the original contribution of the Somali president to the ideology of scientific socialism. He "postulated that the classless nature of Islam" and its egalitarianism made it compatible with scientific socialism.

According to the president in 1971 the socialism of Somalia would not take ownership of livestock away from the herders (who still make up a substantial majority of Somalia's population) or ownership of small shops away from the petty traders (who form the bottom layer in the country's rural commerce). Private ownership was to be allowed "provided that such wealth [was] not used against the interest of the Somali people."

In 1975, however, the secretary of state for trade said the government's willingness to allow small businessmen to function was based on the belief that this social class did not represent any real counterrevolutionary threat to the SRC since its members lacked the ability to act against the government. It was not clear whether this comment indicated a disparity of views within the leadership or an evolution of its views.

A belief in God, a willingness to recognize a debt to religion, a tolerance of some degree of private enterprise, and an emphasis on diversity within the Marxist-Leninist community—all these clearly distinguished Somalia from the Soviet Union and, except perhaps in the last case, from the Asian communist states as well. There were other significant differences. Despite President Siad's statement during a state visit to Moscow in 1971 that "every Soviet victory is a victory for all progressive forces," Somalia avoided efforts to align the country on the Soviet side against the PRC. Reflecting this, the president's only state visits beyond Africa and the Arab world had been to the PRC, the Democratic People's Republic of Korea (North Korea), and the Soviet Union (see ch. 10).

Many Somali statements favorable to the Soviet bloc (for example, one by the president that "Somalia was sure to benefit from the Soviet experience in constructing a classless communist society") had to be considered in the light of the country's heavy dependence on aid from the Soviet Union. In addition to the general question of aid the Somali military leaders were particularly in debt for the form of aid that had been given in two difficult situations—the large-scale assistance in combating the worst effects of the 1974-75 drought and the grant of military equipment for use against Ethiopia in the 1963-64 period.

The warm regard expressed for Somalia by a Soviet bloc leader in describing the country's government as a "fraternal socialist state" had to be balanced against evident and widespread reports of the opposition by Somali at all levels to the heavy Soviet presence in the country and to the overbearing personalities of many in the large Soviet community.

CHAPTER 10

FOREIGN RELATIONS

During most of its postindependence years one issue—pan-Somalism—dominated Somalia's international politics and had an impact not only on its relations with neighbors but also, indirectly, on its associations throughout Africa and the world. After nearly eight years of relative quiet that issue was again coming to the fore in 1976.

Somalia is surrounded by the states and territories of Kenya, Ethiopia, and the French Territory of Afars and Issas (FTAI, formerly French Somaliland), all of which include ethnic Somali in their populations. The Somali governments have continued to see this fragmentation as a result of an unjust division of the Horn of Africa by the colonial powers (see ch. 2). Between 1960 and early 1967 Somali antipathy for these colonial divisions led to almost constant conflict of varying intensity with neighboring states that considered Somali irredentism the cause of the difficulty. The Somali, however, did not directly claim sovereignty over land but rather demanded that the Somali of the adjacent territories be granted the right of self-determination. Somali leaders asserted that they would be satisfied only when their fellow Somali had the opportunity to decide for themselves what their status would be.

After the election of a new government in June 1967 Somalia adopted a fresh attitude toward the importance of good relations with its neighbors. Beginning at a meeting of African heads of state under the auspices of the Organization of African Unity (OAU) in September 1967 the government made strong efforts, even in the face of vigorous internal opposition, to ease the strains with Kenya and Ethiopia. Although many problems remained, by late 1968 major steps toward improving relations had been carried forward, and an end had been brought to the state of near war that had previously existed along both sides of the borders.

The military leaders who came to power as the Supreme Revolutionary Council (SRC) in October 1969 also sought to avoid conflicts with the three neighboring states. The right of self-determination for all Somali, however, continued to be the dominant international issue in Somalia. In 1976 the potential for conflict over the pan-Somali issue was again increasing because of the projected withdrawal of French control over the FTAI. France had announced in December

171

1975 that it would end its rule over the territory after a plebiscite to determine the territory's future. Ethiopia sincerely feared Somali control over the small territory's vital port city, Djibouti, which serves as Ethiopia's major outlet to the sea.

In addition to pan-Somalism the country is strongly affected by two other transnational currents, pan-Africanism and pan-Arabism. At the juncture between the Arab world and black Africa, Somalia draws inspiration from and gives at least vague allegiance to both. The country's détente with its neighbors was at least partly motivated by a desire to find a place for itself in the OAU and to promote its economic development by taking part in the trade zone created by an East African economic community. Although the community itself had encountered major problems and Somalia's intention to join it was never carried out, the SRC continued to place considerable importance on ties with the OAU, and Somalia's president, Major General Mohamed Siad Barre, achieved a prominent position in that organization.

Somalia is also bound by historical and religious ties with the Arab world, particularly to the Arabian Peninsula with which it also has important trade ties. Significant aid and technical assistance have been provided by Egypt, Saudi Arabia, and Kuwait and were expected by Somalia to increase significantly after the country became the only non-Arab member of the League of Arab States (Arab League) in 1974. Many Somali, particularly among the more religious, felt that ties with the Arab world should be given even higher priority.

Beginning in 1962 Somalia's need for an expanded military force to support its irredentist claims led to growing military ties with the Soviet Union. By 1968 more than 800 Somali had received military training there, and the army had been entirely equipped with Soviet arms. The army officers who seized power from the civilian government in October 1969 were led by men who were ideologically disposed toward some form of Marxism-Leninism. They sought to establish what they labeled a scientific socialist state. Continuing Soviet military aid flowed in, and Soviet nonmilitary aid also was extensive. In Western eyes the culmination of the Somali-Soviet relationship was the establishment after 1973 of a naval supply and missile storage base at the port of Berbera, which served as the main resupply point for the Soviet Union's small but politically strategic Indian Ocean fleet. Despite the ideological affinity and the close dependence on Soviet assistance, Somalia's leaders laid heavy emphasis on a policy of nonalignment and sought and received a major portion of its nonmilitary assistance from Western Europe, with which it continued to have its most important economic ties.

ORGANIZATION OF THE FOREIGN MINISTRY

Major foreign policy decisions were taken by the country's executive: the SRC until July 1976, the Council of Ministers thereafter.

172

Routine matters were handled by the Ministry of Foreign Affairs, which was headed by a senior member of the cabinet. From the inception of the SRC in 1969 until mid-1976 the post was held by Omar Arteh Ghalib, with the title of secretary of state for foreign affairs. Ghalib lost the post just before the major reorganization of the government in July 1976; thereafter the heads of all ministries were given the title of minister.

The structure of the ministry was established by presidential decree in May 1972. The senior permanent employee of the foreign ministry, its director general, was a civil servant. The ministry's staff of seventy in Mogadishu worked in the director general's office and six departments. Three departments dealt with relations with countries grouped into major geographic divisions: Europe and the Americas, Asia and the socialist countries, and Africa. The fourth department handled international organization affairs, although it apparently shared responsibility for inter-African organization affairs with the Africa department. Of the remaining departments one was responsible for protocol and public relations, and the other dealt with legal and research matters. As of mid-1972 there were ninety-six diplomats stationed outside the country in Somalia's eighteen embassies and one consulate general; at least two embassies were added between that date and mid-1976. Several of the embassies included military attachés appointed by the army (but under embassy control) and cultural attachés appointed by the Ministry of Culture and Higher Education.

The Somali government did make use of its foreign posts to send potential opponents out of the country. Thus former Prime Minister Mohamed Ibrahim Egal, detained for five years after the 1969 revolt and then held in jail for another two years pending prosecution for alleged corruption, was appointed ambassador to India within six months of his release in 1976. His minister of education, with a similar detention record, was appointed ambassador to Pakistan at the same time. Reportedly, army officers who were restive were assigned to military attaché posts or sent with some frequency to the Soviet Union for training programs (see ch. 15).

The twenty-four embassies in Mogadishu included seven from the communist bloc countries, eight from the Arab and Muslim world, and six from the West. Ambassadors were also exchanged with Ethiopia and Kenya.

PAN-SOMALISM

The issue that dominates all other considerations of foreign relations for the majority of Somali is the status of their fellow Somali in adjacent countries: the Northern Frontier District of Kenya (NFD, in the 1970s part of Kenya's North-Eastern Province); the Ogaden and Haud regions of Ethiopia, generally called simply Ogaden; and the southern half of the FTAI around the port of Djibouti (see fig. on distribution of clan-families and ethnic groups, ch. 4). Somali occupy roughly one-fifth of Kenya, perhaps one-quarter of Ethiopia, and nearly one-half of the FTAI. The inclusion of the contested areas in Somalia would roughly double its size and increase its population by 50 percent; this addition, however, would not necessarily increase the national wealth since, with the exception of the built-up areas of Djibouti, the contested areas are at best dry pastureland and at worst absolute desert. (There was some hope of finding exploitable oil sources in the Ogaden region.)

This preoccupation with the pan-Somali issue was emphasized by the formation of the country's institutions. The exact size of the National Assembly at independence was not established by law, in order to facilitate the inclusion at some time in the future of representatives of the contested areas after unification. The national flag is dominated by a five-pointed star whose points represent the portions of the country to be united. Moreover the Constitution of 1961 stated prominently in its introduction that "the Somali Republic promotes by legal and peaceful means, the union of the Somali territories," and its fundamental laws continue to provide that all ethnic Somali, no matter where they reside, are citizens of the republic.

Despite the importance of the unification issue, the government after 1967 generally placed particular emphasis on carrying it out by peaceful means. In its international presentations the government has insisted, not on the right of all Somali to be united under one government, but on the right of the Somali in the three contested areas to self-determination in line with the provisions of the United Nations Charter. All three Somali governments in power since mid-1967 have insisted that they would be satisfied with any decisions resulting from internationally supervised impartial plebiscites in the areas, even if these plebiscites resulted in conclusions unfavorable to Somalia. They maintained that such plebiscites should offer three alternatives—continued direct or federated ties with the states to which they are now attached, separate independence, or unification with the Somali Democratic Republic. The Somali governments, however, expressed confidence that any such vote would result in unification.

The Northern Frontier District Conflict

At the time of European colonization at the turn of the twentieth century the Somali were still on the move in the south, expanding into or strengthening their position in the area then called the Trans-Juba, extending from the Juba River southwestward to the northern shore of the Tana River in present-day Kenya. The entire area was at first claimed by the British as part of Kenya. In 1916, however, they agreed to split it in half along the present-day internationally recognized boundary line. The northern half was ceded to the Italian colonial authorities as part of Great Britain's settlement for Italy's entry into World War I (see ch. 2).

By the time colonial control was solidified after 1925, Somali dominated most of the area north of the Tana River, having driven all the weaker ethnic groups southward or westward. To prevent further interethnic warfare the British authorities set up a line, virtually an internal frontier, beyond which the Somali were not permitted to travel. Other barriers were set up by the Kenya colonial authorities to set the Somali permanently apart from the rest of the African population. For example, the Somali were taxed at a rate higher than that set for the African population.

These distinctions, all of which at least indirectly recognized the foreign nationality of the Somali and therefore their basic ties with Somalia, remained in effect until Kenya's 1963 independence, continually reinforcing the Somali sense of exclusiveness. The Somali of the NFD were convinced that their interests had been neglected while they had been a part of the Kenya Colony, and they expected to be similarly neglected by the postindependence government. They looked to their politically and economically advanced fellow Somali across the international boundary for leadership, particularly after Somalia's independence in 1961.

In 1961 the political leaders of the NFD demanded at the Kenya independence talks in London that the British arrange the NFD's separation before Kenya gained its independence. The British appointed a commission to ascertain the desires of the population in the NFD. The results indicated that separation from Kenya was almost unanimously supported by the Somali and their fellow Muslim nomadic pastoralists, the Galla. The two peoples represented a clear majority of the population of the NFD.

Despite considerable diplomatic activity by the Somali government, Great Britain did not act on the results of the commission's findings. The leaders of Kenya's two major political parties were opposed to giving away any part of the country that was shortly to be theirs. This opposition continued despite visits by the parties' leaders to Mogadishu to hear the Somali arguments in full. The British were reluctant to oppose the Kenyans and felt that the federal format then proposed in the Kenya constitution would provide a solution. The North Eastern Region, composed of the Somali district of the NFD, was established as a federal unit; it was thought that this arrangement would retain Kenya's unity while accommodating the Somali's sense of separation from the rest of the country. This solution, however, did not ease Somali demands for unification, and the modicum of federalism disappeared after the new Kenya government opted for a strongly centralized constitution in late 1964.

The denial of Somali claims led to steadily increasing hostility between the Somali and the Kenya government. The Somali in the NFD, brought up in the difficult life of nomads in the semidesert region, adapted easily to life as guerrillas, or *shifta* (bandits) at the Kenyans called them. They conducted a campaign against the Kenyan police and army for more than four years. The Kenyan government claims that well over 2,000 *shifta* were killed by security forces in the NFD between 1963 and 1967. The rebels were armed with a variety of older military equipment, most of it manufactured in the Soviet bloc or the People's Republic of China (PRC). Their most effective tactic was mining desert trails. The Somali government denied Kenyan government claims that the rebels were trained in Somali army camps, were armed with weapons provided by the Soviet military assistance program to the Somali army, or received their instructions from Mogadishu. The Somali government, however, did not deny that the Voice of Somalia radio in Mogadishu was able greatly to influence the level of guerrilla activity by the tone of its broadcasts, particularly through the traditional medium of war poetry (see ch. 7).

Under OAU auspices a number of efforts were made to end the conflict between the two countries. Most of the earlier attempts concentrated on a mutual lowering of the level of hostile propaganda. The resulting agreements were usually honored until some reported act in the NFD inflamed Somali or Kenyan public opinion, after which the propaganda level would rise again and with it the level of the hostilities. This situation eased only after the change of Somalia's government in mid-1967.

The Conflict with Ethiopia

The conflict with Ethiopia is even more complex than that with Kenya, although the basic problem is the same. Two factors complicate the issue further, and both involve questions of the location of the border between the two countries. In the south the doubts result from a historic disagreement between Ethiopia and Italy, largely hinging on whether the northern tripoint between the British, Italian, and Ethiopian possessions was located at 47° or 48° east longitude.

In the north the official location of the international frontier is agreed upon, but the Somali contend that it was unfairly placed so as to exclude the herdsmen residing in Somalia from their very important seasonal grazing lands in the Haud, now within Ethiopia, even though the region had historically been administered by the British as an integral part of British Somaliland. The British did not withdraw from the Haud until 1955 and even then stressed its importance to Somalia by requiring the Ethiopians to guarantee the Somali access to the grazing lands.

176

The Somali refused to recognize the relevance of any preindependence treaties defining the Somali-Ethiopian borders for three reasons: first, they maintain that treaties that gave away territory claimed or populated by Somali clans were not in accord with the agreements by which the clans placed themselves under Colonial protection; second, the Somali were not consulted on the terms of the agreements and in fact were not even informed of their existence; and third, such treaties violate the principle of self-determination. Because recognizing the validity of these treaties would indirectly recognize Ethiopia's sovereignty over the area, the Somali government has persisted in refusing to do so, even going so far as to refuse to acknowledge the British treaty guaranteeing grazing rights in the Haud, despite the need for access to preserve Somali herds.

Military incidents in the Haud began within six months after Somali independence. At first the incidents were confined to clashes between Ethiopian forces and armed groups of Somali nomads, usually arising over such traditional sources of conflict as smuggling, stock theft, or tax collecting rather than over modern nationalistic issues. In Somalia, however, despite their actual causes, the clashes tended to be viewed as expressions of nationalism. A hostile radio campaign by both sides further inflamed the feelings of the Ethiopians and Somali in the contested region. Incidents grew slowly in scale until the end of 1963 and gradually came to include limited confrontations between Somali and Ethiopian armed forces along the border. In February 1964 this confrontation became an armed conflict, and it quickly extended along the entire length of the Somali-Ethiopian frontier. The Ethiopian air force conducted raids on targets well within Somalia (see ch. 15).

Open hostilities were brought to an end in April by a cease-fire arranged under the auspices of the OAU by the Republic of the Sudan. The terms of the cease-fire called for an end to inflammatory radiobroadcasts, the setting up of a joint commission to examine border incidents, and the creation of a demilitarized zone six to nine miles deep on each side of the frontier. Although no further military confrontations occurred, the verbal hostility and the potential for future armed clashes remained high.

Between 1967 and 1969 the Egal government, as part of its overall policy, sought to reduce tensions with Ethiopia: it had considerable success. The SRC government generally continued this policy.

Improved Relations with Its Neighbors, 1967-75

At the beginning of 1967 the republic was faced with crises on all three borders. Because Somalia's demands for unification were among the most important issues affecting public opinion among Somali both within the republic and in the contested areas, there was little chance of ending these tensions. Yet it was clear to many Somali leaders that there were more important immediate issues to be faced by the republic as well as by its neighbors, particularly improvement of the economic position and welfare of the population. The search for solutions to these more important issues was being postponed as the border conflicts exhausted the slender reserves of both skilled manpower and financial means. Expenditures for defense were far above the combined total for education, labor, and health. Loans received in 1965, for example, for military equipment to expand the armed forces equaled more than a third of the government's total annual income.

Although still devoted to the concept of a unification of all Somali under one government, the government elected in mid-1967 under President Abderashid Ali Shermarke and Prime Minister Egal realized that it was not immediately attainable and was not likely to be obtained by force of arms. It therefore preferred to look for solutions to Somalia's other problems. In order to end tensions and ease the drain on the nation without renouncing the popular demands for unification, the government stressed that the issue was one amenable to peaceful solution by turning it over to the OAU as an intermediary.

Other factors contributed to this basic change in foreign policy. Somalia had been unable to obtain any important diplomatic support for its claims. The communist powers were willing to provide military supplies but did not wish to go further and antagonize Ethiopia and Kenya. The Arab states to which Somalia had first turned were sympathetic but were not really interested in affairs on this far edge of the pan-Arab world. The other group with which Somalia was naturally connected was the African states. Somalia was a charter member of the OAU, and pan-African ties are enshrined in the Somali constitution. Most African states, however, were alienated by what they saw as Somali irredentism and feared that, if Somalia were successful in detaching the Somali-populated portions of Kenya and Ethiopia, the example might inspire their own restive tribal minorities divided from their brothers by frontiers imposed in the colonial period. In addition, in President Jomo Kenyatta of Kenya and particularly in Emperor Haile Selassie of Ethiopia, the Somali had taken on two of Africa's most important elder statesmen.

At the same time regional cooperation was becoming an important economic consideration. This resulted in part from the fact that the United States and a number of international agencies had come to prefer providing economic and technical assistance for projects involving regional cooperation. Simultaneously the project for an East African common market took a long step forward with the agreement for the creation of the East African Community (EAC) during the summer of 1967. Membership in the EAC, initially composed of Kenya, Uganda, and Tanzania, was later to be opened to applications from Somalia, Ethiopia, and other countries of eastern Africa. The creation of the EAC seemed to offer Somalia increased expectations of new or continued preferential trading rights in external markets. Although the EAC later was largely to prove a failure, Somalia's expectations of an area common market continued into the 1970s. A final factor was the personal inclination of Egal, a British-educated pragmatist who had developed pan-African sentiments during his student days in London, where he had been a student with the late Kenyan political leader Tom Mboya.

The Egal government began to seek support for regional détente by including improved relations with the neighboring states in a program that obtained a parliamentary mandate in August 1967. In September Egal attended a meeting of the OAU heads of state at Kinshasa and took advantage of Haile Selassie's presence to propose that meetings be held at the ministerial level in order to seek ways to end their longstanding armed confrontation. Talk held in the Ethiopian capital resulted in a renewal of earlier agreements to ease tensions, including the ending of hostile broadcasts.

Under the sponsorship of Zambia's president, Kenneth Kaunda, the Kinshasa meeting also served as an arena for discussion between Egal and the leader of the Kenya delegation, Vice President Daniel arap Moi. This meeting was followed in October by a formal meeting at Arusha, Tanzania, between Egal and Kenyatta, again with Kaunda as host. The leaders signed a memorandum of understanding at the end of the meeting. The memorandum stated that Somalia and Kenya recognized the need to restore peaceful good-neighbor relations by stopping all hostile propaganda, gradually ending the state of emergency existing in border areas, reopening diplomatic relations, creating a committee to review periodically the ways and means of furthering and continuing good relations, and encouraging the development of economic and trade relations.

The memorandum caused an uproar among opposition leaders in Somalia who claimed an abandonment of the Somali in Kenya, but Egal won a vote of confidence on the issue. Relations between the two countries continued to improve during 1968 and the first half of 1969. The improvements included a restoration of trade, an ending of the activities of the Somali guerrillas, the lifting of the four-year-old state of emergency in the entire NFD, and the proclamation of amnesty for all guerrillas.

The progress of détente with Ethiopia was slowed, as it had been before, by popular reaction to incidents between Somali nomads and Ethiopian security forces. The northern Somali have a centuries-old tradition of conflict with Christian Ethiopia and have not always been responsive to the demands for moderation issued from Mogadishu. At least one of these leaders had demanded independence for the region from Somalia as well as from Ethiopia. Nevertheless slow progress was made, climaxed by an official visit by Egal to Addis Ababa in

September 1968. The agreement reached by the two governments at that time provided for commercial air and telecommunications connections, trade agreements, and the ending of the state of emergency in the border regions, all of which were aimed at decreasing the number of hostile incidents.

These steps toward peace improved Somalia's position in pan-African circles. The country had become a member of the loose organization of east and central African governments, which met frequently to discuss matters of common interest. It was also elected a member of the OAU's African Liberation Committee and declared itself strongly opposed to continued racial minority rule in southern Africa.

In October 1969 the Somali military leaders seized control of the government and imprisoned the previous civilian leaders (see ch. 9). Although the large army had been created specifically to carry out the actions required by the country's pan-Somali objectives, the new leaders made it immediately clear that they would adhere to Egal's policies toward Kenya and Ethiopia. The military government warmly welcomed the replacement of the Ethiopian emperor in 1974 by a military group that, like the SRC, pledged to bring about revolutionary changes in the society and to create a socialist state.

Friendly words, however, were accompanied by a continuing growth in the size and capability of the Somali armed forces, which by 1976 left Somalia with a significantly greater chance of success if it chose to rekindle the border wars (see ch. 15). The implications of this growth were not lost on Ethiopia or Kenya.

Nor were the Somali government leaders' comments always reassuring to their neighbors. For example, in 1973 at the annual meeting of the heads of state of the OAU, President Siad again raised the issue of Somalia's claims to Ogaden, spurred apparently by new reports about the imminent discovery of oil and natural gas deposits in the region. The government leaders claimed that Somalia's position did not place it in conflict with the OAU's policy regarding the inviolability of colonially imposed national borders because, as they saw it, theirs was not a border claim but rather a problem resulting from "continuing colonial occupation." In another instance, while reassuring outsiders that Somalia believed in peaceful coexistence and rejected the use of arms to resolve the differences over Ogaden and the NFD, the foreign minister concluded by saying that, if peaceful means did not succeed, Somalia would use other means. Thus despite significant improvements in Somalia's relations with its neighbors, the underlying major differences and the potential for renewed conflict remained.

The Djibouti Question

In contrast with the general improvement of relations between Somalia and Ethiopia, one issue continued—that concerning the small portion of the Horn of Africa over which neither country exercised control. This area was the French possession of some 8,000 square miles centered on the strategic port of Djibouti. In the mid-1970s the question of the ultimate disposition of this area, the FTAI, was the major problem facing Somalia's foreign policymakers.

Originally called French Somaliland, the area was officially called the French Territory of Afars and Issas after December 1966. Since 1958 the territory has been part of the French Republic, with elected representation in the French National Assembly in Paris. This smallest fragment of the Horn of Africa is worth fighting over because it contains the important modern port of Djibouti, which serves as the terminus of the Franco-Ethiopian Railway. The railroad, running from the port to the Ethiopian capital of Addis Ababa, is the irreplaceable main route for most of Ethiopia's foreign commerce. For this reason the territory is of strategic importance to Ethiopia, and any change in its status must take Ethiopian reactions into consideration. Given its disagreements with Somalia over present-day boundaries and the hold Somalia could exert over Ethiopian foreign trade if it possessed Djibouti, informed observers considered it probable that the Ethiopians would be prepared to go to war rather than permit the area to pass into Somali hands when the French forces left.

The territory is not of great economic importance to Somalia, and its Somali population is minuscule compared with perhaps 1 million Somali in Ethiopia and Kenya combined. Any Somali efforts to annex Djibouti after the French departed would be motivated primarily by the popular reaction within the country against allowing any further area inhabited by Somali to fall into Ethiopian hands and by the belief that control over Djibouti would allow the Somali government to exert pressure on Ethiopia for a lessening of its control over other Somali-populated areas.

The strategic portion of the territory is very open to Somali influence. For nearly the first 100 miles of its length the railroad lies within ten to twenty-five miles of the Somali border. Somali are probably in the minority among the population of the territory as a whole, but nearly all the people of the southern areas through which the railroad runs are Somali, principally of the Issa section of the Dir clan-family. In Djibouti the Somali probably represent the major portion of the population. The largest population group in the territory is the Afar (Danakil), ethnically closely related to the Somali but historically their enemies.

The urbanized Somali of Djibouti hold most of the lower echelon semiskilled and skilled positions in public and private enterprise. Yet even those with such apparently permanent ties to an urban life and to the French enclave are legally Somali citizens and generally maintain a second home within the republic, to which they remit much of their earnings. The level of opposition to French rule was first demonstrated by prolonged rioting in Djibouti on the occasion of President Charles de Gaulle's visit in late 1966. After the riots, in which a demand for an immediate end to French rule was the main issue, all Somali who could not prove their citizenship were expelled from the territory. A plebiscite was held under French supervision in March 1967 and resulted in a victory for those supporting continued ties with France. The Somali government refused to recognize the validity of this plebiscite, claiming that the election was unfairly conducted. Riots and violence between the Afars and the Issas continued over the next decade.

In 1968 a legislative council was created in the FTAI with broad responsibility for most internal matters. Twenty-six of thirty-two seats in the chamber went to the Afar Party, led by Ali Aref Bourhan. Ali Aref was able to develop some Issa support, forming a government composed of eight Afars and three Issas. The French government, represented by a high commissioner, retained control of foreign, defense, and security affairs and of the currency. It also controlled the court system, law enforcement, and citizenship, the last a vital matter as it left in French hands the decision over who in the highly fluid population had the right to vote.

A new legislative council, this time with forty members, was elected in November 1973. Ali Aref's party won all the seats, although it was widely believed that the opposition's supporters had been blocked from reaching the polls on the grounds that they were citizens of Somalia, not of the FTAI. France granted the new council and its cabinet of ministers additional powers, including control over the police.

The legal opposition party, left without an elected post, was the African People's Independence League. The Somali government provided support to one exile party, the Front for the Liberation of the Somali Coast (FLSC); Ethiopia harbored a second, the Djibouti Liberation Movement. The FLSC claimed that its use of violent means to call attention to its demands was forced on it by the repressive actions taken by the FTAI government. In order to prevent violence and to prevent an influx of Somali, a fortified barrier fence had been established around Djibouti. Nevertheless, in February 1976 FLSC supporters seized a bus filled with thirty French schoolchildren, threatening to slit their throats unless all political prisoners were released. The kidnappers attempted to drive the bus with the children on board into Somalia but were stopped and later killed on the frontier by French troops who also fired on the Somali border post, killing a number of Somali police and some civilians.

In December 1975 the French government had announced plans to grant the FTAI its independence as part of France's efforts to end the last of its colonial ties, long criticized in the rest of Africa. Independence was to follow a referendum intended to let the voters decide on the territory's future disposition. The initial French government statement, saying that its decision had been taken at the request of Ali Aref, seemed to indicate that France planned to continue to station defense forces there in order to block any postindependence military actions by Somalia or Ethiopia; it would also continue to use the port as a naval base. Other French comments, however, left a continuing military presence in doubt.

Ali Aref had lost much of his political support among the Afars between 1973 and 1976 and was forced to resign in July 1976. The opposition party, which gained Afar supporters as Ali Aref lost power, demanded immediate independence and an end to the French military presence, although it also opposed unification with Somalia.

The short-term expectation of independence for the pivotal territory, particularly in light of a possible withdrawal of French forces, led immediately to renewed and major tensions between Ethiopia and Somalia. Ethiopia accused Somalia of encouraging Somali to enter the FTAI in order to swell the rolls of supporters of unification in the expected referendum. Before the OAU it demanded that Somalia agree to guarantee the future independence of the FTAI. Somalia refused arguing among other things that such a joint guarantee would constitute an infringement on the future country's sovereignty. At the July 1976 summit meeting of OAU heads of state, however, Somalia again asserted that it would honor the territory's freedom.

Ethiopia clearly remained skeptical about Somalia's intentions toward the territory. In May and June 1976 the Ethiopian government was engaged in a major and costly effort to reduce the forces of the secessionists' movement in its Eritrean province. Like the Ethiopian Somali farther to the south, the Eritrean movement was associated with a nomadic Muslim people who could expect support from their coreligionists in the nearby Arab countries; Somalia was frequently accused of involvement with the Eritreans.

TIES WITH THE ARAB WORLD

Somalia's long-recognized ties with the Arab world are religious and historic as well as geographic and economic. The Somali were introduced to Islam centuries ago by religious teachers from the Arabian Peninsula, and Islam and Islamic culture are very strong common influences on the majority of Somali (see ch. 5). On the African continent the Somali lands were separated from the rest of the Arab world by the ancient Christian kingdom of Ethiopia, but on the north the Red Sea and the Gulf of Aden served as links, rather than barriers, to connect the area to Arabia and Egypt. Ties with Egypt began with the spice trade in early times, although commerce in this direction is of little modern importance; the Arabian Peninsula, however, was by far Somalia's largest export market in the 1970s, taking roughly half of its total exports. For a number of years British Somaliland had been administratively linked to Aden, which had a sizable colony of Somali—perhaps 20,000.

After independence the Republic of Somalia turned to the Arab world for diplomatic and economic support. In its support of pan-Arabism Somali political opinion is influenced by several factors, the first directly linked to long-standing cultural and religious influences: political ties to the Arab world are seen as strengthening Somalia's religious legitimacy. For those who support the achievement of Somali unification by the most radical means, including resort to violence and continued warfare, pan-Arabism is seen as the counterweight to the pan-Africanist policy, which requires that Somalia's international position be strengthened by gaining friends through relaxing tension with Kenya and Ethiopia.

Throughout the 1960s Somalia generally sided with the Arab cause on Middle Eastern questions. It invariably opposed Israel, primarily because of its own Arab connections but also because Israel provided military assistance to Ethiopia. Somalia's adherence to the Arab world was inhibited, however, by its desire to demonstrate its independence from outside control and to go its own way, and different political groups exhibited varying degrees of warmth toward the Arab countries. Most sensitive were relations with Egypt, then striving to be the leader of the Arab world. Egypt sought to increase its internal political influence in the country with mixed results. During the 1960s Egypt was the primary Arab supplier of aid. Its embassy maintained contacts with Somali religious leaders, and its propaganda had widespread dissemination and appeal. After 1967, however, Egyptian foreign policy in general adopted a lower profile.

The post-1969 military government continued the former government's policy toward the Arab countries, stressing cultural and other ties while seeking to remain at arm's length. Its relations with specific states were affected by its self-proclaimed scientific socialist position. Somalia thus came into conflict with the conservatism of many Arab states, particularly the wealthier ones, while also rejecting the Arab socialism of Egypt and the religious puritanism of Libya. The SRC did feel some affinity, however, with such radical Arab governments as those of Syria and the People's Democratic Republic of Yemen [Yemen (Aden)]. Saudi Arabia's conservative influence on Somalia's religious leaders was apparently feared by the government, which on occasion accused Saudi Arabia of interfering in Somali affairs. The most notable instance involved the clash between religious leaders in Mogadishu and the government over improved rights for women in January 1975, which culminated in the execution of ten mullahs, the most patently violent action the SRC took during its nearly seven years in power (see ch. 9). Charges of Saudi Arabian instigation of the mullahs, made at the time, were later downplayed by the president.

In the 1973 Arab-Israeli war Somali offered to send troops to the Egyptian front but did not; it did allow the Egyptian navy to use Berbera as if it were an Egyptian naval base. When the world oil crisis began to develop after the boycott and raising of prices by the Arab oil producers in late 1973, Somalia chose to accept the offer of membership in the Arab League that had been extended to it years before but had never been acted upon.

Somalia's decision to join the Arab League was announced suddenly on February 16, 1974, without the prior public discussion that characterized most other major decisions. The government then and later laid heavy stress on the long existence of religious, historic, and cultural associations as well as on past trade ties and future economic relations. League membership was accompanied within a year by substantial increases in foreign assistance. In return for the assistance and investment that the oil-rich peninsular states could provide, President Siad sought to stress his country's agricultural potential (see ch. 13). The moneyed but agriculturally poor states of the Persian Gulf were attracted by the possibilities of Somalia, which could be for them a nearby food source responsive directly to their future needs.

President Siad also stated that Somalia would give greater support to the Arab cause against Israel, apparently including a military commitment. In addition he sought to stress Somalia's usefulness as a link between the African and Arab worlds, especially during the year after entry into the Arab League when he held the post of president of the OAU. President Siad attempted to combine the roles by urging the Arab oil producers to seek African support against Zionism. In order to keep the African support they had gained after the oil crisis, the Arab states had to understand the problems the African states were encountering as a result of the rise in energy costs and respond to those problems by appropriate meaningful economic gestures. He also urged the Arab states to step in to replace the technical assistance programs many African states had received from Israel until they had voted to support the Arab side in the United Nations Middle East debates.

RELATIONS WITH THE COMMUNIST STATES

The government of Somalia from 1960 to 1969 was in the hands of men who generally regarded communism as in basic conflict with the strong religious convictions of their people. Moreover many of them were well disposed toward the Western states with which they were most familiar, particularly Italy and Great Britain. Nevertheless, as a reflection of their primary objective—demonstrations of Somali independence and self-reliance—the Somali government established diplomatic ties with both the Soviet Union and the PRC by 1961.

The PRC's embassy in Mogadishu was one of the first in Africa. By 1969 it had contributed considerable aid, totaling about US$23 million in grants and loans. Significant PRC aid continued in the 1970s, highlighted by funding and technical assistance for the construction of the first all-weather road linking Mogadishu to Berbera and thus connecting the northern portion of the country with the country's southern heartland and capital (see ch. 14). The PRC had also been active in the medical field and in 1976 was erecting a maternity and pediatric hospital in Mogadishu.

In 1976—in addition to the Soviet Union and the PRC—Bulgaria, Czechoslovakia, Cuba, the Democratic People's Republic of Korea (North Korea), and the German Democratic Republic (East Germany) had diplomatic missions in Mogadishu. North Korea was also providing aid, including construction of a cement plant, an iron foundry, a vegetable oil factory, and a technical college.

The major foreign influence on Somalia in the mid-1970s was clearly the Soviet Union. The growth of this influence began in the early 1960s when the Soviets agreed to provide Somalia a loan equivalent to US$32 million to finance the equipping and training of an expanding army, at a time when the expansion of the army was the most important national issue. By 1969 a large number of Soviet officers were serving as advisers in the Somali force, which was equipped almost entirely with weapons of communist manufacture (see ch. 15).

Beginning in 1961 the Soviets also provided a large amount of nonmilitary assistance. The first loan agreements were signed in June 1961 and by 1969 aid had included at least 450 scholarships for university-level and technical studies in the Soviet Union, assistance in agricultural and industrial development, and the provision of presses for the government printer and of broadcasting units for the national radio station.

The Soviet military aid was regarded by the Somali as support against Ethiopia. The Soviets' image was further enhanced by their lack of connection with colonial efforts in Africa. Some conservative Muslims tended to look on the Soviets not as atheists but as neutrals in the religious conflict with Christianity.

The major Soviet success occurred through their association with the army's leadership. By 1969 more than 800 Somali had received military training in the Soviet Union. The officer corps had become completely acclimated to a Soviet presence. Many of the officers, including the majority of the leaders of the 1969 coup, had become ideologically disposed to some form of Marxist-Leninist philosophy and saw in scientific socialism the best means for ending their country's abysmal poverty (see ch. 10).

The SRC military government, therefore, was inclined to turn first toward the Soviet Union for advice and assistance; the response was prompt and substantial. Between 1970 and 1975 supplies were provided to nearly double the size of the army, from 12,000 to 23,000 men. The supplies included 100 newer model tanks and twenty-four MiG-21 aircraft. The increased capability provided by the postcoup aid made Somalia's armed forces a considerably greater threat to neighboring countries (see ch. 15). From the Soviet point of view it bound the Somali much more firmly to dependence. It appeared that this dependence would continue to exist for as long as Somalia felt constrained by the threat of war with its neighbors to maintain what was, in proportion to the economy and population, the enormous burden of a very large army.

Soviet military aid went further than simply the supply of arms. Soviet training and tactical doctrine prevailed in the army. In 1975 an estimated 1,000 Soviet military advisers were present at all levels of the 23,000-man armed forces, and an average of 170 secondary-school graduates were being sent yearly to study in Soviet military schools (see ch. 15).

Soviet civil aid was also extensive after the SRC came to power. The Soviets, apparently spurred to compete with the impact of the large PRC roadbuilding project, began construction of an important hydroelectric and irrigation dam on the Juba River, Apparently their greatest success in cementing relations, however, had come from extensive humanitarian assistance to Somalia during the disastrous 1974-75 drought. The Soviets provided relief supplies and transportation in the form of an airlift and a gift of a large number of trucks to move 110,000 refugees to better lands in the country's south. The movement, which the Somali would otherwise have been unable to accomplish, both ameliorated the refugee problem and dovetailed neatly with the government's long-range plans to resettle large numbers of nomads in the southern agricultural zone. The Somali government appeared very grateful for this assistance.

Soviet aid was estimated to total about US$145 million through 1974, the majority of it nonmilitary (see ch. 12). Such large-scale aid obviously created links between the Soviet and Somali governments. The real form and substance of these links was clouded, however, and it was not entirely clear just how closely aligned with the Soviet bloc Somalia was. The Somali, always eager to stress their independence, must be resentful of the nearly perpetual burden Soviet aid places on their economic future in the form of loan repayments. The Somali, whose egalitarianism is exceeded only by their pride, find themselves in constant conflict with the pedantic and often arrogant Soviets, and widespread dislike of the Soviets is frequently made quite plain. According to President Siad a major reason for his government's close ties with the Soviet Union was that they "have not asked anything of Somalia in return for the unconditional aid they offer us."

The president's remarks brushed aside an issue of great interest, the Soviet navy's use of the port of Berbera. The Somali government continually denied assertions by the United States that it was allowing the Soviets to build a naval base at Berbera. The assertions, at first general, were documented in United States Congress hearings in June 1975. Their timing was resented by the Somalis because they came just as Somalia was most in need of more foreign assistance to combat the critical drought. The Somali government leaders continued to deny strongly that a Soviet base existed at Berbera and invited the United States Senate Armed Services Committee to inspect the site. They stated in their invitation not only that "the Somali government categorically denies the existence of a Soviet base in Berbera as elsewhere in Somalia," but also that the country "would never allow its soil to be used by [a] foreign power for the storage or deployment of means of destruction."

Nevertheless, when the congressional committee officials accepted the invitation and visited Berbera in July 1975, they concluded that there was a significant military facility and that much of it was under the control of, and the rest was used by, the Soviet navy. The committee was not able to determine, however, why the Somali government would continue to deny that the faciltiy existed while opening it almost without reservation to inspection. Despite the committee's detailed revelations, Somalia continued to deny that a base existed.

The basis for Somali-Soviet military cooperation in the mid-1970s was the formal Treaty of Friendship and Cooperation signed in July 1974 during the visit of the Soviet president to Somalia. Article 9 of the treaty states that Somalia may not enter into any military agreement with any country with which the Soviet Union is in disagreement, although the Somali in 1975 and 1976, in countering the accusations about the Soviet navy in Berbera, voiced offers to extend equal facilities to American naval vessels.

RELATIONS WITH THE WEST

Somalia's relations with West European countries and the United States have varied considerably in warmth but have remained important despite the SRC's close ties with the Soviet Union and other communist states. Resentment against Great Britain and Italy as the former colonial powers was not in evidence. Yet a considerable coolness toward Great Britain resulted from that country's incidental involvement in pan-Somali matters. The British government was blamed for the failure of efforts to reunite the Somali-populated areas of Kenya with the republic and for the loss of the important Haud region to Ethiopia. Diplomatic ties with Great Britain, broken over the Kenya issue, remained severed from March 1963 until January 1968. Once restored, relations with the British did not again become significant.

Despite some unfortunate experiences under Italian rule before independence, Somalia's relations with Italy since independence remained consistently good. Italian influences generally continued in the modernized sectors of social and cultural affairs. Until a script for the Somali language was finally agreed upon in 1972, Italian remained one of the country's four official languages. Italian economic assistance between 1960 and 1966 totaled more than a quarter of all the civil foreign assistance received, and Italy continued to fill a vital foreign aid role in the 1970s, largely through the European Economic Community (EEC, also known as the Common Market).

The number of Italians resident in Somalia had dropped from a maximum of 30,000 in the colonial era to 3,000 in 1965, but Italians still dominated much of the country's economic activities until after the 1969 revolution and were still influential in 1975.

Through Italy's sponsorship Somalia became an associate member of the EEC. This membership provided the country with another source of technical and economic aid but, more important, it kept open West European markets for Somalia's key exports (see ch. 12; ch. 14). After 1971 the SRC's nationalist and socialist policies had a decidedly adverse impact on the remaining Italian residents and investors. By the mid-1970s the share of Somalia's imports from Italy had declined markedly from that of a decade earlier. Nevertheless Italy remained an important market, second only to Saudi Arabia and surpassing all the communist states combined (see ch. 12; ch. 14).

The Federal Republic of Germany (West Germany) provided Somalia with a moderate amount of aid, notably sharing with Italy the training of the police force. Somalia's relationship with France centered on opposition to the continued French presence in the FTAI. A low point was reached after the March 1967 referendum that led to French retention of the territory, but Franco-Somali relations profited from the relaxation of border tensions under Egal. He emphasized this improvement by a state visit to Paris in September 1968. The SRC government also refrained from hostile activities toward the territory. Control of Djibouti, however, remains potentially the most explosive issue in the Horn of Africa, and in 1976 future Franco-Somali relations depended on a smooth French disengagement from the small but volatile territory.

During the 1960s the United States was the second largest supplier of nonmilitary aid to Somalia, a very large proportion of it in the form of grants. In 1966 there were thirty-six Somali on scholarships at universities in the United States as well as a significant number of

Peace Corps volunteers working as teachers in Somalia. The United States was also the major source of financial and technical assistance for the Somali national police. Trade between the United States and Somalia was negligible, however.

The image of the United States in the eyes of most Somali was more influenced by its support for Somalia's rivals, Ethiopia and Kenya, than by any American assistance to Somalia. The Somali were aware that the United States considered Ethiopia one of the most strategically important countries in Africa and that more American investments had gone to Kenya than to any other country in black-ruled Africa. The large scale of United States military aid to Ethiopia was particularly abhorrent: the fact that the aid had begun long before the Somali-Ethiopia conflict and was based on other considerations did not impress the Somali as long as the aid continued. Nevertheless relations with the United States did improve in the late 1960s as the threat of armed conflict with its neighbors diminished. A high point was reached in 1968 and 1969 with a state visit by Vice President Hubert H. Humphrey to Mogadishu and two visits by Prime Minister Egal to Washington.

The coming to power of the SRC brought an immediate decline in relations with the United States. The SRC's ideology oriented it strongly in several ways: toward the communist bloc and aginst the United States as the leader of the capitalist world; toward the Arab bloc and against the United States as Israel's primary benefactor; and toward the radical African bloc and against the United States as one of the states that maintained ties with the white regime of southern Africa. The SRC also suspected that the United States, as an active supporter of the previous democratically elected government, would involve itself on the side of any anti-SRC elements. It was presumably such suspicions that led the government to expel the Peace Corps program in December 1969 and five employees of the United States embassy and the Agency for International Development in April 1970 after accusing them of engaging in counterrevolutionary activities. The low point in relations with the United States, however, came as a result of an issue far removed from these. As a revenue-raising measure, Somalia had allowed itself to be used as a "flag of convenience" state for ships owned by corporations in other countries. When the Somali government continued to allow ships registered under its flag to carry cargoes to the Democratic Republic of Vietnam (North Vietnam) over United States protests, the latter announced that, in line with congressional directives, its aid would be halted within one year.

The aid that was terminated by June 1972 had included technical assistance programs in agriculture and education as well as self-help assistance and food distribution under the Public Law 480 (Food for Peace) program. Two projects under way—the US$9.5 million aid toward the construction of a water supply system for Mogadishu and the reconstruction of the port of Kismayo—were allowed to continue until they were completed. United States bilateral assistance to development projects had not been restored as of mid-1976, despite the end of the Vietnam conflict and the interest expressed by the Somali government in a renewal of aid. The question of the Soviet base at Berbera clearly troubled relations between the two countries, despite President Siad's offer while visiting Washington in 1974 to allow United States naval vessels to call at Somali ports. A considerable amount of assistance from the United States continued to reach Somalia throughout this period, however, in the forms of contributions to multilateral aid programs and indirect disaster relief grain shipments.

CHAPTER 11

COMMUNICATION AND PUBLIC INFORMATION

The significant features of public information and communication in Somalia in the mid-1970s were that all modern media were completely in the hands of the government and its agencies and that the news and information broadcast or carried in the very few domestic publications were limited to what the government considered to be good for the Somali people. Mitigating this situation was the possibility for the educated elite to secure information from usually uncensored foreign publications available within Somalia and for anyone possessing a radio receiver to listen to a variety of foreign programs. Any information obtained from these outside sources, however, could be transmitted further only by word of mouth.

The most important medium was the radio. There were an estimated 200,000 widely distributed sets, including many owned by the nomadic population. Recognizing the value of radiobroadcasting, the government in the fall of 1975 almost doubled program time in Somali to fourteen hours a day. The printed media were still sources of information for only a comparatively small portion of the population. This situation was bound to change, however, as growing numbers of children in schools and adult literacy programs provided a larger reading population for materials printed in the new Somali script.

Oral communication, almost the sole channel for news until well after the end of World War II—except in Mogadishu and possibly one or two other towns—in the mid-1970s probably still constituted a major means for the dispersal of information, especially among the nomadic population. This was a natural consequence of the proverbial Somali interest in news and the penchant for collecting interesting information to relay as valuable gifts to relatives and even to strangers met in the course of travel. Such information might be expected to include in particular news outside the scope of the usual controlled radiobroadcasts. In the early 1970s, according to one report, the government tried to discourage the oral transmission of information it felt conflicted with its own views. The military regime's broadening of the governmental base in 1972 through the establishment of village and district councils may have introduced controls over certain kinds of word-of-mouth communication, but specific information relating to this situation was not available in mid-1976 (see ch. 8).

THE GOVERNMENT POSITION ON PUBLIC INFORMATION

The revolutionary government's approach to public information since 1969 has been that the basic aim is orientation to its values and policies. This view was summarized by President Mohamed Siad Barre in a speech in early 1971: "We have made it our duty to inform our people of whatever we believe to be of interest to them and to the country." Some indication of the government's basic concept was also reflected in the title of the agency, the Ministry of Information and National Guidance, which was charged with disseminating to the people through the mass media "what is good and what is in their interest" and advising them on "politics, life, and government laws."

Reorganization of the mass media after 1969 was intended to make them into instruments for the development of "ideological awareness" and the molding of a "collective conscience," in essence to encourage cohesiveness and cooperation in attaining economic, social, and political goals. In the process, however, improvements in such things as radio programs appear also to have occurred. In the National Theater a shift from foreign to national production, reflecting what was called the task of national reorientation, resulted in new opportunities for Somali artists, musicians, and poets. Many of the new works, including dramas, sketches, and songs, had revolutionary themes; some of these works were reportedly of high artistic merit.

Although in early 1971 President Siad expressed the belief that only through the Ministry of Information and National Guidance could the Somali people be united and news and proper guidance be given them, local political centers under the direction of the Ministry of Interior were also highly impor ant points of contact with the population. These centers, established in all villages and towns and in the quarters of Mogadishu, were first known as public relations offices but by 1972 had been designated guidance (sometimes also called orientation) centers. They were designed as places for social activities of all kinds—meetings, literacy classes, cultural events, and so on—but had the principal purpose of facilitating the indoctrination of the local population in the aims of the government and scientific socialism (see ch. 9).

THE PRINTED MEDIA

Newspapers and Periodicals

During the nine years of civilian government after independence the literate portion of the population had access to a varying number of daily, weekly, and monthly newspapers and periodicals that presented relatively freely the views of all significant elements in Somali politics. Because of the lack of a nationally accepted orthography for Somali, however, these publications appeared in English, Italian, or Arabic—one was also in Osmanya (a form of Somali orthography)—and their readers probably constituted little more than 3 or 4 percent of the population (see ch. 7). In 1968 some fifteen periodicals appeared fairly regularly. Four had estimated circulations of over 1,000 copies; three of these were owned by the government, and the fourth belonged to the dominant governing party, the Somali Youth League (SYL). The majority of publications, however, had very limited circulations and for financial reasons were often short lived.

After the military takeover in October 1969 independent periodicals ceased publication, and by late 1970 all newspapers and periodicals appeared to be issued either by the Ministry of Information and National Guidance or by other governmental bodies. Included among ministry publications were the daily *October Star* in English, similar dailies in Italian (*Stella d'Ottobre*) and Arabic (*Nagmat Uktubir*), and a weekly, *The Dawn*, in English. The ministry also published the magazine *New Era* in English and an Italian version, *Nuova Era*. An English-Arabic weekly *Horseed* (Vanguard—*Al-Taliah* in Arabic), which identified itself as independent, was also appearing.

A major change in the press was effected by the government in early 1973 when the new Somali national script was introduced. For domestic purposes use of languages other than Somali was considered irrelevant, and from late January a new newspaper in Somali, the daily *Xiddigta Oktoobar* (October Star), replaced the foreign-language editions; *The Dawn* was also discontinued. *Horseed*, which had added Italian as a main language, continued, however.

In early 1976 the domestic press consisted of the two newspapers *Xiddigta Oktoobar* (estimated circulation 12,000) and *Horseed* (4,000). The former was of tabloid size and usually of four pages. Some foreign news was carried and attributed to such sources as Agence France Presse (AFP), Reuters, and the Soviet news agency TASS, among others. Local news, at least in part, came from the Somali National News Agency (SONNA). *Horseed*, published every Friday, was also of tabloid dimensions and ordinarily eight pages in length. Usually half the newspaper was devoted to articles in Italian, the other half in Arabic. On occasion items appeared in English concerning the Communist Party of the Soviet Union, activities of Soviet leaders, and information on other East European communist states. Materials from the Democratic People's Republic of Korea (North Korea) were also in English. Many of these items were releases furnished by communist embassies. The news was highly politicized, and comments and articles showed a strong Marxist-Leninist orientation. The newspaper carried in its masthead the statement in Italian (and a similar statement in Arabic) that it was an "independent weekly in Italian and Arabic." Informed observers, however, were strongly of the opinion that the newspaper was controlled by the Ministry of Information and National Guidance.

In 1976 the Ministry of Information and National Guidance continued to publish New Era in English, Italian, and Arabic editions primarily for distribution abroad; a Somali edition was also issued. Total circulation was about 8,000 copies. The several other periodicals published in Somalia dealt with specific fields, such as banking, economics, education, and law. The government also issued an official gazette, Faafin Rasmi ah (earlier called the Bollettino Ufficiale), which was published on a regular monthly basis although the number of supplements varied from month to month. After April 1973 the materials carried were usually in Somali, but items in Italian or Arabic occasionally appeared.

The Somali National News Agency

The press and the Somali Broadcasting Service (SBS) were furnished with domestic and world news by SONNA, which also published a daily news bulletin in English (about 200 copies a day in early 1976) providing information on Somalia to the foreign community. Formally established in July 1963, although it first began operations only in mid-1964, SONNA was also designated at its inception as the sole agency for the reception and distribution in Somalia of foreign press agency services, a provision that remained in effect in 1976. During the 1960s several international wire services maintained offices in the country, but none did so in mid-1976. In the mid-1970s only TASS was reported to have a representative in Mogadishu; other services covered events in Somalia through correspondents stationed in East Africa.

Books and Printing

In mid-1976 the country's printing industry was completely in government hands, the result of nationalization in October 1972. The organ in charge was the State Printing Agency, established originally in 1967 but reorganized as an autonomous body in January 1971. Information on existing facilities was meager. The principal printing establishment was the government printing house in Mogadishu, a main part of which had been constructed and equipped by the Soviet Union and given to the government in 1964. The Development Program 1974-1978 envisaged a considerable expenditure, concentrated in the first three years of the program, to provide additional machinery and equipment for expansion and modernization to meet current and anticipated requirements.

One of the major reasons for the 1972 nationalization was the coming introduction of the new Somali script, scheduled for January 1973, and the anticipated tremendous demand for new textbooks and literacy materials that would have to be printed as quickly as possible. It was reported that during 1973 almost 263,000 textbooks for elementary, intermediate, and secondary schools and more than 1.2 million books designed principally for planned literacy campaigns were published (see ch. 7). The Development Program 1974-1978 projected an output of materials in these categories, as well as various government publications and other books, of about 24.5 million units annually during the program period. In mid-1976 the lack of any reports on actual production prevented assessment of the progress being made.

BROADCASTING

Radio Service to 1969

The country's first radio service was initiated by a British army 100-watt transmitter set up in Hargeysa in 1943. Known as Radio Kudu (after the Kudu antelope then common in northern Somalia), its program consisted of little more than British Broadcasting Corporation (BBC) news rebroadcast in Somali, Arabic, and English. In 1944 the British military administration took over the operation. The broadcast range was increased by installation of a 600-watt unit (at which time the station was renamed Radio Somali); this was replaced a year later by a one-kilowatt transmitter. No further increase in power output occurred until 1957, when a five-kilowatt unit was installed.

By the 1950s programs had been expanded to include, in addition to news, presentations of Somali classical and modern poetry, music, and other cultural items. Materials and information on Great Britain were also regular parts of the broadcasts. The British colonial administration, which had assumed control of operations in 1948, permitted substantial freedom to the Somali broadcasters in handling programs. It also endeavored to increase the listening public by establishing community listening centers in the principal towns and by distributing battery sets to district offices, police posts, and village leaders. The community centers drew large audiences, and enterprising coffee shop operators soon installed radios as a customer draw; during the late afternoon local program broadcasts, most of the male population of the northern towns could be found either in coffee shops or at listening centers.

The first station in the southern part of the country, which again came under Italian administration as a United Nations trusteeship in 1950, was established in Mogadishu in 1951. This was a small unit of only 200 watts and of very limited range. It was the territory's sole broadcasting facility, however, until 1959, when it was replaced by a five-kilowatt transmitter. Its programs included news in Somali and Italian and Somali cultural features—songs, music, and poetry—as well as, later, some informal educational broadcasts. Efforts by some staff members to secure permission to broadcast in Central Somali, the dialect used by the Rahanwein, who constituted most of the local listening audience, met with opposition from both the Italian administration and other Somali staff members who used the more prevalent Common Somali; this reduced the radio's effectiveness (see ch. 4). Receiving sets were scarce because of costs, and the Italian administration did little to popularize the radio. A limited number of outdoor listening places, however, were set up in Mogadishu, and a loudspeaker-equipped set was given to each district commissioner.

In 1960 facilities at Hargeysa were expanded by the addition of a ten-kilowatt shortwave transmitter provided through British funds. This began operating in 1961. The addition was apparently the result of British interest in improving favorable broadcasting in the eastern African area to counter increased programming to Africa by countries of the East European communist bloc. British activities at Hargeysa ceased, however, with the breaking of relations by Somalia in 1963 (see ch. 10). (When the British withdrew, they also dismantled a powerful radio facility they operated at Berbera.)

A major improvement in facilities occurred in 1965, when a fifty-kilowatt transmitter constructed by the Soviet Union went into operation at Mogadishu. Operations of Radio Mogadishu (then Radio Mogadiscio) were further advanced in 1966 by completion of several modern, fully equipped studios provided as a gift by the Federal Republic of Germany (West Germany). Because of the lack of adequately trained Somali technicians, however, operation of the transmitter remained in the hands of a Soviet engineer for some years, and a program adviser and a studio engineer from West Germany ran the studios until 1970. Both, meanwhile, provided on-the-job training for Somali.

The new transmitter improved radio reception in Somalia to a limited extent only; because it was used primarily for the country's external service, domestic listeners had to rely largely on the five-kilowatt transmitter emission from Mogadishu and the ten-kilowatt transmission from Hargeysa for their programs. Some effort was made at this time to improve the staff, and program offerings were expanded. Programs were basically designed to entertain the listener or, in the case of educational and informative materials, to spread general knowledge rather than to promote governmental goals.

Broadcasting under the Supreme Revolutionary Council

In early 1976 radiobroadcasting was carried out by the SBS under the direction of the Department of Broadcasting in the Ministry of

Information and National Guidance. Radio Mogadishu was served by three shortwave transmitters. One of five kilowatts and a second of fifty kilowatts were used in the national home service. The third transmitter, of fifty kilowatts, had been installed under the Development Program 1974-1978 and was employed in the country's external service. Radio Hargeysa in the northwestern part of the country continued to use the two shortwave transmitters, one of five kilowatts and the other of ten kilowatts, that it had operated since the early 1960s.

In late 1975 Radio Mogadishu was broadcasting thirteen hours daily in Somali and Radio Hargeysa four hours daily. The foreign service operated almost six hours daily and included, in addition to programs in Somali, offerings in Arabic, Afar, Amharic, Galla, Swahili, French, English, and Italian. The domestic service had about forty regular feature programs each week covering a variety of topics. These included livestock and agricultural information and educational materials, sports, a children's program, and a program on women's activities—the home, nutrition, and the like, as well as information on women's rights and responsibilities in the new socialist society. Another feature presented top songs; this also included songs of a revolutionary and patriotic nature and dramas and sketches explaining and furthering government policies. Other regular features highlighted government activities, workers, and Somali culture, and several brief broadcasts daily dealt with the Quran and religious matters. The programs were designed to be entertaining, but underlying all was the philosophy that a major purpose of radio programming was to inform and familiarize people with, and encourage them to promote, the aims of the revolution. Accordingly this theme was interwoven in varying degrees in just about every broadcast (see The Government Position on Public Information, this ch.).

Foreign Broadcasts

In mid-1976 listeners could receive broadcasts in Somali from a number of foreign countries. The home service programs of the neighboring states of Ethiopia and Kenya and the French Territory of Afars and Issas (FTAI), broadcast to the Somali populations within their own borders, were audible throughout all or much of Somalia. Great Britain (through the BBC), Egypt, and the Soviet Union each broadcast one hour daily in Somali, and Italy provided a regular program in Somali for half an hour each day. In early 1976 the Voice of America (VOA) did not carry a Somali program, but its one-hour-a-day broadcast in Swahili to East Africa could be heard by Swahili-speakers in Somalia—found chiefly in the southern coastal region.

The most extensive foreign-language broadcasts by non-African countries that could be readily heard in Somalia were those of the

BBC in English (about eighteen hours a day) and of VOA (more than ten hours daily). Both the Soviet Union and the People's Republic of China (PRC) also broadcast English-language programs to the area, Italy broadcast over an hour a day in Italian, and the PRC specifically aimed a daily Italian-language broadcast of one and one-half hours at Somalia. There was no information on the extent of listening by Somali to any of the non-Somali broadcasts, but it seemed likely that at least the more educated portions of the population tuned in such programs.

FILMS

According to a United States Information Service (USIS) report, Somalia had about thirty-three motion picture theaters with a total seating capacity of some 45,000 at the end of 1975. All theaters appeared to be in urban areas—mostly in the southern part of the country—where they constituted the major source of entertainment for the urban population; attendance was estimated at over 8 million annually in the mid-1970s.

The production of films in Somalia was negligible and consisted almost entirely of documentaries; one feature film of unknown length was reported to have been made in the early 1970s, but no information on further production was available in mid-1976. American Westerns appeared to be extremely popular in the early 1970s, but later information was also lacking. About 450 commercial films were imported annually in the early 1970s. In 1975 approximately 50 percent of the total imports were of American make with Italian soundtracks; films produced in India constituted another 30 percent (it was not known whether these were dubbed in Italian). Of the remaining 20 percent about half were of Italian origin, and the other 10 percent came from the Soviet Union, the PRC, and other communist countries. Films from communist states were also ordinarily dubbed in Italian. The importation and distribution of films was in the hands of the Somali Film Agency, an autonomous body set up in 1971.

Since independence the government has censored films shown in the country. Throughout the 1960s a commission, on which the Ministry of Information was represented, was charged with preventing the screening of any film that might be damaging to morals, public order, or religion. During the decade, however, commission members did not engage full time in these duties, and few actions appear to have been taken. In January 1971 a new law established the Central Censorship Board, which had broader responsibilities that included film censorship. Under the provisions of the same law regional and district boards were also to be constituted. In March 1971, a few days after actual formation of the central board, a senior government official stated that from that point on no theatrical performance could be staged, no film shown, and no publication circulated without the prior approval of the board. Considerable detail on how censorship was to be effected, however, had to be worked out before the board could function properly. How effectively censorship was being carried out was unclear in mid-1976.

SECTION III. ECONOMIC

CHAPTER 12

CHARACTER AND STRUCTURE OF THE ECONOMY

Reliable statistics are lacking on the structure of Somalia's production and the progress of its economic activity. As a Least Developed Country (LDC), however, it is thought to be among the ten poorest on the United Nations (UN) list of twenty-nine; its per capita gross domestic product (GDP—see Glossary) was estimated at about US$80 in 1975. About 70 percent of the population was thought to be living at subsistence level.

Pending publication of data from the 1975 census, reliable information was also lacking on the occupational structure of the labor force. A manpower survey project in 1972 estimated that 6 or 7 percent of the economically active were engaged in industry and 11 to 13 percent in trade, transport, and services. Until the 1974 drought—the worst in living memory—left many northern nomadic families without livestock, some 60 percent of the population were thought to be nomads or seminomads relying primarily on stockraising for their livelihood and about 15 to 20 percent to be fully settled smallholders deriving subsistence and in good years a little cash income primarily from their crops (see ch. 13). In mid-1976 it was still unclear how the drought might affect this pattern. Past severe droughts had occurred in the north about every five years. After each one most of the nomads affected had rebuilt their herds, and livestock population had soon surpassed its previous size. In each instance, however, some nomads had lost their stock and had been obliged to migrate to the towns, where they swelled the ranks of the unemployed.

After the Supreme Revolutionary Council (SRC) government came to power on October 21, 1969, its earliest economic policy move was to launch crash programs for agriculture, public works, and community development. To absorb unemployment and avert delinquency numbers of young men were employed on self-help projects or on the state farms, where the harvests were in principle to be distributed to the workers in proportion to their contribution. State subsidy maintained these farms and three crop-farming settlements created in mid-1975 on the Shabelle and Juba rivers in the south for some 110,000 northern nomads made destitute by the drought (see ch. 13). Another 18,000 had opted to become fishermen. Some unemployment was also absorbed by significant recruitment into the army and the police.

A majority of the nomads in the relief camps, particularly those who had some stock left, had preferred to return to the pastoral life in the north. Only time would tell whether, once back on their feet, those who had turned cultivators or fishermen would also begin to think in traditional terms and wish to restore their lost herds. The British authority I.M. Lewis of the London School of Economics had suggested in 1972 that planned settlement of nomads may be most quickly and smoothly achieved when the initial incentives are pragmatic and survival oriented but that later the entrepreneurial appeal or profit potential must be stressed because pastoral nomads are "some of the thickest-skinned capitalists on earth, people who regularly risk their lives in speculation." He also noted, however, that past spontaneous settlement of nomads has often been associated with ideological change, as in the movement to religious communes (see ch. 5).

The 1972 manpower survey estimated that by 1971 nationwide employment (excluding family workers and plantation workers) included 67,203 private sector employees, 5,900 crash program employees, and 35,273 other public sector employees (including autonomous public entities). It predicted that by 1976 there would be 84,476 private employees, 13,900 crash program employees, and 69,569 other public employees. A May Day rally in 1976 was told that there were some 142,262 employees in the public sector as a whole and an additional 95,919 employed on periodic public projects.

Crash program self-help projects were of two kinds. Short-term projects to accomplish specific tasks, such as the stabilization of sand dunes and the rural literacy campaign, mobilized students, civil service workers, or army personnel for specified periods on what one aid mission described as "a more or less 'voluntary' basis." The anticommunist British journalist Brian Crozier alleged that jail terms await those who fail to "volunteer" for spare-time labor when requested. Recruitment for these projects puts the ideological objective of teaching social equality and dignity of labor uppermost. According to some reports the crash programs were also designed to avert delinquency and urban unrest. One source reported that many of those "recruited" were from the class of servants, shoeshine boys, and others in urban fringe occupations who were left idle when urban affluence was reduced by the anticorruption drive and the pay cuts for civil service and private employees in 1969 and 1970. They were rounded up on the streets of Mogadishu and sent to join work gangs.

In the second kind of crash program, for agriculture and public works, the objectives of providing employment and increasing production are reportedly dominant. One London journal reported in 1972 that the jobs created were only a drop in the ocean of unemployment, which had reached frightening proportions.

In the intensive public relations campaign that followed the 1969 coup President Mohamed Siad Barre explained the need for the coup in terms of national pride. He affirmed that the past regime, corrupt and servile, had shamed the nation and permitted undue interference by foreign aid donors. Use of foreign aid funds was alleged to have been riddled with self-interest, tribalism, and nepotism. The new government's approach, Siad said, would emphasize self-reliance and the broadest possible popular participation. Self-help efforts, as exemplified in the crash programs, combined these objectives and maximized use of the resource in most abundant supply, unskilled labor.

The regime's official philosophy of scientific socialism was declared in the first of its development programs to have the ultimate aim of building a completely socialist economy in which the state would control the means of production. The statement recognized, however, that the problems of limited resources and administrative capacity made it necessary to have some private and foreign investment and made "the continued existence of a mixed economy, as a transitional stage, inevitable." Moreover the new society was to be based on broad popular acceptance and would therefore require a massive preparatory educational effort.

Explaining the government's gradual economic policy approach retrospectively in 1975, President Siad stressed that the first five years of SRC rule had been needed "to mobilize the people, prepare and guide them." Thereafter the government's task would be "to mark out a clear path for the implementation of scientific socialism."

Later in the year he declared that the political awareness of the workers had not yet reached the required level. Many of the self-help projects were being inefficiently run. In the first five years of SRC rule things had not worked out as planned; the reason, he said, was insufficient understanding of scientific socialism and the failure of officials to understand their responsibilities. There was still evidence of such lingering evils as regionalism, tribalism, and nepotism.

Although bureaucratic corruption and duplication of effort had not been entirely eliminated by mid-1976, most reports found that they had been visibly reduced. The government had greatly improved fiscal performance in mobilizing domestic resources for development, at least in the years 1971 through 1973, when for the first time the current budget, instead of being in deficit, had yielded a surplus that could be used for self-financing of nearly one-third of development expenditure. Despite the strong emphasis in official rhetoric on self-reliance, the government had also been highly active in mobilizing foreign assistance. This proved particularly advantageous in 1974 and 1975, when import prices were soaring and government spending was diverted to drought relief. Many of the development achievements highly publicized in the 1971-75 period, however, had originated in planning, feasibility studies, or construction undertaken by foreign aid in the 1960s, a fact discreetly glossed over in publicity.

There was more continuity in development policies in the 1960s and 1970s than was generally realized, but on some of these policies action had been dilatory under the parliamentary regime. For example, a draft land tenure law under study in 1966 had placed a lower ceiling on arable holdings than that of 1975; the latter, however, was enacted and might well be enforced. In some other respects the SRC regime found itself facing the same constraints and delays that had plagued the development plans of the 1960s. For example, the irrigation projects proclaimed as the major focus of the Development Program 1971-1973—which had also been proclaimed as the main tasks of the First (Five-Year) Plan 1963-67—were not even started during the 1971-73 plan period but had to be carried forward once again. The need for sophisticated feasibility studies in advance of foreign aid commitments was a continuing irritant to the policymakers, impatient for progress.

Although the crop and livestock economy remained primarily subsistence oriented, improved government price policy had some success in increasing the production of cash crops and the supply of cattle to the state cannery. Earnings from the major exports—livestock, bananas, and livestock products, in that order—had been increased. Reliance on food imports remained fairly heavy, however (see ch. 14). Subsidized large-scale state farming had reportedly produced low crop yields but was effecting some income redistribution and teaching young nomads farming skills and the values of collectivism. These values were less readily assimilated by smallholders, whose integration into the cooperative system had been disappointingly slow. Progress in this sphere was a central objective of the Development Program 1974-1978.

ECONOMIC POLICIES

In its early months in office the SRC made few economic policy declarations, concentrating on its "accounting without shame" campaign against corruption, accompanied by highly publicized arrests. Corruption had been an acknowledged problem in the late 1960s: former Prime Minister Mohamed Ibrahim Egal, in a mid-1969 speech, had attributed his difficulty in mobilizing fiscal resources to corruption among customs officers, allegedly bribed to turn a blind eye to smuggling. In November 1975 President Siad in his turn was obliged to issue a decree prohibiting high officials from meeting their families beyond airport customs barriers, complaining that many had encouraged their wives to engage in an active smuggling trade. Other sources reported that corruption had been reduced, however, and civil servants were reportedly working harder, although duplication of effort by scarce trained manpower remained a bureaucratic problem.

In the first year of SRC rule the definition of future policy direction was vague. The government had taken over 51 percent of Somali Airlines in December 1969, but in a November speech President Siad had disavowed any intention of nationalizing other business and had specifically reassured traders. Despite some uncertainty among foreign residents and businessmen, the foreign exchange controls imposed to prevent capital flight after the coup could be removed a month later.

On May 7, 1970, however, the government announced its decision to nationalize banking, insurance, electric power, the local distribution chains of foreign oil companies, and the sugar estate and refinery at Jowhar, semipublic since 1963 but one-half owned by an Italian firm. The Jowhar complex was the country's largest industrial producer; the four other large manufacturing plants had been built in the 1960s explicitly for state ownership and operation, but their production was still on a preliminary pilot scale in 1969 (see ch. 14). Some sources refer to the 1970 measures as nationalization of all Italian-owned firms, but in fact private Italian and other foreign-owned firms were still operating in Somalia in 1976. In addition to Italian firms, two British-owned commercial banks and the Shell-Caltex distribution network were nationalized in 1970. Somali and Italian banana planters were assured that their estates would not be nationalized, and at least the producing acreage remained intact in 1976 (see ch. 13). The Italian government expressed confidence that promised compensation for nationalized firms would be forthcoming and signed a technical cooperation agreement providing for more aid (see ch. 10).

The largely foreign-owned import sector began to lose confidence, correctly anticipating that as in other African countries the wholesale and retail trades would probably be the next taken over. In fact state monopoly of export trade in bananas and hides and skins, assumed in 1970, was followed by import monopoly in several products, further extended in January 1972 to monopoly of import, wholesale, and retail trade in key consumer goods. In October 1975 the government assumed an official monopoly in the import of most goods from motor vehicles to cooking pots; it also announced that the government would henceforth take over all retail sale of textiles and clothing. This measure would presumably affect a multitude of small-scale operators. A committee was to implement the measure and allocate compensation to the firms expropriated. In late 1975 the government also took over all foreign trade representation (see ch. 14).

Stagnation of business and imports in 1970 cut fiscal receipts, and aid inflow showed what proved to be a temporary decline. Since the coup relations had been deteriorating with the United States, which in June 1970 announced that all its economic development aid would be withdrawn within a year over the issue of trade with the Democratic

Republic of Vietnam (North Vietman) carried by ships flying the Somali flag of convenience (see ch. 10). The International Monetary Fund (IMF) had granted Somalia a special standby credit because a hiatus in foreign aid and export earnings was expected, but the exceptionally large aid inflow of 1969 remained to be disbursed, and ongoing aid projects were not interrupted.

A major expense incurred had been for the crash programs launched in February 1970. A 1967 aid mission had recommended seeking food rations from the World Food Program (WFP) to support the intensified program of self-help activity that was made an important element of the Second (Short-Term) Plan in 1968-70. The Development Program 1971-1973, prepared in 1970, declared that the experiment had been a success but denounced the previous government's self-help program as "limited in perspective and utility by the lack of a national objective." The statement added that in their self-help efforts "the people had to await the October revolution to receive guidance and encouragement for the energies they were willing to put out." The foundation for these allegations was not entirely clear, but the new government did establish a national committee to coordinate self-help efforts, and its recruitment, reportedly less voluntary than in the 1960s, had been more successful. The program became an important motif in President Siad's economic policy and in the government's image at home and abroad. In 1970 there was said to be a quickening of development activity both within and outside the framework of the 1968-70 plan carried over from the previous regime. By late 1970 self-help efforts showed readily visible signs of success in new irrigation ditches, rural centers, and upgraded local roads.

As a result of declining fiscal and foreign aid receipts and mounting expenditure on self-help and other programs, the government in August 1970 found itself faced by a sizable budget deficit. Italy had pledged to continue the budget support it had provided during the 1960s, but this would not have accorded with President Siad's views. In September 1970 the government consequently announced an austerity program to raise duties and taxes on luxuries and to reduce civil service pay scales.

The same statement announced that all private firms must cut pay scales and contribute the proceeds to a government development fund; this became known as the development levy. They were also ordered to free their employees at 2:00 P.M. for "voluntary social work," but one source indicated that this provision was allowed to lapse after four weeks. The development levy has continued to apply as a kind of extra income tax to all nongovernment employees, including those of public entities as well as of private firms. It is exceptional in affecting the lowest wage class but is highly progressive, ranging from 5 percent on the lowest wage to 45 percent on the highest salary. It was also intended, when first devised, to make the system equitable, as it corresponded in amount to the cuts effected in the civil service pay scale. As civil service pay has risen since 1970, however, the development levy has come to constitute an inequitable income tax burden on non-civil-service employees compared with that on civil service workers or the self-employed. Providing differential returns to those employed in different sectors may distort income distribution and resource allocation.

Under the previous government the deficit on the current operating budget had been reduced from Sh51.2 million in 1960 to Sh13.6 million in 1969 (for value of the Somali shilling—see Glossary). The budget deficit in 1970, at Sh16.8 million, had proved to be lower than expected, and for the 1971-73 period it was converted to a large current surplus that could be used to help finance the development (capital) budget. The 1970 civil service pay cut, though largely offset by increased spending on newly enacted pensions and other social services, reduced total current operating expenditure by 4 percent in 1971. Thereafter government current expenditure expanded rapidly, but the growth in imports, heavier taxation of imports, and the increase in direct taxes brought a rise in the current surplus from Sh38.5 million in 1971 to Sh53.3 million in 1972 and Sh71.6 million in 1973. Defense and police expenditure totaled some 40 percent of revenue during most of this period, constituting a more severe drain on public resources than in the majority of developing countries.

Austerity and self-reliance, reportedly major elements in President Siad's personal code, became watchwords of the new regime and, visible in practice, made an important contribution to its image at home and abroad. Because domestic resources were meager in relation to the lag in development and incomes, reliance on domestic financing for development remained limited but had been improved in the 1971-73 period relative to the performance of the 1960s. More important than financial constraints were those in skilled manpower, management experience, planning, and advance preparation of projects. An earlier decree on December 15, 1969, had restricted employment of foreigners to positions for which no nationals could be found, but more such positions remained than could be filled even with generous technical assistance from abroad.

The number of Soviet advisers increased from 190 before the coup to 800 or 900 in 1970 and to several thousand by 1975; many, but not the majority, were military advisers (see ch. 15). Italy supplied technical assistance for education, budget management, and public accounting, and technical assistance was received from a variety of other aid sources.

Self-help efforts maximized use of the most abundant resource, unskilled labor, but could be derailed by constraints in scarcer resources. One source reported that, although such projects flourished in every village and town, many were wasted because of lack of planning experience or lack of teachers for newly built schools. The labor-intensive intermediate technology favored in theory was not always preferred in practice. For example, irrigation and large-scale mechanized farming, adopted on state farms and as an eventual goal for the entire rural cooperative system, were more capital-and foreign-exchange-intensive than the simple dryland farming improvements for smallholders introduced by United States aid in the 1960s. In the mid-1970s these improvements were reportedly still providing the smallholders concerned with protection against crop failure in poor years and with yields twice those from traditional methods (see ch. 13).

On October 21, 1970, President Siad proclaimed Somalia a socialist nation in which the means of production were to be controlled by the state to free the masses from exploitation and to distribute the national income more equitably. By 1971 recent nationalizations and higher employment at previously nationalized plants had brought employment in the public sector to 38 percent of total employment excluding family workers. It was expected to be at least 50 percent by 1976.

In 1971 speeches interpreting scientific socialism for the people, President Siad declared that the state would not expropriate small-scale retail shops (see ch. 9). The October 1975 announcement that the government would take over all retail sale of textiles and clothing appeared in conflict with this promise, but it was not yet clear how thoroughly the announced policy would be administered. In Somali towns there are many small-scale textile and clothing shops, ranging down to open-air stalls where shirts are stitched. In 1974 and 1975 the government policy appeared to be one of prohibiting private investment in industrial enterprises of any appreciable size but of permitting small-scale private investment, particularly in joint ventures. Apparently both foreign and domestic investors were included. In 1975 the Somali Development Bank had under consideration applications for private investment totaling Sh28 million, mainly for small-scale import replacement industries for domestic production of beverages, paints, ceramics and tiles, and batteries.

In his October 1970 statement the president had emphasized that any attempt at industrialization would be doomed to failure unless preceded by the transformation of the stockraising and crop production sectors. Plan policy statements later stressed the immediate need to increase state farm acreage and employment and the eventual goal of assimilating all cultivating families into a system of cooperative farms.

The government definition of cooperative farming differs from that favored in most African countries. Participants will be expressly prohibited by law from retaining more than 1.2 acres of rain-fed or 0.5 acre of irrigated land in their individual family plots. Other acreage will be pooled and farmed collectively, using advanced technology.

This provision of the Cooperative Law of October 4, 1974, will apply only in Stage II of the formation of agricultural cooperatives, which will be the stage of full collective farming. Stage I will start with "multipurpose cooperatives" for joint marketing, supply, and community self-help projects and will proceed—once mutual trust and cohesiveness have been established—to the creation in conjunction with each multipurpose cooperative of a "semicollective farm" in which the use of equipment and services will be in common but each family will apparently retain acreage and stock of its own. This semicollective phase of Stage I probably corresponds to the usual definition of a cooperative or group farm. In this stage the government will retain a share in each cooperative, which must comprise at least two to six villages and 500 to 1,500 families, depending on conditions; in the collective farms of Stage II the minimum will be thirty families.

The sixty-five agricultural cooperatives formed by 1974 were just becoming eligible for credit and were not yet involved in marketing (see ch. 13). Despite this disappointing rate of advance, the Land Tenure Law of 1975, by limiting private tenure of arable land to two ten-year concessions, suggests that considerable progress in collectivization is expected by 1995. Some qualified observers, however, believe that the collectivization provisions of the Cooperative Law will never be implemented.

Asked in a 1975 interview why the government favors collective farming and resettlement despite their somewhat dubious results in other countries, the secretary of state for agriculture replied that the choice had been given serious thought and a policy of collectivization adopted because it permitted the use of machinery on large acreages; there was also a long tradition in the country of collective work in farming, if not of the sharing of harvests. This may have been an allusion to traditional religious communities (see ch. 5). In stockraising, resources had been increasingly devoted to government purchase and fattening of young cattle for processing or direct export; herders were in future to be encouraged to form cooperatives and engage in group ranching (see ch. 3).

In view of the need to increase domestic food supply with all possible speed, the government in 1975 was reported to be taking a practical view in not only allowing private investment in mechanized crop farming but even permitting the Somali Development Bank to finance purchases of farm machinery by private entrepreneurs. This policy was no doubt viewed by the leadership as transitional.

Some observers believed that the commitment to collectivization and nationalization would weaken as development progressed and dependence on Soviet assistance dwindled. President Siad was said to be less doctrinaire in regard to orthodox Marxism-Leninism than most of his young aides, but in defining the official orientation of scientific socialism he had on occasion stressed its kinship with the Soviet brand of Marxism and explicitly distanced it from the much milder African socialism espoused by many African governments (see ch.9).

Statements by the president in late 1975 and early 1976 referred to the SRC's initial task of mobilizing the masses and imbuing them with socialist ideology. In November 1975 he said this was not yet accomplished; in early 1976, however, he referred to the nation's readiness for social and economic transformation as "due a great deal to the ideological preparation of our people and to our deep conviction in the indivisibility of the revolutionary process the world over." One source in late 1971 had termed the odds against success of the indoctrination effort formidable, and its success in the mid-1970s was uncertain.

Officials were sent on reorientation courses or to the army for ideological indoctrination. After two years of SRC rule the leaders had reportedly had little success in radicalizing the bureaucracy. In mid-1975 fifty-seven officials were dismissed for "their ineptness in keeping abreast of the ideologies of scientific socialism," and in November the president warned that the government would not hesitate to punish anyone who opposed the policy of the nation.

A goal not stressed in policy rhetoric but pursued in practice was to increase monetization of rural subsistence production. Developing the cash nexus between government and rural activities could facilitate intervention and control of production. The many small subsistence producers could gradually be enlisted into cash marketing and supply cooperatives; by more flexible manipulation of prices the government could determine production options. A law forbidding farmers to retain more than 220 pounds of their combined maize (corn) and sorghum crop per family member had eeen enacted but not yet enforced by mid-1975.

Funneling crop and livestock earnings through the public coffers had also become, for most African governments, a means of determining the allocation of resources among productive sectors and the distribution of income among segments of the society. In the 1960s the allocative and distributive effects of public policies in Africa had often been largely accidental and insufficiently understood; finer tuning of fiscal and economic policies was being adopted in the 1970s just when it was proving less reliable in controlling the business cycle in the industrial countries. In Somalia a predominant share of economic activity is for subsistence; much of the remainder is in government hands. The vagaries of rainfall and seasonal floodwaters are far more important than anticyclical policy in determining the level of activity, of prices, and of living standards. Nonetheless such details of fiscal policy as the development levy and more minute and flexible adjustment of such economic regulators as seasonal crop prices and credit expansion may have a significant effect on resource allocation and on the distribution of income in the society.

212

A practical effect of government policy that might appear to be in conflict with current international neo-Marxist doctrine was its relative success in increasing production for export. For the most part this had not been at the expense of domestic food supply, as it had been in the 1960s, and it was hoped that reliance on food imports could be reduced by 1978. The increase in bank credit through 1973 had gone primarily to banana planters or government enterprise, however, and use of fertilizer and improved seed had been confined largely to production for processing or export. Until the drought rehabilitation projects of 1975, spending on the livestock sector was also largely for export or industry. Emphasis on export production remained a major feature of development planning.

Among longer term development objectives was an increase in the domestic processing content of exports and thus in the share of value added (GDP) accruing to nationals. The resource-based export industries for fish and beef canning had been denounced as white elephants built by a servile prerevolutionary government to placate foreign aid lenders. The onerous project loan debt incurred to the Soviet Union, however, was reportedly canceled in 1974. By 1975, having succeeded in obtaining better export prices from the Soviets and in improving supplies of raw materials, the processing plants were being hailed as significant achievements of the revolutionary government. As elsewhere in Africa, the import-replacement approach to industrialization had failed to yield the foreign exchange gains expected: the sugar complex had been fairly successful through 1969 but had since encountered problems, and the textile mill was still obliged to import some cotton (see ch. 14).

In 1972 industry was thought to account for no more than perhaps 8 or 9 percent of GDP and between 6 and 7 percent of the labor force. Plans for future manufacturing capacity that would replace imports included a cement plant and a refinery to process Iraqi crude oil, hitherto processed and shipped to Somalia by the Soviet Union. The principle that most new manufacturing should be based on the rather scant range of domestic raw materials was represented by a gypsum-producing pilot plant at the cement works and by heavy spending to improve the supply of raw materials to the processing plants built in the 1960s (see ch. 14).

In its foreign economic policy the Somali government has favored a united stand by developing countries that export primary products in pressing the more militant demands inspired by the success of the 1973 oil embargo of the Organization of Petroleum Exporting Countries (OPEC) and expressed in the Manila Declaration of February 1976. Among these are demands for the advanced processing of raw materials within the exporting country; for indexation to make raw material prices move automatically with those of finished products; and for a common fund to support commodity prices by buffer stocks bought at times of oversupply and low prices and sold at times of high demand and high prices. Another demand was the cancellation of all outstanding Least Developed Country (LDC) debts.

By 1975 this controversy had come to dominate international affairs, and the United States was at its center. Recognizing that "economic issues are turning into central political issues," Secretary of State Henry Kissinger, in a May 1975 speech, indicated that the United States might move from its traditional opposition to managed markets, at least far enough to participate in discussions of buffer stocks as a reasonable technique for commodity price stabilization.

At the Fourth Session of the United Nations Conference on Trade and Development (UNCTAD IV) at Nairobi in May 1976, the "Group of 77" developing countries (actually comprising 113 nonaligned nations) had concentrated on pressing its demands for the common fund. The demand was initially rejected by several of the industrial nations, notably Japan and the Federal Republic of Germany (West Germany). There proved to be little ground for agreement between the opposing positions; the outcome was a minimal compromise setting a timetable for voluntary discussions designed to move toward easing debt obligations for the poorest nations and toward piecemeal regulation of commodity prices. Bananas were among the first eighteen commodities that were to be negotiated between September 1976 and February 1978. The United States delegation stated that participation in the commodity consultations would not commit its government to negotiation of final commodity agreements nor would participation in preparatory meetings on the common fund imply any commitment to participation in the common fund negotiating conference. In mid-1976 the United States officially disagreed with the proposed New International Economic Order. Its reservations about the indexation proposal remained unaltered. It did not favor the proposal for blanket cancellation of LDC debts but proposed instead that future aid be on a grant basis.

In Somalia an article in the government-sponsored journal New Era in March 1976 had urged that the developing countries must present a common front in their economic confrontation with the industrialized world at UNCTAD IV. The proposals of the Group of 77 for the New International Economic Order, initially formulated at the sixth special session of the UN General Assembly in May 1974 and reaffirmed in the Manila Declaration, could be won in theory or in practical application only through united action. This foreign policy position makes sense for Somalia: only the relatively few countries possessing high-grade deposits of minerals in limited world supply, such as bauxite, could enforce some compliance with their more militant demands by unilateral action or through producers' associations. Since the Group of 77 had begun pressing its united demands in world forums, however, Somalia's aid position had measurably improved.

An August 1976 article in *West Africa* (London) noted that, in the growing confrontation between rich and poor nations, events since 1973 have provided the nonaligned nations with a satisfying explanation for their economic problems that places the United States and other Western countries in the villain's role, while the People's Republic of China (PRC) and the Soviet Union are often viewed as allies of the poorer countries. This tendency was reflected in a speech by President Siad to the Communist Party congress in Moscow, crediting solidarity among world revolutionary forces with enabling Somalia to recover from the 1974 drought disaster. He also referred to "the economic difficulties exported to the poor nations by the crisis in monopoly capital." The difficulties exported to the poor nations were reflected mainly in the deterioration in their terms of trade (the ratio of export to import prices) as simultaneous inflation and recession hit the industrialized countries in the wake of the 1973 energy crisis.

Besides passing the modified Declaration for the New International Economic Order, the May 1974 UN session on raw materials and development had initiated the UN Emergency Operation to assist those developing countries hardest hit by the decline in raw material prices and the rising cost of oil and manufactures. In May 1975 it became the UN Special Fund for Most Seriously Affected (MSA) countries. By 1976 the list comprised forty-two developing countries that had low per capita gross national product (GNP—see Glossary) and balance-of-payments deficits expected to exceed 5 percent of imports. At the top of the list were Rwanda and Burundi, each with per capita GNP equivalent to US$60; there followed four countries, including Somalia, having per capita GNP estimated by the World Bank (see Glossary) as US$70 in 1973. This put Somalia on the priority list for aid from the OPEC countries, which it received on a bilateral basis (see Uses and Sources of Development Finance, this ch.)

With the exception of hides and skins, Somalia's exports consist almost entirely of foodstuffs rather than industrial raw materials, so that it was not directly affected by the recession abroad, but its domestic economy felt the impact of world inflation. No national accounting aggregates are estimated for Somalia, but the resource gap between domestic supply (GDP) and aggregate demand (expenditure for private consumption, government current consumption, capital formation, and change in inventories) can be measured by the balance-of-payments deficit on goods and services, which increased fivefold from Sh137 million in 1972 to Sh423 million in 1973 and Sh716 million in 1974 (see ch. 14). Although the cost of petroleum fuels and lubricants had quadrupled in 1974, it was a relatively minor factor in the overall rise in imports, which was caused in part by deficiencies in domestic food supply and consumer manufacture and in part by the mounting tempo of development expenditure and spiraling world prices for manufactured goods.

From independence through 1975 all development imports and a portion of imports for current consumption by government and the private sector had been financed by foreign assistance. In the 1968-72 period the current deficits were offset by unrequited transfers (mostly aid grants) and capital inflows (mostly official loans) averaging US$28 million a year. In 1973 and 1974 these receipts increased to US$79 million a year but failed to cover the mounting deficit on goods and services; foreign exchange reserves diminished, and there was some short-term borrowing. In 1975, however, the resource gap was more than adequately covered by foreign grant and loan receipts of more than US$125 million.

During its first three years in office the government had been able to hold consumer prices down. Demand pressure was curtailed by the compulsory pay cuts of September 1970, but rising incomes apparently contributed to the pressure on the internal price level exerted by the rapid rise in import prices after the world energy crisis of 1973. As the pressure mounted in 1974, the government sought to hold consumer prices in line by narrowing profit margins for private traders and government trading agencies. On such government-imported products as wheat flour, maize, sorghum, tea, and sugar, profit margins were eliminated or turned into heavy losses. In effect the government was thus subsidizing consumption—possibly even smuggled exports—of these goods (see ch. 14). The effect on allocation of resources was probably negative. Rural food supply had suffered from the drought, so that the subsidies may have benefited rural consumers in 1974 and 1975, but their net effect was probably to favor town dwellers. Before the end of 1974 the government was obliged to put an upper limit of Sh140 million on subsidies and allow some prices to rise. The result was to produce a black market in food, which reportedly continued after rationing of staple foods was introduced for Mogadishu in March 1975.

Government policies on producer prices in the 1970s had brought some improvement in domestic food supply and in the supply of livestock to the government export cannery at Kismayo. Government regulation of livestock export had increased but, for lack of adequate market information, price adjustments were not flexible enough for optimum influence on supply and earnings. The monopoly grain purchase, storage, and price stabilization system established by UN agencies in 1966 became fully operational in mid-1970 and had reportedly been successful in obtaining supplies in good seasons for distribution in bad years; its storage capacity was to be expanded to permit adequate buffer stocks, and its price adjustments were to become more flexible to improve supply.

USES AND SOURCES OF DEVELOPMENT FINANCE

Development Planning

Lack of statistical data on the origin and use of national product limited the potential for systematic planning in terms of available manpower and material resources. Like those of most emerging African countries in the 1960s and 1970s, each of the four development plans formulated in Somalia since independence had consisted, to varying degrees, of a shopping list of desirable projects that would require financing well in excess of foreseeable availability at the time of plan publication. In such cases plan fulfillment, when expressed as a percentage of listed projects actually completed or in actual spending as a percentage of projected expenditure, is meaningless except as a warning that most development plans cannot be taken as an accurate blueprint for the plan period.

This was particularly true of the First (Five-Year) Plan 1963-67. The foreign financing received probably exceeded the capacity of the economy to absorb it but fell far short of the overambitious requirements projected in the plan. The Second (Short-Term) Plan 1968-70 was formulated as an interim program to continue a number of projects carried over from the first plan and to allow a breathing space that would permit certain administrative reforms required for more rapid development progress. Of the original 1963 list of projects a number were completed by 1969 and a few under the Development Program 1971-1973, but others were carried forward to the Development Program 1974-1978 and had not yet been completed by mid-1976 (see ch. 13; ch. 14).

The short-term plan acknowledged that defects in implementation of the first plan had included wasteful and unproductive use of foreign aid resources. This may have applied in particular to use of the Soviet commodity loan and project loan of 1961 (see ch. 13; ch. 14). Other major drawbacks cited were political preoccupations, deficient planning experience, and the continuing current budget deficit that limited Somalia's own public sector contribution to 15 percent of total development spending between 1963 and 1969. Deficiencies in the administrative machinery of government, however, were named as the single factor most responsible for the disappointing plan performance.

Ironically the planners affirmed in 1968 that attention to development had suffered in the 1963-67 period because first priority had necessarily been given to the achievement of political stability. President Siad, however, in explaining the need for the 1969 coup, later referred to his impatience with the inadequate attention accorded to development under the previous regime.

In announcing the Development Program 1971-1973 he placed great emphasis on the fact that the share of spending directed to the rural sector would be increased. As things worked out, however, this third planning effort encountered some of the same problems as the preceding ones. Its targets, though more modest than those of the 1963-67 plan, were overambitious in terms of available funds and skilled manpower; the dates set for completion of projects were unrealistic in that they failed to allow for advance preparation required.

In view of these constraints the rate of progress achieved was quite good in livestock supply and disease control, in food grain marketing and price stabilization, and notably in expanding the agricultural crash program. The more ambitious the target, however, the greater the apparent shortfall in fulfillment; this was particularly conspicuous in irrigation, which had included some of the most ambitious projects. Most of these—such as the Bardera dam, the flood control project, and projects for irrigated production of cotton, sugar, food grains, and bananas—were carried forward to the Development Program 1974-1978 and were in the course of fulfillment in 1976. Less conspicuous in the statistics but more meaningful in terms of rural living standards and of crop yields was the poor rate of progress in forming cooperatives and providing extension guidance and improved inputs to smallholders, who received no farm credit at all until 1974 (see ch. 13).

Despite these disappointments about two-thirds of planned investment expenditure under the Development Program 1971-1973 had taken place, and one-third of this investment had been financed from domestic resources. Estimates of domestic spending reportedly did not include any attempt at valuation of the labor invested in self-help projects, nor did it include the WFP food rations provided to compensate self-help labor. It turned out that, as in earlier plans, a higher share of actual spending went to basic infrastructure (45 percent) than to the rural sector (20 percent); but some of the spending on infrastructure was for water supply for stockraising. The share of transport and communications infrastructure was 29 percent.

The improvements in basic infrastructure and the other investment effected under each plan increased capacity to absorb and make effective use of the expenditure allocated under succeeding plans. The autonomous agencies for crop and livestock supply and marketing created in 1966 had been expanded to provide the framework for utilizing increased spending in the 1970s. Planning capability had been somewhat improved, although manpower constraints prevented the central planning organ from carrying out many of its functions and capacity for adequate project preparation was still lacking.

The SRC leaders had shown a capacity to learn from the trial and error experience of the 1960s as well as to make political capital from criticizing it. This was evidenced, for example, by the declaration that industrialization could never succeed without prior rural transformation. The tremendous emphasis placed on mobilizing popular opinion, though strongly politically and ideologically motivated, seemed also to reflect the lesson of experience that development, to be effective and lasting, must enlist the broadest possible grass-roots participation and minimize the gulf between the rural producer and the educated urban elite.

In this respect plan preparation was improved in advance of the Development Program 1974-1978, reportedly the first of the four plans to be an essentially Somali product. To ensure participation of the rural areas, multidisciplinary teams led by central planning staff traveled to all parts of the country and had discussions with local councils. The new plan, more production oriented than the previous plans, called for an increased share of investment for the rural sector.

The investment targets set for 1978, however, bore little relation to past performance. Development spending had attained a record high in 1973; at Sh340 million it was thought to be equivalent to about 22 percent of GDP. The plan called for it to be increased to Sh855 million in 1974. Some considered this unrealistic in view of known manpower and planning constraints, and in fact fulfillment during the first year of the plan was markedly low. Tax receipts in 1974 had shown a small decline instead of the large increase projected, and current spending on famine relief alone took Sh168.4 million. For the 1974-78 plan period the internal contribution through public savings was to have been tripled; by 1975 it appeared unlikely that this could be achieved.

When the plan was published in 1974, it was considered by some qualified analysts to be overambitious and inadequately planned. They added, however, that in view of the government's serious commitment to economic development and its record of success in obtaining foreign loan commitments, the plan might have a better chance of fulfillment than past performance would suggest. A number of large and costly projects had reportedly been included primarily because there seemed to be good prospects for foreign financing; this might account for some of the apparent large discrepancies between past performance and projected future progress in such categories as irrigation. By early 1977 the prognosis had greatly improved both for fulfillment of the original plan and for new projects under the drought rehabilitation program formulated in 1975 and 1976. (see ch. 13).

Before the drought rehabilitation program was added, some informed analysts had found the plan somewhat unbalanced and unlikely to promote broad-based rural development. Spending on the livestock sector had been earmarked primarily for government activity; the provision for range regeneration was inadequate to the need, and no funds had been projected for resettlement or other measures benefiting nomads. Spending allocated to the agricultural sector seemed destined to promote large-scale collective farming at the expense of improved crop yields. This outlook was improved to some extent after the drought crisis. Four IDA missions visited the country in 1975 to identify promising projects and coordinate donor financing; the three projects for which financing had been confirmed by mid-1976 seemed likely to accelerate the pace of rural development on a broader base than before (see ch. 13). In 1976 the Development Program 1974-1978 was reportedly undergoing revision to take account of the new order of priorities, reduce the estimate of internal financing, and find new uses for foreign finance.

The Development Program 1974-1978, as published in 1974, specified that 32.6 percent of projected development expenditure was to be covered by domestic financing and 67.4 percent, or Sh2.7 billion by foreign financing. In the absence of better data foreign financing confirmed may offer a relatively meaningful basis for assessing how realistic a plan is when published and what level of fulfillment may reasonably be expected by target date (see table 1).

Of the foreign financing proposed in the plan, 55.2 percent had been confirmed by mid-1975; 61.6 percent had been officially confirmed by September 1976. The 1976 total included some credits that exceeded the projected spending proposed in the plan, including the first phase of the Mogadishu port project, a credit for extension of the port project, and the International Development Association (IDA) credits for the North West Region Development Project.

Press reports also asserted that Arab financing had been obtained for three major projects that account for much of the remaining spending proposed for foreign financing. The reports did not make clear whether these agreements had been signed and the financing decisively confirmed, nor did they specify the amount of financing granted. Nevertheless they have been tentatively included in the estimate of financing confirmed and bring the estimate up to 75.2 percent.

Because of the tighter budgetary situation after 1973 the plan as published probably substantially overestimates the share of spending that can be met by internal financing and thus understates the total of planned foreign financing. Moreover the steep rise of world prices since late 1973 meant that, to achieve the physical targets set when the plan was drafted, total spending might have to be considerably higher than projected.

Projects reported as physically completed by September 1976 accounted for 7.8 percent of total planned expenditure listed in the plan. They included Phase I of the Mogadishu port project, completion of the Kismayo airport, paving of the road between Berbera and Hargeysa, and engineering feasibility studies of the roads from Hargeysa to Borama and from Golweyn to Gelib.

Probably more important in the long run than the foreign loans provided to finance the development program were those for the

Table 1. Somalia, Planned and Actual Development Spending, Selected Years, 1963-78
(annual average in millions of Somali shillings)[1]

	Planned				Actual	
	1963-69	1971-73	1974-78	Drought Program[2]	1963-69	1971-73
Spending by Sector of Activity:						
Stockraising and range development	13.0	23.1	37.9	33.1	8.6	18.7
Irrigation	15.6	13.0	118.3	35.2	3.5	6.2
Agriculture, forestry, and fishing n.e.s.	53.2	37.3	127.0	108.8	52.7	23.0
Water supply	16.8	39.8	27.9	n.s.s.	21.8	35.1
Manufacturing, mining, and power	70.4	42.9	154.1	---	44.0	39.1
Transport and communications	188.3	117.7	188.9	---	103.3	63.6
Education	15.3	16.2	38.2	---	12.6	9.7
Health	12.9	23.7	15.5	8.6	9.9	11.1
Social n.e.s.[3]	21.5	9.5	33.7	---	15.1	4.5
Tourism	---	4.5	2.5	---	---	6.7
Other[4]	7.7	5.5	28.7	---	0.4	1.2
Total Development Spending	414.7	333.2	772.7	185.7	271.9	218.9
Sources of Financing:						
Soviet Union	...	...	48.4	88.3	55.6	...
People's Republic of China	...	...	74.0	---	5.6	...
Democratic People's Republic of Korea	...	...	31.6	---	---	...
United States	...	...	---	---	46.6	...
Western Europe, bilateral[5]	...	...	n.r.	---	27.7	...
European Development Fund	...	...	66.7	---	35.0	...
Other multilateral sources	...	...	74.4	29.1	51.9	...

Table 1. *Somalia, Planned and Actual Development Spending, Selected Years, 1963-78—Continued* (annual average in millions of Somali shillings)[1]

	Planned			Drought Program[2]	Actual	
	1963-69	1971-73	1974-78		1963-69	1971-73
Arab countries[5]	...	...	140.5	68.3	2.1	...
Other or unspecified sources[5]	...	...	8.1	---	6.8	...
Foreign financing confirmed	...	...	443.7	185.7	231.3	153.9
Foreign financing not yet confirmed	...	...	18.9	---	---	...
Planned internal financing, listed	...	...	138.2	n.r.	40.6	65.0
Other projects, financing unspecified	...	...	171.9	---	---	...
Total Development Financing	...	...	772.7	185.7	271.9	218.9

--- means none; ... means none; ... means not reported; n.e.s. means not elsewhere specified; n.r. means not reported; n.s.s. means not separately specified.

[1] For value of the Somali shilling—see Glossary.

[2] Assumes spending is allocated for a four-year period. Assumes Sh352.8 million from Soviet Union in June 1975 was entirely for drought rehabilitation program. Probably an overestimate.

[3] Includes for the 1963-69 period community development (water and other services for nomads and villages); for 1971-78 period housing and labor training.

[4] Includes statistics, mapping, and since 1971 information service.

[5] Financing expected from West European countries in the 1974-78 period is not listed in the plan. In the 1963-69 period the category "other or unspecified sources" included Egypt, Eastern Europe, France, and West European countries other than Italy and the Federal Republic of Germany (West Germany).

Source: Based on information from Somalia, Ministry of Planning and Coordination, *Development Programme, 1974-1978*, Mogadishu, 1974, pp. 18-29; German Planning and Economic Advisory Group, *Report on the Progress of Development Projects in the Somali Democratic Republic*, Mogadishu, 1969; and Ozay Mehmet, "Effectiveness of Foreign Aid: The Case of Somalia" *Journal of Modern African Studies*, London, May 1971, p. 39.

drought rehabilitation program initiated in 1976. Information available in mid-1976 did not specify the time period projected for the three major projects involved; it is assumed to be four years, so that the total of Sh742.7 million received would permit spending averaging Sh185.7 million a year. This calculation also makes the perhaps arbitrary assumption that the Soviet loan of US$60 million provided in mid-1974 was to be spent entirely on drought resettlement and rehabilitation.

Development Assistance

In a 1975 interview President Siad confirmed that the principal objective of SRC economic policy was equitable distribution of income but added that an adequate national income must first be attained through an intensified development effort. He believes that foreign aid often carries strings and makes little contribution to development and improved productivity at the grass roots. The ultimate goal is to make the country independent of world capitalism, but this can best be achieved by accumulation of enough fixed capital and national wealth to make the country self-sufficient. The SRC government therefore recognizes the necessity for foreign aid and limited foreign investment during the period of transition to a socialist society.

During the mid-1970s cabinet officials had made tours to West European and Arab capitals to present Somalia's case for increased aid on concessional terms. This effort had been quite successful; the inflow of foreign capital (largely official) had increased from an annual average of US$39 million a year in the 1963-69 period to US$59 million in 1973 and US$125 million in 1975. About 62 percent of the capital inflow in the 1960s had consisted of unrequited grants; in 1973 about 50 percent was grant aid, but most of the loan aid received has carried soft (concessional) terms with respect to interest rates, amortization periods, and the valuation of repayment in kind.

Comprehensive data that would include aid commitments by Arab countries and the communist world were lacking to substantiate the frequent surmise that Somalia's per capita aid receipts were among the highest in the developing world. Some estimates could be made, however, of the level of communist aid. During the 1960s some US$22 million in economic aid had been received from the PRC and US$66 million from the Soviet Union. For the entire period from independence in 1960 through 1973, commitments of economic aid by the PRC totaled some US$132 million.

International statistics failed to report any new Soviet economic aid commitments to Somalia from 1967 through 1974, although large amounts of Soviet aid were clearly being used on a number of new projects. Most sources said that information on Soviet loans was closely held. One source estimated that Soviet economic aid commitments had totaled only US$90 million for the entire 1960-73 period, in addition to military aid of US$55 million. The United States Department of State reported, however, that in October 1971, shortly after the PRC had committed US$100 million for roadbuilding, the Soviets pledged some US$90 million in loans for projects, including building the Fanole dam. It was not clear whether the US$60 million loan reportedly committed in July 1974 was included in this amount.

Comparison of the sources of foreign financing confirmed for development programs in the 1960s with those for the 1974-78 period shows a pronounced shift away from bilateral financing from Western countries and toward increased future reliance on financing from Arab countries and to a lesser extent from the PRC and the Democratic People's Republic of Korea (North Korea). A different picture emerges from published international sources of aid statistics, which indicate that official bilateral development assistance to Somalia from West European countries averaged US$15.6 million a year from 1970 through 1974 in addition to sizable amounts of technical assistance (see table 2). The data obtainable from international sources are incomplete, however, providing much better coverage of multilateral and Western bilateral official aid than of communist or Arab aid.

Of the foreign financing confirmed for the Development Program 1974-1978 and the drought rehabilitation program of 1975 combined, the Soviet Union was reportedly furnishing 20.1 percent, somewhat less than in the 1963-69 period, when it furnished 24 percent. The share provided by the PRC had increased from 2.4 percent to 11.8 percent, and North Korea was providing 7.1 percent, increasing the total communist share of financing to about 39 percent. The United States, which had financed 20 percent of the total in the 1963-69 period, was no longer supplying any direct aid, although it was a major contributor to the World Food Program (WFP) the World Bank Group (see Glossary), and the UN aid funds. Altogether, from 1954 through 1970, the United States had extended nearly US$80 million in aid to Somalia.

Multilateral agencies were committed to furnishing 16.8 percent of foreign development financing for the 1974-78 period, compared with 22.4 percent in the 1960s. This included some lending by the African Development Bank, but the leading multilateral lender was the IDA, a member of the World Bank Group. The European Development Fund (EDF) of the European Economic Community (EEC, also known as the Common Market) was to provide 15.0 percent, compared with 15.1 percent in the 1963-69 period. The only confirmed bilateral financing from West European countries shown for the Development Program 1974-1978 was Sh20 million from Italy for a banana development project. As projected in the plan, bilateral lending from Western Europe thus falsely appeared to have declined from 12 or 14 percent of total in the 1963-69 period to less than 1 percent in the 1974-78 period.

In 1975 and 1976 the press reported that Arab sources were providing financing for the Bardera reservoir and the Fanole sugar complex, among the costliest projects in the Development Program 1974-1978. If this financing were confirmed, 34.3 percent of total foreign financing for the plan and the drought rehabilitation program combined would be from OPEC sources. With these projects Arab loans officially confirmed constituted 31.6 percent of total confirmed foreign financing. In the 1963-69 period aid from Saudi Arabia had totaled Sh14.6 million, or about 2.1 percent of development financing from foreign sources. Aid had also been provided by Egypt, but it was not reported separately. Aid from unspecified countries amounted to only 3 percent of total foreign financing in the 1963-69 period; so the share of Arab countries cannot have exceeded 5 percent at most; the share financed by bilateral aid from Western Europe cannot have exceeded 15 percent.

Somalia had joined the League of Arab States (Arab League) in February 1974, not long after the successful OPEC oil embargo of 1973 and just a few months before the resulting sixth special UN session on raw materials and development, which was called at the demand of the Group of 77 (see Economic Policies, this ch.). The UN emergency aid program voted at that session had called for major OPEC contributions to the multilateral programs to alleviate the effects of world inflation on countries on the MSA list. At private meetings of the Group of 77 during the special session the OPEC countries had reportedly promised substantial additional aid directly from their own joint or individual aid funds. As one of the six poorest MSA countries and as a member of the Arab League, Somalia was thus well placed to benefit from the compromise reached as a result of the third world demands.

As an MSA and an LDC Somali had received some US$4 million from the UN Emergency Fund by the start of 1975 and was also accorded higher priority for WFP aid. Somalia has received most of its special aid, however, from the new aid funds established by the oil-exporting Arab countries since 1974. The OPEC special fund of US$800 million did not become operational until August 1976; in the interim Somalia had received bilateral loans from OPEC countries and multilateral assistance from the Special Arab Fund for African Countries. Somalia was by no means high on the list of OPEC aid recipients, however. In 1974 it received US$2.0 million from the Arab Fund for Economic and Social Development (Arab Fund), US$30.0 million from Saudi Arabia, US$19.5 million from the United Arab Emirates (UAE), US$17.5 million from Iraq, US$14.0 million from Qatar, US$9.6 million from Libya, and US$7.0 million from Kuwait. Libya and Abu Dhabi were tentatively designated as the largest contributors

Table 2. *Somalia, Reported Foreign Aid Disbursements, 1960-74*
(in millions of United States dollars)

| Year Disbursed or Committed[5] | Official Bilateral Grants and Loans | | | | | Multilateral Aid[1] | |
| | Communist Countries[2] | | OPEC[3] Countries | DAC Countries[4] | | | |
	PRC[6]	Soviet Union		United States	Other	EEC[7]	Other
1960	---	---	n.r.	3.00	18.41	0.06	---
1961	---	57	n.r.	3.00	17.60	1.79	0.82
1962	---	---	n.r.	9.00	13.33	0.27	1.47
Total 1960-62	---	57	n.r.	15.00	49.34	2.12	2.29
1963	22	---	n.r.	7.00	20.33	1.76	1.36
1964	---	---	n.r.	6.00	11.56	2.52	1.60
1965	---	---	n.r.	7.90	17.11	1.77	1.89
1966	---	9	n.r.	6.00	8.26	1.51	2.17
1967	---	---	n.r.	6.00	5.06	1.81	2.17
1968	---	---	n.r.	5.00	5.30	2.03	3.30
1969	---	---	n.r.	7.89[8]	13.41	0.70	11.53
Total 1963-69	22	9	11.2[9]	45.79	81.03	12.10	24.02
1970	---	---	n.r.	--[8]	17.86	0.3	9.65
1971	110	---	n.r.	---	21.74	6.2[10]	2.75
1972	---	---	n.r.	--[8]	11.60	1.3[10]	10.09
1973	---	---	n.r.	---	19.31	14.8[10]	1.20
1974	1	n.r.	36.70	---	7.32	12.91	20.06
Total 1970-74	111	n.r.	n.r.	n.r.	77.83	35.51	43.75

226

- - - means none; n.r. means not reported.

[1] Only multilateral agencies giving credits on concessional terms (grant element of at least 25 percent) are included; these include United Nations agencies, members of the World Bank Group, and the African Development Bank.

[2] US$6 million reported from other East European countries in 1966 not included here.

[3] Organization of Petroleum Exporting Countries.

[4] Development Assistance Committee (of the Organization for Economic Cooperation and Development) DAC member countries granting bilateral official aid to Somalia included chiefly Italy, the United Kingdom, and the Federal Republic of Germany (West Germany). There was a little aid from Switzerland and in 1974 US$20,000 from Japan.

[5] Year in which disbursed. Exceptions: aid from communist countries is reported for year in which committed, and EEC 1971-73 is probably year in which committed.

[6] People's Republic of China.

[7] European Economic Community.

[8] Statistics published by United States government show total economic aid disbursements to Somalia as US$3.5 million in 1969, US $3.0 million in 1970, and US$300,000 in 1972.

[9] Incomplete figure: includes only aid from Saudi Arabia 1960-66.

[10] Data for EEC 1971-73 are probably not on the same basis as other data.

to proposed financing of the Development Program 1974-78; Kuwait and the Arab Fund had granted support for the drought rehabilitation program (see ch. 13).

The Arab loans carry terms somewhat harder than those on credits from the international agencies or the Soviet Union but softer than commercial rates. The 1976 Arab Fund loan for the riverine resettlement projects, for example, carried 4-percent interest and was repayable over twenty-five years after a five-year grace period. During the drought Somali media had carried some criticism—disavowed by the government—of the lag between promises of aid and actual commitments by Libya and other oil-exporting Arab countries. By mid-1976, however, the promised aid was being received in generous quantity. The director of Abu Dhabi's aid fund explained that Arab countries were seeking to coordinate their aid policies, notably to require full project evaluation and preinvestment studies, and that the lack of adequately prepared projects explained the delay in aid commitments.

Medium-and long-term official loans on soft terms from multilateral agencies and from most Western bilateral lenders also require thorough project preparation, and since 1970 the SRC leadership had expressed some impatience with the cost and long delays involved in sophisticated preinvestment planning. This may have contributed to an expressed preference for aid from communist sources, which is unhampered by consideration of future economic return and can consequently be well timed for maximum political impact (see ch. 10). The swiftness of the mid-1975 Soviet gift of trucks and operation of an airlift to relocate nomads from the drought relief camps was particularly appreciated.

Soviet trade credits, such as that provided for the abortive state farm program of the 1960s, sometimes carry hard terms, but the Soviet project loan of 1961 for three processing plants apparently carried the soft terms usual for such loans. Partly because there had been no adequate preinvestment planning, however, it proved difficult to repay the project loan from the initially meager output of the completed plants (see ch. 14). Repayment had to be rescheduled repeatedly. This problem was reported to be common among African countries that received Soviet project loans in the 1960s.

The July 1974 Treaty of Friendship and Cooperation with the Soviet Union, as published in *Pravda,* revealed no details regarding aid arrangements. According to an article in *Conflict Studies* (London), the unpublished clauses included one canceling the equivalent of some US$45 million in outstanding economic debt and US$80 million in military debt. *Africa Research Bulletin* (London) reported this as cancellation of US$100 million in military debt. If the economic debt was indeed canceled, the move was again well timed, since in 1974 leading Western bilateral lenders were resisting rising third world

228

demands for cancellation of outstanding debts (see Economic Policies, this ch.).

Confirmed Soviet financing for projects in the Development Program 1974-1978 totaled some US$38 million, including provision of farm machinery, mapping and surveying, and most notably the Fanole irrigation project on the Juba River, well under way by 1976. In mid-1975 the Soviets had reportedly provided some US$60 million for the drought rehabilitation project involving resettlement of nomads in fishing cooperatives. Some sources reported that the Soviet Union was also increasing oil storage capacity at Berbera port and improving the port and airstrip (see ch. 14). PRC financing had been provided principally for construction of the north-south road from Belet Weyn to Burao. Other PRC loans were for a polytechnic institute and a maternity and pediatric hospital. North Korea was financing construction of a cement plant and gypsum pilot project near Berbera and an irrigated state farm at Balad. Financing from the EDF, the IDA, and OPEC countries was being used for education and for a variety of agricultural and transport projects (see ch. 13; ch. 14).

Somalia's aid receipts had contained a large grant element. Moreover, despite the alleged susceptibility of prerevolutionary officials to bribes and the subsequent impatience of the SRC with the delays involved in Western loans, Somalia had thus far avoided the pitfall of resorting to large amounts of short-term supplier or contractor financing, which often provides favorable surveys and an early start on construction but may create repayment difficulties. It was consequently in a better debt-servicing position than many developing countries, although its aid receipts had been relatively large in relation to national product and export earning capacity.

At the end of 1973 there was some US$17 million of foreign private capital invested in Somalia. Since 1960 the country had received grant aid of US$311 million; debt outstanding for loan aid committed (including undisbursed) was US$268 million at the end of 1973 and US$361 million by late 1975. Debt outstanding for aid received and disbursed totaled US$145 million in mid-1974, of which 38 percent was owed to the Soviet Union, 16 percent to Arab countries, and 11 percent to the IDA. The ratio of debt service obligations to export earnings was on the rise, from a favorable 3.4 percent in 1972 to 5.8 percent in 1974 and 10.0 percent in 1975. It was expected to remain at 10 percent through the 1970s; this is often regarded as the maximum safe debt service ratio, and future loans would have to be sought on soft terms.

The prospect for further aid was favorable, depending chiefly on improved ability to identify and prepare suitable projects (see ch. 13). In other respects the country was considered creditworthy by leading international lenders in view of the government's past fiscal performance. Moreover Somalia qualified for special consideration from almost every possible source. Having a socialist revolutionary government, it could appeal for support from other socialist regimes; it was a member of the Arab League; it was on both the LDC list of twenty-nine least developed countries and the MSA list of forty-two countries most seriously affected by declining terms of trade (see Economic Policies, this ch.). Both multilateral and leading bilateral lenders were pledged to give priority consideration to countries on these two lists.

From 1959 through 1974, as one of the eighteen original African EEC associates under three Yaoundé agreements, Somalia had received economic development aid totaling 82 million EEC units of account (about US$103 million), of which 93 percent was grant aid. This total did not include famine relief totaling 3 million units of account in 1965, 1970, and 1971 and 1.7 million units of account in 1974 and 1975.

Somalia was also among the forty-six African, Caribbean, and Pacific (ACP) countries granted preferential treatment by the EEC under the terms of the Lomé Convention of February 1975 (see ch. 14). The commercial preference for bananas formerly enjoyed by Somalia as one of the eighteen original associates had been somewhat watered down by the entry of so many new countries, but sizable amounts of project aid were being received from the EDF.

Under the export stabilization arrangement established by the Lomé Convention, Somalia was also one of seventeen ACP countries accorded compensation for declining 1975 export earnings from the Stabex fund; under this mechanism, when a country's exports to EEC markets of any one of twelve specified products fall by a certain percentage below the average of the preceding four years, the Stabex fund will make up the difference. The product must have furnished 7.5 percent of the country's export earnings, or at least 2.5 percent in the case of an LDC. For 1975 Somalia received US$1.7 million in compensation for lost banana earnings and US$800,000 for untanned skins. As an LDC it received these sums as an outright grant; countries not on the LDC list are obliged to repay the loan. The decline in exports of hides and skins was attributed to industrial recession on the EEC market. The decline in banana exports was caused by poor rainfall in Somalia but nonetheless qualified for Stabex compensation.

BANKING

In the mid-1970s the wholly nationalized banking system was still in a relatively early stage of development. It comprised a central bank, an investment bank for medium-term and long-term development financing, and two commercial banks with about twenty branches. Little effort had been made to mobilize personal saving through the banking system; it was thought to go chiefly into real estate in Mogadishu, livestock, and purchase of banana plantations.

The Somali National Bank (SNB) had been established at independence to serve as bank of issue and to perform the other usual functions of a central bank. It acted as banker to the government and handled foreign exchange transactions. Its statute gave it the power to regulate credit by setting bank rates, the rediscount rate, and reserve requirements for commercial banks. This power was not flexibly used as an instrument of policy, however, for the commercial banks were usually in a position of excess liquidity. In the 1960s the SNB had effectively used moral suasion to set ceilings on commercial bank credit, but its efforts to curb the increase in credit to the public sector in 1974 had only limited effect. In 1975 it was routinely rediscounting commercial bank credits at 2.5 percent. In the 1960s the central bank had also functioned as a commercial bank in competition with the private foreign banks and at one time was issuing 50 percent of all commercial credit. This function was to have been abolished in 1968 if sufficient staff could be found to administer it separately.

Until commercial banking was nationalized in May 1970, there had been local subsidiaries of two leading Italian banks and a British bank, as well as one Somali-owned commercial bank, Credito Somalo. They were replaced by the Somali Commercial Bank, which took over the assets and liabilities of the foreign banks, and the Somali Credit and Savings Bank, which reportedly took over the commercial banking functions formerly performed by the SNB.

Expansionary demand pressure in the mid-1960s had been attributed largely to the import sector, which at that time was in private hands, and had been effectively stabilized when the central bank curbed its own credit expansion and persuaded the commercial banks to follow suit. After 1969 expansionary demand did not again become a problem until 1973 and 1974. By that time two-thirds of all commercial banking activity was concerned with the public sector, although credit and banking services were still used by private interests in livestock exporting and a few other residual activities. Many public enterprises depended heavily on the banking system for their capital requirements. The strong expansion in 1973 and 1974 again originated in the import sector, by then largely controlled by public agencies. It was attributed partly to their increased import requirements and partly to the steep rise in world prices. After a year of poor rainfall and crop failure large food imports were required, import prices were high, and the marketing agency kept down prices to the consumer and was unable to reduce its debt to the banking system. The food price index nonetheless rose by 34 percent in one year.

In 1968 the former development loan section of the Credito Somalo commercial bank was separated and converted into the Somali Development Bank. Credito Somalo ceased to exist in 1970. Its development loan section had been capitalized by United States government loans of US$2 million. It had financed some precarious ventures, including the brickworks in Afgoi and ill-fated tuna-freezing plant at Ras Filuch (see ch. 13). Attempts were being made in the 1970s to revive both ventures under new management, and they figured briefly in reports of the new industrial capacity created by the Development Program 1974-1978.

The Somali Development Bank retained these liabilities when it took over the loan portfolio of its predecessor, but it was much better capitalized, receiving annual allocations from the central budget and being able to refinance with the central bank or the commercial banks. It played a central role in financing public sector activity, not only providing medium-term loans of up to six years and long-term loans of up to twenty years but also actually setting up and managing industries. Most of its lending had been to public sector industry. Until 1974 its limited lending to agriculture went entirely to private banana planters or for tractors and other agricultural machinery—apparently for private entrepreneurs. In 1974 credit guarantees were provided for cooperatives by the relevant ministries, making them eligible for credit from the development bank. It was also beginning to consider applications for credit for private investment proposals. Government policy permitted private investment only in small-scale ventures.

PUBLIC FINANCE

By its notable achievement in mobilizing fiscal resources through indirect and direct taxation and through public sector enterprise, the SRC government was able to cover expanding current expenditure and attain a growing surplus to cover one-third of development spending in the 1971-73 period. In 1974 the surplus failed to increase as expected, and public sector borrowing from the banking sector expanded. Despite rising import prices and the critical food shortage, the government met its requirements without resort to large-scale inflationary financing.

Budget statistics were still fragmentary in the mid-1970s, but accounting and audit procedures had been greatly improved each year since 1970. In 1972 it was announced that future profits of the public sector entities were to become the principal source of central government revenue. More than twenty such enterprises were then in operation, and their use as a means of resource mobilization was made a leading tenet of scientific socialism. In principle three kinds of contribution to the central government budget are required. Depreciation reserves must be paid into a central development fund, since allocating new investment is regarded as a central government function; each enterprise must pay a turnover tax, which in effect seems to be levied on profits; and 100 percent of profits remaining after various operating and social funds are met is in principle payable to the central government budget. The public entities' contribution was about 6 percent of central government revenues in 1973 but fell short of expectations.

In 1975 the budgets of all autonomous agencies were fully integrated into the central government budget. The local government budgets had been integrated into the budget since 1973. The local councils prepare their own budgets, but these form an integral part of the central budget and must be approved and audited by the central government. Somalia is one of the few countries in Africa where local government taxation generates a surplus; in 1973 it amounted to more than 20 percent of local revenue.

From 1970 through 1974 the administration had succeeded in more than doubling its tax revenues in spite of the very meager tax base in a partially monetized economy in which 70 percent of the people are thought to be living at subsistence level. Perhaps the major source of revenue had been multiple taxes on imports. Imports had tripled in value since 1970, supported by the large inflow of foreign assistance. The stamp tax and excise tax on sugar and a number of tariff rates had been raised, particularly on alcohol, beer, gasoline, and footwear. A major share of the increase in import revenues, however, had come from the responsiveness of tariff yields to the increase in import value. A World Bank report also noted that, in contradiction of all conventional wisdom concerning developing countries with limited administrative capabilities, the SRC regime had succeeded in increasing the share of direct taxes in total tax revenue from 9 percent in 1969 to 19 percent in 1974. The increase had resulted in large part from the development levy imposed since 1971 (see Economic Policies, this ch.).

Central government recurrent expenditure had increased by only about 7 percent a year from 1969 through 1973. Great restraint was shown, particularly in the wage bill and in administration, usually an inflexible item. A wage increase was granted in December 1973. Current spending was thought to have increased by some 30 percent in 1974, owing partly to badly needed spending on social and economic services. Administrative ministries still took 60 percent of current spending, however; defense took 25 to 30 percent and police another 10 percent, rather high for an African state.

Because the per capita GNP is unknown, the country's tax effort cannot be quantified; but the World Bank estimated that in 1974 it was relatively high in proportion to average income, leaving limited scope for further revenue mobilization to meet anticipated growth in future expenditure. Even if debt servicing does not become a serious burden, development progress brings with it heavy obligations for future recurrent expenditure on such needs as maintenance of irrigation projects and education, health, and other social services. The excellent record of fiscal discipline through 1974 thus did not preclude increasingly serious future problems in public finance. The vast expansion of the public sector under the socialist system intensified the central problem of shortage of trained manpower; since 1970 turnover in management had been high, and lack of supervision had sometimes impaired productivity in development projects and public enterprise.

CHAPTER 13

AGRICULTURE

Livestock and land are the nation's most readily exploitable resources and the mainstay of the subsistence economy, providing a scant livelihood to 80 percent of the people in the mid-1970s. Controlled irrigation and mechanized farming were used on state farms and on the private banana plantations along the Juba and Shabelle rivers in the south, but most people were producing by traditional methods and largely for their own subsistence, hoping for a surplus for sale in good years and for survival in the not infrequent years of drought.

The share of population dependent primarily on livestock was thought to have declined from 80 percent in 1960 to about 60 percent in 1973. Before the 1974 drought it was estimated that perhaps 35 to 40 percent of the people were still purely nomadic; 25 to 30 percent were seminomads, practicing cultivation during the year's two rainy seasons but dedicating part of the family or part of the year to transhumant pastoralism; and 15 to 20 percent were settled cultivators. Along the Juba and Shabelle floodplains riverine cultivators grew maize (corn) as the main staple food grain, using uncontrolled seasonal flood irrigation sometimes supplemented by small pumps. The staple crop of dryland (rain-fed) cultivation was drought-resistant durra sorghum, grown in the relatively high rainfall areas in the northwestern highlands and on the interriver plain between the Juba and Shabelle but beyond reach of their floodwaters.

Traditional attitudes had been slowly but perceptibly modified since the mid-1950s. Herders had proved responsive to market and price incentives, increasing the annual rate of offtake for sale or slaughter to 7 to 10 percent. Livestock and livestock products had begun to take first place among exports even before the 1967 Suez Canal closing and loss of protection on the Italian market curtailed banana earnings. Although plans for settlement of nomads failed to materialize until 1975, the rate of unplanned settlement had increased. The ethnic distinction that once prevailed between cultivators and herders had somewhat blurred, and despite the disdain for cultivation taught by pastoral tradition more nomadic families were taking it up on a seasonal basis. Permanent settlements had also increased. The nomads were becoming conscious of new needs and were spontaneously sending their children to town and boarding schools in growing numbers (see ch. 7).

Around permanent settlements overgrazing soon developed, for lingering traditions still favored keeping the largest possible number of animals without regard to their productivity. Moreover harsh experience had taught the pastoralists to place the survival value of a larger herd above immediate return, as from the sale or slaughter of female stock. Thus the people were more receptive to innovations, such as vaccination, that could help increase the size of their herd than to such unfamiliar conservation measures as grazing control, which was badly needed but might be regarded as in conflict with deep-rooted social traditions.

As a result of overstocking, by the late 1960s a growing number of herders had been forced onto marginal grazing lands, becoming more vulnerable to drought. In the north there were severe droughts with heavy loss of livestock in 1950, 1955, 1964, and 1969; in between the rains were often inadequate; the 1974 drought followed several years of poor rains. After each drought numbers of nomads or their children were obliged to migrate to urban settlements, where they often remained without adequate employment. The Agricultural Crash Program was launched by the military government a few months after its advent to power in the October 1969 coup to absorb some of this unemployment. Most of the 5,760 jobs created on ten state farms by late 1974 were filled by former nomads or their sons.

Crash program pioneers showed enthusiasm for farming and communal activity but, while they were acquiring valuable experience, crop yields suffered. Earlier, from 1960 to 1969, yields per acre of sugar and bananas had been greatly improved and costs lowered, but meanwhile larger food grain imports were required each year. The two trends were then reversed; yields and output on the nationalized sugar estate and yields on the private banana plantations fell from their 1969 high, but from 1970 through 1975 banana output was somewhat increased, and large food grain imports were required only in 1971, 1974, and 1975. Yields per acre were low, however, and few state farms could break even; some could not feed their own residents. Measures to improve yields had been minimal and ineffective. The planners sought to focus on expanding irrigated food grain acreage to reduce fluctuations in food supply due to unreliable rainfall.

Although self-sufficiency in staple food grains was cited as an immediate policy goal, in actual practice the government appeared to give lower priority to early improvement of yields and productivity than to broadening popular participation in development, expanding state collective farm acreage, and preparing the way for eventual collectivization of cooperative farming (see ch. 12). At least until the settlement project for nomads in 1975, its greatest achievements had

236

been in fiscal performance and in education, notably the literacy drive (see ch. 7). Improvements in agricultural methods and research in plant varieties and seed had probably gone deeper in the 1960s but were disseminated narrowly if at all. In the early 1970s the effort to reach people was much broader, although it may be that the knowledge disseminated was necessarily spread somewhat thin. By the 1980s it was hoped that more productive techniques could be brought to a broadly literate people indoctrinated in the required social attitudes.

The prevailing assessment was that if improved management of fields, flocks, and rangeland could be introduced and accepted, the country had the potential to meet its food requirement in a good year and afford a reserve for years of drought, flood, locust invasion, and other natural hazards. If social resistance to grazing control could be overcome, the natural bush and pasture could sustain an adequate animal population of improved breed and more productive yield. The involuntary destocking and relocation precipitated by the 1974 drought might afford a unique opportunity to effect the required transformation in the traditional way of life and to tackle the formidable challenge of bringing literacy and improved welfare to the nomadic population.

PASTORAL AND CULTIVATING AREAS

In early 1976 the country had sixteen first-order administrative divisions known as regions that in turn were subdivided into seventy-eight districts (see ch. 3; ch. 8). Because these new regions cut across divisions of climate and terrain, they were not being consistently adopted in economic development sources, which instead often referred to terrain features, past regional names, or English translations of present-day names. For example, the Trans-Juba Livestock Project was designed to assist the nomadic cattle herders whose home wells are in the area west of the Juba River. The Upper Juba Region dryland farming feasibility study became the Bay Region Study when the Upper Juba Region was divided into three smaller regions. Waqooyi Galbeed is translated as North West Region.

The term *north* is loosely but commonly used in an economic context to designate the seven regions from the Waqooyi Galbeed Region to the southern border of Galgduud Region, which was also used to define the southern limit of the six regions most afflicted by the 1974 drought (see fig. 6). The hardest hit were Sanaag, Togdheer, and Nugaal regions, but considerable deprivation was also caused in Bari, Mudug, and Galgduud regions. Mean annual rainfall in these six regions seldom exceeds three or four inches. Nomads afflicted by the 1974 drought were estimated at 700,000. As the same figure was cited for the 1964 drought, this probably represents a rough estimate of the total number of "northern" nomads.

237

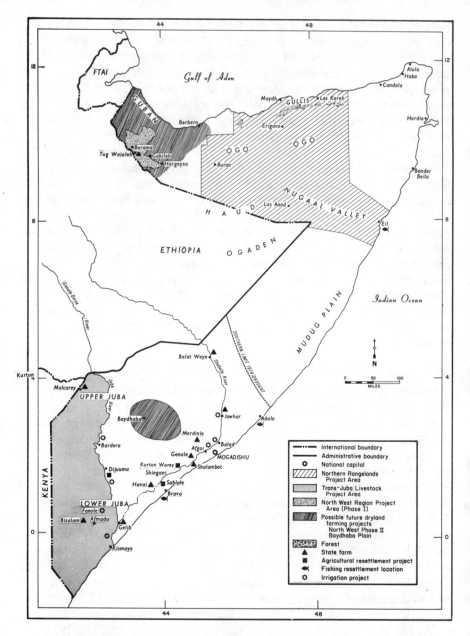

Figure 6. Somalia, Development Projects, Pastoral and Cultivating Areas, 1976

No region was really spared by the 1974 drought, however, not even the Juba-Shabelle (riverine and interriver) area, which has the highest mean annual rainfall in the country. Peripheral information suggests that both spring and fall rains were deficient, resulting in frequent crop failure on rain-fed land. Both the subsistence crops of traditional floodplain cultivators and the food grains, industrial crops, or export crops of state farms and private plantations concentrated along the lower Shabelle suffered when the Shabelle failed to flood in June and again in September 1974.

On average the riverine plains are flooded twice a year. In the spring rainy season (gu) of April through June the Juba overflows its banks in April and May and the Shabelle in June. The second flooding of the Shabelle in September occurs when most of the area is afflicted by the long dry season (hagaa) of July through September, but the Juba floods in the short rains of October to December (dayr).

Bananas, sugar, and citrus had been and would continue to be grown on the large-scale private plantations or government farms under controlled irrigation and mechanized collective farming. The government was to produce an increasing share of food grains—maize, sorghum, rice, and wheat—as well as sugar, cotton, grapefruit, and even bananas. Traditional smallholders produced subsistence food grains, oilseeds, and garden produce. In the 1960s they had been successful in cotton growing, but without improved inputs production fluctuated too radically, and cotton was becoming a government product.

Most of the crash program state farms had been established on land already under controlled irrigation along the lower Shabelle. The high saline content and occasionally inadequate flow of the Shabelle waters had contributed to the decline in sugar and banana yields, and some of the irrigation canals had suffered from flood damage or neglect. The Shabelle floodplain had also been more fully developed than the Juba, which had more unoccupied land available. Because of its higher cost and the need for feasibility studies, however, planned Juba development had been repeatedly deferred since its irrigation potential was studied in 1960 with United States aid and more elaborately in 1963 by a Soviet team. In 1969 it was to have been financed by a consortium of the United States and the European Economic Community (EEC, also known as the Common Market). This agreement may perhaps have lapsed after the October 1969 coup. The study was continued under the Development Program 1971-1973, which stated that the long-term strategy would be similar to that proposed for the Juba in earlier plans but that, in the short term, land on the Shabelle already developed but not under crop would be used.

Of the first eleven crash program state farms, three were on land cleared for state farms in the early 1960s at Tug Wajaleh, Gelib, and Balad—in 1963 Balad was the site of an army-run state groundnut (peanut) farm, which by 1976 had become a cotton project financed by the Democratic People's Republic of Korea (North Korea). The formerly semiprivate sugar estate at Jowhar was fully nationalized. The other Shabelle sites had ongoing irrigation projects: at Belet Weyn, Afgoi-Mordinle, Genale, Shalambot, Havai, and Gelib. In the

1974-78 period the state was to double its acreage and take over some concession land not being actively exploited or in excess of the new maximum size.

The 68 percent of agricultural development spending under the Development Program 1974-1978 allocated to fourteen irrigation projects at first appeared as overambitious as in earlier plans, but by mid-1976 financing was reported to be forthcoming for even the two costliest projects; the proposed Bardera reservoir and the Juba sugar complex near Fanole. It was not entirely clear, however, whether the Arab loan for Bardera and the contract awarded a British firm for the sugar complex involved actual construction or a feasibility study. The Soviet Union was financing and building the Fanole irrigation project; equipment had arrived, presumably to build the thirty-mile canal from the diversion dam at Bardera to the proposed 20,000-acre sugar estate at Fanole, which was also to have a sugar mill and distillery (see ch. 14).

On the Shabelle internally financed projects already under way included a rice production program and, between Belet Weyn and Falcheiro, a canal-desilting and river-dredging operation. Saudi Arabia and Somalia were cofinancing offstream storage at Jowhar to compensate for the low seasonal flow in January through March. To rehabilitate the sugar refinery at Jowhar, the plan allocated some Sh40 million (for value of the Somali shilling—see Glossary). A final feasibility study was proposed for the long-deferred swamp reclamation project on the seasonal course of the Shabelle south of Falcheiro, where malaria and trypanosomiasis had impeded efforts at rice production. The Afgoi-Mordinle project initiated by the United Nations Development Program (UNDP) in 1972 was expanded and conducted jointly by Libya and Somalia for rotation of cotton, rice, groundnuts, and sesame on 2,500 acres. Downstream projects for state banana and grapefruit production were supported by the EEC.

Livestock are not kept on state farms. They are kept primarily by nomads or cultivators of Somali origin and thus of pastoral tradition (see ch. 2; ch. 4). The sedentary riverine peoples are often partly or wholly of remote or recent non-Somali origin, but many keep small herds of cattle and other livestock. Dryland cultivators in the interriver area are usually ethnic Somali, members of Digil or Rahanwein clan-families by either origin or adoption. They include both seminomads and wholly settled farmers, as do the dryland cultivators of the northwest. Both groups keep cattle and other livestock. Of the estimated 500,000 cattle kept north of 4° north latitude in 1973, about 400,000 were probably in the North West Region Project Area. There some livestock were kept by cultivators; about 65 percent of the area's population were nomadic herders.

About 83 percent of the estimated national cattle herd of some 3 million in 1973 were in the southern regions, where perhaps 1.5 million were kept by interriver or riverine cultivators and about 1 million by Trans-Juba nomads of Darod and Hawiya clan-families. Of this group, comprising an estimated 20,000 nomadic families, many had established semipermanent homes in the lower Juba area to take advantage of schools and health facilities. The majority, who remained purely nomadic, had come to regard their cattle primarily as a source of growing cash income, selling 7 to 10 percent a year. Of cattle sold 8 percent went to municipal slaughterhouses, 46 percent went to the marketing agency for the canneries or for export, and 46 percent were sold in Kenya during the seasonal migration.

In 1973 seminomadic pastoralists lived mainly in the southern regions or the North West Region in areas where crop growing and cattle herding were feasible. Throughout most of the arid and semiarid northeastern and central regions water and bush or pasture were barely adequate for wet season extensive grazing of sheep, goats, and camels. Of the estimated national flock of 14 million sheep and goats in 1973, some 11 million were thought to be in the north. The estimated camel herd of 2.5 million was about equally divided between north and south. Most of the northern nomads spent the harsh months of the winter dry season (jilal) of January through March near their home wells in the Guban plain or the Ogo (a zone of broken highlands and valleys), moving east and south with the first spring rains of April into the Nugaal Valley, the Haud, the Ogaden region of Ethiopia, or the arid Mudug Plain (see ch. 3).

A pilot survey of nomadic households in 1973 in Burao (later Togdheer) Region found that 94 percent of households surveyed kept goats and sheep, 65 percent camels, and only 6 percent cattle. The average family in this sample would have had 5.75 people, 110 goats and sheep, twenty camels, and eight head of cattle. This was said to reflect the general pattern of stock ownership in the north.

Camels are usually in the care of boys and unmarried men; sheep and goats move with the wives and the nuclear family. In the dry season cattle can move only two to four days' journey without water, sheep and goats from three days (in the hotter south) to a week (in the north), and camels from a week (in the south) to two weeks (in the north). A few burden camels may be left with the family while the young men take the milch camels in search of distant grazing.

DROUGHT RELIEF, RESETTLEMENT, AND REHABILITATION

For some years the country's rangelands had been providing inadequate nutrition to their human and animal population, particularly in the drought years that occurred in about two years out of five. A survey in 1964 had concluded that even in the high-rainfall Juba-Shabelle area, under optimum conditions in other respects, over an average five-year period dryland cultivation could be expected to yield two good crops, one poor crop, and two years of no crop; floodplain cultivation along the Shabelle could yield three good crops, one fair crop, and one poor crop. Riverine cultivators who did not keep livestock, however, had only one string to their bow: when rainfall was scanty and the river failed to flood, their lot was not enviable. In the interriver area the rains could be so irregular that entire villages of settled as well as semionadic cultivators were sometimes obliged to take to the nomadic life for survival, driving their flocks in pursuit of distant rain clouds.

It is characteristic that each of the four development plans launched in Somalia since independence in 1960 got off to a delayed start attributed to severe drought. Poor rains for two successive years caused heavy livestock losses and famine among the nomads in 1964 and reportedly interfered with progress on the First (Five-Year) Plan 1963-67. President Abderashid Ali Shermarke was touring the drought-stricken regions when he was assassinated in October 1969. The drought of 1969 was blamed by both the old and the new governments for their budget deficits and for delays in their respective development plans, the Second (Short-Term) Plan 1968-70 and the Development Program 1971-1973. As they embarked on their Development Program 1974-1978, Somali authorities complained that the only year of decent rainfall since 1968 had been in 1972, when cyclones ravaged the northeastern coast.

Several years of inadequate rains in six of the northern and central regions inhabited largely by pastoralists culminated in the worst drought in living memory after the short autumn rainy season failed in 1974. In November the government declared a state of emergency. Providentially 25,000 urban secondary students had been sent among the nomads in August 1974 on a combination census and literacy drive (Rural Development Campaign) that quickly turned into a famine relief operation.

Eight relief camps were set up in the afflicted regions. The first 200,000 people succored were mostly women and children, who move closer to watering points with the sheep and goats. The men were ranging over hundreds of miles with the camel herds in search of grazing. At the peak of the relief phase in late May 1975 there were some 270,000 people in the camps, and another 500,000 were receiving food supplies outside the camps. In the south rainfall was deficient, the Shabelle did not flood, and the food grain harvest largely failed. In the country as a whole about 1.2 million people were given food relief. Prompt action by the authorities was thought to have saved many thousands of lives, but there had been some 19,000 deaths due to drought. In July 1975 livestock losses were estimated at 1.0 million cattle, 500,000 camels, and 5.7 million sheep and goats.

The 1975 spring rains in the south and the southwest monsoon rains between May or June and September in the north proved ample and soaked most of the country. As the relief camps were disbanded from June through August, the emergency operation entered the resettlement phase. An advance guard of some 20,000 refugee families was sent south to start the next season's food crop. Aircraft, trucks, and financial aid furnished by the Soviet Union were then used to relocate the rest. Altogether 104,000 to 110,000 nomads who perhaps had lost all their livestock agreed to take up crop farming in the south and another 14,000 to 16,000 to settle as fishermen at Brava and three other ports. More than 100,000, however, opted to return from the relief camps to nomadic herding in the north.

In early 1975 the government sought the assistance of the International Development Association (IDA) in coordinating financing for the rehabilitation phase of the drought emergency operation and in formulating appropriate projects. This process was still under way in mid-1976, and the Development Program 1974-1978 was being revised to take account both of the diversion of internal budgetary resources to drought relief needs and of the increase in the inflow of foreign loans for drought rehabilitation projects, which might make possible more rapid progress in rural development than had been foreseen by informed analysts of the development program in its original, unrevised form. It had contained no provision for funding settlement of nomads, for example, and its provision for range control and management had been criticized as inadequate in view of the need.

Several aid missions had visited the country during 1975 to identify promising projects, and by April 1976 financing had been committed for three major projects under the drought rehabilitation program. The first to obtain financing was the project to settle some 14,000 to 16,000 nomads at fishing ports along the coast. In June 1975 the Soviet Union had agreed to provide a loan equivalent to US$60 million to cover the cost of fishing boats and training facilities and perhaps also to cover the cost of the mid-1975 airlift of nomads to the south. The three cultivating settlements under the Juba-Shabelle Emergency Settlement Scheme would be jointly financed by the Arab Fund for Economic and Social Development (Arab Fund) and the IDA. Kuwait had committed a loan equivalent to US$21 million for the badly needed Northern Rangelands Development Project (see Actual and Potential Land Use, this ch.).

Since the 1950s several aid missions had recommended settlement to give nomads better access to schooling and other services, provide them with a more productive source of income, and relieve the population pressure that had caused extensive overgrazing and progressive deterioration of the northeast and central rangelands. Other experts had advised against starting any settlement of nomads until it had been more convincingly demonstrated that the rain-fed land available could provide subsistence in bad years as well as good. The 1963-67 plan listed a project for settlement of nomads that was not carried out; it stated explicitly that nomads were unlikely to take to crop farming unless it could be made more secure through controlled irrigation. Until 1975 the only other move toward a possible future settlement was a sociological survey of the nomadic zones of the north by a 1971 mission—requested in the 1960s—in line with the recommendations of earlier aid missions (see Actual and Potential Land Use, this ch.).

An early policy statement of the military government referred to the need for settlement of nomads (see ch. 9). As of mid-1976, however, there was no other evidence of any long-term plans for settlement either before or after the Juba-Shabelle emergency scheme. Since the abortive provision in the 1963-67 plan, no development plan had contained any provision for settlement of nomads.

A 1967 study estimated that the annual maintenance cost for controlled irrigation on such projects—which would burden future government recurrent budgets—would amount to about 15 percent of their heavy initial capital cost. In the 1960s it was assumed that the cost of providing and maintaining irrigated farmland for settlement of nomads would be prohibitively uneconomic, and 1975 aid missions formulating rehabilitation measures proceeded on the same assumption. Meanwhile, however, the government started construction of canals to irrigate some 17,000 acres at the three resettlement projects. Less concerned with economic return than its predecessors, the government proposed concentrating on irrigation development and large-scale mechanized farming on its state farms and espoused a similar policy for the resettlement projects. Until the drought victims could produce their own food, moreover, their maintenance was costing US$1.5 million a month (in addition to foreign relief receipts). Work therefore proceeded at once on the projects: by May 1976 a small first crop had been harvested, and a larger second crop was being planted.

The Juba-Shabelle Emergency Settlement Scheme called for the 104,000 to 110,000 nomads relocated at the three agricultural settlement projects to achieve interim emergency food production on about 74,000 acres within four years. The largest (44,000 acres) was at Dijuuma on the middle Juba; two smaller settlements (14,800 acres each) were at Sablale and Kurtun Warey on the lower Shabelle. The riverine locations had been selected by the government with a view to relying on irrigation. Because there was a need for pilot projects to provide more experience in improving the reliability of dryland farming, however, it was finally agreed that one-half the acreage at each settlement would be irrigated and one-half devoted to dryland farming. Maize, rice, vegetables, and cotton would be grown under irrigation and maize and sorghum on the rain-fed land.

Under the agreement announced in April 1976 the IDA provided credits of US$8 million for the dryland farming portion of the projects; the heavier cost of completing irrigation of the other half would be covered by a loan of US$22.4 million in Kuwaiti dinars from the Arab Fund. The aid fund of the African Development Bank provided the equivalent of US$5.5 million to build a hospital in each of the settlements. The government undertook the establishment of an autonomous settlement development agency. The lenders agreed that farming on all three projects would be on a centralized and consolidated basis, at least until the food production targets had been attained. In return the government agreed that among the options it might consider for the rain-fed half of the projects at a later stage would be dividing the land into plots of 988 acres (400 hectares), each of which would be cooperatively cultivated by a group of 100 families. These smaller cooperatives would permit the intensive supervision required to improve dryland farming methods.

There was no provision on the settlements for stockraising, and some people predicted that in time many of the former nomads might seek a return to herding. The British authority I.M. Lewis, however, has pointed out that "under acute ecological pressures Somali pastoralists have in the past proved themselves remarkably adaptable. . . . . The nomad's traditional contempt for cultivation [and fishing] . . . should not be regarded as an absolute impediment to change." In the past these attitudes have not prevented them from adopting crop farming when responsive to their needs and introduced by innovators acceptable to the group.

Since joining the League of Arab States (Arab League) in February 1974 Somalia has received assurances of substantial aid commitments from oil-exporting Arab countries. In mid-1976 the IDA was helping identify and prepare suitable projects to be financed by further Arab loans.

LAND TENURE

A 1975 law imposed statutory limits on size and transfer of arable landholdings, which were henceforth to be parceled out in ten-year concessions by the authorities. The constitution adopted at independence had stated that in principle all land belongs to the state. In practice most arable and pasture land in the interriver and riverine areas had traditionally been regarded as under the effective control of one of the lineages, and their control had thus far been respected. The right to cultivate a holding was acquired by clan members either by birth or by adoption as a client (see ch. 4). The clans that held most of the interriver cultivating land, for example, consisted essentially of various groups of clients in various stages of assimilation into the patron clan. Here a 1964 survey found that the average holding was thirty-four acres, but there was considerable variation: 60 percent averaged five acres, and 40 percent averaged fifty-six acres.

Legislation in the late 1960s had given district commissioners authority to grant ninety-nine-year leases to qualified applicants. The authority was most often used in urban areas. In the interriver area some leases had been granted, and some leaseholders sublet their land to tenant farmers. In the northwest there had been increasing enclosure of both arable and pasture land to the detriment of herders; this practice had been permitted by some district commissioners but discouraged by others.

In the southern river valleys after independence numbers of wealthy Somali entrepreneurs had bought up large landholdings from local clan families for commercial production of bananas and other crops. From twenty-six in 1955 the number of Somali banana planters increased to 147 in 1965, when there were 200 Italian-held banana plantations. The average plantation size was then 740 acres, of which 123 acres were actually planted to bananas. In the 1970s the number of sizable banana plantations in private hands had stabilized at 138, of which fifty were Italian concessionary leaseholdings.

Apparently no land tenure law had been enacted until 1975, although in 1966 a draft law had been under study that provided for a ceiling of fifty acres on holdings of rain-fed land. A Food and Agriculture Organization (FAO) report had recommended that the limit be waived to permit settlement and group ranching by nomads.

Under the Land Tenure Law of 1975 arable land may be held only under ten-year concessions granted by the Ministry of Agriculture. Concessions for plantations are not to.exceed 247 acres (100 hectares). In principle individual cultivating families must also hold their land under ten-year concessions. The prescribed size limit for family holdings is 148 acres (sixty hectares) for rain-fed land and seventy-four acres (thirty hectares) for irrigated land. A family may be given only one concession, renewable for a second ten-year period. Only because of physical disability and with official permission may one farmer sublet the land to another. Mortgage, sale, lease, or other transfer is prohibited. Banks may lend only against the value of improvements and the increased income they produce. On the death of the concession holder the holding may be transferred to his legal heirs. If it is transferred to another, the heirs must be compensated for the value of improvements.

In principle land under pasture or grazing bush is not owned by specific clan groups but open to grazing use by all Somali. In practice, however, there has been a high degree of customary clan usage, dividing water and adjacent pasture into traditional patterns of movement according to the rhythm of the seasons and the status of relations among groups. A customary itinerary is usually closely adhered to and acknowledged by other groups. In the not infrequent years when the pattern or timing of rainfall varies radically, however, the nomadic itinerary may also vary, and competition for wells and pasture will increase.

Under Islam it is considered immoral to deny access to water to thirsty men or animals. In practice this is applied primarily to natural water points, to those constructed by government or foreign aid, and to shallow wells in the coastal areas of the north where water is relatively plentiful just beneath the sandy surface. Other man-made watering facilities are customarily regarded as the property of the lineage, village, or individual who built them. In the inland areas of the northern and central regions the home wells must be deep and often require group effort to maintain and operate. These are often marked with a symbol of lineage ownership backed in times of scarcity by effective fighting strength. Fights have often developed in the dry seasons when herding groups congregate near the home wells and competition for water and grazing is keen.

Government consideration of a draft water law was at an advanced stage in mid-1976. It would seek to safeguard the existing supply of surface and ground water by prohibiting unregulated overdevelopment. The authorities placed much of the blame for localized overgrazing on the irresponsible proliferation of cement tank reservoirs (berkads) during the 1960s by profiteers who sold water to stockraisers. It was alleged that parliamentary deputies of the 1960s sold their votes for cement tank permits or built the tanks with embezzled government funds. Before such commercial reservoirs were banned by the government, they had increased in Burao Region alone from one reservoir in 1954 to 18,000 in 1970. The government planned to build many such tanks itself but to distribute them more rationally. The existence of so many private and public tanks had enabled the government to maximize the store of water in the area at the time of the 1974 drought; enough water was trucked in to fill all the tanks.

ACTUAL AND POTENTIAL LAND USE

Assessments of the country's agricultural potential have ranged from those stressing the relatively favorable ratio of land area to population and the existence of underexploited or still untapped river and groundwater resources to those emphasizing the unreliable rainfall and the depletion or low inherent fertility of most arable soils. Prognoses for the future have depended less on the assessment of physical resources than on evaluation of the chances of introducing improved cultivation and range management practices on a more lasting basis than in the past. Land that can be rendered suitable for cultivation or more productive grazing is quite limited in relation to total land area, but it is thought that with good management it could prove more than adequate to increase export earnings and to supply the country's food requirement in a reasonably good crop year and still afford a surplus for use in years of drought.

Estimates of potential land use in the mid-1970s assumed that about 32 percent of total land area was too arid even for nomadic herding, 55 percent was suitable for extensive grazing, and 12.5 percent was potentially arable (see table 3). The basis for these approximations was not known, and they could not be readily traced to their source, which may have been estimates prepared in the early 1950s by the Italian authorities in the south and the British administration in the north.

The real land use potential of much of the 12.5 percent assumed to be arable had not yet been determined in the mid-1970s. Unexploited production potential was thought to exist primarily along the Juba, on the interriver plain, in the North West Region, and to a lesser extent wherever groundwater was accessible and not too brackish or where there was a *tug* (seasonal freshet in a dry watercourse; pl., *tugag*). The Juba-Shabelle area (riverine and interriver) had the highest cultivation potential in the country, but even here there may have been only about 4.9 million acres suitable for cultivation. This estimate generally cited in 1975 was taken from the agricultural and water survey conducted in the area from 1961 to 1967 for the FAO—the FAO Lockwood Survey. It estimated that in 1963 about three-fourths of the land suitable for cultivation was already occupied—most densely along the Shabelle floodplain and in the dryland farming area around Baydhaba, then known as the Baidoa plain.

Rangeland

Until 1974 range management and grazing control had never been introduced successfully in Somalia. Since 1956 a series of studies by United States and multilateral aid missions had stressed the urgent need for such measures. A 1967 FAO livestock report, based on an aerial survey in February to June 1966 supplemented by spot checks and an overland safari, had found that except for areas with tsetse fly or without water the country's ranges were badly overgrazed or showed evidence of recent overgrazing.

The northern ranges were even then particularly devastated, and four contributory factors were cited. The number of permanent settlements had increased, and their stock grazed the year around on adjacent pasture. Growing numbers of stock grazed the northern ranges on their way to market at Hargeysa or Berbera. Moreover portions of the northern range were being enclosed by privately owned zarebas, or light thorn hedges, and were used not only for private cultivation or grazing but for the sale of forage grass to feed livestock at urban markets. The nomadic pastoralist returning to his traditional home pasture during the winter dry season found it not rested and restored,

Table 3. Somalia, Actual and Potential Land Use, 1974

Use	Acres (in thousands)	Percent of Total Land Area
Potential Land Use:		
Land Suitable for Dryland Farming	19,120.0	12.1
Land Suitable for Irrigation		
Juba	370.6	0.2
Shabelle	197.6	0.1
North	12.3	0.0
Total Irrigable Land	580.5	0.4[1]
Total Arable Land	19,700.5	12.5
Land Suitable for Extensive Grazing	86.500.0	54.9
Other[2]		
Woodland[3]	6,200.0	3.9
Scrub	15,600.0	9.9
Desert and undefined	29,600.0	18.8
Total Other	51,400.0	32.6
Total Land Area	157,600.5	100.0
Actual Land Use		
Area under Dryland Farming	1,359.0	0.9
Area under Controlled Irrigation		
Juba	14.8	0.0
Shabelle	66.5	0.0
North	3.7	0.0
Total under Controlled Irrigation ...	85.0	0.1[1]
Area under Flood Irrigation		
Juba	51.9	0.0
Shabelle	108.4	0.1
North	1.7	0.0
Total under Flood Irrigation	162.0	0.1
Total Area in Crop or Fallow	1,606.0	1.0[1]
Land Available for Irrigation		
Juba	303.9	0.2
Shabelle	22.7	0.0
North	6.9	0.0
Total Available for Irrigation	333.5	0.2

0.0 means less than 0.05 percent.

[1] Figures do not add to total because of rounding.

[2] The 32.6 percent of total land area designated "other" is mostly unsuitable for any form of grazing or cultivation.

[3] The dominant varieties are acacia, euphorbia, and other thorn trees.

Source: Based on information from Somalia, Ministry of Planning and Coordination, *Statistical Abstract, 1968*, Mogadishu, 1969; and Somalia, Ministry of Planning and Coordination, *Draft Development Programme, 1974-1978*, Mogadishu, January 1974, p. 83.

as in the traditional nomadic cycle, but instead overgrazed by others in his absence. His stock nevertheless had to subsist on this depleted range throughout the season, as the home wells provided their only permanent source of water.

The fourth and perhaps the main factor contributing to overgrazing and progressive range deterioration had been the overall increase in livestock numbers resulting from the growth of human population and subsistence needs and made possible by progress in water supply and veterinary disease control. In 1966 the more arid areas from Bari Region to Galgduud Region were thought to contain only 23 percent of the population, but the livestock needed to sustain this population already exceeded the carrying capacity of the unimproved range. The 1967 FAO mission warned that another major drought could be disastrous. It helped the Somali government of the time submit a request for UNDP assistance in surveying the potential for range development and in preparing an appropriate program.

By 1970 a UNDP-FAO rangeland conservation and development survey had begun ecological classification of Somalia's northern rangeland and water resources. As also strongly urged by the 1967 report, two experts from the International Labor Organization (ILO) were invited in 1971 for a sociological survey to precede integrated development of the nomadic zones.

These were among eighteen agencies involved in the 1970s in the program for Ecological Management of Arid and Semi-Arid Rangelands (EMASAR), a UN-sponsored rescue operation to arrest the deterioration of rangeland in thirty-seven countries of Africa and the Middle East. In these countries the natural curb on livestock numbers once exerted by drought, disease, and tribal conflict had been offset by two or three decades of progress in disease control, water supply, and marketing development. Solving the resulting problem of range deterioration had not ranked high among the priorities pressing on African governments concerned until the Sahelian drought cycle of 1966 through 1972 focused world attention on the threat of widespread famine. The EMASAR experts stressed that the trend was readily reversible; the regenerative capacity of deteriorated rangeland under proper management is remarkable, and the technical innovations required are relatively simple. The most formidable challenge involved is overcoming social resistance to unfamiliar conservation methods among peoples whose long pastoral traditions have been reinforced by the teachings of Islam.

In Somalia this kind of social resistance had caused earlier experiments in grazing control to sink without a trace. The first attempt to introduce range management had been in 1956, when a small United States-sponsored pilot project at Afmadu in the Trans-Juba area had effectively but all too briefly demonstrated how rangeland around publicly constructed watering points could be rapidly improved by rotational and deferred grazing. This essentially Western concept failed to reckon with the prevailing custom of free access to public wells, and local authorities declined to intervene when the project, designed to support 3,000 head of cattle, was overrun and devastated by some 30,000 head. The same thing had happened in the 1960s on a government livestock station near Hargeysa supposedly closed to general grazing. Guards were driven from the area, which became just as devastated as the surrounding range. Until 1974 attempts at grazing control had been confined to the south or to the North West and Burao regions, and all had been unsuccessful.

In the light of this experience the FAO survey of 1967 had placed great stress on the need to precede active range management projects by a sociological survey to evaluate the effects on the people of development and settlement of nomads and above all by a massive program of adult education in range management and by practical demonstrations of its benefits, perhaps in conjunction with famine relief. Because the term *grazing reserve* had come into disrepute with the people in colonial times, they were to be called famine reserves or drought reserves. The report, in common with other aid reports, had recommended that development programs not give priority to proliferation of watering points until range control measures could be adopted.

The succeeding three development plans had deferred active range control projects until the proposed ecological and sociological surveys should be completed; but in the meantime they had gone full speed ahead in spending on new watering points and disease control, which increased overstocking of the range. It had been recommended that marketing agency holding grounds and government ranches be established on land not traditionally used by nomadic lineages because of tsetse infestation or lack of watering points. Cattle-fattening holding grounds completed near Kismayo and Mogadishu in the 1960s and near Hargeysa and Burao in the early 1970s, however, were subtracted from traditional nomadic grazing lands in areas of maximum pressure. When work finally began in 1975 on the IDA-financed Trans-Juba Livestock Project, the long-deferred plans to install government breeding ranches and fattening grounds on land newly cleared of tsetse infestation began to materialize.

During the 1950s and 1960s the proliferation of private reservoirs for sale of water had been particularly criticized by aid missions, who recommended that such construction be restricted. A ban on private tank construction awaited enactment of the proposed water law, but profiteering on the sale of water had been eliminated since 1969. Public construction of borehole wells, man-made basins or ponds *(warrs),* and masonry tanks or concrete reservoirs continued, however, and also contributed to the problem of localized overgrazing. It is hoped that future watering points can be more evenly spaced and adapted to the carrying capacity of the range.

The Development Program 1974-1978 in its original unrevised form had allocated most of its livestock investment funds to intensification of the programs for disease control, water supply, marketing, and government cattle fattening that had been featured in the three earlier development plans. Some Sh27.4 million was allocated for expenditure on the UNDP-FAO Rangeland Conservation and Development Project. This was to cover both continuation of the range classification survey throughout the country and simultaneous progress on the second phase of the project, under which 220 grazing guards would be employed to police some 8,260 square miles of grazing reserves. By 1974 twenty-one reserves had already been demarcated; estimates of their effectiveness in time of drought varied widely, but some observers said they were being respected in 1976.

Efforts to counteract soil erosion and improve the range by water-spreading and-retention works were financed from the allocation for forestry and were greatly expanded in the 1974-78 period. The 1967 FAO report had recommended that help be sought from the World Food Program for the ongoing self-help dune stabilization program, which was made part of the 1968-70 plan. The Development Program 1971-1973 affirmed that the dune program had been quite successful under the previous plan and would be continued on a much larger scale. Mainly through the availability of World Food Program assistance, it was hoped to reach the unprecedented target of stabilizing some 5,000 acres of shifting dunes by 1979. Of these some 3,500 acres were to be planted with casuarina between the coast and the lower Shabelle in the Genale area, where shifting dunes had long threatened irrigation projects and in 1975 were endangering the new nomadic settlements (see ch. 3).

The involuntary destocking of range and disruption of the nomadic way of life precipitated by the devastating 1974 drought seemed to offer an opportunity to extend effective range control and to demonstrate its potential advantages. Kuwait assured the necessary financing, at somewhat better than commercial terms, and the Northern Rangelands Development Project, launched in early 1976, became the first comprehensive effort in Somalia to promote range regeneration for the eventual benefit of pastoral herders rather than of government export or breeding programs. It was designed to develop some 35 million acres, or about 40 percent of the total land area suitable for grazing, in a 54,000-square-mile area east of Burao. Intensively grazed until the drought, the area was virtually denuded and would need at least three years to recover.

The project was prepared by the IDA, building on the survey work of the ongoing UNDP-FAO study. It would seek to protect the regeneration potential of the range by locating water development for

252

stock at strategic intervals and establishing drought reserves and grazing reserves patrolled by effective guard units. Drought reserves would give cattle permanent access to water in the dry season but would be closed to all livestock during heavy rains. Stone wall terracing would help retain runoff from bare slopes in the reserves, and forage trees would be planted. The project would establish twenty forage production units irrigated by water harvesting techniques employing runoff from bare slopes, seasonal *tugag*, or flash floods. It would organize herders into grazing associations and provide informal instruction at all levels to promote soil conservation and range management programs.

Irrigated Farming

Estimates of land area suitable for irrigation vary considerably, ranging from about 495,000 to 740,000 acres. In the mid-1970s it was surmised that there might be some 580,500 acres of irrigable land, of which about 247,000 were already under some form of irrigation, leaving roughly 333,500 acres available for irrigation development. The irrigation potential of the Shabelle valley had been more fully exploited in the past because of its proximity to major towns and because irrigation in the Juba valleys required the use of pumps. Much of the irrigated cropland on the Shabelle, however, was using uncontrolled flood irrigation and could potentially be converted to controlled irrigation. Disadvantages were that the Shabelle, although commonly described as perennial, dries up in its lower course during the critical months from January to March every year; the upper course near Balad runs dry once every five or six years; and the Shabelle waters have a higher mineral content than those of the Juba.

Since the FAO Lockwood Survey reported data for 1963, the estimate of land under uncontrolled flood irrigation along the Juba and Shabelle floodplains had declined from 363,000 to 160,300 acres. From 37,000 acres on the plantations in 1963, land under permanent controlled irrigation on the Juba and Shabelle had been increased to an estimated 81,300 acres in the mid-1970s. Much of this growth had taken place during the 1960s, when commercial acreage under bananas, sugar, grapefruit, and some other crops was expanding. A total of Sh25 million in development funds was spent on irrigation development between 1963 and 1969; this was less than one-fourth of the irrigation expenditure projected in the overambitious plan of the period.

Of the Sh31 million investment in irrigation development projected for the 1971-73 period, 48 percent was actually spent, mostly in 1973, the last year of the program. The largest project—for flood control— was not begun at all, and others got off to a slow start.

Official policy has stressed that Somalia needs as much irrigation as can be obtained if fluctuations in food supply are to be reduced; it should be developed not only along the southern rivers but wherever seasonal *tugag* occur. Most international planning advisers apparently concurred in this emphasis, given the variability of the country's rainfall. Wherever mean annual rainfall is below sixteen inches, the rains are so unreliable and the yield capacity of the soil so limited that irrigation is needed if cultivation is to be expanded. Of the total investment expenditure projected for development of livestock and crop farming in the unrevised January 1974 version of the Development Program 1974-1978, some 68 percent was allocated for irrigation development or for crop farming projects that would depend on irrigation.

Dryland Farming

Most of the country's crop farming is without access to irrigation and must depend entirely on the two annual rainy seasons. Dryland farming is practiced throughout the country by seminomads and settled cultivators wherever soils are suitable and mean annual rainfall exceeds twelve inches. Even where rainfall exceeds sixteen or twenty inches, however, dryland farming by traditional methods entails a high risk of periodic crop failure. Estimates of the arable land suitable for dryland farming vary; it is found primarily in the Juba-Shabelle area and in the northwest. In 1974 the Ministry of Planning estimated that there were some 60,000 acres of arable land on the Tug Wajaleh plain northwest of Hargeysa and about 295,000 acres in the North West Region Project Area as a whole, of which one-half had suffered severe erosion. In 1964 the FAO Lockwood Survey estimated that there were some 2.5 million acres of unoccupied rain-fed land in the Juba-Shabelle area that could be used for settlement.

An FAO planning report of 1965 noted that on the Tug Wajaleh plain, where mean annual rainfall is twenty inches, experience showed a probability of drought once every three years. In the Juba-Shabelle area it found that in a five-year period there was drought and famine in 1960 followed by devastating floods in 1961 that reduced sowing for 1962, when there was localized drought; a bumper crop in 1963 was followed by drought in 1964, crop failure, and famine in some areas.

To survive these recurrent natural hazards, dryland farming development requires more complicated techniques than those employed in irrigated agriculture. Trials in the past had been on a project-by-project basis, relying on experience gained in one project to provide the technical knowledge needed in the next. International planning advisers, while acknowledging that the potential for boosting production by dryland farming is modest, nonetheless recommended a sequence of dryland farming feasibility studies and integrated agricultural projects to give greater continuity to progress in rain-fed farming techniques before advances realized in the 1960s were lost or forgotten. The progress of soil erosion in dryland farming areas and the ravages of the 1974 drought, in their view, gave added urgency to the need to formulate a continuing strategy for dryland farming development.

In the unrevised Development Program 1974-1978 published in 1974, dryland farming development was to take place on about 62,000 acres in Phase I of the North West Region Development Project and about 6,180 acres in the Agricultural Crash Program state farms, including notably the one at Tug Wajaleh. Of the 18,600 acres taken over for state farms by 1973, some 10,000 acres were in the irrigated areas and 8,600 acres in rain-fed areas. By 1978 they were to take over an additional 6,180 acres of rain-fed land and 9,260 acres of irrigated land.

Interriver Dryland Cultivation

The FAO Lockwood Survey had found that in 1963 some 2 million acres of rain-fed cropland on the interriver plain had been cleared for about 64,000 traditional family small holdings at scattered settlements. Two-thirds of the traditional interriver cultivators kept small herds of cattle and some sheep or goats, and many families were seminomadic. The wholly settled cultivators lived in villages near a water source, usually a well or a man-made pond. They favored round wattle-and-daub huts, whereas the seminomads often used a portable hut of poles and skins (see ch. 6).

An integrated agricultural development project for the interriver dryland farming area was identified by the government with the help of the World Bank (see Glossary) and assigned high priority, but it was not included in the Development Program 1974-1978. Instead its feasibility was to be assessed along with that of Phase II of the North West Region Development Project after the experience of Phase I had been thoroughly evaluated. The proposed interriver project area would comprise about 14.1 million acres in Baydhaba Region, of which an estimated 1.4 million acres, or 10 percent, were cultivable: about 1.0 million on the Baydhaba plain and 400,000 in the undulating Bur Acaba District.

Pending more thorough adoption of 1976 regional names using the new Somali alphabet, the dryland farming area around Baydhaba was known to planners as the Bay Region or Upper Juba Region project area. It was the main dryland farming area in the country, producing about 80 percent of the total sorghum crop and supporting a settled farming population of some 200,000 in addition to seminomadic cultivators. Of the arable land in crop, 90 percent was planted to sorghum and the rest to maize, cowpeas, groundnuts, and beans.

In this area the Bonka Farmers' Training Center had been largely financed and staffed by United States aid from 1958 through 1969. After 1964 the center (and the training center and research station at Afgoi) had been operated on contract by the University of Wyoming.

Twenty-three Somali participants were sent to the United States for training; by 1969 fifteen had returned to become extension workers.

In the 1960s valuable research work had been performed concerning rain-fed soils, water, tillage, and fertilization, and there had been promising developments in improvement and adaptation of fast-maturing, drought-resistant sorghum, groundnuts, and safflower seed. Dissemination of improved techniques had lagged, however; only fifteen extension workers were stationed in the villages to help cultivators with improved practices. The project agreement had called for an increasing contribution of Somali personnel and counterpart funds; as this was not forthcoming, the United States contribution was to cease by mid-1971.

As it turned out, the United States announced in June 1970 that, because of trade with the Democratic Republic of Vietnam (North Vietnam) carried by ships flying the Somali flag of convenience, all United States economic development aid to Somalia would be terminated within a year (see ch. 10). Ongoing aid projects were not interrupted, but by 1971 dryland farming development had been left more or less in limbo. During the 1960s some 1,100 interriver cultivators had attended two-week training sessions at the Bonka center, where they learned how to grow improved sorghum, groundnuts, and cowpeas; proper seedbed preparation and row planting instead of broadcast sowing; weed control; and manure application. They made their own yokes and trained oxen to draw locally adapted plows and other small equipment. Demonstrations were also conducted on the farmers' fields. In 1974 about half the cultivated area in the project region was still being cropped by traditional methods, but the improved methods used on the other half were ensuring a harvest in poor years when most farmers suffered almost complete crop failure. The proposed Bay Region feasibility study called for detailed analysis of the extent to which local farmers had adopted improved practices and of the results.

Annual rainfall in the proposed project area averaged twenty inches, but the longer spring rainy season failed in one year out of four, and the short fall rainy season failed in one of every two years. When crops failed, farmers often left the region with their cattle for three or four years, leaving their holdings uncultivated. Like the riverine cultivators, traditional interriver farmers relied on the short-handled hoe, at best hoeing the earth into furrows a few inches deep to retain rainwater. The same crop was often planted on a field for several years, sowing was broadcast, and no fertilizer was used. Yields were low, and crop failure was frequent.

North West Region Development Project

A declared goal of policy in 1974 was to reduce the disparity in living standards between south and north. To make the north self-sustaining in food supply a project was prepared by a World Bank mission to redevelop arable land in areas of the high plateau in Borama, Galileh, and Hargeysa districts of Waqooyi Galbeed Region. In 1973 about 65 percent of the people in the project area were nomads who moved with their flocks in the wet season into the northeastern and central regions and into Ethiopia. Since the late nineteenth century, however, some had followed the example of their Darod kinsmen in Ethiopia by settling to cultivate sorghum, using a rudimentary wooden oxplow. Their number had greatly increased since the 1930s; in 1973 the settled population of the three districts was about 160,000, and about 12,000 cultivating families (60,000 people) were thought to have settled in the area.

Landholdings averaged about twenty-five acres (one-third in fallow); annual rain-fed farm income of Sh1,400 (US$230) included subsistence production valued at Sh800 (US$128). The average cultivator was thought to keep about ten cattle, two to four camels, and twenty to forty sheep and goats. Of some 395,000 acres of arable land in the three districts, about 105,000 were probably in fallow and 205,000 in crop (of which 80 percent was planted to sorghum). About 630 small horticultural gardens irrigated from wells fed by seasonal *tugag* occupied about 6,670 acres and grew citrus (1,235 acres), other fruits, vegetables, and coffee.

The region's natural rangeland had been badly overgrazed around the few and poorly distributed watering points by stock being driven to market at Hargeysa or Berbera from the south or from Ethiopia, and stock of both nomads and cultivators was in poor condition even before the 1974 drought. Most of the plateau had been cleared for cultivation since the 1930s. By the late 1960s severe erosion had left only about 510,000 acres of arable topsoil in the entire northern part of the country. Soil and water conservation projects conducted by the British in the 1950s and with United States aid in the 1960s had succeeded in arresting erosion in three districts by bunding (building earth embankments). In Somalia conservation procedures, such as bunding and dune stabilization, that restored land without first reserving it from use, were readily accepted by the local population.

Natural conditions in the area favor dryland farming. Sorghum yields in good years suggest that soils are fertile, and annual rainfall averages sixteen to twenty inches. In years when the rains were scant or poorly distributed, however, crops failed everywhere but on the 50,000 acres bunded in the 1950s and 1960s; there was no known instance of crop failure on bunded land. On about 40,000 acres the bunds had been kept in excellent condition; the North West Region project proposed to restore bunds in disrepair on 5,000 acres and to build new ones on 60,000 acres. Over the six years of Phase I the project would also establish some basic services for the first time and strengthen others that had run down in recent years, reintroducing crop trials for fast-maturing kinds of sorghum, rehabilitating the extension service for dryland farmers, and creating a new extension service for irrigated farms.

Sorghum yields were twice as high on bunded as on nonbunded land. Bunding was to have first priority; thereafter improved practices could be taught that might double the average bunded yield. The objectives of the six-year Phase I program were to make the project area self-sufficient in food grains; to improve the incomes of some 2,500 cultivating families; and to take advantage of valuable experience that could serve as a basis for extension of the program in Phase II to the entire North West Region over a twenty-five-year period and for a similar integrated agricultural project around Baydhaba in the south.

AGRICULTURAL PROGRAMS, INSTITUTIONS, AND GOALS

Reports from Somalia commonly stress the gains achieved since 1970, somewhat obscuring the appreciable element of continuity between development policies before and since the October 1969 coup. Such major foreign lenders as the United Nations (UN), the EEC, the Federal Republic of Germany (West Germany), and the Soviet Union were active in the years from 1960 to 1969, laying the foundations for subsequent development progress. In the 1970s the government had sought to profit by the lessons of the earlier trial-and-error experience in development planning and execution. Its most notable achievements had been in mobilizing more domestic investment resources by promptly raising direct taxes and cutting government and private salaries, in partially reducing bureaucratic duplication and fragmentation, and in initiating the massive educational effort needed to modify social attitudes toward innovation.

The army's own development efforts in the pre-1969 period had taken place through its reserve corps of Young Pioneers on the Soviet model. The young men were given intensive army training and then sent as low-cost manpower for roadbuilding, well-digging, conservation, farming, and construction projects. They helped in flood and drought relief and in stabilizing sand dunes, which became highly publicized features of the post-1969 efforts. The army also operated experimental farms. In February 1970, soon after assuming power, the army officers who formed the Supreme Revolutionary Council (SRC) established an agricultural pioneer corps, recruiting workers for the high-priority Agricultural Crash Program. Like the earlier pioneer corps, it stresses the self-help concept that had been a popular feature of the army's pre-1969 effort and helps mobilize sociopolitical support at the grass-roots level for economic development and nation building.

In the 1960s development spending had gone mostly into roads and ports, in the hope that spending on the rural sector could then be greatly increased in a later phase. The postrevolutionary government resolved to increase spending on the rural sector. Annual spending on livestock development, which averaged only Sh8.6 million in the 1963-69 period, was in fact doubled in the 1971-73 period, but total annual spending on the rural sector declined from Sh64.8 million in the 1963-69 period to Sh47.9 million in the 1971-73 period. The nearly sixfold increase called for in the draft Development Program 1974-1978 was considered unrealistic, but the prognosis improved after the 1974 drought when foreign loans of more than US$100 million were committed.

In colonial times Italy's spending on research and development in the south had been primarily adapted to the needs of the Italian plantations, although efforts were made to introduce indigenous cultivators to oxplows and other improvements. In the Trust Territory of Somaliland under Italian Administration efforts to improve indigenous cultivation and stockraising absorbed a little over half of the modest US$13.7 million provided for several concurrent seven-year plans for 1954 through 1960 administered by UN and United States aid agencies. Grain storage and flood control facilities were built in the Juba-Shabelle area and wells and reservoirs provided in the more arid regions.

Of the projected investment expenditure of Sh572.8 million for stockraising, cultivation, forestry, and fishing listed in the prerevolutionary government's ambitious First (Five-Year) Plan 1963-67, only a fraction had actually been spent by the end of the plan period. The period was one of crises and hardships, starting out with two years of drought, crop failure, livestock loss, famine, and active hostilities on the Ethiopian border that drained budgetary resources. The Second (Short-Term) Plan 1968-70, published in 1968, freely acknowledged, however, that fulfillment of the first plan had suffered from such defects as wasteful and unproductive use of foreign aid proceeds. The short-term plan was formulated as an interim program to permit progress on abandoned or ongoing projects listed under the first plan and to allow the introduction of basic reforms in the administrative structure adapted to more rapid development progress (see ch. 12).

Action on the short-term plan had barely started, however, by the end of 1969. From 1963 through 1969 spending (confirmed foreign financing) on the rural sector was less than 80 percent of the planned sum, and spending on projects actually completed (as well as studied or started) was only 31 percent of total planned spending (see ch. 12). Of the total spent nearly 50 percent had been received in the form of Soviet loans. These financed the purchase of tractors and bulldozers for the state farm and machinery pool projects and the import of consumer goods from the Soviet Union. Sale of consumer imports was to have financed the development of three state farms. The Soviet goods did not sell, however; so no progress could be made in developing the

259

land cleared for two state farms at Gelib on the Shabelle. On the Tug Wajaleh state grain farm in the northwest the area under crop had to be drastically reduced for lack of funds, and in 1966 work was abandoned and the Soviet machinery left to rust.

The projects most frequently criticized in foreign publications as being spectacular failures in 1969 were the state farm program and three expensively built processing plants that were financed from the funds allocated for industry but were unable to repay the loans used to build them because rural planning had failed to ensure an adequate supply of low-cost raw materials. A tuna-freezing plant built with United States aid was bankrupted when the tuna forsook the coastal waters but has since been restored to operation by an Italian firm. The Soviet-sponsored meat cannery at Kismayo and dairy at Mogadishu were also labeled disastrous failures because of their difficulties with supply in 1969, but after heavy investment in cattle marketing the meat cannery has been able since 1971 to export canned stewed beef to repay the Soviet loan (see ch. 14).

Agricultural Programs since October 1969

The fiscal and administrative reforms introduced immediately after the October 1969 coup were said to have produced a perceptible quickening of activity during 1970 on projects both within and outside the short-term plan. In line with the new government's socialist ideology, there was a shift of emphasis in agriculture as in other sectors toward stronger government control of trade and more direct intervention in production.

The autonomous agencies were reorganized to make them more responsive to central government, and President Mohamed Siad Barre called for more to be accomplished by self-help at the local level and by government development expenditure from its own savings. The state farm program was expanded, but plantations were left in operation by Italian or Somali owners; collectivization of small-scale agriculture was to be accomplished piecemeal and by persuasion through an intensive effort to organize agricultural supply and marketing cooperatives that could later be adapted to group farming and in time to full collective farming (see ch. 12).

The first major rural development move was the launching of the Agricultural Crash Program in February 1970. When the initial target for employment on the farms proved overambitious, a crash program for public works was introduced to take up the slack. Those employed were chiefly former nomads who had flocked to the towns from the drought-stricken northern regions after 1964 or 1969. According to I.M Lewis, the crash program was specifically designed to provide work for unemployed nomads, particularly young men.

Most of the early crash program farms were located in the concession areas along the Juba and Shabelle. The short-term plan had noted that sizable areas of well-located land along the river that were still under concession but were not being cropped offered the best potential for a sustained national drive for crop diversification, import replacement, and self-sufficiency. The Development Program 1971-1973 —possibly drafted by the same foreign planning advisers as the earlier plan—noted that the crash program, merged with the state farm program "which has been continuing through the period of the Short-Term Plan 1968-1970," would be expanded in part by stabilization or rehabilitation of existing but underutilized irrigation facilities at Belet Weyn, Genale, Afgoi, and Jowhar.

Part of the state farm at Tug Wajaleh was transferred to the crash program in 1970. Wheat was being grown on 7,000 acres by 1973 and was to be grown on 15,000 acres by 1978, but average yields had declined, and output was affected by drought and disease. Yields had declined drastically since the state took over the sugar estate at Jowhar, once Italian owned but under joint ownership since 1963. One-fourth of the cane acreage had also become unusable because of saline soil, and the proposal for a second sugar complex at Fanole, under study since 1963, was being revived. By November 1974 there were ten crash program state farms employing 5,760 pioneers and some 220 technicians to farm a cultivated area of 19,150 acres.

The Agricultural Crash Program had been almost the only element of the Development Program 1971-1973 to surpass its target; doubling it had high priority in the 1974-78 program. It stressed the principles of self-help and national self-reliance. Its only foreign aid receipts had been the food rations provided by the World Food Program for pioneers working on self-help projects. It was still heavily dependent on government subsidy, but many officials considered this continuing drain on the budget amply justified by the program's value as an experiment in social progress and nation building. Economically it had been more successful in providing employment than in increasing rural production: yields on its farms were thought to be below the low national average, and some farms could not feed their own residents.

Poor management and inadequate supervision were thought to be the main reasons for the poor performance of the state farms. Management turnover had been high, and trained staff was lacking for supervision. This had led to neglect of such practices as adequate land leveling for irrigation, use and care of machinery, use of fertilizer, and use of improved seed. Although their inexperience might retard production, the pioneers were acquiring skills needed for irrigated farming. Perhaps most valuable in the long run might be the program's influence in giving young nomads positive attitudes toward cultivation. From the first day pioneers received a paramilitary and political indoctrination—increasingly ideologically defined—teaching com-

261

munity responsibility and the values of collectivism. They had daily literacy classes. Foreign journalists reported that the most impressive feature of the crash program was the community spirit and enthusiasm displayed by pioneers in self-help building projects and in communal sports, music, and theater.

Similar benefits were claimed from the seven-month, IDA-supported, Rural Development Campaign that sent 25,000 to 35,000 urban students among the nomads in August 1974 to teach the new Somali script (see ch. 7). Its organizers explained that it combined literacy instruction with four other aims: provision of medical care; promotion of political consciousness by inculcating socialist principles; population census; and inventory of national resources, notably livestock population and water supply. The students were supplied with vaccines and pamphlets on hygiene and animal husbandry and were said to have vaccinated "vast numbers" of people and livestock. The campaign had to be shelved on March 7, 1975, but an effort was made to pursue the work in the relief camps.

A major objective of the Development Program 1974-1978 was a massive effort to develop agricultural cooperatives. Little progress had been made since 1970: some sixty-five cooperatives were founded, but they could not obtain credit and had the usual problem of lack of understanding among the farmers. Henceforth the Ministry of Agriculture was to provide credit guarantees and much stricter supervision of cooperatives; a few had already qualified for credit from the Somali Development Bank in 1975. The credit increase since 1969 had gone almost entirely to private plantations and government enterprises.

Great stress was placed on the importance of the Cooperative Law of October 4, 1974, in providing a legal framework to facilitate the development of a pervasive, truly socialist cooperative system that was to contrast with the "token systems" that had survived the 1960s in most other African countries. The law provided for detailed regulation of the contractual relations involved and spelled out the series of stages in which cooperatives were to be developed in each sector of activity.

In the agricultural sector there was to be a period of assimilation in which each farm family would retain its own landholding but marketing, supply, and community self-help projects would be in common. Once mutual trust and cohesiveness had been established, a group farming cooperative could promote common use of equipment and other services. The final stage will be collective farming; the Cooperative Law specified that at this stage a family will not be allowed to retain more than 1.2 acres of rain-fed or 0.5 acre of irrigated land, a few chickens, and handtools (see ch. 12).

By mid-1976 the government, with IDA assistance, was seeking to identify and prepare new projects to utilize foreign loan commitments, and the Development Program 1974-1978 was being revised in the light of drought developments. As originally stated its goals were to increase the number and area of state farms and to make them self-supporting; to attain self-sufficiency in sorghum, maize, cotton, oil-seeds, fruit, and vegetables; to increase domestic production of wheat and rice; and to increase the range and efficiency of agricultural extension, research, and marketing services.

In addition a package program of the kind successful in many other African countries was to be introduced to provide farmers with improved inputs and services. To achieve the most rapid production increase and conserve skilled manpower and other scarce resources, it was to be introduced only in the eight districts that had the most developed infrastructure and the highest output.

Some progress had been made in cash crop policy. The storage and marketing system initiated with UN help after 1966 began gradually to effect some improvements in price and marketing policy that provided incentives to cash production, and more careful adaptation of official producer prices to production needs is a goal of the Development Program 1974-1978. Use of improved inputs has been confined largely to the plantations, but there has been limited government distribution of fertilizer for rice and cotton production. Marketing or distribution of supplies through cooperatives had not yet begun but was to be initiated before 1980. Average yields have remained low, and only in such favorable years as 1972 and 1973 has the country attained self-sufficiency in maize and sorghum.

Conditions for replacing rice and cotton imports are more propitious than for wheat. Variety trials and adaptive research during the 1960s provided a sound basis for expansion of rice and cotton output in the Juba-Shabelle area. In 1969 a rice and tobacco project was started by the People's Republic of China (PRC) on the experimental station at Jowhar. During the period of the Development Program 1974-1978 rice will be grown under irrigation on the Juba-Shabelle Emergency Settlement Scheme and on the Libyan-sponsored Afgoi-Mordinle irrigation project, an expansion of the Shabelle pilot project of the 1960s. Also proposed was the establishment of a large rice development scheme in the swamp area along the lower Shabelle south of Falcheiro under a swamp reclamation project to eliminate malaria and tsetse fly infestation.

Cotton has been grown for centuries for home spinning and in the mid-1960s was grown on a limited scale as a cash crop by small-scale cultivators on both the flood-irrigated and the dryland farming portions of the Juba-Shabelle area. The Somaltex cotton textile mill at Balad was built under the 1963-67 plan with assistance from West Germany and began trial operations in 1968; problems included competition from cheap smuggled imports and deficiency in domestic raw cotton supply. Under the short-term plan land cleared earlier at Gelib for one of the abortive Soviet-sponsored state farms was made into a cotton demonstration project.

Seed reproduction stations established in 1968 at Genale and Camsuma by the EEC developed medium-staple cottonseed for the Shabelle area and long-staple cotton for the Lower Juba (in addition to sesame and grapefruit seedlings). Since 1968 the Agricultural Development Corporation (formerly the Agricultural Development Agency) has been in charge of supplying lint to the factory at Balad and providing supervision and improved supplies to the state farms and smallholders engaged in cotton growing. Like much of the planning and development administration, however, the corporation has admittedly been suffering from technical and organizational dysfunctions, and in the 1970s cotton yields have been poor owing in part to deficiencies in technical supervision and distribution of seed and other improved inputs. Perhaps for lack of these improvements production has fluctuated widely from year to year in response to variations in rainfall, although soils and climate in the area are supposed to be favorable for cotton growing. Large farms have suffered from labor shortages. Although cotton is a very suitable cash crop for smallholders, plans for the 1974-78 period focused on expanding large-scale irrigated production.

In the stockraising sector the policy goals and programs in the original unrevised version of the Development Program 1974-1978 were the same as those of the 1963-67 plan; they had meanwhile been restated and updated in the two intervening development plans. They focused largely on export marketing and disease control, and improvements were to benefit primarily government export earnings, processing factories, and ranches. The improvements in conditions for nomadic herders that were the focus of drought rehabilitation programs in 1975 and 1976 had received rather short shrift in the original program for the 1974-78 period, perhaps pending more detailed census and survey data.

In the 1960s progress had focused on creating the institutional framework for later development in the livestock sector and in conducting predevelopment surveys and studies. By 1969 facilities for livestock marketing, transport, and disease control had been greatly improved.

The Livestock Development Agency, created in 1966, got into gear with an EEC grant of US$5.9 million in mid-1968; by 1969 it had created and stocked holding grounds to supply the Kismayo cannery and organized auction markets in the Trans-Juba area and elsewhere. The Community Development Service, created in 1966, was furnishing nomads with cement tanks, dispensaries, community centers, and welfare facilities. Teacher training and education programs for the nomads had been under way since 1958 (see ch. 7). A training center for those working in hides and skins and leather development had been in operation since 1968. So had the UNDP-financed Training School for Animal Assistants at Mogadishu, which had turned out forty-four assistant veterinarians by 1971.

With this framework in place annual spending on livestock development could be doubled after 1971. The Development Program 1971-1973 noted that the 1967 FAO livestock survey had helped identify major problems, including prevailing diseases; what remained was to press the disease control program forward with greater vigor. With West German assistance an antirinderpest campaign for Somalia, Kenya, and Ethiopia was launched in 1970. By 1973 some 800,000 cattle in the Trans-Juba area had been immunized. The project for intensification of animal health had to be confined to the Gedo, Dijuuma, and Lower Juba regions in the hope of meeting veterinary standards for export of frozen beef from Kismayo to Europe. It was hoped eventually to create a disease-free zone extending into the two Shabelle regions and Hiiraan Region. In 1973 vaccination was made compulsory; henceforth vaccine would be provided free.

Major creations by 1973 included the four-year College of Veterinary Science and Medicine, whose first twenty-one students would graduate in 1978; the 21st October Dairy Farm, established with West German assistance to supply the dairy plant at Mogadishu; and holding grounds at Hargeysa and Burao. Of the Sh189.6 million projected expenditure for stockraising projects in the Development Program 1974-1978, the largest allocations were Sh95.2 million for cattle-fattening projects, Sh24.4 million for animal health, and Sh13.0 million for cattle-marketing improvement.

Organizational Structure

Institutions involved in agricultural development and related services had been proliferating since independence. Most were autonomous agencies under the supervision, rather loosely defined, of the relevant ministry. For the most part they dated from before the revolution; the boards of directors had since been replaced by management committees weighted in favor of lower echelon workers. In mid-1976 the chain of command was still not clearly defined, and the fragmentation of functions among different agencies or ministries was dissipating the efforts of scarce trained manpower, but some amalgamation of staff and functions and tightening of the planning process appeared to be in prospect.

Directly responsible to the SRC were the National Rehabilitation Committee, created in 1975 to supervise the drought resettlement and rehabilitation program, and the Agricultural Crash Program Agency, to which the crash program had been transferred in June 1972 from the Ministry of Agriculture. The commercial banks and the Somali Development Bank, under the Ministry of Finance, were involved in agricultural credit. Trade in farm exports came under the National Banana Board or the National Trading Agency and the ministries of external and internal trade. Drilling and maintenance of wells and boreholes was the function of the Water Development Agency, responsible to the Ministry of Mining and Water Resources.

The Livestock Development Agency and the Agricultural Development Agency, both established in February 1966, had been brought under the supervision of the relevant ministries, expanded and strengthened since mid-1971, when the name of the latter was changed to the Agricultural Development Corporation. Originally created to consolidate gains already made in disease control as well as to rationalize stock routes and marketing and improve cattle supply to the canneries, the Livestock Development Agency had become concerned almost exclusively with factory supply and export of live cattle. Disease control had been expanded under the veterinary department of the Ministry of Livestock, Forestry, and Range. In 1974 the agency was to be restructured to operate production ranches in addition to markets, stock routes, and holding grounds. Financial autonomy and improved organization and management were to be introduced in an effort to correct the agency's inefficient operations.

A government central agricultural machinery pool and rental service, established with Soviet assistance as the National Tractor Hiring Agency in 1963, merged with the Agricultural Development Corporation in 1969 and was restored to autonomous status in 1973. A monopoly grain-marketing and price stabilization scheme initiated by the UN in 1966 had been strengthened, better funded, and moved around in similar fashion. Law Number 51 of July 22, 1971 had given the Agricultural Development Corporation the monopoly of trade in sorghum and maize, and between mid-1971 and mid-1974 its operations, supported by buffer stocks, had reportedly been quite successful. Price stabilization had become a function of the Ministry of Agriculture in consultation with the agency.

The Ministry of Agriculture, responsible for most other functions, was to be reorganized under the Development Program 1974-1978; its efficiency had reportedly been impaired by constant changes in organization and by acute shortage of trained staff at the middle and lower levels. In 1974 a department of agricultural cooperatives was created within the ministry to centralize control and speed development of the still embryonic cooperative system. Its cooperative development fund would receive some Sh48 million of projected expenditure in the 1974-78 period, leaving only Sh43.7 million, or 4 percent of agricultural sector investment, to improve the ministry's extension service, department of plant protection and desert locust control, research department, and meteorological service.

STOCKRAISING

In the early 1970s stockraising was the source of two-thirds of the country's export earnings and an important supplement to the income or subsistence diet of much of the settled population. For the nomadic or seminomadic pastoralists who made up some 60 percent of the population, livestock was increasingly regarded as a source of cash income as well as a traditional unit of social value and pledge of lineage responsibility, a source of daily sustenance, and a last resort against famine in the harsh dry seasons and in the droughts that occur in two years out of five.

The livestock herd is the nation's principal store of wealth and the most readily exploitable resource of much of the population, and its potential effectiveness as a factor of production is therefore a matter of prime concern to development planners. Countless reports and surveys have been devoted to the subject; yet there is little agreement on such matters as the size of the livestock population, the rate of offtake for sale or slaughter, and the attitudes and habits of the herders. Most sources concur in the 1967 FAO survey estimate that the national herd had almost trebled since the late 1950s despite recurrent severe drought. After each drought the herd was rapidly restored to surpass its previous size, despite progressive depletion of pasturage (see Actual and Potential Land Use, this ch.). The ILO mission estimated in 1971 that the total number of animals had risen by 40 to 60 percent in the preceding five years.

Until data from the 1975 census and surveys could become available, information on the age and sex composition of herds and the pattern of their exploitation and sale remained the subject of speculation. One source estimated that the 1973 livestock population included 2.5 to 3.5 million cattle, 8 to 9 million goats, and 4 to 6 million small black-faced sheep, used for meat and milk but of little use for wool. In 1972 estimated offtake peaked at 10 percent for cattle and 35 percent for sheep and goats, then declined to 7 percent for cattle and 30 percent for sheep and goats in 1974. Favorable prices offset part of the decline in live exports from 77,000 cattle and 1.6 million sheep and goats in 1972 to an estimated 25,000 cattle and 1 million sheep and goats in 1974. Exports were expected to decline further in 1975 and 1976 as herds were rebuilt; thereafter the rate of offtake may be increased by improved husbandry and range management.

Consumption of sheep and goat meat is estimated at one animal (perhaps thirty-three pounds) per person per year. Among nomads they are slaughtered for ritual occasions or hospitality, but meat consumption may also increase if milk yields fall below the famine level in the dry season. In the camel and cattle camps milk is the only diet the year around. The family camps retain one or two milch camels as well as burden camels. Their daily diet of goat or camel milk may be supplemented by durra sorghum, dates, and wild berries and by smuggled or locally purchased rice, sugar, and tea.

In the mid-1960s the FAO survey had estimated that a nomadic family wholly dependent on livestock for subsistence, cash, and barter would need a per capita minimum of about ten animals of current quality just to stay alive. The nomads were then thought to be getting less than half their average daily caloric requirement during a normal dry season. Nomadic families interviewed in the 1973 Burao Region pilot study confirmed that a wife and her family of four or five young children at the family camp required a flock of at least fifty to seventy sheep and goats for subsistence, because no more than half of the flock would usually be in milk at any one time. At the end of the dry season milk yields decreased, and survival was a problem for many families (see ch. 6).

The low productivity of livestock in both meat and milk yield results from use of small, low-yielding, unimproved breeds; from the poor grazing and water supply available; and also from frequent use of traditional, unimproved husbandry practices, especially in the north. The traditional system of nomadic rotation is skillfully adapted to the harsh environment and the rigorous alternation of the seasons but is fundamentally oriented toward survival rather than high productivity. In dry seasons watering is kept to a strict minimum. Animals receive little care at birth or in sickness, castration is not regularly practiced, and males and females are not segregated at any time of the year; females are not systematically culled except when sterile or too old. Birthrates are low, death rates high, and animals are often underweight, exhausted, and vulnerable to drought and disease.

As was true for many other African countries in the 1950s and 1960s, far more detailed and thoroughly researched information was published abroad on the traditional role of livestock in the lineage relationships and social system of the Somali pastoralist than on its contemporary significance as a factor of production or a source of income or sustenance. In the early 1970s livestock retained significance as a unit of social value: camels in particular were the main unit of marriage payments and *dia* (blood money) payments (see Glossary). They were a measure of individual wealth and were valued as beasts of burden and as a source of daily sustenance and given priority in watering, grazing, and management. Even camels were commonly sold, however; the FAO livestock survey in 1967 found that few salable bull camels and castrates were retained.

An April 1971 article on nomadism and land use in Somalia by Thadis W. Box contended that contrary to frequent assertions "the Somalis have no hesitation in selling their livestock. Indeed, they are great traders, and the organization of the livestock business in Somalia is, despite the general belief, a highly sophisticated business. . . . . It is not uncommon to find Somali livestock buyers trading with both

Somali and non-Somali peoples in neighboring Kenya and Ethiopia. Livestock cross the borders during annual migration, and it is almost impossible to tell how many of the animals sold from Somalia were actually produced in that country." In 1973 the inflow and outflow of cattle to and from Somalia across the borders were thought to be balancing out as demand and prices in Somalia rose.

The 1972 ILO report on the nomadic zones confirmed that the traditional marketing system was well established and pervasive; there were daily markets in most towns and villages, and traders used trucks or camels to reach nomads in remote areas. A 1975 study noted, however, that stock was priced by the head rather than by weight or quality grade, indicating some survival of the tradition of valuing sheer stock numbers above their productivity.

Little is known of factors that influence herders in selling or retaining stock. On the influence of weather there is some conflict. The 1967 FAO report and 1972 ILO report said that herders are often reluctant to sell in wet seasons if enough grazing is available, but export demand and prices are then highest because stock is in peak condition. This interaction of high demand and low supply results in top prices during the best grazing season: conversely supply increases in dry seasons because of shortage of grazing, but with stock in poor condition export demand slackens. A 1975 report stated, however, that more animals are offered for sale when rains and grazing are good because of lower stock mortality and greater confidence among herders; in drought years fewer animals are sold, because of lower demand and higher stock mortality and because nomads keep as large a flock as possible to ensure survival despite lower yields and high losses. This increases the ratio of stock to pasture at the worst possible time and makes for even higher mortality. This pattern might be studied to see if means could be found to increase offtake and reduce pressure on grazing in time of drought.

The meat yield of animals sold is often low because herders tend to market their most unproductive stock, such as males not required for breeding, old males and females, and females that are sterile and unproductive. The age and sex structure of sheep and goat flocks retained indicates heavy culling of young male stock. The 1967 FAO survey found that very little male stock beyond the weaning stage had been retained. When cattle are killed for consumption, young male calves are slaughtered first, then older males and aged or sterile cows. Some peoples in the south who keep cattle for milk only sold so many male stock that not enough were left to ensure reproduction. In severe drought years all cattle but the most valuable female breeders may be sold, slaughtered, or allowed to die. Some 30 to 40 percent of cattle exported were calves and young bulls; their export was prohibited by a government order of December 1973, when it was planned to buy and fatten young stock for higher export prices. Export of all female animals had been prohibited in the 1960s, reportedly for fear that varieties in great demand on the Arabian Peninsula might be reproduced by breeders there. Much female stock is sold at home, but demand and prices are lower than for males.

Low-yielding but hardy, all five main cattle breeds are derived from the zebu. Most numerous and most used for breeding improved stock are the Jiddu (Suroq) dual-purpose breed, kept by the interriver peoples, and the boran (Havai), kept as a dual-purpose herd in the Trans-Juba area and bred for improved beef stock.

FISHING

After the tuna catch failed in 1963, the government requested the UNDP to conduct a new survey of fishery resources off the country's 1,800-mile coastline. Concluded in 1974, it again assessed the coastal waters as rich in a variety of exploitable species (see ch. 3). Since the third Ming dynasty ethnic minorities on the southern Bajun Islands and at limited settlements along the coasts had conducted a thriving export trade in shark fins, tortoiseshell, and dried fish with China. This trade had been dominated by the merchants of Zanzibar, to whose sultan the Bajun Islands once belonged, and was disrupted by the revolution there in 1964. Fish had been part of the subsistence diet and way of life only among certain non-Somali groups. In 1854 the explorer Richard Burton had found that a common taunt used by ethnic Somali against other groups was "speak not to me with the mouth that eateth fish," and something of this attitude survived a century later. In 1974 about 2,500 full-time and 16,000 part-time fishermen manned about 2,500 small boats. To avoid the monsoons small-boat fishing is confined to the months from October to March. On the north coast some 1,680 traditional fishermen, using about 500 dugout canoes and 215 motorized boats, fish for tuna from November to February to supply the three tuna canneries and one freezing plant.

About 80 percent of the total catch is exported. The tonnage exported in canned form increased from 378 in 1971 to 1,045 in 1973 while the tonnage smoked, dried, fresh, or frozen (including shellfish) declined from 1,045 to 751. Some fish is sold fresh in Mogadishu, but most of the catch by traditional east coast fishermen is smoked and dried for export. All four plants had been operating far below capacity because of a widely fluctuating but consistently inadequate supply from the fishing fleet.

An Italian firm operated a 7,000-ton-capacity tuna-freezing plant at Ras Filuch near Alula and two 7,000-ton-capacity canned tuna and fishmeal plants, built at Habo and Candala in 1936. In the best year processing of the catch used only a fraction of capacity at these plants and at the costly government tuna cannery and fishmeal plant at Las Koreh, which could not pay its way or service the Sh43 million

Soviet loan that built it. The notoriously unreliable migratory habits of tuna shoals, which once idled highly capitalized industries in Norway and on California's cannery row, had bankrupted the Ras Filuch freezing plant after it was first built with United States aid in 1963 and had caused the catch to fail almost entirely in 1966 and 1968.

The 17,474-square-mile continental shelf is covered with coral reefs rich in rock lobster and shrimp. A freezing plant built by a Somali-American firm at Kismayo in 1968 had a highly successful operation flying frozen shellfish to Europe and the United States. Idled by litigation since the October 1969 coup, it was taken over by a Japanese concern in 1975.

Projects for training in improved fishing methods and the introduction of motorboats and other equipment were sponsored by United States aid after 1959 and by the Soviet Union after 1972. A joint Somali-Soviet company created in October 1974 improved supply to the Las Koreh plant; its fleet increased from ten boats in 1973 to seventy in 1974. Ten were trawlers and would inaugurate deep-sea fishing. They would be operated by some 200 men and would be exclusively under the Ministry of Fisheries and Sea Transport. The smaller motorboats would carry 850 men; most would be attached to the canneries. A repair and maintenance base for fishing vessels was to be built at Berbera and fishing ports at Mogadishu, Alula, and Eil. A UNDP-FAO project to assist training, marketing, and boatbuilding was started in May 1969 and was to be extended through 1976. It had helped create twenty-one fishing cooperatives.

An effort had been made in mid-1975 to recruit 78,000 nomads to man the expanded fishing fleet. Only 16,000 finally volunteered, however, because many changed their minds and decided to join the crop farming settlements or return to herding. The 16,000 nomads were divided among four fishing communities and organized into cooperatives, adding to the twenty-one fishing cooperatives already in operation.

FORESTRY

The country's modest forestry potential had been progressively depleted rather than developed in past years. The Development Program 1974-1978 proposed to begin gradual measures to prepare the way for long-term progress in reducing reliance on imports of wood and wood products. This would involve management of three areas of cedar (*Juniperus procerus*) forest totaling some 296,000 acres in the Gullis Range in the northern Sanaag and Bari regions, served by the country's only sawmill, at Erigavo. Government forestry plantations were to be established on some 14,800 acres of coastal plain near Berbera and another 14,800 acres at Gcanlibax. There had been encouraging results in trials of irrigated teak plantations.

An inventory was to be made of the cedar forests and of forestry resources along the Juba riverine floodplain and in the mangrove thickets of the coastal plain (see ch. 3). No forest reserves had yet been established in the south; the possibility of creating extensive reserves was being considered. Protective shelter belts and woodlots would be tried along the Juba; a protective plantation of 5,000 acres at Genale was proposed. In some areas forest reserves might be created to protect watershed areas or to counteract erosion and desert encroachment. The 1969 ban on charcoal exports continued, but charcoal was the main fuel source of the subsistence population and led to much destruction, as did grazing by goats.

* * *

For more comprehensive information on traditional and innovational stockraising and other nomadic activities see the International Labor Office's *Report to the Government of the Somali Democratic Republic on the Integrated Development of the Nomadic Zones.* For informed discussion of crucial economic policy questions see the International Labor Office's "Problems of Nomadism in the Sahelian Region of Africa." For perspective needed to supplement journalistic reports see the Food and Agriculture Organization (FAO) report *Somalia: Livestock Development Survey.* Detailed and most recent available information on traditional and potential land use in the south can be found in *Agricultural and Water Surveys, Somalia*, an FAO publication. (For further information see Bibliography.)

CHAPTER 14

INDUSTRY, TRADE, AND TRANSPORTATION

The predominant pattern of Somalia's trade and transportation in the mid-1970s still largely reflected the superposition of two separate colonial enclaves in north and south on the traditional caravan trade and Arab-dominated dhow trade. In 1960 Somalia had inherited two rudimentary transport systems designed to serve the two export economies that were unified at independence. In the north the rapid growth in livestock exports since the mid-1950s had revived the importance of the port at Berbera, which had served the caravan trade to Ethiopia until the French built a railroad from the neighboring port of Djibouti in the late nineteenth century.

In 1960 roads in the north were mostly impassable in the rainy season. In the south a paved highway from Môgadishu to Ferfer dated from the Italo-Ethiopian war in the 1930s (see fig. 7). The rest of the road system was designed to serve the banana plantations along the Shabelle and Juba rivers. During the 1960s a sizable share of development spending went for transport infrastructure. Paved roads were built from the Juba at Gelib to Kismayo, from the Shabelle plantations to the other banana ports at Marka (Merca) and Mogadishu, and to the grain-farming center at Baydhaba (Baidoa). Deepwater port capacity was built at Kismayo with United States aid and at Berbera with Soviet aid. Engineering studies for the deepwater port at Mogadishu and its construction between 1973 and 1977 were financed by multilateral aid from the International Development Association (IDA) and the European Economic Community (EEC, also known as the Common Market).

In the early 1970s studies were made for new paved roads in the north, and one from Berbera to Hargeysa was completed in 1975. The project repeatedly deferred since 1963 for a modern road from Belet Weyn to Burao was undertaken by the People's Republic of China (PRC) in 1971; construction began in 1973. On its completion in 1978 the road would greatly reduce travel time and increase heavy truck traffic between the hitherto somewhat isolated road systems of north and south. A more direct route from the important towns of the south to those of the northwest would have had to go through Ethiopia— a fact that had long contributed to the isolation of north from south.

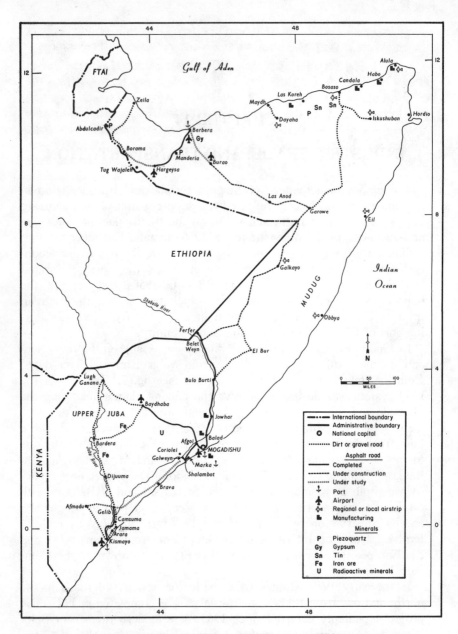

Figure 7. Somalia, Industry and Transport, 1976

A highway program sponsored by multilateral aid had improved the organization, equipment, and training of road maintenance authorities. The self-help effort begun in the 1960s to build more local feeder roads was intensified under the public works crash program launched in 1970, partly by more authoritative recruitment measures and in large part by an increase in the food rations donated by the World

Food Program (WFP) for self-help projects. In much of the country the transport system was still in a rudimentary state of development.

In the 1960s Somalia, like most African recipients of sizable Soviet and other bilateral aid, had put much development spending into the creation of state-owned and -operated processing plants with a capacity well in excess of that required by the immediate market or raw material supply. Accordingly much spending in the 1970s has gone into increasing these plants' supply of cattle, fish, and cotton for processing and into trying to improve their efficiency and reduce their operating losses. In 1974 and 1975 the textile plant at Balad and the sugar complex at Jowhar were being expanded and modernized; new or renovated plants were expanding production of flour, pasta, and corrugated cartons; in March 1976 Iraq committed long-promised financing for a large new refinery to be completed in two years.

Gross manufacturing output expanded strongly from 1968 to 1970 as the large government processing plants came into operation. After stagnating in 1971 and 1972 and declining in 1973, output reportedly picked up in 1974 and 1975 as new plants were completed and renewed agreements with the Soviet Union increased the fishing fleet and restored the lapsed contract for canned-beef exports. Even in 1972, a good year, value added in manufacturing (by compensation of employees, profits, and consumption of capital) was estimated at no more than 8 or 9 percent of gross domestic product (GDP—see Glossary). Mining and quarrying activity was very limited, consisting largely of exploration.

Export earnings had increased through 1974 but less rapidly than the cost and volume of imports, so that the chronic merchandise trade deficit experienced since independence had grown much heavier. Except in 1973 and 1974, however, it has been amply covered by rising grants and loans from abroad under official bilateral and multilateral agreements (see ch. 12). For a time after October 1969 foreign private investment was discouraged, but in the mid-1970s it was reportedly being sought again, although on more strictly supervised terms than in the 1960s.

In addition to heavy spending on measures to increase the volume and lower the cost of banana and livestock exports to make them more competitive, foreign aid and development planning in the 1960s had effected some improvement in diversification of export markets and export products in anticipation of the loss of preference on the Italian market at the end of 1969. The success of these and subsequent efforts seemed apparent by mid-1976. Banana exports to Italy had become less profitable, but exports to Saudi Arabia, Iran, and Kuwait at higher prices had been developed, and both volume and value of exports of bananas and livestock had risen fairly steadily except for temporary setbacks from drought in 1970 and 1973. Other

275

causes, notably fluctuation in raw material supplies, affected the variation in exports of processed fish and meat.

Dependence on aid partly tied to imports, particularly from the Soviet Union, had affected the direction of trade in the 1960s. The only important shifts in direction of trade from 1969 to 1974 were a decline in Italy's share of exports from 26 percent to 15 percent; an increase in exports to the Soviet Union, the German Democratic Republic (East Germany), and the PRC from less than 1 percent to nearly 10 percent of total exports; and a rise in imports from the PRC from 2 percent of total imports in 1969 to 10 percent in 1974, consisting largely of textiles, clothing, and capital equipment for development projects. Significant shifts in imports from the Soviet Union, imports from Italy, or trade with the Middle East had not yet been reflected in the statistics by 1974 but might result from planning implemented from 1974 through 1978.

Government intervention and control of foreign and domestic trade, begun for food grains in the mid-1960s, had been extended by 1972 to all domestic wholesale and retail trade in food grains, key consumer goods, medicine, and petroleum products and to the majority of imports and exports. In September 1975 the government also took over trade representation, and import permits for agents importing on commission were withdrawn.

MANUFACTURING

The country's industrial potential is clearly limited by the small size and relatively low per capita income of its consumer market and by the difficulty in achieving competitive export costs in view of the limitations in resources, skilled manpower, and management and the early stage of development of transport, power, and other infrastructure. Ambitious plans were nevertheless under way for considerable expansion of manufacturing and mineral production.

Manufacturing was not on a large scale by international standards; the largest operation was the sugar factory at Jowhar, which employed 580 full-time workers. The manufacturing sector consisted of a few relatively large government-owned and -operated plants and a larger number of small private establishments employing five or more people (see table 4). Artisan-scale establishments employing fewer than five people are usually not included in the statistics. In 1972 value added in manufacturing establishments employing five or more people totaled some Sh127.1 million (for value of the Somali shilling —see Glossary). Some 89 percent of this value added was in the public sector, and about 75 percent was in food processing.

Gross output and value added in manufacturing had increased considerably since the 1960s. The five largest state-operated plants had been completed in the 1960s, but the four built specifically for state

Table 4. Somalia, Manufacturing and Artisanal Establishments, 1971
(value added in thousands of Somali shillings)[1]

	Food and Drink	Textiles, Clothing, leather, and Footwear	Furniture and Fixtures	Chemicals	Brick, Lime, and Clay Products	Electric Power	Total[2]
Public Sector:							
Number of units	4	2	2	1	1	6	18
Number employed	2,244	911	63	34	20	383	3,735
Value added[3]	89,280	6,140	1,620	500	60	8,800	108,020
Private Establishments Employing Five or More People:							
Number of units	54	16	28	8	32	2	177
Number employed	1,451	172	358	125	288	26	2,879
Value added[3]	7,250	880	1,620	500	1,560	200	14,450
Private Establishments Employing Fewer than Five People (informal or traditional sector)							
Number of units	1,160	1,188	161	4	32	- - -	2,861
Number employed	2,615	1,950	276	7	63	- - -	5,565
Value added[3]	7,850	6,140	830	200	180	- - -	16,830

- - - means none.

[1] For value of the Somali shilling—see Glossary.
[2] Includes miscellaneous establishments not included in categories listed.
[3] Value added consists of compensation of employees, profits, and consumption of capital (depreciation).

Source: Based on information from Somalia, Ministry of Information and National Guidance, *Somalia: Five Years of Revolutionary Progress*, Mogadishu, 1974, pp. 88-89.

operation did not attain full production until after 1969, two of them not until 1974 or later. These four were the Somaltex cotton textile plant of Balad, completed in 1968 with a Sh27.4 million credit from the Federal Republic of Germany (West Germany), and three factories financed by a Sh85.5 million project loan from the Soviet Union. Of the latter the Sh37.5 million beef cannery at Kismayo finished in late 1968 was producing well in 1972, but the Sh43.0 million Las Koreh tuna cannery and the dairy plant at Mogadishu had supply problems.

Of total development spending on industry from 1963 through 1969 of Sh307.9 million, Sh107.7 million was reported to have come from the Somali government, Sh7.2 million from the United Nations (UN), and Sh3.9 million from the European Development Fund (EDF) of the EEC. Financing of Sh12.0 million from the United States probably went to build a shellfish-freezing plant at Mogadishu, which after some years of litigation was taken over by a Japanese firm in 1975; a tuna-freezing plant built earlier with United States aid was being operated by an Italian firm in the 1970s (see ch. 13).

Some Sh23.9 million in financing provided by Italian banks in the 1960s had been used to organize and modernize the sugar refinery at Jowhar. This was one of the main projects for industry under the First (Five-Year) Plan 1963-67, but under the Development Program 1974-1978 Sh40 million was to be spent for modernization and expansion, said to be necessitated by the age of the existing equipment. In 1963 the Somali government, with assistance from the International Finance Corporation, had purchased half ownership of the refinery and associated sugarcane plantation at Jowhar established by the Italian duke of Abruzzi in 1927. At that time it adopted the name National Company for Agriculture and Industry (Societa Nazionale Agricola Industriale—SNAI), apparently retained when the complex was fully nationalized after October 1969. Output declined in the 1970s: one-fourth of cane acreage was lost to saline soils; yield per acre and extraction rates fell drastically; trained manpower and replacement parts for old equipment were in short supply.

The top management of SNAI was said in 1975 to have recently been replaced; as in other public industries, management turnover had reportedly been high and efficiency low. A report on public sector industries, probably unpublished, prepared in 1971 or 1972 by a financial management expert from the United Nations Industrial Development Organization (UNIDO), was said to have led to stricter accounting procedures and improved management performance in public enterprises.

Sugar has always been a most important item in the Somali diet. When output at Jowhar declined from 46,854 tons in 1969 to 34,704 tons in 1973, imports had to be increased to meet domestic demand. Imports have fluctuated strongly from year to year, perhaps owing in part to smuggling caused by price differentials. In the 1960s competition from smuggled imports was a serious problem for SNAI. The SRC government sought to crack down on smuggling of all kinds, but there is a limit to the expansion of border patrols and, when recorded imports of sugar through customs rose from the previous high of 8,528 tons in 1966 to a new high of 23,196 tons in 1973, it was thought that the apparent strong rise in domestic demand must derive in part from smuggled exports. Earlier, when the sugar complex fell badly short of its production quota, there had been unconfirmed rumors of black marketeering of the sugar by officials; public reports said police were investigating charges that saboteurs were involved. When fifty-seven prisoners were later amnestied in October 1975, press reports mentioned that one of them had been jailed for sabotaging the Jowhar sugar factory.

In late 1975 the press reported that a British sugar machinery firm had been given the contract to build a second sugar complex at Fanole on the Juba, where saline soils are not a problem. Recommended by a United States aid survey in 1961 and listed successively in each of the intervening plans, it was to be completed by 1978 and was to comprise a 30,000-acre sugar estate; a 60,000-ton-capacity factory capable of expansion to 100,000 tons a year; a distillery to process molasses; roads and houses for 1,200 families; and ancillary services. It was reportedly to be financed by the Somali government. In January 1976, however, the sheikh of Sharjah, one of the seven member states of the United Arab Emirates (UAE), announced that the UAE was to contribute financing for several projects, including a new sugar factory.

A pamphlet published by the Ministry of Information and National Guidance in 1974 asserted that the country's four major industrial plants—at Las Koreh, Kismayo, Jowhar, and Balad—had been set up by a corrupt prerevolutionary government in order to placate countries donating foreign aid but had been brought into production under the revolutionary government. Similar statements had been made about almost every sector of economic activity; in more cursory writings any reference to pre-1969 origins is commonly omitted, creating some confused impressions in the foreign press.

One objective multilateral report described the Kismayo cannery as well designed and the private Italian-owned cannery at Mogadishu, SOPRAL, as efficient. Problems of cattle supply resulted in part from lack of flexibility in pricing; prices offered for cattle for the canneries were often lower than those for export.

Owing partly to rising prices and partly to heavy ongoing expenditure on development of livestock marketing infrastructure under three successive plans, the cattle supply was improved until in 1974 both plants were operating at or near full capacity. In the 1970-73 period some 15,000 to 50,000 head of cattle a year were purchased by the

Livestock Development Agency for the Kismayo plant. They came entirely from southern nomads.

The Soviet-financed milk processing plant at Mogadishu had never reached full capacity since its establishment in 1965 because of the short supply of milk in the area, particularly during the dry seasons. The nearby 21st October Dairy Farm, financed by West German aid, was to be reorganized, and cattle owners in Mogadishu were to be regrouped in cooperatives in an effort to achieve adequate milk supply that could justify the Sh5 million allocated for modernization of the plant.

The cannery at Las Koreh had suffered from erratic and consistently inadequate fish supply until 1974. The Development Program 1974-1978 allocated Sh6.5 million for modernization of the plant and Sh9.5 million for other fish industry development in addition to Sh40 million to expand the fishing fleet from ten boats in 1973 to seventy in 1974. This project was financed by the Soviet Union and training by the United Nations Development Program (UNDP) and the Food and Agriculture Organization (FAO).

The Somaltex plant at Balad reached record production of 6.4 million yards of cotton cloth in 1972, of which the proportion of bleached and dyed cloth had been successfully increased. Production fell in 1973 because of problems in obtaining spare parts for worn-out machinery. A major modernization program from 1974 to 1978 was intended to increase production.

Fragmentary and often misleading reports available in 1976 made it difficult to determine which manufacturing plants were genuinely new, having been built since 1970, and which were holdovers from the 1960s. Of the plants in operation in the 1960s, some had since gone under, some had remained in continuous operation, and some had suspended operations on the departure of foreign investors but had since been revived or expanded as joint ventures or government operations and were reported as new industrial capacity achieved under one of the two most recent plans.

Under the Second (Short-Term) Plan 1968-70 American and Somali investors were to finance a plant to produce corrugated pasteboard packing material for bananas. This plant may have been deferred until a later plan; in 1974 it was one of the public enterprises receiving a major share of bank credit. A brickyard at Afgoi and a tuna-freezing plant at Alula financed by a forerunner of the Somali Development Bank had closed down but were revived with major new investment in the 1970s.

In 1975 there were also a small electrical goods enterprise and a match and cigarette factory described as recently built. New investment by the Somali Development Bank in the 1970s had focused on expansion of such resource-based industries as the fruit-processing plant at Afgoi, tomato paste canning, and a grain mill at Mogadishu opened in 1972. Reports that a flour and pasta mill entered operation in Mogadishu at about that time may have referred to the same grain mill, to revival of an older flour and pasta mill, or to an entirely new operation to produce wheat flour and pasta. There were also to be new grain mills at Hargeysa and Kismayo and a third in either Baydhaba or Berbera.

The Somali Development Bank had been playing a predominant role in the financing of new industry since 1970. Toward the mid-1970s somewhat more encouragement was being given to private investment, domestic or foreign, but it was under consideration only for smaller scale industries, largely designed to replace imports of beverages, batteries, paints, and tiles and ceramics. UN financing and Yugoslav technical assistance had built a US$6 million iron foundry at Mogadishu. Using charcoal and domestic scrap, it was designed to turn out some 500 tons of cast iron products a year for use in construction or by households.

After three years in the doldrums gross manufacturing output increased in 1974 to Sh309 million, of which Sh43 million was exported. Gross output includes the cost of domestic and imported raw materials and intermediate materials in addition to the factor payments that make up value added. The strong growth of 1974 may therefore have included an element of inflation. It took place despite the effect of the drought on raw material supply to the Kismayo cannery, the Jowhar sugar mill, and the Balad textile plant.

MINERAL ACTIVITY

The mining code introduced by the new government is designed to elicit quick results from companies seeking concessions that might otherwise prolong the exploration stage to gain tax relief at home. A prospecting concession may be granted for an initial two-year term and may be renewed for three more one-year terms; it may not exceed five years in all. A company must also spend a minimum of Sh21 for each square mile of the concession area. A new unit was created in the Ministry of Mining and Water Resources to exercise close supervision over petroleum exploration by foreign firms. In 1974 four foreign firms were exploring for oil, and several others had reportedly applied for concessions, but in early 1976 only one, a consortium including a French group and Standard Oil of New Jersey (EXXON), was actively exploring. No oil had been found, but gas showings indicated a potential for oil in large areas of the country.

Before the UNDP began its Mineral and Groundwater Survey in 1964, mineral exploration in Somalia had reportedly been perfunctory. There were numerous known mineral occurrences, however, notably in the northern regions (see ch. 3). Most of the minerals found in quantity have been in abundant world supply, and the closer investigations made since independence indicated that they could probably not be exported at cost competitive with those of more accessible supplies in other countries.

A tin mine at Majayahan in Bosaso District and salt pans at Hordio had been abandoned or destroyed during World War II. In the 1960s mineral production was confined to salt, meerschaum (sepiolite), limestone, sandstone, and clay. Some 30 tons of meerschaum a year had been produced in Galgduud Region and some exported to the United States for pipe manufacture, but in the 1970s it was produced only for local artifacts.

Because of the scarcity of trained manpower the first phase of the UNDP survey, financed under the 1963-67 plan, was confined to general exploration of what was then the Upper Juba Region, comprising Bur Acaba and Baydhaba districts. The survey found sizable deposits of low-grade iron ore and deposits of radioactive minerals, including uranium, thorium, and such rare earth minerals as europium and yttrium. The iron ore, at 30 to 40 percent iron content, was too low in grade to repay the cost of extraction and transportation, but in the mid-1960s there had been high hopes that the uranium deposits at Alio Gelle and elsewhere might prove a lucrative new source of export earnings. The second phase of the UNDP survey, which was carried over from 1969 to 1971, consequently provided for test drilling and evaluation of the radioactive deposits as well as for preinvestment studies of the gypsum and tin deposits and other known mineral occurrences identified by the British surveys in the northern regions in the 1950s.

By the mid-1970s hopes appeared to have faded for commercial exploitation of the uranium deposits, at least under prevailing world market conditions. Of the three foreign firms that had prospecting concessions in the Bur Acaba area in the 1960s, the only one still actively exploring in 1976 was Italy's National Hydrocarbons Agency (Ente Nazionale Idrocarburi—ENI). Meanwhile the UNDP survey in the north had found large areas of pegmatites having veins of extra-grade piezoquartz suitable for use in electronic or optical instruments. At Bur Mado the deposits covered an area of some 965 square miles; there were smaller deposits at Manderia and Abdulcadir.

The 1963-67 plan had proposed that Sh12 million be spent on a project to mine gypsum at Suria Malableh, about ten miles southeast of Berbera. The 1968-70 plan noted that the project had not found financing for lack of an apparent market for the product and proposed that gypsum be used as the base for fertilizer manufacture, which could transform the output and export structure of Somalia's economy in less than a decade. Under the Development Program 1971-1973 a more modest gypsum pilot project was to have been financed by UNIDO, but the assistance failed to materialize, and progress was negligible. At 7 million tons the Suria Malableh deposit was finally assessed as among the world's largest. The pilot project to test the commercial viability of gypsum as a domestic building material became part of a joint venture with the Democratic People's Republic of Korea (North Korea) for a cement plant at Suria Malableh to begin production in mid-1977.

Under a bilateral agreement with Bulgaria another pilot project launched under the Development Program 1974-1978 had begun test production of tin at the Majayahan mines, abandoned since World War II. The ore remaining in this deposit was said to be of low grade, but a larger tin deposit had been discovered ten miles away at Dalan in Las Koreh District and was to be the subject of a feasibility study. In February 1976 a Bulgarian team announced that it had found occurrences of unspecified nonmetallic minerals in the same vicinity. The plan also allocated Sh500,000 for further investigation into the potential for iron mining. The UNDP team had concluded that the small size (33 million tons) of the deposits of marketable grade would not justify the cost of upgrading and transport. The Somali government, however, keeping in view the prospect of creating a sizable iron-based industrial complex, wanted to reassess possible exploitation of the deposits "by alternative technology suitable to the conditions existing in the area."

The plan also affirmed that in the course of the UNDP survey since 1974 enough Somali geologists, chemists, and other professionals had been trained to launch a national geological survey on termination of the UNDP project in March 1974. During the plan period two teams would explore what had been the Upper Juba Region, two would prospect in the north, and one would assess known deposits of nonmetallic minerals, including talc, feldspar, kaolin, vermiculite, graphite, mica, and asbestos. In 1974 construction began on a factory to produce corrugated asbestos sheets, a joint venture of the Somali Development Bank and an Italian firm.

FOREIGN TRADE

Recurrent severe drought and frequent variations in rainfall between droughts make it difficult to select "normal" years to illustrate shifts in Somalia's pattern of foreign trade. Time series for such data as banana and cattle exports may also be subject to such radical revision that conclusions can vary considerably depending on the data selected. The value of 1965 banana exports, for example, was reported in 1968 as Sh108 million but in the 1970s was being given as only Sh62.9 million (see table 5). If the latter figure is the accurate one, it appears that the value of banana exports was only moderately affected by the closing of the Suez Canal in mid-1967 and the loss of Italian subsidy at the end of 1969.

Table 5. *Somalia, Composition of Foreign Trade, Selected Years, 1965-74* (in millions of Somali shillings)[1]

International Trade Classification	1965	1968	1969	1971	1972	1973	1974
Exports							
Bananas							
To Italy	62.9[2]	58.3	54.9	40.5	39.1	35.3	n.s.s.
To Middle Eastern countries	- -	1.4	5.3	22.0	31.6	32.3	n.s.s.
To East Germany[3]	- -	- -	- -	1.4	7.5	- - -	n.s.s.
Total Bananas	62.9[2]	59.7	60.2	63.9	78.2	67.6	80.2
Livestock and Products							
Cattle	14.5	14.3	11.8	18.5	23.8	35.0	n.s.s.
Sheep and goats	52.8	98.6	104.5	88.2	123.5	138.2	n.s.s.
Camels	13.5	11.5	15.7	16.6	14.7	23.3	n.s.s.
Total Livestock	80.8	124.4	132.0	123.3	162.0	196.5	222.4
Hides and skins	13.1	11.0	17.1	18.1	17.7	13.1	14.2
Canned meats	0.8	2.8	2.8	21.4	22.7	22.5	n.s.s.
Total Livestock and Products	94.7	138.2	151.9	162.8	201.8	232.1	n.a.
Fish and Fish Products	1.5	- - -	2.9	2.8	5.3	13.5	n.a.
Charcoal[4]	12.0	5.0	5.8	- - -	- - -	- - -	- - -
Frankincense, Myrrh, Gum Arabic, and Other Forest Products[4]	- -	- -	- -	- - -	4.5	5.2	n.a.
Exports n.e.s.	20.9	9.1	11.1	16.5	10.1	22.0	...
Total Exports (from customs records)	192.0	212.0	231.9	246.0	299.9	340.4	390.6
Imports							
Foodstuffs							
Rice	29.8	19.9	16.0	36.2	26.6	29.7	n.s.s.
Wheat flour and products	11.1	7.5	7.7	22.7	20.9	10.6	n.s.s.

Import Category						
Sorghum, maize, and other cereal products	21.1	7.6	24.9	52.2	9.5	48.2	n.s.s.
Sugar	3.9	6.8	0.1	1.0	14.9	23.4	n.s.s.
Tea	3.7	6.0	11.6	12.1	16.3	8.9	n.s.s.
Fruits and vegetables	13.0	10.7	13.6	16.6	9.9	13.7	n.s.s.
Other food (including live animals)	18.8	15.3	20.4	12.1	24.4	11.3	n.s.s.
Total Food Except Fats and Oils	101.4	73.8	94.3	152.9	122.5	145.8	212.1
Fats and Oils	16.4	7.1	9.3	16.6	15.2	8.3	n.s.s.
Total Foodstuffs	117.8	80.9	103.6	169.5	137.7	154.1	n.s.s.
(as percent of total imports)	(33.3)	(23.8)	(28.0)	(37.8)	(26.3)	(22.7)	(21.2)[5]
Other Consumer Goods							
Beverages and tobacco	10.7	10.0	14.3	13.6	13.7	27.3	n.s.s.
Textiles	27.0	43.6	24.3	38.6	38.0	57.0	n.s.s.
Clothing and footwear	8.5	14.5	10.7	11.8	14.6	22.1	n.s.s.
Pharmaceuticals	5.6	8.6	10.7	15.1	15.1	38.0	n.s.s.
Soaps, cleansers, and polishes	2.8	4.9	2.2	2.0	2.9	8.1	n.s.s.
Total Other Consumer Goods	54.6	81.6	62.2	81.1	84.3	152.5	118.0[5,6]
(as percent of total imports)	(15.4)	(24.0)	(16.8)	(18.1)	(16.1)	(22.5)	(11.8)
Petroleum Fuels and Lubricants	16.4	14.3	19.1	18.9	24.6	28.8	120.3
(as percent of total imports)	(4.6)	(4.2)	(5.2)	(4.2)	(4.7)	(4.3)	(12.0)
Development Goods							
Cement	9.2	9.5	7.5	11.5	8.7	8.0	n.s.s.
Base metals and semimanufactures	11.8	2.8	8.6	13.6	17.5	17.5	n.s.s.
Metal manufactures[7]	11.7	9.3	12.1	12.1	22.0	25.1	n.s.s.
Electrical machinery and appliances	9.3	8.6	12.1	8.3	26.5	26.6	n.s.s.
Nonelectrical machinery and equipment	46.8	22.8	31.4	20.4	45.6	70.6	n.s.s.
Transport equipment	27.4	31.4	46.4	30.2	56.2	85.0	n.s.s.
Miscellaneous manufactures[7]	15.6	30.7	25.0	32.5	42.5	44.8	n.s.s.
Total Development Goods[7]	131.8	115.1	143.1	128.6	219.0	277.6	419.6[5]
(as percent of total imports)	(37.3)	(33.9)	(38.7)	(28.7)	(41.8)	(41.0)	(42.0)

Table 5. *Somalia, Composition of Foreign Trade, Selected Years, 1965-74—Continued*
(in millions of Somali shillings)[1]

International Trade Classification	1965	1968	1969	1971	1972	1973	1974
Imports n.e.s.[8]	33.1	47.9	41.8	49.9	58.5	64.4	130.2
Total Imports (from customs records)	353.7	339.8	369.8	448.0	524.1	677.4	1,000.2[9]
Adjusted Data (exchange basis)[9]							
Bananas	n.a.	41	43	45	89	75	74
Livestock	n.a.	147	167	160	206	182	249
Other	n.a.	31	32	67	99	101	79
Total Exports Adjusted	n.a.	219	242	272	394	358	402
Total Imports Adjusted	n.a.	333	396	398	503	704	1,045
Trade Deficit	n.a.	114	154	126	109	346	643
Services Deficit	n.a.	49	18	5	29	77	73

--- means none; n.s.s. means not separately specified; n.a. means not available; ... means not applicable; n.e.s. means not elsewhere specified.

[1] For value of the Somali shilling—see Glossary.

[2] Data are reported to be customs statistics, but customs records gave banana exports as Sh108.2 million in 1965 and a similar sum in 1964.

[3] German Democratic Republic.

[4] Charcoal exports were prohibited in 1969; data reported here as charcoal probably include exports of aromatic gums.

[5] 1974 data are preliminary Somali government estimates, and definitions of categories may differ from earlier years. For 1974, for example, total foodstuffs excludes animal and vegetable fats and oils, which may be included in "other consumer goods."

[6] The Somali government definition of "consumer goods," used for 1974, is unknown; it would give Sh90.2 million in 1971, Sh87.2 million in 1972, and Sh142.9 million in 1973.

[7] Includes both consumer goods and development goods.

[8] Imports n.e.s. consist chiefly of paperboard manufactures, chemicals, and timber.

[9] Data have been adjusted to payments basis by the Somali National Bank. Exports are f.o.b. (free on board), imports c.i.f. (cost, insurance, and freight).

The principal exports, livestock and bananas, were both affected by the severe droughts of 1964, 1969, and 1974, and food imports were particularly high in 1965, 1971, and 1974, including increased rice imports from Thailand and other Far Eastern countries and food imports from African countries. Imports and exports of cattle from and to Kenya and Ethiopia, insofar as they show up in official statistics at all, may show extreme variation from year to year because of price differentials. Of the years commonly selected to illustrate the pattern of foreign trade, 1968 was a year of business recession, weak world prices, and high freight rates after the Suez Canal closing; 1969 and 1974 were years of severe drought in the north; 1972 was a good crop year; and 1973 was a year of poor rainfall and setbacks in manufacturing.

According to the final adjusted data bananas accounted for about 18 or 19 percent of export earnings in 1968 and 1969 and for 21 or 22 percent in 1972 and 1973. Although sales of livestock increased by 23 percent over the five-year period, they accounted for only 51 or 52 percent of export earnings in 1972 and 1973. More meat was being exported in processed form, however, and exports of hides and skins had somewhat improved; altogether livestock and livestock products were furnishing two-thirds of export earnings.

Export value increased by 15.8 percent a year from 1968 to 1972; the trade deficit was reduced from Sh114 million to Sh109 million. Poor rainfall in 1973 reduced export volume, and retooling under way at the sugar and textile factories made it necessary to import more of these products; in 1973 export value fell by 9 percent, import value rose by 40 percent, and the Sh346 million deficit in merchandise trade was twice the size of the previous record deficit of 1966. The 1974 drought reduced export volume for both bananas and livestock, but much better livestock prices and the continuing shift in banana exports from Italy to higher priced markets in the Middle East restored export earnings in 1974 to slightly above their 1972 high. Imports, however, had risen by another 48 percent in 1974, and the deficit was an unprecedented Sh643 million.

Somalia has always been a net importer of agricultural crops and crop products, notably rice, wheat flour, and pasta, and at times when the rains are inadequate is obliged to import even sorghum and maize (corn), the staple crops of most domestic producers. In 1972, an exceptionally good crop year, the achievement of self-sufficiency in sorghum and maize was highly publicized, but imports had to be resumed in 1974. Among the goals of the Development Program 1971-1973 and the Development Program 1974-1978 were complete self-sufficiency in maize and sorghum and progressive replacement of rice and wheat imports by domestic production (see ch. 13). Domestic production of fruits and vegetables was to be promoted, and the plans for a second sugar complex at Fanole were designed to eliminate the heavy sugar imports that resumed in 1972 and 1973.

Among the other consumer imports to be replaced after completion of investment allocated under the Development Program 1974-1978 are dyed and printed cotton fabrics, cotton yarn, and knitwear. The government already had its own animal serum and vaccine laboratory in Mogadishu; but when cattle vaccination was made compulsory and free in 1973, the laboratory could not keep up with the demand, and imports of veterinary drugs rose to Sh6 million. The project for a large-capacity refinery to use Iraqi crude oil should help curb the steep rise in import costs.

After 1978 cement imports will probably be replaced by production from the plant being built at Suriah Malableh. Most other goods classified as for development, however, must continue to come from abroad.

The category "miscellaneous manufactures" consists in part of consumer goods and in part of such wares as optical instruments and navigational aids. If this group is included, development goods have been responsible for much of the rise in imports after 1971. There had been a temporary hiatus in foreign aid receipts after the October 1969 coup, and the Development Program 1971-1973 got off to a slow start, most of the projected spending taking place in its last year.

From independence through 1975 all development imports and a portion of imports for current consumption by government and the private sector had been financed by foreign assistance. Except in 1973 and 1974 receipts of grant aid and long-or medium-term official loans had amply covered the deficit on goods and services, so that foreign exchange reserves could be built up slightly. In 1973 and 1974 there was a little short-term borrowing from abroad; foreign exchange reserves were reduced by US$7 million in 1973 and US$9 million in 1974. Although imports were high in 1975, there were unexpectedly large livestock exports, and the current deficit was more than offset by US$130 million in foreign grants and loans.

In 1975 officials and their wives were denounced for smuggling on air voyages, but there was little information on either traditional smuggling or legitimate trading by migrating herders or coastal dhows (small lateen-rigged Arab coastal vessels). Reports from the Arabian Peninsula in the mid-1970s said that the dhow trade was on the decline.

The area now occupied by Somalia is often identified with the land of spices known in the Bible and in Greek and Roman sources as the best source of frankincense and myrrh in the ancient world. A thriving Indian Ocean trade in ancient and medieval times followed the monsoon winds from Arabia down the northeastern coast of Africa and across to India and the Persian Gulf along much the same route followed by the small sailing dhows of the twentieth century. Written descriptions dating from the third century A.D. or earlier tell of well-developed ports with pre-Islamic Arab or Persian settlements (see ch. 2).

With the exception of slaves, ivory, and gold, the products exported from the area in ancient and medieval times were still on the export list in the late 1960s: aromatic gums, gum arabic, tortoiseshell, ambergris, and leopard skins. The gulf coast trade declined at the end of the nineteenth century when the railroad was built from Djibouti, but the traditional export trade continued, and cotton cloth, sugar, and dates were still the staple imports of the dhow trade and the barter trade of Arab merchants with the interior. Since the third Ming dynasty ethnic minorities on the Bajun Islands and at limited settlements along the coast had exported tortoiseshell, shark fins, sea cucumbers, and dried fish to China. This trade had been dominated by the merchants of Zanzibar, to whose sultan the Bajun Islands had once belonged, and was interrupted by the Zanzibar revolution in 1964. Trade in frankincense and myrrh had gone by way of the merchants of Aden and may have been disrupted by the revolution there.

Government monopoly of foreign trade, which had begun in the early 1960s with imports of tractors and food grains, was further extended after the October 1969 revolution to exports of bananas and hides and skins and to imports of petroleum products, pharmaceuticals, and film. These products were handled by autonomous government agencies. The National Trading Agency, created in 1962, had handled only goods imported under commodity loans from communist countries, but in January 1972 a new law extended government monopoly to import, wholesale, and retail trade in a range of key consumer goods, including tea, coffee, sugar, pasta, confectionery, soap, rubber sandals, and radio batteries. These goods are imported by government in a number of other African countries. The objective was to reduce profit margins or divert them to national purposes (see ch. 12).

In September 1975 the government announced that it would take over the administration of trade representation and withdraw licenses from all foreign traders operating on a commission basis. Agents importing on their own account, retailers, and government agencies would still be allowed to import directly and maintain normal communication with their suppliers.

In October 1975 the government assumed official monopoly of the import of most goods from motor vehicles to cooking pots, and it took over all retail sale of textiles and clothing. The latter measure might affect a multitude of small-scale family operations. A committee was to implement the measure and allocate compensation to the firms expropriated.

Direction of Trade

The diversification of export markets beginning in the late 1960s resulted mainly from lower banana prices on the Italian market, which caused Italy's share of Somalia's exports to drop beginning in mid-1967 (see table 6). The increase achieved in volume and prices of banana exports to Middle Eastern countries is not fully reflected in the data because 1968 and 1969 were years of high livestock exports to Saudi Arabia and the Persian Gulf countries and 1973 and 1974 were years of low livestock exports. Exports to Egypt were curtailed in 1973 because Egypt, accustomed to bilateral barter agreements, resisted Somalia's demand for payment in convertible currency; they were resumed in 1974. It is expected that during the period of the Development Program 1974-1978 Somalia's production and export capability will fall far short of meeting the rapidly expanding demand for both bananas and livestock in the Persian Gulf states and other Middle Eastern countries. Growth in demand is expected to be particularly strong in Egypt.

The share of exports going to the socialist countries increased rapidly once the meat, fish, and dairy processing plants built with the Soviet project loan of 1961 began to come into production in the 1969-71 period. The project loan could be repaid in Somali goods, but any portion not covered by such exports had to be repaid in convertible currency (see ch. 12). After a grace period of two years after the end of each project, the loan was to be repaid in twelve annual installments. A moratorium was granted in 1966 until the end of 1969 and another in 1971 extending until 1976. The debt was reportedly canceled in 1974.

The original agreement had assumed that the debt for construction of each processing plant would be repaid in its finished products. Because of the dearth of raw material, however, output was inadequate. The long-term contract with the Soviet Union had called for annual export of 16 million cans of stewed steak from Kismayo. The price fixed, however, was below world market level, so that the cannery could not offer a price for cattle purchases that could compete with prices for export on the hoof. Since the objective of building the costly Kismayo cannery in the first place had been to increase the export earnings and national income generated by livestock—the nation's principal resource—this arrangement was less than satisfactory.

The agreement for the Kismayo cannery had provided that it would be managed by a team of Soviet experts until 1976. The procedures followed were not always efficient. Until 1972 the plant operated at a loss, despite the low prices paid for cattle, and was unable to meet its quota for exports to the Soviet Union. Plans for greatly increased production and cattle supply were made in conjunction with the Trans-Juba Livestock Project (see ch. 13).

In 1972 the Kismayo cannery entered into cooperation with SO-PRAL, the privately owned Italian cannery in Mogadishu that exports corned beef to Italy and Belgium. The Italians were to provide management expertise and joint marketing. In 1972, for the first time, the Kismayo cannery produced at full capacity, met its quota for stewed steak exports to the Soviet Union, and made a profit of some Sh2 million, which sufficed to service the debt. In addition it sold 600,000 cans of cooked corned beef to African and Mediterranean markets. Prices obtained for this product compared favorably with those for the same product of Argentine origin and permitted purchase of adequate cattle supplies. Since there is no market for canned stewed steak outside the Soviet Union, it was determined that future expansion would be in the production of corned beef.

The contract with the Soviet Union lapsed in 1973, adding to the various problems afflicting overall manufacturing and export in that year. In 1974, however, prices received for canned steak exported to the Soviet Union were brought approximately into line with world market prices. In May 1976 it was announced that over the next five years Somalia would supply the Soviet Union with 60 million cans of beef and 5 million cans of fish.

Plans to improve export earnings from the livestock-processing sector would involve some shift to more lucrative markets. Veterinary standards had been improved, and uncooked beef could therefore be exported to such Mediterranean countries as Italy, Greece, Cyprus, Lebanon, Egypt, and Libya as well as to traditional livestock markets in Saudi Arabia, Kuwait, and other Persian Gulf countries. Completion of the Libyan-financed airport at Kismayo would permit air freight of chilled or frozen beef, which might become one of the factory's major activities.

There were also plans to increase exports of livestock on the hoof to the traditional Middle Eastern markets and to improve the quality and meat yield of the animals exported so as to afford a higher contribution to export earnings and national income. In December 1973 the government had prohibited export of calves and young steers in order to purchase them itself for fattening on its three extensive holding grounds before export or sale to the cannery. Growing interest in cattle fattening had also led to an increase in private domestic demand for young stock. The Trans-Juba Livestock Project alone was expected to provide some 25,000 fattened steers by 1980, supplemented by eventual establishment of private fattening operations in the Kismayo area.

By 1975, however, the government was reconsidering its ban on the export of calves. Because of inadequate forage the cost of maintaining and patrolling the holding grounds at Galaday near Hargeysa, for example, had not been repaid by the weight gain achieved. Moreover this calculation does not include the social cost of depriving the area's

Table 6. *Somalia, Direction of Trade, Selected Years, 1965-74*
(in millions of Somali shillings)[1]

Area of Origin or Destination	Exports				Imports			
	1965	1968	1973	1974	1965	1968	1973	1974
European Economic Community[2]								
Italy	93.4	64.9	77.3	59.9	101.2	111.2	226.6	239.2
Other	0.5	1.4	8.0	32.0	61.1	52.6	96.7	83.4
Total EEC	93.9	66.3	85.3	91.9	162.3	163.8	323.3	322.6
(as percent of total)	(48.9)	(31.3)	(25.1)	(23.5)	(45.9)	(48.2)	(47.7)	(32.2)
Socialist Countries								
People's Republic of China	1.3	0.3	7.2	8.0	13.7	9.8	85.9	105.8
Soviet Union	}0.1	}0.2	11.7	13.3	28.0	20.7	36.7	37.1
Other[3]		0.0	17.9	17.5	2.6	1.6	2.9	2.9
Total Socialist Countries	1.4	0.5	36.8	38.8	44.3	32.1	125.5	145.8
(as percent of total)	(0.7)	(0.2)	(10.8)	(9.9)	(12.5)	(9.4)	(18.5)	(14.6)
African Countries	6.9	1.5	14.5	18.4	36.5	22.3	44.4	67.0
(as percent of total)	(3.6)	(0.7)	(4.3)	(4.7)	(10.3)	(6.6)	(6.6)	(6.7)
United States	2.9	0.8	0.5	0.0	18.2	32.4	15.4	10.6
(as percent of total)	(1.5)	(0.4)	(0.2)	(0.0)	(5.1)	(9.5)	(2.3)	(1.1)
Middle East								
Saudi Arabia	46.7	106.0	110.1	104.6	3.6	n.a.	1.7	2.9
Yemen (Aden)[4]	28.2	26.4	35.4	41.6	16.4	8.0	6.1	6.6
Other	9.8	5.2	47.4	66.9	12.1	12.3	9.1	14.9
Total Middle East	84.7	137.6	192.9	213.1	32.1	20.3	16.9	24.4
(as percent of total)	(44.1)	(64.9)	(56.7)	(54.6)	(9.1)	(6.0)	(2.5)	(2.4)

Asian Countries								
Japan	- -	0.1	0.1	8.4	18.8	33.3	89.8	126.8
Thailand	n.a.	0.0	0.0	0.0	5.0	3.7	3.7	28.3
India	n.a.	0.1	0.0	0.0	8.0	6.7	6.8	13.3
Pakistan	n.a.	0.0	0.2	0.0	n.a.	4.5	5.2	28.9
Other	n.a.	0.0	5.7	15.2	3.9	11.1	16.6	11.0
Total Asia	n.a.	0.2	6.0	23.6	35.7	59.3	122.1	208.3
(as percent of total)	...	(0.1)	(1.8)	(6.0)	(10.1)	(17.5)	(18.0)	(20.8)
Countries Not Elsewhere Specified ..	2.2	5.1	4.4	4.8	24.6	9.6	29.8	221.5[5]
TOTAL[6]	192.0	212.0	340.4	390.6	353.7	339.8	677.4	1,000.2

- - - means none; 0.0 means less than half the unit; n.a. means not available; ... means not applicable.

[1] For value of the Somali shilling—see Glossary.

[2] Nine-member European Economic Community (EEC, also known as the Common Market).

[3] Includes the Democratic People's Republic of Korea (North Korea), the Democratic Republic of Vietnam (North Vietnam), and all of Eastern Europe except Yugoslavia.

[4] People's Democratic Republic of Yemen.

[5] Imports from other countries in 1974 included Sh170.1 million (possibly fishing boats) from Norway, usually a minor import source.

[6] From customs records.

pastoral population of some 37,000 acres of the best grazing land in a region under intense grazing pressure.

In the past from 90 to 99 percent of all exports of livestock on the hoof had gone through Berbera. Trucks were used to transport sheep and goats overland, but cattle were usually trekked over distances as great as 600 miles and upon arrival were often underweight, exhausted, and susceptible to disease. Saudi Arabian shipping companies had a near-monopoly of livestock transport from Berbera; ships were dilapidated and ill ventilated; weight loss and mortality were high, and it was not uncommon for the boats to sink en route.

The Saudi lines had also imposed differential freight rates to make it more costly to ship stock to destinations other than Saudi Arabia. It was hoped that reopening the Suez Canal would break the near-monopoly of Saudi cattle carriers and permit other shipping lines based around the Mediterranean to compete again at lower cost. Somalia had established its own National Shipping Line and chartered two fast, refrigerated banana ships; in 1975 it owned only one small and rather old cattle boat because it had not yet been able to find and buy the proposed two used livestock carriers, each to have a capacity of either 2,600 head of cattle or 15,000 sheep and goats. The shipping line had been created as a joint venture with Libyan participation; Somalia thereupon became a member of the Association of Arab Transport Companies and the Maritime Academy of the League of Arab States (Arab League).

A special berth usable only for loading livestock had been built in the new deepwater port of Mogadishu so that more cattle from the south could be exported direct without making the long trip to Berbera. It was also hoped, however, that on completion of the newly improved road from Belet Weyn to Burao in 1978, more cattle, sheep, and goats from the south could be transported to Berbera by heavy truck and arrive in better condition.

A 1975 aid mission report had pointed out that most areas of the world, notably the Middle East, do not consume much beef. Ambitious plans for more lucrative beef export should therefore not be given too much priority over the continued and expanded export of sheep and goats to traditional markets.

Italy had retained its importance as a source of imports. The composition of these imports had remained fairly constant, suggesting that they might consist in large part of supplies for Italian factories and plantations still operating in Somalia. Imports from the Middle Eastern countries, never very important, were furnishing a slightly lower share of the total in 1973 and 1974 than in 1969, perhaps because of loss of contact with merchants in Aden or other centers that had ties with Somalia's Arab trading community. The United States had been replaced as a source of imports by Japan, which furnished chiefly iron and steel manufactures and semimanufactures. West Germany remained a source of road motor vehicles and equipment. Imports from socialist countries had been boosted by Soviet shipments of petroleum fuels and lubricants, by imports of earthmoving and construction equipment for the Soviet-financed Fanole dam, and by imports from the People's Republic of China (PRC) of textiles and clothing and of equipment and materials for the Belet Weyn-Burao road. According to one source the Soviets had imported refinery products from Iraq, which was to build the Mogadishu refinery at the instance of the Soviet Union. The Soviet Union would import Iraqi crude oil for the refinery after it was built, so that the direction of trade would not change.

Imports from Asian countries vary markedly from year to year, depending in large part on domestic food supply. Rice is imported from Thailand; Sri Lanka furnishes tea; and it may be surmised that large imports occasionally recorded from India, Singapore, and Hong Kong include quantities of cotton fabrics.

Banana Exports

In the 1950s and 1960s measures designed to reduce dependence on Italian subsidy had improved yields and reduced the cost of banana exports. From 1930 to 1942 and from 1950 to the end of 1969, a major share of the bananas exported had been produced by Italian concession holders, and all banana exports benefited from special protection on the Italian market; sales to Italy averaged more than 90 percent of banana exports, which until the late 1960s consistently accounted for about 45 percent of export earnings and were thought to provide a direct or indirect livelihood for 35 percent of the settled population.

Until 1964 annual agreements with Italy had fixed an export quota and a minimum export price. From 1964 to late 1969 the subsidy took the form of a special reduction in Italian sales tax on the first 100,000 tons of bananas imported from Somalia. Under pressure in world trade forums, Italy had agreed in 1964 to terminate this discriminatory practice altogether by the end of 1969 (the initial deadline of 1967 having been extended after the Suez crisis). Thereafter Somalia enjoyed only the same preference on West European markets accorded to the other seventeen African countries associated with the EEC. These seventeen included such efficient competitors as Ivory Coast, and under the Lomé Convention of February 28, 1975, the benefits of association have been extended from the original eighteen to forty-six African, Caribbean, and Pacific (ACP) countries exporting tropical products. On the EEC market these producers enjoy exemption from the common external tariff of 20 percent on bananas.

All the banana plantations along the Juba were destroyed by flood in 1961. By 1966 the country's total area planted to bananas had been reduced from nearly 30,000 acres to about 18,500 acres. Average yield per acre had been greatly improved, however, plantings replaced by a less fragile variety, and the proliferation of middlemen and high cost of transport modified. The 3,700 acres of banana plantations restored along the Juba since 1961 had been modernized and gave yields twice as high as the average in the Afgoi-Genale area of the Shabelle. Credits for rationalization of banana production in the 1960s were furnished by Italy and by the EDF. In 1967 the FAO reported that Somalia's banana exports had become competitive in cost with those of all its principal rivals except perhaps Ivory Coast.

Shortly thereafter bananas from Ecuador and Central American countries gained a foothold on the Italian market when Somalia's exports were disrupted by the closing of the Suez Canal in mid-1967. By the end of 1967 the volume of banana exports to Italy had returned almost to previous levels, but the price obtained had been lowered by more stringent competition. In 1969, however, the International Monetary Fund (IMF) reported that by chartering faster and better equipped ships Somalia had reduced spoilage to manageable proportions and achieved a lower unit cost for shipping bananas around the Cape of Good Hope than it had formerly paid for shipment through the canal. It thus appeared equipped to compete without the aid of subsidy.

In addition to its credits for improving banana production, the EDF had provided funds for diversification into plantation production of grapefruit. The EEC had also initiated antitrust action against United Brands (formerly the United Fruit Company), which was fined US$4 million for using its monopoly position to undercut Somali bananas and capture 90 percent of the Italian banana market.

Because of price competition, Somalia's banana exports to Italy had become less profitable, and a growing share of the steadily mounting banana exports since 1968 had been exported to new markets in the Middle East that offered higher prices and rapidly rising demand. The market for Somali bananas in Italy was estimated at about 100,000 tons in the mid-1970s and, with the rising demand in the Middle East, export potential thus exceeded current production of bananas of export grade, which reached 116,500 tons in 1972. By 1974 the area under bananas had been increased to 24,215 acres, but 4,450 acres were still immature, and export yield per acre was thought to have declined. Yields were also affected by saline soils along the Shabelle, and exports fell because of drought in 1973 and 1974. The number of Italian concession holders had decreased from about 100 in the early 1960s to fewer than fifty in 1975 and, when marginal producers for the domestic market, who accounted for 25 to 35 percent of production, were eliminated from the census, the reported number of Somali banana growers was reduced from 350 to about ninety.

Banana growing and transport had been left in private hands, but banana trading was nationalized in 1970 under the National Banana

Board. In 1974 the board was allocated Sh20 million to establish its own model plantations of 600 acres each at Golweyn and Kalenji to increase exports and to serve as demonstration farms. It was projected that private plantation acreage would increase by 2,700 acres and banana exports to 150,000 tons by 1978. J.R. de Benoist's article in *Afrique Contemporaine* affirmed in mid-1975 that the government had been gradually taking over the banana plantations as Italian planters left the country.

TRANSPORTATION

Roads

In 1975 there were some 8,700 miles of dirt roads and tracks, 630 miles of gravel roads, and 660 miles of asphalt-surfaced first-class roads and highways. At the outset of the First (Five-Year) Plan 1963-67 there had been only 370 miles of paved (asphalt-surfaced) roads, including a 135-mile stretch from Jowhar to Belet Weyn that was in poor repair. The plan had called for improving this stretch and upgrading to first-class paved status some 1,500 of the country's remaining 7,000 miles of second- through fourth-class dirt and gravel roads.

The prohibitively costly construction program proposed in 1963 has been carried over to subsequent plans and is being implemented piecemeal. By October 1969, however, there were some 540 miles of paved first-class roads. Those built from 1963 to 1969 included the seventy miles from Kismayo to Gelib, financed by West Germany; the forty miles from Shalambot to Afgoi, financed by the EDF; and sixty-five miles of the 135-mile road from Afgoi to Baydhaba, center of the main grain-producing region, financed by IDA and EDF. The paved road from Afgoi to Mogadishu had been resurfaced with Italian aid. The first phase of the IDA-financed Highway Development Program had created a maintenance department, trained Somali personnel, and provided equipment. A self-help program had been launched to build rural and other local roads using army pioneers and local residents.

Foreign loans or grants financed more than 97 percent of the development spending of Sh312.7 million on road motor transport reported for the period 1963 through 1969. This probably overlapped the sum of Sh139.7 million spent on road transport development under the Second (Short-Term) Plan 1968-70. This included the cost of building bridges at Hargeysa, Lugh Ganana, and Balad; Sh50.0 million from West Germany for intensive strengthening of the Kismayo-Gelib road built earlier; and Sh83.9 million for increasing the total of paved first-class road from 540 miles in October 1969 to 625 miles in March 1971. This included the seventy remaining miles of the Afgoi-Baydhaba road, opened to traffic in April 1971, and the stretch from Shalambot to Golweyn on the lower Shabelle River. Food aid was obtained from the World Food Program (WFP) for self-help activity to stabilize sand dunes that endangered the road between Gelib and Shalambot, but this was not included in transport spending.

The only road construction completed under the Development Program 1971-1973 was resurfacing of the segments from Jowhar to Bulo Burti and from Afgoi to Shalambot. The Sh74.4 million spent on roads went mainly for surveys and engineering studies for future roads, including notably the 1971 and 1972 portions of IDA and EDF loans of Sh20.2 million for the Berbera-Hargeysa road and of a PRC loan of Sh24.0 million for the Belet Weyn-Burao road. Construction began on both roads in 1973. Expenditure of Sh3.0 million on the public works crash program included only the Somali government contribution; food aid from the WFP was not reported. IDA lending of Sh6.8 million went for the second phase of the Highway Development Program.

The Development Program 1974-1978, the most ambitious since the 1963-67 plan, proposed to increase the total paved road mileage by 1,063 miles in five years and nearly to triple annual spending on road development. Of the projected five-year total of Sh635.9 million, only Sh22.4 million was to come from domestic financing (for bridge building and an intensified self-help crash program). Some 95.6 percent was to come from foreign credits. By mid-1976 such financing had in fact been found for many of the costly projects proposed, most notably Sh360 million in credit, engineering, and labor provided by the PRC for the 649-mile north-south road from Belet Weyn to Burao. In mid-1976 construction was proceeding on schedule, and the road was expected to be completed by 1978.

Paving of the ninety-eight-mile dirt road from Berbera to Hargeysa, financed by credit from the IDA and the African Development Bank, was completed and the road opened to traffic by September 1975. By then feasibility and detailed engineering studies for the Hargeysa-Borama road, also financed by IDA, had been completed, and the building phase was awaiting approval. In January 1976 the United Arab Emirates (UAE) had agreed to finance a seventy-mile road from Berbera to Burao. In January 1974 engineering studies were under way for upgrading the unpaved 168 miles between Gelib and Golweyn, unusable in the rainy seasons, and the heavily traveled and often flooded roads from Arara to Jamama on the lower Juba and from Danow on the lower Shabelle to Coriolei in an important food-grain belt.

By 1975 the transport features most vital to foreign trade and industry had been modernized, and the time required to drive from south to north was at last to be substantially reduced; but sizable areas of the countryside remained without all-weather roads, and many rural settlements had access only to rudimentary dirt tracks. This was said to impede food distribution and development of fishing and mining activity. Moreover it was of political as well as economic concern to the government. The development program published in January 1974 stressed that "in building a socialist system, transport and communication is a vital means for reaching the people through dispersion of information, for facilitation of government intervention, and for promoting balanced development."

The high cost and repeated delay in roadbuilding projects had derived partly from the shopping-list character of successive plans and the need to find foreign financing and partly from the nature of the terrain and climate. In 1974, however, it was also attributed to the fact that the government lacked the capacity for preparation of engineering and feasibility studies; no reputable international construction company would adopt less than a minimum standard too luxurious for local conditions or for the needs of sparsely populated areas. When the second phase of the IDA Highway Development Program was completed in 1974, road maintenance had been greatly improved and the nucleus of a road construction and rehabilitation unit established in the Ministry of Works; the Arab Fund for Economic and Social Development provided Sh16.8 million for equipment, and the unit's capacity was to be developed.

Seaports

There are said to be twenty-seven harbors along Somalia's long coastline, but more than 95 percent of the country's overseas trade is handled by four ports—Berbera, Kismayo, Mogadishu, and Marka. The rest are usable in season for the dhow trade or small-boat fishing. The only three naturally sheltered harbors are Berbera, Kismayo, and Hordio; Hordio has no economic hinterland, and its port was never rebuilt after its giant saltpans were destroyed or sequestered during World War II. Berbera serves the northern region and also handles 90 percent of all exports of livestock on the hoof, sometimes driven north from as far as 600 miles away. In the 1960s most bananas were exported through Marka or Kismayo, some through Mogadishu. Kismayo's importance as a meat-processing and export center has since been developed. Mogadishu handles two-thirds of all imports and about 5 percent of exports.

The number of ships calling or refueling at the major ports may increase with the reopening of the Suez Canal. This prospect has also sharpened the political controversy surrounding the Soviet presence at Berbera (see ch. 10; ch. 15). By January 1969 some 1,150 feet of deepwater wharves for ships of up to thirty-two-foot draft had been built at Berbera with Soviet aid and turned over to the Somali government. At Kismayo four deepwater berths for vessels of up to 10,000 tons had been provided by United States aid by the same date. Work on ancillary facilities continued at both ports under the 1968-70 plan. The Soviet navy retained refueling facilities at Berbera.

In early 1972 a London economic quarterly reported that Soviet aid was to double goods-handling capacity at Berbera port, then about 200,000 tons a year. No such project has shown up in either the Development Program 1971-1973 or the Development Program 1974-1978. In September 1975 a Moscow journal reported that petroleum storage facilities and other economic facilities at the port were being built or expanded with Soviet assistance. A British source reported that Soviet engineers were then also building an airstrip at Berbera.

The first deepwater berth at Mogadishu had been completed in June 1976; three more were to become available in August, November, and December 1976 and a fourth in April 1977. Plans for a deepwater port at Mogadishu, first formulated in 1963, had been deferred for lack of financing and pending technical study. Some improvements at the port had been effected by 1966. In late 1964 the World Bank (see Glossary) made a technical assistance grant of US$311,000 for a preliminary engineering study. Spending on port development by the World Bank from 1963 through 1969 was reported as Sh118.9 million. The 1968-70 plan had called for completion of construction during the three-year plan period. This was too ambitious a target, but the subsequent plan reported in 1971 that the final design and engineering study had been completed. Construction was again delayed for technical modifications, however, and the Sh32.7 million spent on the project under the Development Program 1971-1973 went for further studies. Thus in 1973 large ships were still obliged to anchor offshore in open road-steads for loading and offloading by lighter; turnaround time for shipping averaged seven days. Damage and delays in handling of perishable bananas and other cargo were particularly costly from June to September when high monsoon winds made for rough seas.

The engineering studies for the Mogadishu port project had been financed by the IDA and the EDF. For construction the EDF had provided a grant of US$11.5 million in 1973 and the IDA a credit of US$12.9 million. Construction by an Italian contracting firm began in 1973 but was some six months behind schedule because of late equipment orders and the southwest monsoon. In the meantime imports had risen more rapidly than anticipated, and by 1974 tonnage handled at Mogadishu had almost reached the level projected for 1977. On September 25, 1975, the IDA granted a supplementary credit of US$5.2 million for extensions, notably an additional berth. The original project had been completed by mid-1976; the extension would be completed in early 1977.

Mogadishu's old port was to be turned into a fishing port. The new port of Mogadishu, on completion in 1977, will have a sheltering breakwater more than half a mile long; three general cargo berths with a depth of thirty-three to forty feet; a specialized berth for livestock and another for bananas; marshaling yards for livestock; two transit sheds; and a warehouse. It will be equipped to continue to handle 66 percent of all imports and 33 percent instead of 5 percent of exports. It is hoped that live animals from the surrounding area can be shipped from Mogadishu instead of Berbera. It is expected that reopening the Suez Canal will increase the number of ships calling but not the tonnage handled, as each ship may carry less cargo. A joint venture agreed on with Libya in 1974 created a national shipping line to operate banana, livestock, and general cargo ships.

Through 1975 Somalia had been one of the leading nations providing "flag of convenience" registry for some 250 foreign ships wishing to avoid the more stringent regulations of major shipping nations. In November 1975 the Somali government decided to abolish the practice of registering foreign-owned ships in order to "safeguard its integrity."

Civil Aviation

At last report, in 1975, there were airports of international standard at Mogadishu and Hargeysa, and a third was almost complete at Kismayo. In mid-1976 Somali Airlines had eleven aircraft, including two Boeing 720-Bs, two Viscounts, three DC-3s, and four Cessnas. It operated domestic flights to the three major airports and fourteen other airports, fields, and landing strips. Internationally it operated a scheduled weekly flight to Rome by way of Jeddah and Cairo and was the only airline to provide regular direct service between Europe and Abu Dhabi and between Nairobi, Muscat, and Abu Dhabi.

Somali Airlines was founded in 1964 as a joint venture between the Somali government and the Italian airline Alitalia, which is goverment operated but privately owned. It received considerable assistance from Italy over the years. Its losses, which in the early 1970s averaged Sh2 million to Sh3 million a year, are covered by the Somali government, which owns 51 percent of the shares. In 1969 management, training, and all personnel were still being provided under contract by Alitalia, but Somali Airlines has since become one of the first African airlines in which all crew members and most of the ground staff are nationals. The Somali government appoints the chairman and two members of the airline's administrative council, Alitalia the vice chairman and two other members. The 1963-67 plan had called for the Somali government to take over full operation of the line, but it was still in need of external assistance and expertise in 1975.

The airline began operations in 1964 with only the DC-3s for domestic flights and the Cessnas for domestic air-taxi service. The two Viscounts were acquired in 1968 and 1969, and international flights were inaugurated, at first going only to neighboring countries and to Aden. Two Boeing 720-Bs were bought in 1976; one had been on lease since 1974. Two Fokker F-27s ordered in 1975 were to be delivered in mid-1977 to replace the DC-3s and the Viscounts.

During the period from 1963 through 1969 Italy had provided some Sh17.2 million for Somali Airlines; the EDF had provided Sh18.5 million to modernize Mogadishu airport; and Saudi Arabia had lent Sh17.2 million to improve the runways at Hargeysa, Burao, and Baydhaba (then Baidoa). The runway at Hargeysa was used for Viscount flights to Djibouti and Aden. The Baydhaba runway was completed at a further cost of Sh2.0 million under the Development Program 1971-1973, which also spent some Sh14.0 million for construction at Kismayo airport beginning in 1972. The Development Program 1974-1978 allocated Sh8.8 million to complete the Kismayo airport, providing an air terminal, navigational aids, and a runway capable of taking Boeing 707s. Another Sh19.3 million was allocated to build a new runway of international standard parallel to the existing one at Hargeysa. A study was also under way preparatory to relocating Mogadishu airport at a preselected site that would permit construction of a longer runway with unobstructed approaches. No funds were provided for this project under the plan.

COMMUNICATIONS

From 1967 to 1970 there were about five telephones for every 1,000 inhabitants. Radio was the main means of communication; in 1970 there were an estimated fifty receiving sets for every 1,000 people; presumably transistor sets have since become more common (see ch. 7). The manual telephone exchange at Mogadishu had been replaced by an automatic exchange in 1965. In 1966 a telecommunications project to improve exchanges and connections elsewhere and to link all the populous areas of the country by radiotelephone was submitted to the EEC.

In July 1971 the EEC committed Sh41.2 million in grant and loan aid for a telecommunications project, on which only about Sh900,000 had been spent by the end of the Development Program 1971-1973. Because of rising world equipment prices in the interim, the plan had to be modified to stay within the funds provided. Existing high-frequency systems were to have been replaced by microwave systems; but in the revised project high-frequency systems would be used to link Mogadishu with Baydhaba, Belet Weyn, Galkayo, Bosaso, Burao, Hargeysa, and Berbera. Modern sophisticated systems (presumably microwave) would link the capital with Jowhar, Balad, and points to the south: Afgoi, Coriolei, Marka, Genale, Gelib, Kismayo, and Jamama. Modern exchanges were to be established at Hargeysa and Kismayo. Some 1,000 new telephone lines were to be added to the 3,000 already in use at Mogadishu. Hargeysa was to have 100 lines and Kismayo 200. Existing high-frequency international connections via relay stations at Nairobi and Rome were to be replaced by direct microwave connections.

SECTION IV. NATIONAL SECURITY

CHAPTER 15

THE ARMED FORCES

By 1976 the Somalian military establishment, always large compared with those of other black African countries, had expanded from 5,000 at independence in 1960 to more than 23,000 troops. This included a tank force and an air force unsurpassed in size and matériel in eastern Africa. The infantry was largely mechanized, and the army could call upon reserves and the police force in the event of a national emergency. The armed forces were maintained by voluntary enlistment. Recruits found an army career attractive in part because of the emphasis on military virtues in Somalia's predominantly nomadic culture and in part because of the economic hardships of life in the country's interior.

Somalia's military patron is the Soviet Union, which has provided the base, through financial support and supply of hardware, for the increase in Somalia's military establishment. This patronage, begun in 1973, hinged during the 1970s on an arrangement of mutual advantage: Somalia was able to maintain an army large enough at least to defend its borders; the Soviet Union had the use of naval port, supply, and missile storage facilities on the Indian Ocean, enabling it to exert influence there, particularly on the traffic routes through the Suez Canal and from the Persian Gulf. From Soviet influence there has followed Somali adoption of Soviet techniques and doctrine, reinforced by Soviet training.

The most significant change in the mission of the armed forces since the military takeover in October 1969 has been the extension of military authority into phases of national domestic life where it was previously absent. Not only have military officers come to dominate the government, but they have also assigned the army a significant role in internal development programs, such as construction and literacy campaigns.

THE ARMED FORCES IN NATIONAL LIFE

Military virtues have always figured prominently in Somali life, and the armed forces have enjoyed correspondingly high prestige. Since the military takeover the army's prestige, aided by the regime's public relations efforts, has increased to a higher level than ever before.

The ruling Supreme Revolutionary Council (SRC), composed solely of military officers, knew what role it wanted the armed forces to play in the nation and did its best to ensure that they fulfilled that role. The SRC's conception of its regime was a revolutionary one, that of adapting to Somalia the principles of scientific socialism.

The government's official view was that underdeveloped states unavoidably tend to continue patterns that developed during their colonial period. Although neither a strong entrepreneurial bourgeoisie nor a true class-conscious proletariat forms, there emerges a bourgeoisie composed of civil servants and the educated elite. This class makes an accommodation with the colonial regime because its members reap economic rewards, which they are intent on keeping after independence. Thus economic and social structures remain unchanged and have to be destroyed if any real advance is to be made. No group other than the army is sufficiently organized to break the old superstructure and establish the new, for in the nation at large national relations are less important than family, community, or tribal relations. It is in the army that members from all segments of the population mingle and become aware of their national identity. Therefore it is the army that becomes the revolutionary vanguard and establishes links with the people. But since a military regime can also be oppressive, the degree to which the army fosters socialist revolution rather than oppression hinges on the level of political consciousness of its officers. It is therefore essential to purge from the army and the police any corrupt or reactionary elements. This has been the view of the Somali army's revolutionary role as expressed by its leaders.

In fact within a year of the coup the army did begin to resemble the people's army of the regime's ideal. The SRC attacked corruption and nepotism with varying degrees of success, and it established firm control of the government at all levels. Unexpectedly it continued the previous regime's policy of eschewing an adventurous, militaristic foreign policy. Most important the army became more involved in civil tasks, such as building roads, schools, and health facilities and providing education to illiterate segments of the population. The identification between the military and the people was further strengthened by the provision of paramilitary training to increased numbers and by economic self-help programs run by the military organization.

Military Tradition and History

Each year at the time of the seasonal new year (*dabshid*) a festival is held at Afgoi near Mogadishu on the Shabelle River. It is called the *istunka* and consists of a mock battle between groups of men from both sides of the river. Although the affair has calmed down a great deal since World War II, it used to be quite bloody because the young men were armed with sticks.

There are different explanations for the origin of the *istunka*. One story holds that it grew from training that was to prepare warriors to repel the forces of an invading sultan; according to this legend the training was successful. Another tradition places the origins in a battle over water rights during the dry season. Whatever the explanation, the festival is a reminder of the importance of military virtues in Somali life.

Somali society has always been predominantly nomadic. Despite attempts since independence to settle nomads and defeat tribalism, the nomadic element remains strong. The assumption that "might makes right" has had marked influence on social attitudes, and force is often resorted to with little provocation. Except for a few men devoted to religious life, all Somali males were traditionally considered warriors. Aggressiveness and military prowess were rewarded, for among the nomads force or the potential for exerting force usually decided who would prevail.

Nomadic life required a familiarity and ability with weapons to be used for war and hunting, for protection against wild animals, and sometimes as tools. The chief weapons historically involved in Somali military activity were the spear and the shield. The spear was iron tipped and had a staff of knotted wood; it was used mainly for protection against wild animals. Shields were small (about twelve inches in diameter), round, and made of rhinoceros, giraffe, or oryx skin. The Somali warrior also used a bow made of wood with a camel-gut or -tendon bowstring. Iron-tipped arrows were carried in wooden or leather quivers. Poison-tipped arrows, used since at least the sixteenth century, were apparently in use as late as the 1930s. Their use was prohibited in that decade, however, and bows and arrows in general were largely replaced by rifles.

Knives are early weapons still used today. They are doubled edged and are carried in leather cases attached to the belt. Before the introduction of firearms Somali nomads also used swords. These had long, narrow blades and horn handles and were carried in leather sheaths.

Some matchlock guns may have been used by Somali as early as the sixteenth century, but even by the late nineteenth century rifles were not in general use. A few tribal chieftains received them as gifts from European explorers but used them as prestige symbols rather than as weapons. Firearms became more numerous in the Horn of Africa in the 1890s when they were supplied to Ethiopian Emperor Menelik II through the port of Djibouti. Some of these rifles ended up in Somali hands, and significant numbers came into use in the jihad (holy war) of Sayyid Mohamed ibn Abdullah Hassan against British overlordship from 1899 until his death in 1920 (see ch. 2). After 1920 possession of firearms was common among the Somali.

The appearance of firearms in great numbers over such a brief period of time upset the established balance of power among the clans. Firepower replaced numbers as the main determinant of a clan's strength. The colonial governments sought to disarm the nomads, so that by the mid-1970s there were fewer rifles among that population than earlier in the century.

Warfare had always been important in Somali society both in relations with other groups—for example, the Ethiopians and the Galla—and in relations among Somali clans and clan segments (see ch. 2; ch. 4). The decision to go to war was one of considerable importance. The warring group might be responsible for the payment and receipt of *dia* (blood compensation—-see Glossary) for damages inflicted or received during the war. Since the entire group was responsible for the *dia*, war began only with the unanimous approval of participating members (see ch. 4).

Peace was usually restored after a meeting of elders of the involved groups. They would determine which party was responsible for beginning the war and assess compensation—generally in livestock—for the damages incurred. Usually only the party judged responsible for starting the war would be fined—unless, presumably, they emerged the clear-cut victors.

Readiness for armed conflict thus flourished throughout a long history of foreign invasion and colonial occupation. By the end of Mohamed Abdullah's jihad against the British, the nomads often were more heavily armed than the colonial forces that were responsible for maintaining public order.

The need of the Italian and British colonial regimes to establish order and control in their respective territories led to the formation of police forces into which Somali were recruited, although it was not until after World War II that Somali functioned as officers. The British and Italian forces underwent a series of changes through the years, but in practice they served as police rather than as military units (see ch. 16).

At the time of independence in 1960 most of Somalia's borders were still in dispute (see ch. 2). The provisional government therefore requested the permission of the United Nations Trusteeship Council to establish a national army to protect its frontiers. Permission was granted, and the new army was born under the threat of frontier claims and the growing popularity of a quest for ethnic and political union of all Somali peoples, including those in Kenya, Ethiopia, and French Somaliland (present-day French Territory of Afars and Issas —FTAI).

In 1960 a small army, the core coming from the Mobile Group (Darawishta Poliska, commonly called Darawishta), was created in the Trust Territory of Somaliland under Italian Administration a few months before independence. Immediately before the Trust Territory gained its independence from Italy, the British gave up control over British Somaliland. Additional troops from the British Somaliland Scouts combined with the troops in the Trust Territory to form a 5,000-man army. The commander was Colonel Daud Abdullah Hersi, who had served with the Somalia Gendarmerie, the police force of the British Military Administration. He remained commander until his death in 1965, when he was succeeded by Mohamed Siad Barre (see ch. 16).

The Constitution of 1961 urged the union of all Somali territories but renounced war as a means of settling international disputes. The maintenance of a national military service, with implied civilian supremacy in matters of military policy and operation, was sanctioned to safeguard the republic's sovereignty. The National Army, however, grew unusually large compared with those of other African nations south of the Sahara, even though the personnel of the armed forces never exceeded 1 percent of the population.

Although much military aid was supplied by other countries, military expenditure remained a major item in the Somalian budget. The newly independent government made these economic sacrifices for several reasons. First, almost all of Somalia's borders were the subject of dispute. Second, the neighbor with which Somalia shares its longest common border, Ethiopia, had one of the largest armies in sub-Saharan Africa. This undoubtedly led to fears of retaliation should Somalia attempt to settle the border problem by force, a feeling reinforced by a Kenyan-Ethiopian defense agreement in 1963. Third, despite the constitutional renunciation of war, Somalia did follow an aggressive policy aimed at unifying all Somali—including those living in neighboring countries—under its rule. Somalia supported this policy with military and paramilitary actions along its borders.

The rivalry with Somalia's neighbors reached its height in 1964. Relations between Somalia and Ethiopia, tense since independence, broke into open conflict. A Somali guerrilla leader in Ogaden, the Ethiopian territory claimed by Somalia, initiated a rebellion against Ethiopia in June 1963 after Ethiopian Emperor Haile Selassie had rejected the demand of the Ogaden Somali for self-government. Somalia refused to give the guerrillas official support; but in January 1964, after Ethiopia responded to guerrilla successes by reinforcing Ogaden, Somali staged ground and air raids across the Ethiopian border. Ethiopia retaliated, destroying by air two Somali frontier posts.

Heavy fighting began with a large-scale Somali attack on the Ethiopian frontier post of Tug Wajaleh from February 7 to 10. Subsequent Somali attacks were launched against Ethiopia farther east along the border on February 11. Ethiopia responded with punitive air strikes across its southwestern frontier against Ferfer and Galkayo.

On February 15 the two nations agreed to a cease-fire, but fighting broke out only hours after the truce began. The cease-fire was again established, only to be broken several times during March. On March 25 a conference of the two nations opened in Sudan. On March 30 both sides agreed to withdraw behind their frontiers and submit the dispute to discussion by the Organization of African Unity (OAU). The final cease-fire began on April 2, 1964.

Both sides probably exaggerated their successes, and both lumped together enemy civilian and military casualties in their public reports. The Somali apparently destroyed Ethiopian installations and equipment, but their personnel losses seem to have been far greater than those of the Ethiopians. More telling, by the end of the conflict the heaviest fighting was reported in the area where it had initially broken out. This suggests that, even using their tanks and heavy weapons on ground of their choosing, the Somali were unable to advance into Ethiopia. They could not defend against Ethiopian air raids, and they certainly did not extend their control over Ogaden Somali. On balance, Somali military performance must be judged to have been disappointing. This judgment is confirmed by Somalia's subsequent reluctance to resort to military action against its neighbors, preferring to disrupt them by supporting guerrilla activities in their territories. The government of Abderashid Ali Shermarke and Mohamed Ibrahim Egal, elected in 1967, officially eased tensions with Ethiopia because of the failure of aggressive policy and the ruinous expense such a policy required (see ch. 2; ch. 10).

Despite the easing of tensions and the cessation of military actions by the end of the 1960s, the military establishment continued to be highly regarded by the population. Even before the October 1969 coup the prestige of a military career ranked higher than that of many civilian occupations. The reason for the widespread acceptance of the National Army was still largely based on the recognition of its major role if the unification of all Somali was to be realized (see ch. 10).

The Military in the Government

Before the successful military coup of October 21, 1969, Somalia's civilian government had constitutional control of the military. Twice in the decade after independence, in 1961 and 1967, ineffective military coups d'etat had been attempted. These had been sparked by alleged favoritism shown veterans trained by the Italians over those trained by the British. Otherwise the armed forces, respectful of the traditions taught by their Western mentors, had been content to let civilian rule take its course.

When after the military coup of October 1969 the SRC was established, it had twenty-five members, all of them military officers. The SRC had a balance of northern and southern officers and representatives of the major clans. It also contained a high proportion of younger officers of the generation that had provoked the earlier coup attempts.

By mid-1976 there had been no additions to SRC membership. Three of the original members had been executed because of their involvement in countercoup attempts, and one had left because he had fallen out with the majority of the SRC over matters of policy. Nineteen of the original members remained.

Recognizing that as military and police officers they had limited experience in government, the coup's leaders set up under the SRC the Council of the Secretaries of State (CSS), composed primarily of civilians. The SRC, however, ruled the country directly and by decree until July 1, 1976, when its power was transferred to the Supreme Council after the formation of the Somali Socialist Revolutionary Party (SSRP) (see ch. 8; ch. 9).

All actions of the civilian authorities were subject to military approval. Although ideally the military refrained from interfering in day-to-day administration, it did closely supervise the implementation of its programs. SRC members conducted tours of inspection to ensure compliance with SRC decrees. The Ministry of Interior, which ultimately supervised compliance with government directives, was always headed by a police general. Although the predominantly civilian CSS would occasionally consider matters in joint session with the SRC, the CSS was chaired by President Siad, a military man; and until 1974 SRC members held the key ministries in the CSS.

Despite the regime's refusal to tolerate dissent, the military government has remained popular. Troops, much in evidence immediately after the coup, were applauded in the streets; and a tight curfew instituted at the time of the coup was soon lifted. By 1973 the visible military presence, even in Mogadishu, had markedly declined.

After 1969 military officers replaced the civilian regional governors and district commissioners of the parliamentary regime. The military men remained in charge of local administration in mid-1976.

Rather than dismiss civil servants, the military government chose to reorient them to revolutionary principles. Civil servants were given a political orientation course at Camp Halane (formerly Bottego Training Camp). The course devoted time to paramilitary training including the use and assembly of rifles and various kinds of machine guns, but the practical value of this training, particularly for senior civil servants, was questionable.

Three-month training courses were required of all state officials, students, and those involved in public service, such as teachers or doctors; even ambassadors regularly returned from their foreign assignments to participate. The course included paramilitary training and weapons familiarity. Trainees were required to wear military uniforms.

Attendance at training and reorientation courses was not limited to public officials. All age-groups and social classes received training and indoctrination; the government emphasized the military flavor of this training. For example, 5,000 children from ages five to nine were organized as the Children of the Revolution. Not all such training took place at Camp Halane: by mid-1973 national guidance centers had been set up in thirteen districts of Mogadishu and throughout the country as well. They were centrally organized, were responsible to the SRC, and could accommodate all ages. These centers provided a basic introduction to scientific socialism and supplied other services as well, making them centers for all community activity. Civilian drill instructors at the centers taught children to march. It was proposed in 1973 that all students spend a year at a center for political and military training on leaving school. They would spend a second year of national service as teachers, as medical assistants, or in the armed forces. By mid-1976 national military service had not been instituted, but military training was required of all students over the age of eighteen.

Between 1971 and 1973 seven youth camps were built, and in 1973 seven more were projected for completion by 1975. More than 1,850 students had been enrolled in these camps by 1973. They received a general education, including practical instruction, in agriculture and livestock raising, as well as political orientation and military training.

The Military in Foreign Affairs

The size of Somalia's military establishment, a burden on so poor a country, reflected its relations with its neighbors (see ch. 10) Somalia's borders were drawn during the colonial occupation, and those who determined the borders had little sensitivity to ethnic considerations. The result was the division of the Somali, the only homogeneous group of people in the Horn of Africa, among five jurisdictions (reduced to four when British Somaliland and the Trust Territory were united in 1960) (see ch. 2).

The presence of large numbers of Somali in Kenya, Ethiopia, and the FTAI has created tension along Somalia's borders ever since independence. The Somalian government has never given up the hope of unifying all Somali within its borders; yet it has voiced a fear of the counterclaims made by Ethiopia against Somalian territory. Ethiopia, with the largest army in the Horn of Africa, has posed the only military threat to Somalia.

Both to support the policy of Somali unification and to protect its territorial integrity, Somalia created a large army that has continued to expand. During the 1960s the parliamentary government made active use of the army, supporting an aggressive policy against Somalia's neighbors.

Military incidents with Kenya began in 1963 after the British refused to grant a separate independence to the Northern Frontier District of Kenya, whose population included a substantial number of

Somali. The Somalian armed forces did not actively participate, but Somalia supported the efforts of Somali guerrillas, called *shifta* (bandits) by the Kenyans, who battled Kenyan security forces with Soviet- and Communist Chinese-made equipment until 1967. More than 2,000 guerrillas were killed during those engagements.

Beginning in 1960 there were clashes between Ethiopian forces and Somali nomads over traditional problems, such as smuggling and theft of livestock, which the Somalian government chose to interpret in nationalistic terms. Incidents continued to grow in scale until the armed forces of both sides clashed in early 1964. The fighting reached its greatest intensity in February and March of that year. With the election of a different government later in 1964 a truce was arranged, but détente was not achieved until Prime Minister Egal's government came to power in 1967. By this time it was clear that the campaign to unify the Somali was a failure, and Somalia was heavily burdened with defense expenditures that consumed about 30 percent of the budget.

It was probably these financial constraints that led the military government after 1969 to continue its predecessor's policy rather than again resorting to military action in pursuit of a greater Somalia as some had expected. The enthusiasm for Somali unification was in no sense extinguished, however.

Tensions again increased along the Somalian-Ethiopian border in the 1972-73 period. Both countries at that time reinforced their military units in the area. Additional fears of armed conflict were raised by the discovery in 1973 of natural gas and in 1974 of oil in Ogaden, the Ethiopian territory claimed by Somalia.

The size of the Ethiopian army is a factor in forcing Somalia both to maintain a large army and to exercise restraint in its use. Although Ethiopia has had to use part of its army to deal with internal opposition, notably from rebel groups in Eritrea, the total number of troops in that army is almost double that in Somalia's army. Until the 1970s when the Somali army expanded dramatically because of aid from the Soviet Union, the disparity was even greater. Experts feel, however, that the obsolescence of Ethiopian equipment may have tipped the military balance in Somalia's favor as early as 1970. Certainly by 1976 Soviet assistance had strengthened Somalia to the point that the United States felt compelled to supply the Ethiopian armed forces with more modern equipment at an anticipated cost of almost US$200 million. In 1976 it appeared that even the Kenyan army, previously no military threat whatever to Somalia, was to be supplied with twelve United States fighter aircraft to help fend off threats from Somalia and Uganda. This contribution to arms escalation in the Horn of Africa, particularly supplying arms to Kenya, represented a change in United States policy, which could be taken as a fair indicator of how the West viewed the relative military strengths of Somalia and its neighbors in mid-1976.

The Somalian army has not been active against the French in the FTAI, although the threat remains that Somalia will attempt to annex the southernmost portion of that territory, including Djibouti. This section of the country has a predominantly Somali population. A French withdrawal from the area would make it the likely scene of an Ethiopian-Somalian military clash, because it has been defined as a vital interest by each. The display of Ethiopia's weakness in trying to end the Eritrean rebellion in the spring of 1976 heightened fears that Somalia would risk warfare with Ethiopia to acquire Djibouti. Somalia already permits the Front for the Liberation of the Somali Coast (FLSC), a guerrilla group fighting for FTAI indenepdence from the French, to use Hargeysa as its base.

In late 1975 there were incidents along the FTAI border: French troops were accused of firing on a Somali police station, and there were several violations of Somali airspace by French aircraft. The most serious border incident occurred in February 1976. On a raid inside the FTAI the FLSC seized a school bus filled with French schoolchildren and took it to the Somalian border. French troops staged a raid to rescue the children, in the process killing six of the Somali guerrillas and wounding some of the children and some Somali in the area. This guerrilla raid was in one sense counterproductive: on the day after the French reprisal 800 French reinforcements were sent to the Djibouti garrison. Border tensions had early been responsible for the construction of a defense system around Djibouti itself that included barbed wire, mines, and the use of passes.

Against Kenya and the FTAI, Somalia has supported guerrilla efforts in the territories it has hoped to annex. Although by 1976 increasing numbers of Somali-backed insurgents were moving into southern Ethiopia, Somalia's support of guerrillas in Ethiopia has traditionally been in a territory to which Somalia made no claim. Somalia has given significant support to Eritrean rebels, whose secession movement has absorbed the major effort of the 41,000-man Ethiopian army and has left it unable to bring its full military weight against Somalia.

Direct involvement of the Somalian military in furtherance of foreign policy goals has been confined to the Horn of Africa. Although sympathetic to the Arab world, Somalia played no active military role in the Arab-Israeli war of 1973. The government did, however, give Egypt logistical support by allowing units of the Egyptian navy to enter and to operate the port of Berbera on the Gulf of Aden as if it were an Egyptian port (see ch. 10).

Possessing a small navy effective only for coastal patrol, Somalia has not attempted to project her power seaward. Nonetheless Somalia has claimed a territorial sea to the extent of 200 nautical miles from

312

her continental and insular coasts (see ch. 3). Foreign warships are not allowed to pass through this area unless authorized by the Somali government. Any ship exercising the right of innocent passage is required to fly its national flag and is considered to be under Somali jurisdiction for the duration of its passage. The government can suspend the right of innocent passage at any time.

The Military in the Economy

Since the formation of the National Army in 1960 the cost of maintaining the Somali military establishment has been high compared with other expenditures in the national budget. Even before the 1969 coup brought the military to power, defense costs consistently exceeded the combined amounts budgeted for health, education, and labor. Although the armed forces never exceeded 1 percent of the total population, the ratio of military personnel to population was higher than in any other sub-Saharan nation. In 1973 public expenditure on the military was the equivalent of US$5 per capita, whereas public expenditure for education was US$2 per capita and for health US$1 per capita.

Military expenditure increased at an average of over 9 percent per year from 1963 through 1973, a time when the gross national product (GNP) grew at an annual rate of just under 3 percent. The consistently high level of the defense burden on the national economy ranked the Somalian military among the most costly in Africa.

During the 1960s the United States and the Soviet Union competed in aid to Somalia, the United States supplying the Somali police force and the Soviet Union supplying the armed forces. Since the 1969 coup d'etat the Soviet Union has overwhelmingly been Somalia's major outside supplier.

It appears that military closeness with the Soviet Union has been an important factor in Somalia's receipt of nonmilitary funds. From 1971 through 1975 Somalia received an estimated US$32 million in economic aid from the Soviet Union, and under the terms of an agreement signed in 1975 it was expected to receive an additional US$58 million for nonmilitary development projects (see ch. 14).

Perhaps the most significant difference in the army's role in the economy since the coup has been the extent of its involvement in civil projects. Previously the army's mission centered on border disputes. It was to lend a hand in the event of national emergencies or natural disasters, but most of its activities were in anticipation of combat. The military government added to the army's mission a significant role in internal development.

The army played an important part in evacuating nomads from the regions of the country stricken by drought. The Soviets supplied six aircraft and 165 trucks for this effort. These transports were also used to distribute food, medicine, and other supplies to the refugee camps where the nomads awaited resettlement. A significant proportion of the administrators of at least some of the camps and transshipment points were soldiers.

In addition to its major contribution to the resettlement effort, the army has been involved in crash programs and self-help projects. The military government introduced crash programs to create employment, increase the country's independence from outside sources of aid, and emphasize the dignity of labor. The programs use labor-intensive methods for such projects as agricultural improvement, road-building, and rural development. Work on these projects is on a more or less voluntary basis. The hope is to provide for Somalia's needs to the greatest extent possible from its own resources (see ch. 12).

Initially the army concentrated on self-help projects to improve its own facilities. New barracks were constructed in Benadir and Mogadishu to relieve overcrowding, and roads to Camp Halane were built. Additional lodgings for up to 200 soldiers were built in both the north and the south of the country; and garages, paving, and other improvements were added at various installations.

After working on its own facilities the army became involved in construction in the civilian sector. Some of its projects included cleaning up towns and villages, digging and maintaining wells and irrigation canals, and stabilizing sand dunes. Members of the armed forces also worked on the National University, hospitals, prisons, orphanages, and factories; they contributed to scores of projects in all. Even in districts where the army did not formally participate, those who worked in the crash programs were frequently supervised by district commissioners, all of whom were military men, or by sergeants or lieutenants. The governors received training in the Democratic People's Republic of Korea (North Korea), studying the cooperative movement there as a model for Somalia's own.

MISSION AND ORGANIZATION

Since independence the armed forces' primary responsibility has been to protect national territorial integrity. Assistance to the Somali police force in maintaining internal security constituted a secondary mission. After the 1969 coup the government made it clear that the army's task was not limited to national defense, stressing the civil functions of the army.

Major General Mohamed Ali Samantar, the army's commander, set forth in 1972 directives that were to constitute "advanced guidance" for the armed forces. These gave as the functions of the army a commitment to develop the revolutionary conquests and strengthen ideological preparation within the army, to fight illiteracy, to upgrade the military technically and operationally, and to return to and increase participation in self-help and crash programs. Clearly the emphasis of these directives was on the civil rather than the combat mission of the army. This is in keeping with the view of the army as the vanguard of scientific socialism in underdeveloped countries (see The Armed Forces in National Life, this ch.).

In 1976 the defense establishment was composed mainly of ground forces. The total size of the armed forces was just over 23,000. Most of these—about 20,000—were in the army. The second largest branch was the air force, approximately 2,700 strong. The navy had only about 300 men. There also were about 3,000 paramilitary troops, including border guards and the People's Militia, as well as the 1,000-man Darawishta, the mobile unit of the police force that may serve as an army unit in time of crisis (see ch. 16).

In mid-1976 the military command structure was simple and direct. Major General Samantar was not only commander of the National Army—and therefore commander of the organizationally subordinated navy and air force—but also secretary of state for defense and a vice president of SRC and thus a member of the major decisionmaking body of the government. Holding the two highest defense posts, he stood alone in the command structure between the army and President Siad, the head of state. When in July 1976 the SRC relinquished its power to the newly established SSRP, Samantar retained the portfolio of the Ministry of Defense. The country's real power appeared to be in the SSRP's Politburo, of which Samantar became a vice president.

Strength and Tactical Organization

Before the military coup, command channels ran directly from the commander of the National Army to army sector commanders who exercised authority over military forces stationed in the field, and by 1968 combat units had been reorganized along Soviet lines. There is no indication that either the chain of command to lower echelons or the organization of combat units has changed significantly since the coup.

The army consisted in 1976 of six tank battalions, nine mechanized infantry battalions, two commando battalions, five field artillery battalions, and five antiaircraft artillery battalions. Originally much of its equipment consisted of World War II weapons received before 1963 from British, Italian, and Egyptian sources. After 1963 the Soviets became Somalia's major supplier, although not until the 1970s did Somalia receive substantial amounts of more modern equipment.

One notable feature of the Somalian army was its large tank force. In 1975 it had approximately 250 Soviet medium tanks. About 150 of these were older T-34s, but between 1973 and 1974 the army received about 100 of the newer T-54s and T-55s. This gave Somalia the largest armored force in black Africa, in 1975 more than three times the size of Ethiopia's force. A considerable portion of Somalia's advantage may have been offset by the difficulty of maintaining its tanks, however. It was suggested in 1973, for example, that as few as thirty of the 150 T-34s were serviceable and that even these could run neither far nor long in combat.

The Soviets have also supplied Somalia with: armored personnel carriers, over 300; 76-mm and 100-mm guns, 100; 122-mm howitzers, 130; and antiaircraft guns of varying sizes, about 150. Yet not all of this equipment is serviceable, and spare parts are in short supply.

The air force was a part of the army. Its primary mission was to support ground forces in maintaining internal and border security. In 1976 it had fifty-two combat aircraft, including a bomber force consisting only of one three-plane squadron of Ilyushin-28s. These are short-ranged bombers that could most effectively be used in a ground support role. But Somalia also had a total of twenty-five MiG-15s, MiG-17s, and MiG-19s (nineteen were MiG-17s) and during 1974 and 1975 acquired one squadron of twenty-four MiG-21s from the Soviet Union. There also was a six-plane transport squadron (three An-2s and three An-24s and An-26s) and a helicopter squadron. The amount and quality of the air force's matériel, especially with the addition of the MiG-21s, compared favorably with the strongest of the other sub-Saharan states, although like the army the air force had problems obtaining spare parts and keeping its equipment in operating condition.

Probably the best indication of what the size of the air force meant can be gained by comparing it with the air forces of Somalia's neighbors. In mid-1976 Ethiopia had the next largest air force in the Horn of Africa, consisting of 2,300 men and thirty-seven combat aircraft; the fighters were mainly American F-86Fs and F-5As. Concern over Somalia's increasing military capabilities is reflected in the United States sale to Kenya of twelve F-5 fighters in spite of the avowed desire to reduce the arms race in northeastern Africa. The F-5s are comparable in performance to the MiG-21s, the MiGs having a speed advantage; the F-5s have greater range and versatility. The F-86Fs are comparable to Somalia's MiG-15s and MiG-17s.

The navy was organized to support army forces in maintaining coastal security and was established with the aid of the Soviet Union in 1965. In 1976 there was some disagreement among leading sources on the size and composition of the navy's complement of ships. It included two Soviet OSA II guided missile boats, armed with the surface-to-surface Styx missile system, and four antiaircraft guns. It also included four to six Poluchat-class patrol boats, each carrying two 25-mm antiaircraft guns, and a number of Soviet P-4 and P-6 torpedo patrol boats, each carrying machine guns and two torpedo tubes. The navy has been reported to have two SOI-class submarine chasers,

316

each with four machine guns and antisubmarine rockets. The total number of these combat ships has been variously reported as ten to twelve. The navy also has four Soviet T-4 landing craft. Like the other services, the navy was plagued with insufficient spare parts and a poor rate of serviceability.

Logistics

In the mid-1970s the military services relied almost exclusively on external sources for logistical support. Almost all equipment came from the Soviet Union. Some of the Soviet equipment is relatively sophisticated, forcing the Somali to depend on the Soviet Union for training in its operation and maintenance.

The existing training arrangement with the Soviet Union was reinforced by the twenty-year Soviet-Somali Treaty of Friendship and Cooperation signed in Mogadishu in July 1974. Article 4 specified that the Soviets were to give assistance in training Somali military personnel in perfecting the use of Soviet weapons and armaments.

The precoup logistical system was centralized in Mogadishu. Under the control of a combined logistics-administrative staff within army headquarters, support flowed to units in the field through a relatively direct channel. The logistics organization coordinated the requirements for motor transportation and vehicle maintenance; supervised the centralized equipment and spare parts warehouse; established operating procedures for motor pools; and provided all quartermaster functions, including the central issue of personal clothing, combat weapons, and ammunition. Supplies were channeled directly from Mogadishu to battalions located in various regions of the country. It was felt that the system functioned adequately in peacetime but would be unable to provide effective logistical support under the emergency conditions of war.

There is no indication to what extent, if at all, the logistics organization has been changed since the 1969 coup. The distribution of supplied throughout the country has been made easier by the construction of new roads and by the addition of transport aircraft and trucks given to the army by the Soviet Union to aid in the nomad relocation effort (see ch. 14).

Manpower and Composition of Forces

In 1960 the armed forces totaled 5,000. In 1970, the year after the military coup, they numbered 12,000, and by 1976 they exceeded 23,000. During some years the annual growth rate was estimated to be as high as 10.1 percent.

Strength levels of the armed forces have always been maintained on a voluntary basis. In 1966 a modified policy of universal compulsory military training was approved by the National Assembly. By presidential decree all students over the age of eighteen who intended to apply for government educational scholarships were required to produce certificates from the National Army as evidence that they had completed short-term military training. There has been no indication that this requirement was rescinded after the coup.

The military regime introduced basic military and paramilitary training to large segments of the population through orientation courses. The practical value of this training was questionable, and its actual extent may have been exaggerated for propaganda purposes.

Procurement and Training of Officers

During the decade before the coup most of Somalia's higher ranking officers were veterans of duty with British or Italian colonial units that operated in the area. Others, including those who came to hold the highest positions in the army, were officers in the colonial police forces who transferred to the army at the time of independence, thus giving it experienced leadership. For a time after independence officer transfers between the army and the police force were not unusual.

The army relied on two sources for its officer personnel before the coup: volunteers for officer candidate training and outstanding noncommissioned officers of the army or the police force. To fill unit vacancies for officers of lower rank the Ministry of Defense usually advertised through the mass media. Announcements were in the form of specified numbers of vacancies in the Somali Army Officers' Academy. To be eligible, applicants had to be citizens, be between seventeen and twenty-eight years of age, and be willing to serve for four years.

Completion of the third level of middle school (seven years of education) constituted the minimum acceptable academic experience for officer training, although it was desirable for officers to have a diploma from upper middle school or its equivalent. Officer candidates were given written tests covering mathematics, language, and general information. High moral standards were required; convictions for acts against the state, offenses against other persons, or violations of marriage laws disqualified an applicant. He could also be barred for previous expulsion from a military organization or educational institution for disciplinary reasons. Physical qualifications for officers included good health and a minimum height of five feet six inches. A physical examination was required.

To qualify for pilot training it was necessary to have high scholastic standing, an interest in flying, and a basic technical ability. Physical requirements were more stringent than for duty with ground force units. Before 1963 pilots were trained in Italy, Egypt, and Ethiopia. Since 1963, with the advent of large-scale Soviet military aid, Somali army pilots have received flight training from Soviet instructors in the Soviet Union and in Somalia.

There was no indication that the official requirements for a commission had changed substantially since the coup. It may be assumed that, with the introduction of the new Somali orthography in 1973, literacy in Somali either replaced or was added to the requirement for literacy in English, Italian, or Arabic.

At least one source suggests that the officer corps has tended to be staffed by members of lower middle-class urban families or families of traders from the interior. The corps offered both of these groups prestigious careers.

The training Somali officers had received before the coup, in the Soviet Union and in Gamal Abdul Nasser's Egypt, helped shape their ideological outlook. They at least became familiar with alternatives to parliamentary government and to capitalism. These influences made themselves felt as the parliamentary government demonstrated its corruption and difficulties in governing effectively.

Since the coup the major changes in the officer corps appear to have been in ideology and politics rather than in the specifics of rules and regulations. Most of the young officers are well-schooled Marxists and are familiar with major communist writings.

At the beginning of 1971 it was made possible for anyone, even noncommissioned officers or lower level enlisted men, to reach the army's highest ranks by virtue of merit. "Merit" in this case includes such things as adherence to scientific socialism and devotion to the regime's revolutionary principles. One commentator favorable to the revolutionary government noted that when the political factor became the first principle of assessment, the quality of the officer corps started to change, presumably with more motivated and capable officers replacing elements that in the past had supported the neocolonialist power structure left over from the British and Italian occupations. Because the army has been untested since the coup, it is impossible to determine whether this is actually the case or whether increased politization has merely meant the advance of officers good at politics but not necessarily qualified militarily.

As the political factor became predominant, training was instituted to help form the attitudes of both officers and enlisted men toward the army's revolutionary role. Instruction in the mid-1970s was given in economics, history, and politics or on the working-class movement or socialism—always approached from a Marxist standpoint.

Some things were less quickly changed. The Somali have always been sensitive to matters involving the relative strengths and representation of their clan-families (see ch. 4). Despite the regime's attempts to politicize the officer corps and to eliminate tribalism in the country, balanced clan representation remained a sensitive issue. Any recruitment notice, whether for officers or for all ranks, specified the proportional number of men to be recruited from each district, establishing a de facto clan balance. This practice was in effect at least as late as October 1971. President Siad himself noted that the general public expected the SRC to follow the practice of precoup governments by being equally representative in clan composition.

I. M. Lewis, a leading authority on Somalia, observed in 1972 that the population continued to interpret changes in the composition of the SRC and in the ranks of its members as attempts to achieve a workable clan balance. The changes could be explained by this reasoning, suggesting that the influence of clan balance throughout the army and officer corps remains stronger than the government would like and may in the final consideration count for as much as political conformity.

Whether the importance of clan balance decreased under the pressure of the intense antitribalism campaign is unclear. Coup attempts against the military government in April 1970 and May 1971, both led by officers in the SRC, were probably brought on by overrepresentation of the Darod clan-family among the country's rulers. Although the leaders of the second attempt were charged with engineering a plot to kill the revolution, their executions and funeral arrangements were orchestrated especially to emphasize antitribalism. Still, clan-awareness is deep seated and had as of the mid-1970s survived the coup attempt and its repercussions.

Procurement and Training of Enlisted Personnel

The overwhelming proportion of the Somalian armed forces are Somali, so the tribal quotas used by many other African nations were replaced by a proportional representation of all Somali clans whenever possible. Before the coup traditional group animosities created disciplinary problems where serious clan imbalance occurred. These situations usually resulted in transfers and efforts to correct the imbalance through localized recruiting efforts.

Both before and after the coup recruiting announcements always specified the proportional number of men to be recruited from each district. This procedure had the advantage of decreasing tensions by maintaining clan balance, but it also allowed the military government to mix recruits from all over the country to impress on them the precedence of national loyalty over clan loyalty.

Basic enlistment was for four years. Prerequisites for joining any branch of the armed forces were that a man had to be between seventeen and twenty-five, physically fit, of high moral caliber, and have a "youthful vigor." He had to be at least five feet six inches tall and unmarried. Beyond these, requirements varied according to the category in which a recruit enlisted. Before the coup there were three such categories: general duty with a line unit, military administration, or assignments requiring technical skills. Recruits for administrative positions had to have an elementary education, and those for technical positions needed a government certificate attesting to their special qualifications. There were no special requirements for line duty.

Once accepted for the service, the recruit proceeded on a six-month training course conducted by the appropriate service. Elimination of illiteracy from the ranks was a primary army goal, and garrisons and detachments provided educational improvement courses for new recruits. Attendance for illiterate recruits was mandatory.

Noncommissioned officers received leadership training at a special school in Mogadishu. Other specialized instruction included commando, artillery, and driver training.

In 1961 the Women's Auxiliary Corps was established. Recruits were selected and trained to fill positions in administration, personnel, and military welfare. Qualified enlistees received a five-month period of instruction in basic military discipline and training in typing, recordkeeping, and related administrative subjects. Enlistments were for two years. The corps was small, and most duty assignments were with National Army Headquarters in Mogadishu or with subordinate headquarters in the field.

Just as the officer corps drew its members from the urban middle class or from traders, the enlisted men tended to come from the bush or from nomadic life. Lewis has suggested that this was a direct reflection of the pressure of population on resources in the nomadic regions. It is the nomads who are most likely to gravitate toward government employment in general, but it might be argued that the esteem in which warriors are held in nomadic society makes the army a particularly attractive choice. One group that was noticeably underrepresented in recruitment was the cultivators from southern Somalia, a group with a relatively high standard of living.

Reserves

Somalia first felt compelled to organize a reserve force during the 1964 border clashes with Ethiopia. At that time the National Assembly passed legislation authorizing the mobilization of large numbers of volunteers to be trained by the National Army at special camps in the regional capitals. A force of about 3,000 irregulars was hastily recruited, but these troops were not needed in the border war and were subsequently released from duty. These men received cards identifying them as reservists, but they received neither pay nor training and had no official status.

The Home Guard was established in 1967 when 3,000 men were called up for six months' duty and training. When they had completed their tour, they were discharged but were carried in a reserve pool while 3,000 more were called out for the next six months. This system was in effect at least as late as 1974.

The Young Pioneers were created several years after independence to help solve the problem of developing a reserve element without excessive cost. Patterned after its Soviet counterpart, this group was a quasi-military unit with a civil development role. After a period of intense military training conducted by members of the army, Young

Pioneers worked on national development projects, such as road or housing construction or work on state agricultural farms.

The Young Pioneers appear to have been reorganized in August 1972 as the Victory Pioneers (Gulwadayal). Officially these young people of both sexes are primarily engaged in drumming up support for self-help schemes. Another of their duties is to help the armed forces if necessary. In actuality they serve as a police force, and one observer speculated that they were created to give the SRC an alternative to complete dependence on the national police (see ch. 16).

MORALE AND CONDITIONS OF SERVICE

The best testimony to the appeal of service in the Somalian armed forces is the fact that the large military establishment is maintained on a voluntary basis. Although military life is often arduous, the serviceman has generally been rewarded with fair treatment and recognition of his efforts.

The government standardized the rights and treatment of the armed forces for the first time in 1966. Military pay rates were increased, and the National Assembly passed a defense law regulating the juridical status and conditions of service for all personnel in the armed forces, the police, and the prison guards. This legislation corrected numerous inequities and deficiencies in the defense establishment. Recruiting methods were standardized on a national basis; procedures for promotion, discharge, and decorations were detailed. Policy on all matters pertaining to pay and allowances was delineated. Extensive disciplinary regulations governing military life were enumerated; offenses were defined and punishments prescribed.

Rations before the 1969 coup had been generally better than those in the civilian sector—or at least in those nomadic sectors from which the bulk of recruits were drawn; where economic conditions were better, recruits came forth less readily. Postcoup government surveys of dietary requirements resulted in better balanced meals for servicemen.

After the military takeover, however, pay rates were cut. In 1969 monthly pay rates ranged from Sh105 (for value of the Somali shilling—see Glossary) for recruits to Sh315 for first sergeants; warrant officers received Sh370 and major generals Sh2,000. The austerity measures of the government were responsible for a drastic reduction in army salaries by late 1971. In mid-1973 a journalist alluded to the extremely poor pay of the military.

Other factors mitigated this slashing of pay, however. First, all government employees received salary cuts, so the soldier's position may not have changed very much in relation to that of civil servants and of the population at large. Second, physical conditions of service life were improved. Previously the army had inadequate, overcrowded facilities. Through self-help programs after the coup, the army built new barracks and dormitories, mess facilities, and offices. In any case military service still appeared attractive to the nomadic recruit whose alternative was eking out a meager existence in the interior. This may in part account for the army's increase in size during the drought of the mid-1970s.

The army remained a prestigious career. With the opening of higher rank to anyone on the bases of merit and political conformity, the army may have begun to provide a greater measure of social mobility than in the past. Certainly with its emphasis on literacy and its exposure to administrative or technical training, it provided some preparation for civilian careers.

Before the military takeover military justice was administered through civil rather than military courts; regional courts in Mogadishu and Hargeysa served as the primary courts in prosecution of military offenses. The two courts of appeal had military penal appeals sections in which military officers served as assistant judges.

At the time of the coup the SRC assumed all judicial powers and all jurisdiction over civil, penal, administrative, and accounting matters. The National Security Court, directly under the SRC, has tried both military men and civilians accused of political crimes. After 1970 crimes by members of the military that did not fall into this category were tried by the Military Supreme Court, which was established in that year.

The army wore summer uniforms of khaki and winter uniforms of olive drab. The Darawishta wore the headdress of Mohamed Abdullah's warriors. The Women's Auxiliary Corps wore buff skirts and jackets, and the Victory Pioneers wore green uniforms. Chevrons indicated enlisted ranks, and combinations of stars and shields indicated commissioned officer ranks (see fig. 8).

FOREIGN INFLUENCE IN THE MILITARY

In the mid-1970s Soviet influence in the Somalian armed forces was great. The Somali were bound to the Soviets by their need for financial aid, equipment, matériel, replacement parts, and training on the hardware supplied. Moreover the officers controlling Somalia professed an ideological bond with the Soviet Union.

The close tie between Somalia and the Soviet Union began in the early 1960s just after independence. Because of its own territorial ambitions and the tense relations with neighboring countries, Somalia decided that its interests demanded a 20,000-man army. Government leaders first sought financial support for the army from the United States. But the United States, already a large arms supplier to Ethiopia, would not support the establishment of so large a Somalian army and offered instead to provide enough aid to support 5,000 men. So-

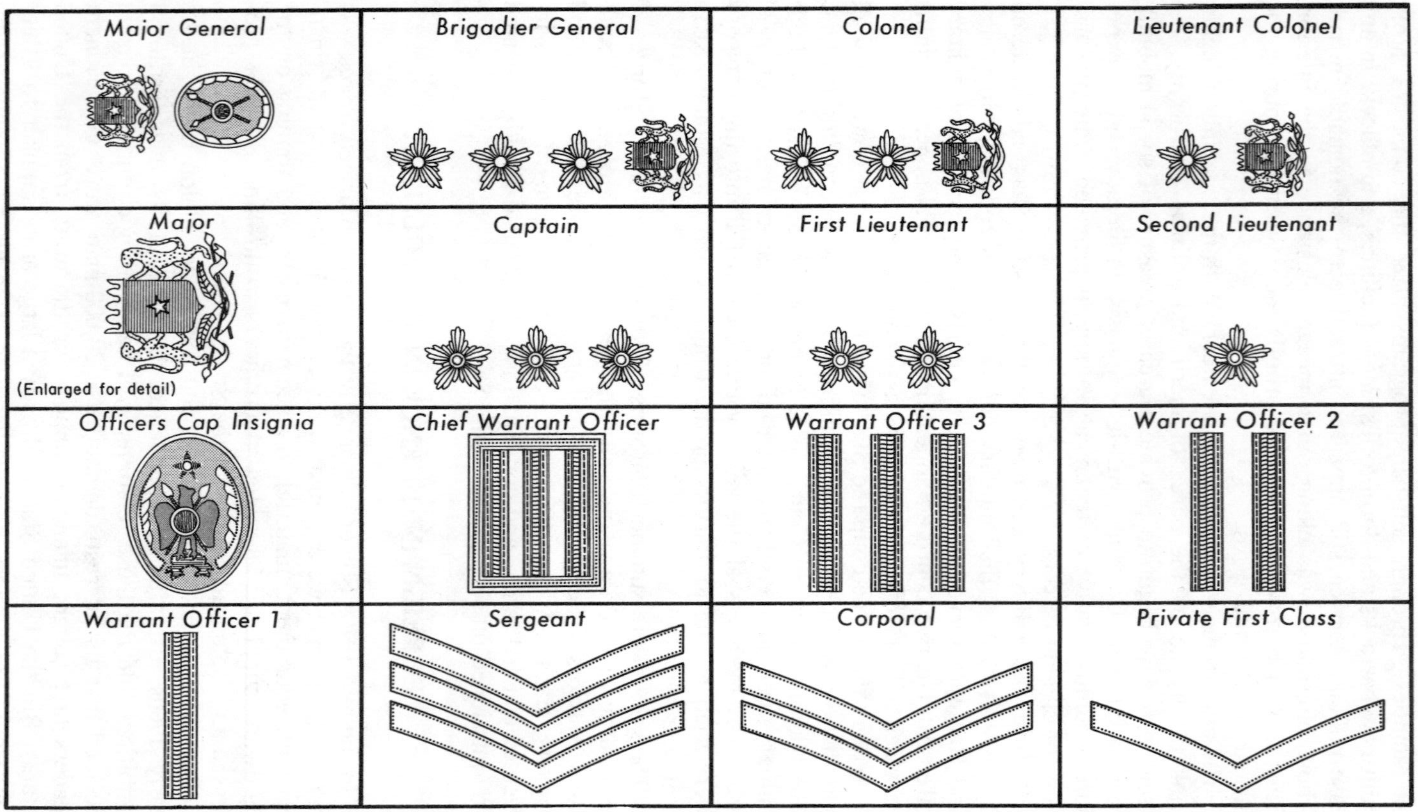

Figure 8. Somalia, Army Ranks and Insignia, 1976

malia looked elsewhere and in 1962 found the Soviet Union ready to grant loans worth US$32 million to develop the Somali army. The loan later was increased to US$55 million, and the Soviets began to equip and train an army scheduled to reach a size of 14,000. By the mid-1970s the size was increased to around 20,000. The loan was made unconditionally, and the Soviets allowed a leisurely repayment schedule over as much as twenty years.

During the rest of the 1960s the Soviet Union supplied Somalia with automatic small arms and artillery as well as a substantial number of T-34 tanks, armored personnel carriers, and MiG-15 and MiG-17 aircraft. About 300 Soviet advisers undertook to train the army and a new armored brigade. More than 500 Somali pilots, officers, and technicians took training in the Soviet Union.

Until the coup Soviet aid to the army was counterbalanced to some extent by two factors: the Somalian government had Western political inclinations, and the police force received aid from the United States and the Federal Republic of Germany (West Germany). But by 1969 the army had become dominant over the police. With the coup the Soviet Union became incontestably Somali's major supplier of military goods. Soviet aid between 1963 and 1973 totaled US$87 million, although not all of this was military expenditure. In the mid-1970s the Soviet Union remained the only important supplier of the Somali military.

In February 1972 Soviet Defense Minister Andrei Grechko visited Mogadishu. From this visit came the Soviet-Somali agreement to improve and modernize the port of Berbera in return for use of the Berbera facility for communication, docking, and repairs (see Mission and Organization, this ch.) (see ch. 10). This agreement was a marriage of, mutual advantage. The Somali wanted military equipment, and the Soviets wanted an Indian Ocean base from which to show their flag and to counter the United States deployment of the Polaris A-3 missile, which they viewed as having made the Arabian Sea a possible launching site for a strike against the Soviet Union. The Berbera facilities acquired additional importance when the Soviet Union was expelled from Egypt in July 1972 and when the Suez Canal was reopened in 1975 and oil shipments from the Persian Gulf through the canal increased.

The port facilities at Berbera attracted considerable Western attention in mid-1975 when United States reconnaissance photographs indicated the existence of a substantial Soviet base with communications, radar, and surface-to-air missile handling and storage facilities. The Soviets' development of Berbera was not new; they had been working on the port in 1965 while the United States was developing Kismayo. Nevertheless the United States Congress sent an inspection team to Somalia that confirmed the existence of a Soviet base with a missile facility, a runway that could accommodate large bombers, and a communications facility. After this visit the Somali continued to invite others to inspect for themselves. The Somali and many of these visitors denied the existence of a Soviet base.

The Somali denial appeared to be based on the technicality that the Soviet Union was merely using and developing Somalian facilities and that these facilities were not "sufficient" to constitute a base. Moreover it was unlikely that the Soviet Union would have remained in Berbera had the Somali wished them to leave. But in practical terms the Soviet Union did seem to have full control over the facility; it was described as almost entirely Soviet run, down to the sweepers of the office floors.

Yet the Soviet Union has been careful to respect Somali sovereignty. Despite Somalia's apparent adherence to scientific socialism and reliance on the Soviet Union for matériel, Somalia's leaders were clearly independent.

As principal supplier of armaments to Somalia the Soviet Union exerted great influence; militarily there is evidence that this may be a restraining influence. The Soviet Union supplied the entire Somalian navy, but the navy was not large enough in the mid-1970s to permit independence from the Soviet fleet for missions other than coastal patrol. Dependence on the Soviet fleet was in fact encouraged by more than sixty visits by Soviet warships to Somalian ports from 1968 through July 1975, including the appearance of two warships off Mogadishu during the threat of an upheaval in Somalia's government in October 1970 and another warship during the coup attempt of 1971. Analysists, such as Helen Desfosses, have suggested that the Soviets had no desire to become involved in Somalia's border disputes but were concerned instead with injecting their naval presence into what was formerly a United States preserve. To do so they have provided Somalia's armed forces with enough equipment to impress them with Soviet friendship and to permit them to create a viable defense system but not enough to permit sustained offensive action. Some writers believe that shortages would prevent a Somalian-Ethiopian war from lasting longer than a week without additional great-power support. As the source of ammunition and spare parts, the Soviets can restrain Somali military activity.

The 1974 Treaty of Friendship and Cooperation reflects Somalia's relationship with the Soviet Union. The Soviets agreed to train Somali military personnel and supply arms to the Somali defense forces, but each country pledged only to refrain from participation in any hostile activity directed against the other.

Soviet influence affected the Somali military in more subtle ways, primarily through the Soviet training of Somali personnel. Not only did this training lead to the adoption of Soviet organization and tactical thought, but it also exposed as many as 60 percent of Somali officers to the Soviet Union and the Soviet system. There were two mitigating factors, however. First, there was evidence that some of the trainees Somalia sent to the Soviet Union were potential troublemakers whom the regime wished to have out of the country. Second, students in Moscow from other African countries have been alienated by their hosts' racial discrimination—a factor that may eventually diminish Soviet influence.

The Soviet Union also provided the training and the organizational model for the Somali army's intelligence service and for the National Security Service (NSS). There is little additional information on army intelligence, but the NSS was directly under the SRC until the SRC gave way to the SSRP in July 1976. There was no indication that the Soviets had any continuing control over these intelligence organizations (see ch. 16).

Other communist countries have offered advice and training to Somalia. North Korean military advisers have been reported in Somalia, and in 1976 Secretary of Defense Donald Rumsfeld testified before the United States Congress that 1,000 Soviet advisers were in Somalia on a permanent basis and that Cuba had about fifty advisers there. The Somali government has repeatedly denied the presence of Cuban advisers; if in fact they were in Somalia, it was improbable that they exerted significant influence on the military. In addition, as late as 1973 Somali naval personnel were sent to Egypt for training.

CHAPTER 16

PUBLIC ORDER AND INTERNAL SECURITY

Somali have a history of fierce independence. They submitted to the authority, or at least the arbitration, demanded in their traditional kinship arrangements, but even after Somalia's independence in 1960 allegiance to an organized national authority as opposed to allegiance to specific descent groups (clans and lineages) not only went against the Somali's traditional social values but was considered a reminder of the country's colonial past (see ch. 4).

Between 1960 and 1969 parliamentary governments provided a penal code, a criminal procedure code, and a loyal, highly respected police force. The codes were an amalgam of laws introduced in the British and Italian colonies adapted to accommodate such traditional forces as Islamic law (sharia) and Somali custom. By 1969 the government had managed to extend its rule of law to most of the country's urban inhabitants and had even achieved some success in bringing law and order to the vast interior.

Still, at the end of the 1960s the traditional way of life persisted among most of the people. Even under modern administration groups protected their rights primarily by force. Fights and small wars were not infrequent. Nomads retained a firm conviction that they were individual masters of their own actions and subject only to the authority of God.

This Somali tradition of independence made it difficult to assess accurately the effectiveness of the measures taken by the military government that gained power in 1969. The government claimed and observers agreed that it had taken significant steps since then to replace tribalism with the government's rule of law. It claimed to have significantly reduced nomadic conflicts and extended its control into the hinterland. The military government had probably succeeded to a substantial degree in all these endeavors; it sometimes used substantial force to demonstrate that its edicts must be followed; it made a concerted effort, unlike previous Somali governments, to eliminate or curtail rival sources of authority; it took advantage of a severe drought to extend its authority over nomads even as it made efforts to save them. Some reports from Somalia stated that the police maintained close surveillance of the public, that nothing went on without the knowledge and sufferance of the government.

Meanwhile other sources suggested that, for all its measures, the government was unable to alter the basic Somali attitude of personal independence. For example, the regime's Victory Pioneers (Gulwadayal) were everywhere, acting as policemen on the street, but it was reported that their authority was not infrequently ignored and that Somali continued to do largely as they pleased (see The Somali Police Force, this ch.) (see ch. 15).

It is likely that governmental measures have not changed basic Somali patterns of behavior. At the same time the military government seems to have greater control over the country than previous governments. The state and its law are replacing more traditional forms of authority.

The government also strove to eliminate sources of internal political opposition. Apparently many internal security measures adopted were purposely vague concerning what specifically constituted a threat to the state. Determination of the existence and degree of such a threat was left to the Supreme Revolutionary Council (SRC) or to appropriate government officials. The Victory Pioneers, in addition to performing routine law enforcement duties, were to watch for activities considered harmful to the state. There was also a security service personally loyal to President Mohamed Siad Barre that was concerned with internal threats and subversion. From 1969 to 1976 no political parties were allowed in Somalia; in mid-1976 the Somali Socialist Revolutionary Party (SSRP), dominated by the men who had previously formed the SRC, was established as the sole legitimate party. Reports from some visitors, however, indicated that, just as the Somali's personal independence had not been eliminated, neither had his outspokenness. It was said that frequent criticisms of the government could be heard anywhere, even among officials. If there is freedom to criticize, it may have developed only since 1972, after the government recovered from a surprise 1971 coup attempt and began to feel more secure in its position.

Actually, there is little or no apparent internal threat to the regime, and there has been none since the defeat of the 1971 coup attempt. In some instances the military regime has given posts to former opponents after a suitable period of "reorientation" or "rehabilitation" in training camps or prisons. Thus some opposition is neutralized by being included in the government. Furthermore the regime's performance has made it relatively popular with most Somali and is perhaps its best guarantee against any threat of overthrow or subversion.

PUBLIC ORDER AND THE INCIDENCE OF CRIME

Public order was the legal responsibility of the minister of interior, regional governors, and district commissioners. The Ministry of Interior controlled the police force at highest levels. Local authorities controlled the regional and district police commands. Any of these authorities could request the intervention of the army or of any other of the state's military or paramilitary organizations.

Public order laws allowed government control over public meetings and associations. According to the law, public meetings could be held without governmental disruption as long as prior notice was given the district commissioner and the meeting complied with any restrictions he required. The district commissioner could place restrictions on a meeting only for reasons of health, safety, morality, order, or security. In practice, meetings in which political views contradictory to the government's might be expressed would not be authorized.

The secretary of state for interior could dissolve by decree any parties or associations operating against public order or morality. Prior authorization was not required to form nonpolitical organizations, but within a month of their formation such organizations had to submit to the appropriate regional governor their constitutions, lists of their officers, and the locations of their headquarters and branches.

The government could maintain public order by imposing certain restrictive measures in either individual territories or the entire state. A court could require a socially dangerous individual to post a bond as security for good behavior. The parliamentary regime had been able to hold people without trial for up to ninety days during a state of emergency; the military government removed most legal restrictions on preventive detention. After the coup a local revolutionary council or the National Security Service (NSS) could detain anyone felt to be conducting himself in a manner dangerous to peace, order, or good government or contrary to the aims and spirit of the revolution (see Internal Security, this ch.). Once the detaining body notified the SRC of its action, the SRC could continue the individual's detention as long as desired. The SRC's decision could not be appealed.

Until the SRC was disbanded in July 1976, the head of state could declare a state of war with prior approval from the SRC. He could also proclaim a state of emergency when the emergency affected the entire nation. When it affected only certain areas, a state of emergency for the affected area could be proclaimed by the secretary of state for interior or the appropriate regional governor. Once the decree was issued, the regional governor could restrict freedom of movement. He could order the search and arrest of persons suspected of a crime or of activities that threatened public order and security and could also requisition the use of property or services without compensation.

The military government was particularly rigorous in dealing with major obstacles to its conception of public order, including possession of firearms, drunkenness, and livestock theft. In 1970 the SRC required all firearms to be turned in to the government except those kept by regional governors and district commissioners, nomads, foreigners working in remote areas, diplomats, and tourists. To discourage outbreaks of violence over possession of livestock or grazing and water rights the SRC in March 1971 imposed a new law with stiff penalties for stock theft and looting. Conviction of stealing livestock could be punished by prison terms of from three to five years, and looting could be punished by imprisonment for five to ten years.

In August 1973 the SRC attacked drunkenness with a four-point law. To reduce the availability of alcohol to the public, all but one of the manufacturers of alcoholic drinks were closed; all beverages from this one producer had to be exported or sold to the Ministry of Tourism. Drunkards in the government were dismissed and tried by the National Security Court (NSC), and alcoholics unable to stop drinking were placed where they could be medically treated. The number of reported drunkenness offenses increased by almost 60 percent from 1971 to 1973, perhaps as a result of strict enforcement of this new law. The number of reported incidents of drunkenness in 1973 was 453. Just over 500 people were arrested in these incidents, and 365 of them had been convicted by the end of the year.

In the 1960s such felonies as armed robbery, rape, and other crimes involving violence or threatened violence were not widespread, and there was no indication of a trend toward general lawlessness, although some homicide, often in the course of conflict between nomadic groups, did occur. A higher rate of burglary and theft occurred in densely populated urban centers.

After independence in 1960 the police discerned a slight increase in the crime rate. They attributed this both to the influx of disaffected nomads into urban population centers and to the resulting disruption of traditional family solidarity.

Quarrels and fighting among the large nomadic population over grazing and water rights as well as illegal activity along the stretches of unsettled border presented formidable obstacles to the maintenance of public order. Smuggling and illegal traffic in contraband constituted the foremost criminal activity. Armed gangs of smugglers often engaged in vicious fights with the police, and organized contraband rings existed in most urban centers.

Available figures were incomplete and probably not very reliable, but they suggested that under the military regime—specifically between 1971 and 1973—the number of ordinary crimes in categories ranging from homicide to receiving stolen goods reported to and verified by the police decreased by more than 26 percent. The number of rapes declined by more than 25 percent and of murders by almost 40 percent, although the number of attempted murders increased. There were significant decreases in all crimes related to theft: simple theft, burglary, robbery, animal theft, and receiving stolen goods (see table 7).

Table 7. Somalia, Major Ordinary Reported and Verified Crimes, 1971 and 1973

Category of Crime	1971	1973
Murder	88	53
Attempted murder	20	55
Rape	93	68
Hurt	1,404	1,773
Affray	1,136	393
Threat	169	114
Simple theft	911	569
Burglary	2,066	1,548
Theft of animals	480	198
Robbery	111	47
Receiving stolen goods	187	80
TOTAL	6,665	4,898

Source: Based on information from Somalia, Ministry of Planning and Coordination, Statistical Abstract, 1971, VIII, Mogadishu, August 1972; and Somalia, Presidency of the Supreme Revolutionary Council, Statistical Abstract, 1973, No. 10, Mogadishu, September 1975.

Smuggling remained a major problem, or at least a major embarrassment, to the military regime. In 1971 the government claimed that smuggling had been brought under control and the flow of contraband reduced to a trickle. Police procedure at that time was to apprehend and try the smugglers and auction the goods to the general public. But despite the government's claims it appeared that, although most of the goods were indeed seized, the smugglers escaped and the goods spoiled because it took so long to auction them.

Still more embarrassing was the fact that in late 1975 wives of senior officials frequently smuggled goods in their suitcases; their husbands would meet them at ports, airports, or border points and use their positions to inhibit customs inspection. On October 10, 1975, President Siad told national security forces, police, and customs personnel that they need fear no reprisals from anyone, however senior his position, if they performed their duties. Officials were in turn forbidden to receive persons at points of entry to the country.

At least as late as 1972 there was evidence that the military government had not completely ended the corrupt practices of public officials, a major complaint against the parliamentary governments. In that year the SRC prohibited all government officials, senior civil servants, and others who handled public funds from purchasing or building new houses. The law also required that these officials declare all properties owned either by them or by their families.

One writer claimed that corruption was even more widespread. He reported that Somali officials were probably engaged in black-marketing sugar and other commodities.

333

In November 1972 Siad launched an anticorruption campaign because officials in the districts and in parastatal organizations were stealing public funds. The government intended to create committees to monitor government expenditure at local levels and in publicly owned corporations by the end of the campaign, but the campaign had no scheduled ending date and was expected to continue for some time.

THE SOMALI POLICE FORCE

The Somali Police Force grew out of police forces employed by the British and Italians to maintain the peace in British Somaliland and Italian Somalia. Both European powers used Somali as armed constables in rural areas, and Somali eventually staffed the lower ranks of police forces officered by Europeans.

From time to time there were organizational distinctions between colonial armed forces and colonial police forces, but in practice these distinctions were blurred. Especially before World War II, units tended to perform the same general functions regardless of whether they were intended to be police or military forces.

The leading personnel of both the army and the police force after independence had served in colonial police forces. Most of those who became senior officers and commanders in the police and the army had begun their careers in the Somalia Gendarmerie under the British Military Administration (BMA) during World War II.

By the time of the military coup of October 1969 the police had grown from a force of about 3,700 at independence to 6,000. They had not further increased in number by 1975. After independence the Somali Police Force received most of its aid from the West, notably the United States and the Federal Republic of Germany (West Germany). The United States terminated its aid in 1970 (see ch. 10). In the mid-1970s West Germany continued to provide financial and matériel support, and Italy helped train Somali police officers.

Historical Development

The earliest of the forces responsible for maintaining public order in Somalia was an armed constabulary of about fiften men established by the British in 1884. Their primary duty was to police the northern coast. In 1910 the British formed the Somaliland Coastal Police, and in 1912 they formed the British Somaliland Camel Constabulary to cover the interior. The camel constabulary took part in operations against Sayyid Mohamed ibn Abdullah Hassan but were ambushed in 1913, losing their leader and most of their 150-man force (see ch. 2). They were later re-formed and continued to operate until 1920.

In 1926 the British formed the first properly constituted police force in their colony, the Somaliland Police Force. Somali held ranks of inspector, noncommissioned officer, and constable, but British officers led the force. Law enforcement, however, remained the responsibility of British district commissioners. They were aided by a uniformed and armed rural constabulary (*illalo*). These men brought offenders to court, guarded prisoners, patrolled local townships, and accompanied nomadic tribesmen over grazing areas.

As in the British protectorate, the Italians brought military force to their colony to maintain public order. They first established a small coastal police and then in 1914 a rural constabulary (*gogle*) to assist Italian residents. This was similar to the rural constabulary of British Somaliland. By 1930 this force comprised about 500 men.

With the advent of fascist influence in Italian Somalia the military uses of the armed forces became more important. In 1923 Italian administrators reconstituted the former Somali Police Corps into a more efficient colonial arm, the Corpo Zaptié. The ranks of the older police corps were purged, and Somali, Eritrean, and Arab troops were recruited to bring the strength of the Corpo Zaptié to about 800. Barracks were built, and schools teaching language and military tactics were organized. Italian carabinieri officers trained and supervised the new corps.

The Corpo Zaptié was at first used to disarm the nomadic population of the Benadir, Obbya, and Mijerteyn interior. These efforts led to rebellions and a series of defeats for the corps. Because it proved ineffective, it was used to defend military garrisons while askaris (policemen) recruited from local clans continued the disarmament effort. Armed bands of these askaris had by 1926 defeated the major nomadic forces in Ogaden (inhabited by Somali but formally part of Ethiopia).

At the end of January 1935 Benito Mussolini's military leaders began preparation for war with Ethiopia. Somalia was a major landing area for Italian troops. Somali colonial troops eagerly fought against their traditional enemy, although some individuals and clan-families fought with the Ethiopians. During the war the Corpo Zaptié expanded to about 6,000 Somali. A total of over 40,000 Somali participated in the campaign, many as porters and laborers.

In the eighteen years of fascist rule Italian forces were able to reduce interclan warfare but often only after using considerable brutality. Although a large number of Somali served in the military force and as irregulars, few were trained for skilled positions. Most served in a capacity similar to that of the traditional askari. They were given commands only at the lowest echelons.

In 1941, after an initial defeat and expulsion from the Horn of Africa, the British returned to crush Italian forces in the area. They then established the BMA over both the protectorate and what had been

335

Italian Somalia. The Italian colony's police force was disbanded and replaced in both territories by the hastily recruited Somalia Gendarmerie under British officers. This force had by 1943 expanded to more than 3,000 Somali enlisted men led by 120 British officers. From this organization would grow the National Army and the Somali Police Force twenty years later. In 1948 the Somalia Gendarmerie was redesignated the Somalia Police Force. Somali served as inspectors, noncommissioned officers, and constables. The British completely changed the Italian colony's central police force, but they took over the rural constabulary without major alteration since it resembled their own.

A school was opened for training Somali officers and noncommissioned officers, both to increase Somali military efficiency and to provide a security force for the future. By 1949 a few of the Somali who attended this school had reached the rank of chief inspector, the highest noncommissioned rank.

A major concern of the British on their return to the colony was the availability of weapons. In addition to those that found their way into the hands of nomads during Mohamed Abdullah's jihad, large stores of weapons and ammunition were discarded in the northern portion of the colony during the fighting with the Italians. The Somalia Gendarmerie, once it grew large enough, successfully disarmed the bulk of the population and was able to control a number of pro-Italian guerrilla groups in the interior. In the northern part of the colony Somali members of the former camel constabulary reported for duty armed with Italian weapons and were sent to disarm the nomads in their sector. By 1942 the Somalia Gendarmerie was in a secure position to maintain civil order throughout the colony.

Between the end of World War II and Somalia's independence, military forces were maintained in both the northern and the southern regions. In the north the British developed a regiment known as the British Somaliland Scouts. In the south the Somalia Gendarmerie, renamed the Somalia Police Force, performed police duties.

When in 1950 the southern area became the Trust Territory of Somaliland under Italian Administration, Italian carabinieri officers and Somali personnel from the Somalia Police Force formed the Police Corps of Somalia (Corpo di Polizia della Somalia). Although Italian officers once again commanded Somali troops, command this time proved transitional. In 1958, two years before independence, a Somali commandant was appointed, and the police were completely somalized and made responsible for all law enforcement in the Trust Territory. At this time the force was redesignated the Police Force of Somalia (Forze di Polizia della Somalia).

Similar progress was not made in British Somaliland. Somali did not receive high command until just before independence. Only in

1960 were British officers withdrawn. At that time the forces of the northern and southern regions were integrated.

The Modern Force

The size of the police force at the time of independence was about 3,700. About 1,000 of these were the Mobile Group (Darawishta Poliska, commonly called Darawishta), a force used to keep peace between warring tribes in the interior. The new government could also call on it for assistance in military actions near Somalia's disputed borders.

Frequent disputes over water and grazing rights often led to fighting between rival clans or lineages, forcing the police to cope with armed conflicts involving large numbers of men. A serious situation of this sort erupted near Hargeysa in late 1965. After several months of attempts at pacification and mediation the police declared a state of emergency and restored order with a large force employing infantry tactics. In such situations military units of the National Army were available to support the police.

A police air wing equipped with Cessna light aircraft and one Douglas DC-3 was established in 1961. The unit was able to operate from improvised landing fields near most of the remote police posts. The air wing provided assistance to the field police units and to the Darawishta through airlift of supplies, reconnaissance, and the transport of personnel.

A small unit of policewomen was formed in 1961. They were generally needed in investigation, inspection, and interrogation of female offenders or victims. Policewomen were also assigned to cases involving female juvenile delinquents, ill or abandoned girls, prostitutes, and child beggars.

General Mohammad Abshir Musa commanded the Somali Police Force from 1959 until he resigned in early 1969. Under his command the force expanded to 6,000 men and acquired a reputation for professionalism and excellence. The police remained committed to the rule of law and respectful of basic civil liberties. To a remarkable extent they were able to remain above the nation's internal political struggles. Abshir frequently complained of political interference with the judiciary, and during Somalia's last national election in 1969 the police did much to preserve order. Abshir finally resigned as a result of his conflict with Minister of Interior Yassin Nur Hassan over the use of the police for political purposes. His resignation greatly demoralized the police force.

Organizationally the police force has since 1960 been part of the armed forces, ultimately commanded by the head of state, who was also commander in chief of the armed forces. The police commandant was under the Ministry of Interior, although the force was answerable to various organs of justice.

Under the parliamentary regime police were trained in West Germany and received matériel aid from West Germany and the United States. The regime was able to use the police to counterbalance the Soviet-supported army (see ch. 15). Nevertheless in October 1969 no police commander actually opposed the army's coup, although not all favored it. It was reported that much of their docility was a result of Major General Siad's skill in negotiating.

The popular Abshir was arrested shortly after the coup even though he no longer held the post of police commandant. The commandant at the time was General Jama Ali Korshel, who was made the first vice president of the SRC. Within a year of the SRC's establishment Korshel was accused of leading a countercoup attempt, but policemen seemed generally satisfied with their inclusion in the government (see Internal Security, this ch.).

After the coup the police force remained responsible to the Ministry of Interior and was headquartered in Mogadishu. The force was organized into various departments known as divisions, which had branches in all jurisdictions throughout the country. The commandant with his deputy commandants and police chiefs usually remained in the capital except when conducting inspection tours. In 1976 the police commandant was Colonel Abdullahi Mahmud Hassan.

Each region had a regional commandant, and other commissioned officers commanded in each of the country's districts. After 1972 the police outside Mogadishu comprised group commands, divisional commands (corresponding to the regions), subdivisional commands (corresponding to the districts), station commands, and police posts. The responsibilities of officials commanding police stations in districts and villages varied in the individual jurisdictions.

The mobile police comprised the Darawishta and the Riot Unit (Birmadka Poliska). The Darawishta operated in remote areas and along the frontier. The Riot Unit rated as a crack unit for emergency action and also provided honor guards for ceremonial functions.

Technical and specialized units included the Tributary Division, the Criminal Investigation Division (CID), the Traffic Division, a communications unit, and a training unit. The CID was the best known of these, for it handled investigations, fingerprinting, criminal records, immigration, and passports and operated in both rural and urban areas. It had modern equipment and was described by Somali as one of the mainstays of the force. Although headquartered in the capital, the CID had a communications network that allowed it to communicate with any outlying station. It maintained close liaison with medical authorities involved in legal medicine and forensic science.

Service units included the Transport Department (Gadidka Poliska), Central Stores, and the health service. The Transport Department had a sizable fleet of motor vehicles by 1971. Modern cars with radiotelephones patrolled Mogadishu, able to respond rapidly to any calls for help. In late 1973 the police force received an additional twenty trucks, forty Land Rovers, twenty-five motorcycles, and eighty-three tons of spare parts from West Germany. In 1971 the police also had an air wing, which flew reinforcements anywhere in the country and helped bring the sick and injured to centers for medical care. There was no mention of this unit in Law Number 2 of December 23, 1972, on the organization of the police force. The government made extensive use of police transport in moving food, medicine, and other supplies to refugee camps during the drought of the early 1970s.

In a speech President Siad paid tribute to the Police Custodial Corps. These men were prison guards, and the president described theirs as the most difficult of all police jobs, for they had to look after men who were clever and full of deceit. Their duties also included orienting prisoners and teaching them trades.

Police ranks were divided into six major groups (see table 8). Inspectors were apparently considered the equivalent of warrant officers in the armed forces. Whenever possible, positions were filled by members of the force. Qualified Somali citizens could be recruited when necessary; qualifications were successively more stringent for askaris, noncommissioned officers, inspectors, and commissioned

Table 8. Somalia, Ranks of the Police Force, 1973

Category	Ranks
General officers	
Senior officers.................................	Colonel
	Lieutenant colonel
	Major
Junior officers.................................	Captain
	Lieutenant
	Second lieutenant
Inspectors	Chief inspector
	Inspector
	Sub-inspector
Noncommissioned officers	1st sergeant
	Sergeant
	Cadet officer
Askaris	1st askari
	Askari
	Recruit

Source: Based on information from Somalia, "Law No. 2 of December 23, 1972: Organization of the Police Force," *Bollettino Ufficiale*, Mogadishu, January 17, 1973, pp. 98-109.

officers. Pay and allowances were the same as for members of other Somali armed forces except that there were allowances for certain specified kinds of duty.

Recruits to the police force had to be between seventeen and twenty-five years of age, of high moral caliber, and physically fit. After joining they received six months' training at the National Police Academy in Mogadishu. Once this training was completed, recruits sat for an examination. If they passed, they served two years on the force. When this service was completed, the policeman could request renewal of his contract. Officers underwent a stiff training course of nine months' duration. The force emphasized supervision of policemen's field performances and provided for their periodic retraining.

Darawishta police received special training in a six-month tactical training course, and Riot Unit police were trained in public order and riot control. Training on the local level was increased after the military takeover, and selected officers went abroad for special training. In early 1976 forty-five officers were being trained in Italy.

At least until 1972 no one with a university education had ever applied to join the police, although some policemen had earned degrees while serving. The police force still had a policy of recruiting secondary school graduates as cadet officers, but by 1972 the trend was toward making officers of men who had earned their secondary school education while serving in the force. Recruiting from the ranks undoubtedly improved morale and meant that more officers had previous police experience.

During 1971 and 1972 newspapers reported abuse of citizens' rights by police. There were also complaints that policemen had not been reoriented since independence to respect these rights, that they continued to treat Somali as if they were subjects of the colonial period rather than citizens. Major General Jama Muhammad Ghalib, police commandant in 1972, admitted that reports of maltreatment or of gruff, arrogant behavior by police might have been true in isolated circumstances but stated that police training stressed that policemen were servants and not masters of the people. It was also customary for policemen to solve problems involving minor infractions on the street rather than bring violators into an already crowded police station for detention and trial. Such solutions might occasionally require the use of force.

Both Ghalib and President Siad suggested that public cooperation with the police was inadequate. Ghalib pointed out that people usually reported crimes committed against them but would not report crimes they saw committed against others, not wanting to testify against the perpetrators. Siad addressed the larger problem of parents' creating in the minds of their children a feeling of intimidation by policemen; they did not teach children that the policeman is a friend. This attitude fostered antagonism between policeman and citizen.

The military government has claimed that the redeployment of security forces to principal trouble spots brought an almost immediate stop to tribal fights. This is quite probably true, at least where the fights were large enough and lasted long enough for policemen to get to them. In such incidents the police would arrive (by air if the territory was suitable for landing their DC-3) and break up the fight. They might seize livestock belonging to the fighting parties if possession of the livestock was disputed or if reprisals against the herds were feared. They would hold the livestock until the matter had been properly adjudicated. This was the procedure before the military coup, and laws in effect since the coup allowed similar police action. There was no indication to what extent such action remained necessary in the mid-1970s—after the drought, after the government's attack on tribalism, and after the increasing penetration of state authority to local communities and nomadic groups on a regular basis.

The Victory Pioneers were a revolutionary group composed, according to government statements, of youth, workers, peasants, and intellectuals (see ch. 15). They were a wing of the army organized by the SRC in August 1972. They worked under the supervision of the Political Bureau of the Presidency of the SRC. Officially their duties were to aid in self-help schemes; to spread principles that would encourage progress; to fight laziness, the misuse of public property, and reaction; and to promote and defend Somali culture and traditional heritage.

Actually the most visible duties of the Victory Pioneers involved law enforcement. They essentially served in the role of the policeman on the street. They had authority to perform such duties as checking contacts between Somali and foreigners. They had powers of arrest independent of the police. In rural areas they formed vigilance corps, performing police and guard duties over grazing areas and in towns. Although members of the police force were not much in evidence, the green-uniformed Victory Pioneers were apparently highly visible in 1976. In early 1975 it was reported that both officials and ordinary members of the public were constantly under their scrutiny.

In the early 1970s there were complaints about crowded conditions in police stations that were too small. Between 1970 and 1972 many police stations were modernized, although overcrowding remained a problem in older stations. Considerable construction was carried out in Mogadishu, and modern stations were built in Borama, Las Koreh, Gelib, Bur Acaba, Bohodleh, and Afmadu. Other regional stations were renovated. Police funds were raised to pay for projects at Genale, Wenle Weyn, Bosaso, and Candala.

Even before the coup the police, along with the army and the Victory Pioneers, were active in initiating self-help projects (see ch. 15). Since 1970 they have promoted such projects as cleaning towns and villages, constructing roads, and building infirmaries and schools.

THE CRIMINAL JUSTICE SYSTEM

Over centuries Somali evolved a system of handling disputes or acts of violence, including homicide, as wrongs involving not only the parties immediately concerned but also the groups of which they were members. The offending party and his group would pay *dia* (blood compensation, often in the form of livestock—see Glossary) to the injured party and his group (see ch. 4). The British and Italians enforced criminal codes based on their own judicial philosophies in their respective colonies but did not seriously disrupt the *dia*-paying system.

After independence the Somali developed their own law codes and procedures, which were largely syntheses and integrations of the codes introduced by Great Britain and Italy. There was no attempt to develop a system of criminal law uniquely Somali. Court procedures mirrored those acquired during colonial occupation, but *dia*-paying arrangements continued to play an important role in the actual administration of justice.

The military government changed remarkably little of the criminal justice system it inherited. It did make slight adaptations in the penal code to allow for the existence of a new central government, but the code as a whole appears to have been retained in its essentials at least as late as 1972. For all its talk of expelling foreign, neocolonial influences, the government directed a major campaign against *dia* and the whole concept of collective responsibility for crimes. This concept is the most distinctly Somali of any in the criminal justice system. The government instead concentrated on increasing and extending the influence of the laws introduced by Somalia's colonial overlords. This had the very practical value of decreasing the importance of a system of dispute settlement over which the government had no control. Therefore the government was able to extend its control over an important area of national life previously regulated largely by custom.

The Penal Code

The Somali Penal Code, enacted in early 1962, was the first codification of laws and sanctions designed to protect the individual and to ensure the equitable administration of justice for all inhabitants of the republic. It was approved by the National Assembly and translated into English, Italian, and Arabic. In December 1962 the public was advised through the press and radio that the code would become effective nationwide on April 3, 1964.

The essential basis of the code was the constitutional premise that the state and the relationships of all its citizens were subordinated to the supremacy of the law. The code placed responsibility for determining offenses and punishments exclusively on the written law and

342

the republic's judicial system and excluded all penal sanctions formerly observed in unwritten customary law. Nonetheless the legal authorities who drafted the code did not completely disregard the people's past reliance on traditional rules and sanctions. Some of the authority expressed by customary law and by sharia was written into the code.

The penal laws applied to all nationals, foreigners, and stateless persons living within the republic. Ignorance of the law was ruled out as a reason for nonobservance of the law or an excuse for committing an offense, but extenuations and mitigating factors were considered. Penal responsibility was personal, and collective punishment of any sort was prohibited. This provision was contrary to the traditional sanctions of *dia*-paying groups, and the code dealt directly with this issue. It stipulated that, if the offense constituted a violation of the code, the perpetrator had committed an unlawful act against the state and was subject to its sanctions. Judicial action under the code, however, did not rule out the possibility of additional redress in the form of *dia* through civil action in the courts. The military government attacked this tolerance of *dia* and forbade it entirely.

To be criminally liable a person must have committed an act or omission that caused harm or danger to another's person or property or to the state. Further, the offense must have been committed willfully or as the result of negligence, imprudence, or illegal behavior. Under Somali penal law the accused was assumed to be innocent until proved guilty beyond reasonable doubt. In criminal prosecution the burden of proof rested with the state.

Because the code established that a person's guilt derived from his capacity for understanding and volition, liability for an offense was excluded under certain subjective conditions. Offenders were not liable if they were adjudged to suffer total mental deficiency, total intoxication from alcohol or narcotic drugs, or deafness. Children under the age of fourteen were exempt from liability under all circumstances. For offenders between the ages of fourteen and eighteen a special inquiry into their capacity for understanding and volition was required. Their punishment was reduced even if the outcome confirmed their culpability.

The penal code classed offenses as either crimes or contraventions. Apart from the difference in the nature and seriousness of the offenses in each category and of the punishments, the code defined a crime as an offense that involved criminal intent. Contraventions were legal violations in which the offender merely acted knowingly and willfully without criminal intent.

Death by shooting was the sentence only for crimes against the personality of the state, such as espionage, promoting armed insurrection, devastation, or pillage, and for crimes against human life, such as pollution of water and food or murder. Even homicide would not draw a death penalty if the act involved killing a person with his consent or if the murderer killed a female blood relative engaged in fornication, the man with whom she was fornicating, or a child born of that act immediately after its birth.

An offender could also receive life imprisonment for a crime. Lesser terms of imprisonment could be from five days to twenty-four years, and fines ran from Sh10 to Sh15,000 (for value of the Somali shilling—see Glossary). For contraventions an offender could be imprisoned for from five days to three years with compulsory labor or be fined from Sh2 to Sh10,000. The code usually prescribed a maximum and a minimum punishment and left the actual sentence to the discretion of a judge.

The penal code comprised three books. The first of these delineated the general principles of juridical science upon which the provisions of the penal laws were based. Book II defined criminal offenses and specified punishments for offenders found guilty. Many crimes listed in this section, such as those dealing with personal honor, had their roots in sharia and Somali customary law. Book III contained sixty-one articles regulating contraventions of public order and tranquillity, safety, morality, and health.

The penal code recognized the social character of punitive measures. In punishing violators for acts that damaged or endangered organized society, the state was less concerned with the traditional concept of punishment than with restoring the offender to a useful place in society. The military government also on occasion returned prisoners who had formerly held governmental positions to official life after they had served time and in theory been rehabilitated in prison.

On the basis of the Quranic precept that paternal authority is sacred, the code considered it an extenuating circumstance if the offender was the father or husband of the injured person. Further examples of the effect of Muslim belief on the modern law were prohibitions on the sale or consumption of alcoholic beverages. These offenses were punishable as crimes regardless of nationality or religious belief.

The military government had not substantially changed the penal code by at least as late as 1974, and there was no indication that it had done so by 1976. Some changes were made to allow for the introduction of new official agencies, such as those associated with the SRC. The SRC also passed additional laws where a need was perceived, such as the law to curtail drunkenness or that completely prohibiting *dia*.

Criminal Procedure and Courts

Matters relating to arrest and trial were governed by the Criminal Procedure Code, adopted by legislative decree in June 1963 and applicable in all regions since April 1964. Conforming to British patterns, the code prescribed the kinds and jurisdictions of criminal courts, specified the functions and responsibilities of judicial officials, outlined rules of evidence, and regulated the conduct of trials. A special section provided guidelines for extradition and other judicial relations with foreign authorities.

Ordinarily a person could be arrested only if caught in the act of committing a crime or upon issuance of a warrant by the proper judicial authority. The Criminal Procedure Code adopted from the British the writ of habeas corpus. The Supreme Court or a regional court of appeal could order the release of any person held either in arbitrary detention or for reasons other than those provided by law.

When a suspect was arrested, the personal possessions he carried with him—shoes, cigarettes and matches, belt, watch, and the like were routinely confiscated. All belongings were registered and were returned upon his release. Some citizens found this practice degrading, but in 1972 Police Commandant Ghalib stated that it was only a security precaution designed to prevent accidents.

Those arrested had the right to be taken before a judge within twenty-four hours. A prison was not to accept a prisoner directly from a police station without a judge's order for his incarceration; this was to prevent imprisonment without trial or detention for an excessive time before trial. Usually those arrested did receive a hearing within twenty-four hours except in cases where the arrest occurred outside an urban center. Even these people went before a judge within a reasonable amount of time, allowing for their transport to the nearest court.

Trial procedure borrowed heavily from that of a British assize court. The judge read and explained the charges to the accused in open court. The accused could enter his plea or any objections but, if the charges were serious, involving more than ten years' imprisonment, the trial was held regardless of the plea. The prosecution opened the case and was followed by the defense. Each side was allowed to cross-examine witnesses called by the other. Rules of evidence also reflected British influence: they were taken from the rule originally provided for India in 1872, used also for British Somaliland, and retained by the Somali after independence. The verdict could be appealed to the appropriate regional court of appeal or to the Supreme Court (see ch. 8). The appellate court could reverse the decision or order a new trial.

The prosecutor general handled cases for the government. He controlled all investigations, drew up the charges, and presented the case.

The court structure after the coup remained much as it was under the parliamentary regime. The major difference was the diminution of the responsibilities of the qadi courts and the introduction of the National Security Court (NSC). The NSC was outside the rest of the legal system, being subordinate only to the SRC. It tried serious cases both political and nonpolitical, although its origins were political (see ch. 8).

Otherwise there were four levels of criminal courts. At the lowest level were the criminal sections of district courts. Next were the regional courts' assize sections, which considered only criminal cases in which the offense was punishable by more than ten years in prison.

Regional courts of appeals were at the third level. They had two sections—one that heard appeals from decisions of the district courts and another that heard appeals from the regional assize sections. At the fourth and highest level was the Supreme Court, the duty of which was to ensure exact observance and uniform interpretation of the law. It heard appeals from decisions and judgments of lower courts and settled questions of court jurisdiction.

The Prison System

Somalia inherited a penal system that did not meet the needs of the new nation. The few prisons that existed before 1960 had been established during the British and Italian colonial administrations. By the time of independence these facilities had deteriorated and were inadequately staffed.

When the Italian south became a trust territory in 1950, United Nations delegations visited the penal institutions. These inspectors revealed prisons that were overcrowded, inadequately lighted, and poorly ventilated. Moreover the prisons lacked an organized daily routine for rehabilitation of inmates. With United Nations backing the Italians began improving conditions in the existing prisons and built several new ones.

Aware of the deficiencies of its prisons, the government at independence included in the constitution an article asserting the premise that criminal punishment must not be an obstacle to moral reeducation of the convicted. This article implied a complex form of prison organization and a strong emphasis on prisoner rehabilitation.

In 1962 the Somali Penal Code laid down the underlying principles for reorganizing the prison system. The code required that prisoners of all ages work during prison confinement. In return for labor on prison farms, construction projects, and roadbuilding, prisoners were paid a modest sum, which they could spend in prison canteens or retain until their release.

According to the penal code, juvenile offenders were not to be imprisoned with adult offenders. In practice they were usually segregated in special juvenile sections of the Mogadishu and Manderia central prisons.

By 1969 the quality of the penal system had improved, but the parliamentary government's program for prison reform was incomplete.

Mogadishu's central prison was the best equipped correctional center of the forty-nine in the system. It employed modern penological techniques. All inmates received elementary school instruction, and many learned skills that would enable them to earn a living after their release. The prison had an adequate infirmary and the services of a qualified doctor.

There was no indication that penal policy altered significantly after the military coup of October 1969. New prisons were constructed at Gelib and Jamama, and extensions were made to the central prison at Mogadishu.

The military government in its official literature claimed credit for opening a youth reformatory in Afgoi, on the outskirts of Mogadishu, but this facility appears to have been used during the time of the parliamentary regime. Young boys in the reformatory received basic education and vocational training.

The military government has retained compulsory labor as part of prison sentences because of its concern with the rehabilitation of prisoners. The SRC apparently held the same view as the parliamentary government: that labor contributes to rehabilitation by guarding against idleness and promoting socially constructive activity for inmates.

The parliamentary government granted two general amnesties, one at the time of independence and another in mid-1966. The military government has used grants of general amnesty more frequently for crimes other than those that threatened the Somali state. Political prisoners, such as former Prime Minister Mohamed Ibrahim Egal, were released from prison individually rather than under general amnesties. The government explained these amnesties as opportunities to give culprits, whether convicted, still in custody, on bail, or in prison, a chance to rehabilitate themselves. The amnesties occurred at the beginning of the military regime and on occasional anniversaries of the military coup.

INTERNAL SECURITY

After the coup of October 21, 1969, the military government lost no time in instituting measures to protect itself against possible threats within the country. Many of the leaders of the previous government were incarcerated in Afgoi. Leading lawyers, businessmen, and senior military personnel who did not support the coup were also arrested; the total number was probably about sixty. Moreover the SRC concentrated in its own hands the control of all legislative, administrative, and judicial functions.

In April 1970 the SRC created the NSC, originally to try the cases of the political leaders of the parliamentary regime. The duties of the NSC were later broadened, but it always tried cases deemed important to the SRC. There was no appeal from the NSC decision except to the SRC, the ruling body reserving for itself the ultimate disposition of any case in which it chose to take an interest.

In September 1970 the SRC proclaimed a new law designed to protect the security of the nation. Any person who harmed the unity, peace, or sovereignty of the nation could be sentenced to death. Heavy punishment could also be meted out to anyone who spread false propaganda against the revolution.

The government sought to achieve internal security by politically reeducating the entire country; this reeducation included orientation courses for the general public and was characterized by the application of carrot-and-stick methods. Within two months of the October 1969 coup President Siad declared the third amnesty in Somalia's history. It applied to all convicts still in custody, on bail, or behind bars except those who had committed crimes capable of endangering the existence or unity of the state. It did not apply to public officials who had committed crimes against public administration, and members of the previous government were not amnestied.

In the spring and summer of 1970, however, the military regime held the first public executions in Somalia's history. The number of executions within the first year (five by the end of June 1970) was far larger than under the parliamentary government, which rarely if ever resorted to execution and never to public execution. The first executions were carried out primarily against murderers rather than against those who had committed political crimes, although at least one man convicted of espionage was publicly executed. The executions appeared to have made the point that the government would not hesitate to employ such measures. Executions occurred from time to time through the mid-1970s, although not with the regularity suggested by the SRC's first year in power. They reportedly were well attended.

The most serious threat to the military government's security was a coup attempted in 1971. There may also have been an attempt in 1970.

In April 1970 the SRC had General Korshel arrested on charges of organizing a coup to restore the neocolonialist power structure. I.M. Lewis, a noted authority on Somalia, speculated that the real reason for the arrest may have been to correct a perceived overrepresentation of the Darod clan-family in the SRC.

The 1971 coup attempt was a complete surprise. The government's explanation was that the coup was aimed at protecting the interests of the trading bourgeoisie and the tribal structure. Many expected that the government would announce clemency for the conspirators. Instead they were executed at Hamar Jajab with thousands looking on. Many Somali considered this an act of revenge inconsistent with Islamic principles and with past standards of justice in the country.

348

Some observers have suggested that Siad was counseled by his Soviet advisers to make an example of the men.

These incidents constituted the only organized internal opposition to the SRC from 1969 to mid-1976. Dissenters had been removed from authority and punished. Many who had either served parliamentary governments or fallen from the SRC's favor were given official posts after they had gone through orientation courses and reconciled themselves to the military government (see ch. 15). The inclusion of possible rivals in government posts may have lessened internal opposition.

In 1974 all government employees were required to sign statements of intent to abide by security regulations. Contacts with foreigners had to be referred to the foreign ministry; this measure was apparently sometimes ignored, but Somali who had contacts with non-Soviet foreigners reportedly did so carefully. By one account security officers conducted monthly interviews with government workers in which questions were asked about the loyalty of the workers' families and acquaintances.

Reports stated that by 1974 the government appeared stable and the SRC united. Although there were exiles who opposed the SRC's socialist policies, there was no organized internal opposition, either overt or covert, to the government. There was no indication that such opposition had developed by 1976.

The SRC has tried to strengthen its position by extending its authority and control as much as possible throughout the country. Concurrently it has undermined rival sources of authority, the two most important of which were the Islamic religious leaders and traditional allegiances to descent groups of varying size and scope (see ch. 2; ch. 4; ch. 5). The regime took great care not to alienate Somali religious leaders. It took even greater pains to convince the Somali that scientific socialism was not only compatible with Islam but indeed identical with Islam. Nevertheless the regime did not want religious leaders interfering in politics.

In January 1975 the SRC ordered the execution of ten men. Ostensibly their offense was opposing on religious grounds a law that increased the rights of women.

Similarly the military government has tried to substitute allegiance to the nation for traditional descent group allegiance, which could be used as a rallying point for opposition to the military government. A 1973 law banned weddings, burial of the dead, and religious rites carried out on a clan or lineage basis. The SRC has also consistently stressed individual responsibility for all offenses, undermining the concept of collective responsibility that grew from tribal society and was the basis for the existence of *dia*-paying groups. By 1975 political imprisonment and imprisonment on charges of tribalism were reported to be accepted features of life under the regime. In the mid-1970s the persistence of clan-related loyalties was described as the problem causing the most concern to the government, which continued to meet certain manifestations of such loyalties with severe prison sentences.

Close police surveillance was reportedly maintained in parts of the country. For example, in 1974 drivers entering or leaving Mogadishu had to show identification papers to a military guard at the city's gates. The Victory Pioneers were reported to be keeping both officials and members of the general public under close scrutiny.

Another organization that monitored possible threats to the regime was the National Security Service (NSS). The NSS was organized on the lines of the Soviet security agency, the KGB, a result of advice from Soviets in the country. Headed in 1976 by Colonel Ahmed Suleiman Abdulle, President Siad's son-in-law, the NSS had broad powers of arrest and investigation. It was staffed by men from the army and police chosen for their loyalty to President Siad. Colonel Abdulle also headed army intelligence and was believed to have his own KGB advisers.

One of the duties of the SRC's Committee for Defense and Public Security was to assist in the prevention of crime and the maintenance of public order. Originally the committee had rather free powers of arrest, but in September 1975 the government removed its power to arrest anyone without complete reports from his district that he was a dangerous and corrupt element. After the disbanding of the SRC in mid-1976 a security committee headed by Captain Hamsa Mohamed Abdi was formed under the new Somali Socialist Revolutionary Party (SSRP).

BIBLIOGRAPHY

Section I. Social

Abdillahi, A. M. *The Best Short Stories from the Land of Punt (Somalia)*. Mogadishu: 1970.

Abir, M. "Ethiopia and the Horn of Africa." Pages 537-577 in Richard Gray (ed.), *The Cambridge History of Africa*, IV: From 1600 to 1700. Cambridge: Cambridge University Press, 1975.

African Statistical Yearbook, 1974. Addis Ababa: United Nations Economic Commission for Africa, July 1975.

Andrzejewski, B. W. "The Art of the Verbal Message in Somali Society." Pages 29-39 in J. Lucas (ed.), *Neue-Afrikanistische Studien*. Hamburg: Deutsches Institut für Afrika-Forschung, 1966.

————. "The Introduction of a National Orthography for Somalia," *African Language Studies* [London], 15, 1974, 199-203.

————. "The Position of Galla in the Cushitic Language Group," *Journal of Semitic Studies*, IX, No. 1, Spring 1965, 135-138.

————. "The Role of Broadcasting in the Adaptation of the Somali Language to Modern Needs." Pages 262-273 in W. H. Whiteley (ed.), *Language Use and Social Change: Problems of Multilingualism with Special Reference to Eastern Africa*. London: Oxford University Press, 1971.

————. "Speech and Writing Dichotomy as the Pattern of Multilingualism in the Somali Republic," *Conseil scientifique pour l'Afrique: Coloque sur le Multilinguisme* [Brazzaville], July 1962, 16-23.

Andrzejewski, B. W., and I. M. Lewis (eds.). *Somali Poetry: An Introduction*. Oxford: Oxford University Press, 1964.

Archer, Geoffrey, and Eva M. Godman. *The Birds of British Somaliland and the Gulf of Aden*, I and II. Edinburgh: Gurney and Jackson, 1937.

————. *The Birds of British Somaliland and the Gulf of Aden*, III and IV. Edinburgh: Oliver and Boyd, 1961.

Artan, A. *Somali Folklore: Music, Dance, Song*. Mogadishu: The National Theatre, n.d.

Battista, Piero. *La Somalia: Nelle sue Genti e nella sua Vita, Storia, Folklore, Tradizioni*. Rome: Angelo Signorelli, 1969.

Breutz, P. L. "Zum Problem des Tribalismus," *Afrika Forum* [Munich], 6, Nos. 7 and 8, July-August 1970, 412-468.

Cahill, Kevin M. "Africa's Flight from Drought Ends in Somalia," *New York Times Magazine*, July 13, 1975.

———. "Studies in Somalia," *Transactions of the Royal Society of Tropical Medicine and Hygiene* [London], 65, No. 1, 1971, 28-40.

Cassanelli, Lee Vincent. *The Benaadir Past: Essays in Southern Somali History*. Ph.D. dissertation, University of Wisconsin, 1973. Ann Arbor: Xerox University Microfilms. 74-9171.

Castagno, Margaret. *Historical Dictionary of Somalia*. Metuchen, New Jersey: Scarecrow Press, 1975.

Cerulli, Enrico. "Islam in East Africa." Pages 203-219 in A. J. Arberry (ed.), *Religion in the Middle East, II: Islam*. Cambridge: Cambridge University Press, 1969.

———. *Somalia: Scritti vari editi ed inediti*, I. Rome: Istituto Poligrafico dello Stato, 1957.

———. *Somalia: Scritti vari editi ed inediti*, II. Rome: Instituto Poligrafico dello Stato, 1959.

———. *Somalia: Scritti vari editi ed inediti*, III. Rome: Instituto Poligrafico dello Stato, 1964.

Chittick, Neville. "An Archaeological Reconnaissance of the Southern Somali Coast," *Azania* [Nairobi], 4, 1969, 115-130.

ı Clark, John D. *The Prehistoric Cultures of the Horn of Africa: An Analysis of the Stone Age Culture and Climatic Succession in the Somalilands and Eastern Parts of Abyssinia*. (Reprint of 1954 ed.) New York: Octagon, 1972.

Clarke, J. I., et al. *An Advanced Geography of Africa*. Amersham, England: Hulton Educational Publications, 1975.

Clauser, Fabio, Salvatore Dell'Oca, and Mario Pavan. *Foreste, fauna, parchi nazionali e consequente sviluppi turistici in Somalia*. (In Italian and English, Forests, Fauna, National Parks, and Relative Prospects for Tourism in Somalia.) Rome: N. pub., 1969.

Contini, Paolo. "The Evolution of Blood-Money for Homicide in Somalia," *Journal of African Law* [London], 15, No. 1, Spring 1971, 77-84.

Davidson, Basil. "Somalia in 1975: Some Notes and Impressions," *Issue*, V, No. 1, Spring 1975, 19-26.

———. "Somalia: Towards Socialism," *Race and Class* [London], 17, No. 1, Summer 1975, 19-37.

Decraene, Philippe. "Multifaceted Evolution under Revolutionary Regime," *Le Monde*, Paris, March 26, 1975, 1-2; and March 27, 1975, 7. Translated by U.S. Department of Commerce. Office of Technical Services. Joint Publications Research Service (Washington). JPRS: 64548, No. 1580, April 15, 1975.

Demographic Yearbook, 1974. New York: Department of Economic and Social Affairs, Statistical Office, United Nations, 1975.

Doornbos, Martin R. "The Shehu and the Mullah: The Jehods of Usuman Dan Fadio and Muhammed Abd-Allah Hassan in Comparative Perspective," *Acta Africana* [Geneva], XIV, No. 2, 1975, 7-31.

Drysdale, John. *The Somali Dispute.* New York: Praeger, 1964.

Fagotto, Flavio. *Il Bufalo Cafro in Somalia: Habitat, Abitudini e Distribuzione.* Catania: N. pub., 1971.

Farah, Nurruddin. *From a Crooked Rib.* (African Writers Series, No. 80.) London: Heinemann, 1970.

Fisher, Humphrey. "The Western and Central Sudan and East Africa." Pages 345-405 in P. M. Holt, Ann K. S. Lambton, and Bernard Lewis (eds.), *The Cambridge History of Islam, II: The Further Islamic Lands, Islamic Society and Civilization.* Cambridge: Cambridge University Press, 1970.

Freeman-Grenville, G. S. P. "Some Aspects of the External Relations of the East African Coast: Before 1800." Pages 69-83 in K. Ingham (ed.), *Foreign Relations of African States.* London: Butterworth, 1974.

Funaioli, Ugo. *Guida Breve dei Mammiferi della Somalia* (Brief Guide to the Mammals of Somalia). Florence: Biblioteca Agraria Tropicale, Istituto Agronomico per l'Oltremare, 1971.

Gallo, Pia Grassivaro. "The Age at Menarche in Somalia," *Annals of Human Biology* [London], 2, No. 2, November 2, 1975, 197-200.

Goody, Jack (ed.). *Literacy in Traditional Societies.* London: Cambridge University Press, 1968.

Griffiths, J. F. 'The Horn of Africa." Pages 133-165 in J. F. Griffiths (ed.), *Climates of Africa.* (World Survey of Climatology, Vol. 10.) Amsterdam: Elsevier, 1972.

Griffiths, J. F. (ed.) *Climates of Africa.* (World Survey of Climatology, Vol. 10.) Amsterdam: Elsevier, 1972.

Grottanelli, Vinigi L. "The Peopling of the Horn of Africa," *Africa* [Rome], 27, No. 3, September 1973, 363-394.

Hance, William A. *The Geography of Modern Africa.* (2d ed.) New York: Columbia University Press, 1975.

Hancock, Graham. "Somalia Introduces Its First Dictionary," *African Development* [London], 10, No. 6, June 1976, 616.

Hess, Robert L. *Italian Colonialism in Somalia.* Chicago: University of Chicago Press, 1966.

―――. "The Poor Man of God: Muhammad Abdullah Hassan." Pages 65-108 in Norman R. Bennett (ed.), *Leadership in Eastern Africa.* Boston: Boston University Press, 1968.

International Labour Office. "Problems of Nomadism in the Sahelian Region of Africa." (Technical meeting held in Niamey, September 9-20, 1968.) (mineo.)

―――. *Report to the Government of the Somali Democratic Republic on the Integrated Development of the Nomadic Zones.* (Regular Programme of Technical Assistance, ILO-OTA/Somalia R. 6.) Geneva: 1972.

Johnson, John W. *Heellooy Heelleellooy: The Development of the Genre Heello in Modern Somali Poetry.* Bloomington: Indiana University Press, 1974.

Johnson, John William. "Research in Somali Folklore," *Research in African Literatures,* 4, No. 1, Spring 1973, 51-61.

Kinnanne, Derk. "How Somalia Put Its Native Language down on Paper," *UNESCO Features* [Paris], Nos. 695 and 696, 1976, 11-13.

Konczachi, Z. A. "Nomadism and Economic Development of Somalia." *Candian Journal of African Studies* [Montreal], 1, No. 2, 1967, 163-175.

Lacouture, Jean. "La Corne Rouge de l'Afrique," *Le Nouvel Observateur* [Paris], November 24, 1975.

Lapiccirella, Francesca Romana. *Luci della Somalia.* (2d ed.) (In Italian, English, and French.) Rome: Edizioni lo Scaffale, 1969.

Laurence, Margaret. *New Wind in a Dry Land.* New York: Knopf, 1964.

———. *A Tree for Poverty: Somali Poetry and Prose.* Nairobi: Eagle Press, 1954.

Lavrencic, Karl. "Somalia Winning Resettlement Battle to Counter Drought," *African Development* [London], 10, No. 1, January 1976, 75-76.

———. "Spotlight on Somalia," *Africa: An International Business, Economic, and Political Monthly* [London], No. 50, October 1975, 95-109.

"Law No. 37 of September 10, 1972: Law on the Somali Territorial Sea and Ports," *Bollettino Ufficiale* [Mogadishu], IV, No. 1, Supplement No. 7, July 21, 1973, 244-249.

Legum, Colin. "Somali Liberation Songs," *Journal of Modern African Studies* [London], 1, No. 4, December 1963, 503-519.

Legum, Colin (ed.). *Africa Contemporary Record: Annual Survey and Documents, 1974-75.* New York: Africana Publishing, 1975.

Legum, Colin, and John Drysdale (eds.). *Africa Contemporary Record: Annual Survey and Documents, 1969-70.* Exeter: Africa Research, 1970.

Legum, Colin, and Anthony Hughes (eds.). *Africa Contemporary Record: Annual Survey and Documents, 1970-71.* London: Rex Collings, 1971.

———. *Africa Contemporary Record: Annual Survey and Documents, 1971-72.* New York: Africana Publishing, 1972.

Lewis, Herbert S. "The Origins of the Galla and Somali," *Journal of African History* [London], VII, No. 1, 1966, 27-46.

Lewis, I. M. "Conformity and Contrast in Somali Islam." Pages 253-267 in I. M. Lewis (ed.), *Islam in Tropical Africa.* London: Oxford University Press, 1966.

———. "Dualism in Somalian Notions of Power," *Journal of the Royal Anthropological Institute of Great Britain and Ireland* [London], XCIII, Pt. 1, January-June 1963, 109-116.

———. "From Nomadism to Cultural Cultivation: The Expansion of Political Solidarity in Southern Somalia." Pages 59-77 in Mary Douglas and Phyllis M. Kaberry (eds.), *Man in Africa*. London: Tavistock Publications, 1969.

———. "Literacy in a Nomadic Society: The Somali Case." Pages 265-276 in Jack Goody (ed.), *Literacy in Traditional Societies*. London: Cambridge University Press, 1968.

———. *The Modern History of Somaliland: From Nation to State*. New York: Praeger, 1965.

———. "Nationalism and Particularism in Somalia." Pages 339-359 in P. H. Gulliver (ed.), *Tradition and Transition in East Africa*. Berkeley: University of California Press, 1969.

———. *A Pastoral Democracy*. London: Oxford University Press, 1961.

———. *Peoples of the Horn of Africa: Somali Afar, and Saho*. (Ethnographic Survey of Africa, edited by Daryll Forde, "North Eastern Africa," Pt. I.) London: International African Institute, 1955.

———. "The Politics of the 1969 Somali Coup," *Journal of Modern African Studies* [London], X, No. 3, October 1972, 383-408.

———. "Sheiks and Warriors of Somaliland." Pages 204-223 in M. Fortes and G. Dieterlen (eds.), *African Systems of Thought*. London: Oxford University Press, 1965.

———. "The Somali Conquest of the Horn of Africa," *Journal of African History* [London], I, No. 2, 1960, 213-229.

———. "Spirit Possession in Northern Somaliland." Pages 188-219 in John Beattie, et al. (eds.), *Spirit Mediumship and Society in Africa*. New York: Africana Publishing, 1969.

Lewis, I. M. (ed.). *Abaar: The Somali Drought*. London: International African Institute, February 1975.

Lewis, Ioan M. "Sufism in Somaliland: A Study in Tribal Islam," *Bulletin of the School of Oriental and African Studies* [London], 17, No. 3, 1955, 581-602.

———. "Sufism in Somaliland: A Study in Tribal Islam," *Bulletin of the School of Oriental and African Studies* [London], 18, No. 1, 1956, 146-160.

Lupi, Ermano. "A Revolution Attacks the Ancient Tribal Order," *L'Unita* [Rome], October 1, 1973, 3.

McEwen, A. C. *International Boundaries of East Africa*. Oxford: Clarendon Press, 1971.

Mountjoy, Alan B., and Clifford Embleton. *Africa: A New Geographic Survey*. New York: Praeger, 1967.

Mueller, Josef (ed.). *Functional Literacy in the Context of Adult Education*. (International symposium held in West Berlin, August 15-26, 1973.) N.pl.: German Foundation for International Development, n.d. (mimeo.)

Mumin, Hassan Sheikh. *Leopard among the Women, Shabeelnaa-good: A Somali Play*. (Trans., B. W. Andrzejewski.) London: Oxford University Press, 1974.

Nicholls, C. S. *The Swahili Coast*. London: George Allen and Unwin, 1971.

"Notes on Somali Culture," *Afrique Actuelle* [Paris], No. 6, March 1966, 45-48.

Nuh, Omar Au. *Some General Notes on Somali Folklore*. Mogadishu: 1970.

"Official Re-orientation," *Africa: An International Business, Economic, and Political Monthly* [London], No. 6, 1972, 39-41.

Oliver, Roland, and Brian M. Fagan. *Africa in the Iron Age*. Cambridge: Cambridge University Press, 1975.

Pestalozza, Luigi. *The Somalian Revolution*. (Trans., Peter Glendening.) Paris: Editions Afrique, Asie, Amérique Latine, 1974.

Prins, A. H. J. "Notes on the Boni: Tribe of Hunters in Northern Kenya," *Bulletin of the International Committee on Urgent Anthropological Research* [Vienna], No. 3, 1960, 25-28.

Prothero, R. Mansell. *Public Health, Pastoralism, and Politics in the Horn of Africa*. (Sixth Melville J. Herkovitz Memorial Lecture given October 9, 1967.) Evanston: Northwestern University Press, 1968.

Puzo, William Daniel. *Mogadishu, Somalia: Geographic Aspects of Its Evolution, Population, Functions, and Morphology*. Ph.D. dissertation. University of California at Los Angeles, 1972. Ann Arbor: Xerox University Microfilms. 73-10465.

Rattray, J. M. *The Grass Cover of Africa*. Rome: Food and Agriculture Organization, 1960.

"Regional Sports Tournament Confirms National Unity," *New Era* [Mogadishu], 4, No. 31, March 1976, 36-379

Rice, Edward. "Somalia," *Vista*, 6, No. 4, March-April 1971, 34-40.

Robinson, Robert S., Jr. *Educational Integration in Somalia, 1960-1969*. Ph.D. dissertation, Department of Education, University of Michigan, 1971. Ann Arbor: Xerox University Microfilms. 72-14976.

Sharabi, Hisham. "Islam and Modernization in the Arab World." Pages 26-36 in Jack H. Thompson and Robert D. Reischauer (eds.), *Modernization of the Arab World*. New York: Van Nostrand, 1966.

Shenk, David Witmer. *A Study of Mennonite Presence and Church in Somalia*. Ph.D. dissertation, New York University, 1972. Ann Arbor: Xerox University Microfilms. 73-08193.

Siad Barre, Mohamed. "Great Successes Have Been Achieved in the Socialist Construction of the Country," *New Era* [Mogadishu], No. 19, November 1974, 26-28.

Simoons, Frederick J. "Rejection of Fish as Human Food in Africa: A Problem in History and Ecology," *Ecology of Food and Nutrition*, 3, No. 2, 1974, 89-105.

Somalia. Ministry of Education. *Statistical Survey of Education in Somalia, 1969-70.* Mogadishu: May 1970.

Somalia. Ministry of Education. Department III. *Current Statistical Trends in Somali Education.* Mogadishu: 1971.

Somalia. Ministry of Foreign Affairs. *The Somali People's Quest for Unity.* Mogadishu: 1965.

Somalia. Ministry of Health. Nutrition Department. *Deficiency in the Somali Diet: Survey and Evaluation.* Mogadishu: 1972.

Somalia. Ministry of Information and National Guidance. *Beautiful Somalia.* Mogadishu: 1972.

————. *The Revolutionary Generation of Tomorrow: Youth, Sports, and Manpower.* Mogadishu: June 1974.

————. *Somalia: Five Years of Revolutionary Progress.* Mogadishu: 1974.

————. *Somalia's Socialist Revolutionary Construction, 1969-73.* Mogadishu: October 1973.

————. *Somalia Today: General Information.* (Rev. ed.) Mogadishu: 1970.

Somalia. Ministry of Planning and Coordination. *Development Programme, 1971-1973.* Mogadishu: 1971.

————. *Draft Development Programme, 1974-1978.* Mogadishu: January 1974.

Somalia. Ministry of Planning and Coordination. Central Statistical Department. *Statistical Abstract, 1971,* VIII. Mogadishu: August 1972.

Somalia. Planning Commission. *Short Term Development Programme, 1968-1970.* Mogadishu: August 1968.

Somalia. Presidency of the Supreme Revolutionary Council. General Directorate of Planning and Coordination. Central Statistical Department. *Statistical Abstract, 1973.* (No. 10.) Mogadishu: September 1975.

"Somalia: A Sort of Marxism," *Africa Confidential* [London], 14, No. 25, December 14, 1973, 1-3.

"Somalia Fights the Shifting Sands," *African Development* [London], 10, No. 5, May 1976, 535.

"Somali Democratic Republic," *Africa* [London], No. 26, October 1973, 55-72.

"Somalie," *Jeune Afrique* [Paris], No. 560, September 28, 1971. Supplement, I-XXII.

"Somali Music, Dance and Song," *New Era* [Mogadishu], No. 3, March 1971, 13-16.

Thompson, B.W. *Africa: The Climatic Background.* Ibadan: Oxford University Press, 1975.

Touval, Saadia. *Somali Nationalism: International Politics and the Drive for Unity in the Horn of Africa.* Cambridge: Harvard University Press, 1963.

Trimingham, J. Spencer. *Islam in East Africa.* Oxford: Clarendon Press, 1964.

————. *The Sufi Orders in Islam.* Oxford: Clarendon Press, 1971.

Triulzi, Umberto. "L'Italia e l'economia Somala dal 1950 ad Oggi," *Africa* [Rome], 26, No. 4, December 1971, 443-462.

Turton, E.R. "Bantu, Galla, and Somali Migrations in the Horn of Africa: A Reassessment of the Juba-Tana Area," *Journal of African History* [London], XVI, No. 4, 1975, 519-537.

————. "The Isaq Somali Diaspora and Poll-Tax Agitation in Kenya, 1936-41," *African Affairs* [London], 73, July 1974, 325-346.

United Nations. Department of Economic and Social Affairs. Statistical Office. *Population and Vital Statistics Report: Data Available as of 1 January 1976.* (Statistical Papers, XXVIII Series A, No. 1) New York: 1976, 8-9.

United Nations Development Programme. *Mineral and Groundwater Survey: Report on Uranium, Thorium, and Rare Earths at Alio Ghelle, Somalia.* Mogadishu: May 1968.

United Nations Economic Commission for Africa. "Censuses Undertaken," *African Census Programme Newsletter* [Addis Ababa], No. 14, June 1975, 1-2.

United Nations Educational, Scientific and Cultural Organization. *Survey on the Scientific and Technical Potential of the Countries of Africa.* Paris: 1970.

United States Information Service. *Somali Democratic Republic: Country Data.* Mogadishu: January 1, 1976.

U.S. Department of State. Bureau of Intelligence and Research. The Geographer. *International Boundary Study: Kenya-Somalia Boundary.* (Series No. 134.) Washington: May 14, 1973.

————. *International Boundary Study: Ethiopia-Somali Boundary.* (Series No. 153.) Washington: November 5, 1975.

U.S. Department of State. Bureau of Intelligence and Research. Office of Strategic and Functional Research. The Geographer. *International Boundary Study: French Territory of Afars and Issas-Somalia Boundary.* (Series No. 87.) Washington: December 30, 1968.

Wilson, P. J. "Status Ambiguity and Spirit Possession," *Man* [London], 2, No. 3, September 1967, 366-378.

(Various issues of the following periodicals were also used in the preparation of this section: *Arab Report and Record* [London], March-November 1975; *Guardian* [London], January-December 1975; *Le Monde* [Paris], January 1970-June 1976; *Le Monde Diplomatique* [Paris], January-December 1975; *Le Nouvel Observateur* [Paris], January-December 1975; and *Neues Deutschland* [East Berlin], January-July 1976.)

Section II. Political

Administrative Changes in Somalia: October 1971-October 1972.
Mogadishu: Somali Institute of Public Administration, 1972.

Andrzejewski, B.W. "The Role of Broadcasting in the Adaptation of
the Somali Language to Modern Needs." Pages 262-273 in W.H.
Whiteley (ed.), *Language Use and Social Change: Problems of Multilingualism with Special Reference to Eastern Africa.* London:
Oxford University Press, 1971.

Bell, J. Bowyer. "Strategic Implications of the Soviet Presence in
Somalia," *Orbis*, XIX, No. 2, Summer 1975, 402-411.

Castagno, A.A. "The Horn of Africa and the Competition for Pow-
er." Pages 155-180 in Alvin J. Cottrell and R.M. Burrell (eds.), *The
Indian Ocean: Its Political, Economic, and Military Importance.*
New York: Praeger, 1972.

Crozier, Brian. "Soviet Presence in Somalia," *Conflict Studies*
[London], No. 54, February 1975, 1-20.

Decraene, Philippe. "Aspect Specifique du Situation Somalie," *Revue
Française d'Etudes Politiques Africaines [Paris], No. 115, July
1975, 29-40.*

Desfosses, Helen. "Naval Strategy and Aid Policy: A Study of Soviet-Somali Relations." Pages 183-201 in Warren Weinstein (ed.),
Chinese and Soviet Aid to Africa. New York: Praeger, 1975.

Drysdale, John. *The Somali Dispute.* New York: Praeger, 1964.

Ganzglass, Martin. *Penal Code of the Somali Democratic Republic.*
New Brunswick: Rutgers University Press, 1971.

Hancock, Graham. "Somalia Introduces Its First Dictionary, "*African Development* [London], 10, No. 6, June 1976, 616.

Head, Sydney W. (ed.) *Broadcasting in Africa: A Continental Survey
of Radio and Television.* Philadelphia: Temple University Press,
1974.

Laitin, David D. "The Political Economy of Military Rule in Somalia,
The Journal of Modern African Studies [London], 14, No. 3, September 1976, 449-468.

Legum, Colin (ed.). *Africa Contemporary Record: Annual Survey and
Documents, 1974-75.* New York: Africana Publishing, 1975.

Legum, Colin, and John Drysdale (eds.). *Africa Contemporary Record: Annual Survey and Documents, 1968-69.* London: Africa Research, 1969.

———. *Africa Contemporary Record: Annual Survey and Documents, 1969-70.* Exeter: Africa Research, 1970.

Legum, Colin, and Anthony Hughes (eds.). *Africa Contemporary
Record: Annual Survey and Documents, 1970-71.* London: Rex
Collings, 1971.

———. *Africa Contemporary Record: Annual Survey and Documents, 1971-72.* New York: Africana Publishing, 1972.

Legum, Colin, Elizabeth Clements, and Richard Synge (eds.). *Africa Contemporary Record: Annual Survey and Documents, 1972-73.* New York: Africana Publishing, 1973.

———. *Africa Contemporary Record: Annual Survey and Documents, 1973-74.* New York: Africana Publishing, 1974.

Lewis, I.M. "The Politics of the 1969 Somali Coup," *Journal of Modern African Studies* [London], X, No. 3, October 1972, 383-408.

MacManus, James. "Somalia Comes Out of Its Shell." *Manchester Guardian Weekly* [London], 112, No. 13, March 29, 1975, 8.

Mumin, Hassan Sheikh. *Leopard among the Women, Shabeelnaagood: A Somali Play.* (Trans., B.W. Andrzejewski.) London: Oxford University Press, 1974.

Noor, Muhammad, Haji N.A. "The Legal System of the Somali Democratic Republic." In Kenneth R. Redden (ed.), *The Legal Systems of Africa Series.* Charlottesville, Virginia: Michie, 1972.

Pestalozza, Luigi. *The Somalian Revolution.* (Trans., Peter Glendening.) Paris: Editions Afrique, Asie, Amérique Latine, 1974.

Roppa, Guy M. "Communication for Modernization in a Nomadic Society: Conditions and Prospects in Somalia." Unpublished Master's thesis. Bloomington: Department of Journalism, Indiana University, March 1970 (mimeo.).

Siad Barre, Mohamed. *My Country and My People: Collected Speeches, 1970-1971,* II. Mogadishu: Ministry of Information and National Guidance, October 1971.

———. *My Country and My People: Collected Speeches, 1971-1972,* III. Mogadishu: Ministry of Information and National Guidance, October 1973.

Somalia Laws, Statutes, etc. "Decree of the President of the Supreme Revolutionary Council of 8 May, 1972, No. 126. 'Organization and Establishment—Ministry of Foreign Affairs,'" *Bollettino Ufficiale* (Mogadishu), III, No. 9, Supplement No. 4, September 28, 1972, 969-979.

"La Prima Carta della Rivoluzione," *Bollettino Ufficiale* (Mogadishu), I, No. 1, October 21, 1969, 1-5.

"Law No. 34 of September 22, 1974: Ordinamento Guidiziario," *Faafin Rasmi ah* (Official Bulletin) (Mogadishu), Second year, No. 10, Supplement No. 1, October 11, 1974, 470-485.

"Law No. 36 of April 26, 1973: Foreign Service Law," *Bollettino Ufficiale* (Mogadishu), IV, No. 5, May 2, 1973, 494-507.

Somalia. Ministry of Information. *The Development of Broadcasting in Somalia.* Mogadishu: 1968.

Somalia. Ministry of Information and National Guidance. *The Portion of Somalia Territory under Ethiopian Colonization.* Mogadishu: 1974.

———. *Somalia: Five Years of Revolutionary Progress.* Mogadishu: 1974.

———.Somalia's Socialist Revolutionary Construction, 1969-73. Mogadishu: October 1973.

———. *Somalia Today: General Information.* (Rev. ed.) Mogadishu: 1970.

———. *Somalia under the Revolution: Two Years of Progress.* Mogadishu: 1971.

Somalia. Ministry of Information and National Guidance. Broadcasting Department. *Broadcasting Handbook.* Mogadishu: 1972.

Somalia. Ministry of Planning and Coordination. *Development Programme, 1971-1973.* Mogadishu: 1971.

———. *Draft Development Programme, 1974-1978.* Mogadishu: January 1974.

"The Soviet Presence in Somalia," *Conflict Studies,* No. 54, February 1975, 1-20.

"Le Territoire Francais des Afars et Issas," *Revue Française des Etudes Politiques Africaines* [Paris], No. 85, January 1973, 38-83.

Torgerson, Dial. "3rd World Media: Glory to Government," *Washington Post,* August 10, 1976, A-14.

Touval, Saadia. *Somali Nationalism: International Politics and the Drive for Unity in the Horn of Africa.* Cambridge: Harvard University Press, 1963.

U.S. Congress. 92d Session. House of Representatives. Subcommittee on Africa. *Faces of Africa: Diversity and Progress.* (Report of Special Study Missions to Africa, February and August 1971.) Washington: GPO, 1971.

U.S. Department of Commerce. Office of Technical Services. Joint Publications Research Service—JPRS (Washington).

The following items are from the JPRS series:

Translations on Africa.

"Efforts Made to Involve the Educated in Socialist Development," *Al-Taliah,* Mogadishu, October 3, 1975, 1. (JPRS: 66184, No. 1627, November 20, 1975.)

"Government's Ruling Techniques Revealed, Discussed," *L'Unita,* Rome. October 7, 1971, 3. (JPRS: 54466, No. 1081, November 11, 1971.)

"Growing Cooperation Cited," by Umar Al-Maghribi, *Al Fajr Al-Jadid,* Tripoli, September 6, 1975. (JPRS: 65956, No. 1621, October 17, 1975.)

"Multifaceted Evolution under Revolutionary Regime," by Philippe Decraene, *Le Monde,* Paris, March 26, 1975, 7. (JPRS: 64548, No. 1580, April 15, 1975.)

"Progress Achieved by Somali Government Described," by Philippe Decraene, *Revue Française d'Etudes Politiques Africaines,*

Paris, July 1975, 29-40. (JPRS: 65586, No. 1611, September 2, 1975.)

"Somalia President Outlines Duties of Political Officers." (JPRS: 60719, No. 1405, December 27, 1973.)

"Somalia's Unique Socialist Experiment," *Le Monde*, Paris, December 26, 1973, 1, 3. (JPRS: 61069, No. 1423, January 25, 1974.)

"Somali Minister Outlines Foreign Policy," by Umar Al-Magharibi, *Al Fajr Al-Jadid*, Tripoli, August 28, 1975. (JPRS: 65755, No. 1616, September 25, 1975.)

United States Information Service. *Somali Democratic Republic: Country Data.* Mogadishu: January 1, 1976.

World Radio-TV Handbook, 1976. (Ed., J.M. Frost.) New York: Billboard Publications 1976.

(Various issues of the following periodicals were also used in the preparation of this section: *Africa Research Bulletin* [Exeter], January 1969-May 1976; *Horseed* [Mogadishu], January 1971-November 1975; *Library of Congress Accessions List, Eastern Africa* [Nairobi], October 1968-July 1975; and *New Era* [Mogadishu], February 1970-March 1976.)

Section III. Economic

Betz, Fritz H. *Entwicklungshilfe an Afrika.* Munich: IFO-Institut
für Wirtschaftsforschung, 1970.

Box, Thadis W. "Nomadism and Land Use in Somalia," *Economic
Development and Cultural Change,* 19, No. 3, April 1971, 222-228.

Crozier, Brian. "Soviet Presence in Somalia," *Conflict Studies*
[London], No. 54, February 1975, 1-20.

De Benoist, J.R. "La Somalie Veut Suffire à Ses Besoins," *Afrique
Contemporaine* [Paris], 14, No. 80, July-August 1975, pp. 16-20.

Di Giorgi, Umberto. "Somalia: Learning from the Disaster," *Ceres*
[Rome], 8, No. 3, May-June 1975. 41-42.

Food and Agriculture Organization. *Agricultural and Water Surveys,
Somalia.* (Prepared for the Government of Somalia by the Lockwood Survey Corporation.) Rome 1967.

————. *Agricultural Development Planning.* (Report to the Government of Somalia by K. Basak, No. ETAP 2007.) Rome: 1965.

————. *Date Production.* (Report to the Government of Somalia by
V.H.W. Dowson, No. ETAP 1731.) Rome: 1965.

————. *Desert Locust Control.* (Report to the Government of Somalia by Sardu Sigh Pruthi, No. ETAP 1987.) Rome: 1965.

————. *Food Consumption Survey.* (Report to the Government of
Somalia by M.C. Malakar, No. ETAP 2042.) Rome: 1965.

————. *Somalia: Livestock Development Survey.* Rome: 1967.

————. *The World Banana Economy.* (Commodity Bulletin Series,
No. 50.) Rome: 1971.

German Planning and Economic Advisory Group. *Report on the Progress of Development Projects in the Somali Democratic Republic.*
Mogadishu: 1969.

"IDA Joins Arab and African Funds to Support Somalia's Drought
Rehabilitation," *IDA News Release,* No. 76/15, April 15, 1976.

International Labour Office. "Problems of Nomadism in the Sahelian
Region of Africa." (Technical meeting held in Niamey, September
9-20, 1968.) (mimeo.).

————. *Report to the Government of the Somali Democratic Republic
on the Integrated Development of the Nomadic Zones.* (Regular
Programme of Technical Assistance, ILO-OTA/Somalia R.6.) Geneva: 1972.

International Monetary Fund. "Somalia." Chapter 10 in *Surveys of
African Economies, II: Kenya, Tanzania, Uganda, and Somalia.*
Washington: 1969.

Laitin, David D. "The Political Economy of Military Rule in Somalia," *The Journal of Modern African Studies* [London], 14, No. 3,
September 1976, 449-468.

Lavrencic, Karl. "Spotlight on Somalia." *Africa: An International*

363

Business, Economic, and Political Monthly [London], No. 50, October 1975, 95-109.

Legum, Colin (ed.). *Africa Contemporary Record: Annual Survey and Documents, 1974-75.* New York: Africana Publishing, 1975.

Legum, Colin, and John Drysdale (eds.). *Africa Contemporary Record. Annual Survey and Documents, 1968-69.* London: Africa Research, 1969.

———. *Africa Contemporary Record: Annual Survey and Documents, 1969-70.* Exeter: Africa Research, 1970.

Legum, Colin, and Anthony Hughes (eds.). *Africa Contemporary Record: Annual Survey and Documents, 1970-71.* London: Rex Collings, 1971.

———. *Africa Contemporary Record: Annual Survey and Documents, 1971-72.* New York: Africana Publishing, 1972.

Legum, Colin, Elizabeth Clements, and Richard Synge (eds.). *Africa Contemporary Record: Annual Survey and Documents, 1972-73.* New York: Africana Publishing, 1973.

———. *Africa Contemporary Record: Annual Survey and Documents, 1973-74.* New York: Africana Publishing, 1974.

Lewis, I.M. "The Dynamics of Nomadism: Prospects for Sedentarization and Social Change." Pages 426-442 in Theodore Monod (ed.), *Pastoralism in Tropical Africa.* (Studies presented at Thirteenth International African Seminar held in Niamey, December 1972.) London: International African Institute, 1975.

Lewis, I.M. (ed.) *Abaar: The Somali Drought.* London: International African Institute, February 1975.

Louis, R. "La Nouvelle Loi Coopérative en République Démocratique de Somalie," *Revue des Etudes Coopératives* [Paris], No. 178, Fourth Quarter 1974, 43-57.

Mehmet, Ozay. "Effectiveness of Foreign Aid: The Case of Somalia," *Journal of Modern African Studies* [London], 9, No. 1, May 1971, 31-47.

Organization for Economic Cooperation and Development. *Development Assistance: 1972 Review.* Paris: 1972.

———. *Development Cooperation: 1975 Review.* Paris: November 1975.

———. *Flow of Resources to Developing Countries.* Paris: 1973.

———. *Geographic Distribution of Financial Flows to Developing Countries: Data on Disbursements and Commitments in 1974.* Paris: 1976.

———. *Geographic Distribution of Financial Flows to Less Developed Countries, 1966-1967.* Paris: n.d.

———. *Resources for the Developing World: The Flow of Financial Resources to Less Developed Countries, 1962-1968.* Paris: n.d.

"Rescuing Africa's Rangelands," *Africa: A Business, Economic, and Political Monthly* [London], No. 54, February 1976, 24-25.

Siad Barre, Mohamed. "Somalia Is Part of the World Revolutionary Movement," *New Era* [Mogadishu], Fourth Year, No. 31, March 1976.

―――. "We Intend to Base Our Development on Agriculture and Animal Husbandry," *Ceres* [Rome], 8, No. 3, May-June 1975, 42-25.

Siad Barre (Somalie) a l'Express: "Inféodés, nous...?" *L'Express* [Paris], June 21-27, 1976, 48.

Somalia. Ministry of Information and National Guidance. *Agriculture in the Service of the Nation: More Production with More Efforts.* Mogadishu: June 1974.

―――. *Somalia: Five Years of Revolutionary Progress.* Mogadishu: 1974.

―――. *Somalia under the Revolution: Two Years of Progress.* Mogadishu: 1971.

Somalia. Ministry of Mining. *The Mineral Resources of the Somali Democratic Republic: Summarized Information on the Principal Mineral Occurrences.* (Compiled by R. Landcastle, OPEX Director of Mines.) Mogadishu: July 1970.

Somalia. Ministry of Planning and Coordination. *Development Programme, 1971-1973.* Mogadishu: 1971.

―――. *Development Programme, 1974-1978.* Mogadishu: 1974.

―――. *Draft Development Programme, 1974-1978.* Mogadishu: January 1974.

―――. *A Macroeconomic Approach to Development Planning in the Somali Democratic Republic,* Pt. I: Estimate of Some Basic Data. (Prepared by Dr. Hendrikson of German Planning and Economic Advisory Group.) Mogadishu: August 1970.

Somalia. Ministry of Planning and Coordination. Central Statistical Department. *Statistical Abstract, 1968,* V. Mogadishu: 1969.

―――. *Statistical Abstract, 1971,* VIII. Mogadishu: August 1972.

Somalia. Planning Commission. *Short Term Development Programme, 1968-1970.* Mogadishu: August 1968.

"Somalia since the Revolution: Special Survey," *African Development* [London], 7, No. 11, November 1973, S3-S17.

Somali Republic. Planning and Coordinating Committee for Economic and Social Development. *First Five Year Plan: 1963-1967.* Mogadishu: N. pub., July 1963.

Treakle, H. Charles. *The Agricultural Economy of Somalia.* (ERS-Foreign 310.) Washington: Economic Research Service, U.S. Department of Agriculture, May 1971.

United Nations Economic Commission for Africa. *Summaries of Economic Data, Sixth Year.* (Somalia, No. 9.) Addis Ababa: January 1975.

―――. *Survey of Economic Conditions in Africa, 1973,* Pt. I. New York: 1974.

U.S. Department of Commerce. Office of Technical Services. Joint Publications Research Service—JPRS (Washington).
The following items are from the JPRS series:
Translations on Africa.
"Measures Taken to Curb Smuggling by Officials," *Al-Taliah*, Mogadishu, October 10, 1975. (JPRS: 66184, No. 1627, November 20, 1975.)
"Somalia on the Way to Emergence," by A. Nicolas. *Remarques Africaines*, Brussels, November 1973. (JPRS: 61343, No. 1437, February 27, 1974)
U.S. Department of State. Agency for International Development. *An Evaluation of Agricultural Services: Somali Republic.* Washington: August-September 1969.
————. *Inter-River Economic Exploration: The Somali Republic.* Washington: ICA, January 1961.
————. *U.S. Overseas Loans and Grants and Assistance from International Organizations, July 1, 1945-June 30, 1973.* Washington: May 1974.
U.S. International Cooperation Administration. *Forestry and Range Management Survey: Somalia,* by Marvin Klemme. Rome: United States Overseas Mission, 1957.
Warsame, Abdullah Salad. "A Common Front of the Third World for a New Economic Order," *New Era* [Mogadishu], Fourth Year, No. 31, March 1976, 32-33.
Weinstein, Warren (ed.) *Chinese and Soviet Aid to Africa.* New York: Praeger, 1975.
World Bank Annual Report, 1975. Washington: International Bank for Reconstruction and Development, 1975.
(Various issues of the following periodicals were also used in the preparation of this section: *Africa: An International Business, Economic, and Political Monthly* [London], January 1974-July 1976; *African Development* [London], January 1973-July 1976; *Africa Research Bulletin* [London], January 1974-July 1976; *Arab Report and Record* [London], January 1975-July 1976; *Direction of Trade* [Washington], annual issues No. 5, 1963-67, through No. 9, 1969-73; *IMF Survey* [Washington] (January 8, 1973-September 6, 1976; *International Financial Statistics* [Washington], March-July 1976; *Quarterly Economic Review, East Africa* [London], No. 1, 1968, through No. 4, 1973; *Quarterly Economic Review: Uganda, Ethiopia, Somalia* [London], No. 1, 1974, through No. 1, 1976; and *West Africa* [London], January 1974 through September 1976.)

Section IV: National Security

Abir, Mordechai. *Oil, Power and Politics: Conflict in Arabia, the Red Sea, and the Gulf.* London: Frank Cass, 1974.

Allott, A.N. (ed.) *Judicial and Legal Systems in Africa.* London: Butterworth, 1970.

"Arab Summit," *Africa: An International Business, Economic, and Political Monthly* [London], No. 47, July 1975, 41-42.

Bartlett, Dewey F. *Soviet Military Capability in Berbera, Somalia.* (Report to Committee on Armed Services, Untied States Senate.) Washington: GPO, July 1975.

Bayne, E.A. *Somalia and the United States: The Somali Predicament.* (American Universities Field Staff. Fieldstaff Reports. Northeast Africa Series, XIV, No. 1.) Hanover, New Hampshire: AUFS, April 1967.

————. *Somalia on the Horn: A Counterpoint of Problems Confronting One of Africa's New Nations, Pt. I: The Policeman.* (American Universities Field Staff. Fieldstaff Reports. Northeast Africa Series, VII, No. 5.) Hanover, New Hampshire: AUFS, March 1960.

————. *Somalia's Myths Are Tested. (AMERICAN* Universities Field Staff. Fieldstaff Reports. Northeast Africa Series, XVI, No. 1.) Hanover, New Hampshire: AUFS, October 1969.

Bell, J. Bowyer. *The Horn of Africa: Strategic Magnet in the Seventies.* (Strategy Papers.) New York: Crane, Russak, 1973.

————. "Strategic Implications of the Soviet Presence in Somalia," *Orbis,* XIX, No. 2, Summer 1975, 402-411.

Booth, Richard. *The Armed Forces of African States, 1970.* (Adelphi Papers, No. 67.) London: International Institute for Strategic Studies, May 1970.

Castagno, A.A. "The Horn of Africa and the Competition for Power." Pages 155-180 in Alvin J. Cottrell and R.M. Burrell (eds.), *The Indian Ocean: Its Political, Economic, and Military Importance.* New York: Praeger, 1972.

————. "Somalia Goes Military," *Africa Report, XV, No. 2,* February 1970, pp. 25-27.

————. "The Somali-Kenyan Controversy: Implications for the Future," *Journal of Modern African Studies* [London], II, No. 2, July 1964, 165-188.

————. "We Want to Restore Dignity and Confidence to the People: Somalia's President Talks to A.A. Castagno," *Africa Report,* XVI, No. 9, December 1971, 23-25.

Castagno, Margaret. *Historical Dictionary of Somalia.* Metuchen, New Jersey: Scarecrow Press, 1975.

Clapham, Christopher. "Ethiopia and Somalia." Pages 1-24 in *Conflicts in Africa.* (Adelphi Papers, No. 93.) London: International Institute for Strategic Studies, December 1972.

Couhat, Jean Labayle (ed.). *Combat Fleets of the World, 1976-1977: Their Ships, Aircraft, and Armament.* (Trans., James J. Mc-Donald.) Annapolis: U.S. Naval Institute, 1976.

Crozier, Brian. "Soviet Presence in Somalia," *Conflict Studies* [London], No. 54, February 1975, 1-20.

Culmie, Afrah Hussein. "The Blue Berets of the Somali Republic" *International Police Academy Review,* I, No. 2, April 1967, 1-3, 16-17.

Davidson, Basil. "Somalia in 1975: Some Notes and Impressions," *Issue,* V, No. 1, Spring 1975, 19-26.

Decraene, Philippe. "Scientific Socialism: African Style," *Africa Report,* XX, No. 3, May-June 1975, 46-51.

Desfosses, Helen. "Naval Strategy and Aid Policy: A Study of Soviet-Somali Relations." Pages 183-201 in Warren Weinstein (ed.), *Chinese and Soviet Aid to Africa.* New York: Praeger, 1975.

"Djibouti: Time Bomb," *Africa: An International Business, Economic, and Political Monthly* [London], No. 56, April 1976, 43-44.

Dupuy, Trevor N., and John A. Andrews (eds.). *The Almanac of World Military Power.* (3d ed.) New York: R.R. Bowker, 1974.

"Eastern Advances," *Africa: An International Business, Economic, and Political Monthly* [London], No. 21, May 1973, 48-50.

Ganzglass, Martin. *Penal Code of the Somali Democratic Republic.* New Brunswick: Rutgers University Press, 1971.

Hess, Robert L. *Italian Colonialism in Somalia.* Chicago: University of Chicago Press, 1966.

Jane's Fighting Ships, 1975-76. (Ed:, John E. Moore.) London: Jane's Yearbooks, 1976.

Joshua, Wynfred, and Stephen P. Gilbert. *Arms for the Third World: Soviet Military Aid Diplomacy.* Baltimore: Johns Hopkins University Press, 1969.

Jukes, Geoffrey. *The Indian Ocean in Soviet Naval Policy.* (Adelphi Papers, No. 87.) London: International Institute for Strategic Studies, May 1972.

Labayle, Jean. "Somalie: Au sujet de Berbera," *Défense Nationale* [Paris], XXXI, October 1975, 186-187.

Lavrencic, Karl. "Djibouti: An Afro-Arab Solution?" *Africa: An International Business, Economic, and Political Monthly* [London], No. 57, May 1976, 63-66.

Legum, Colin (ed.). *Africa Contemporary Record: Annual Survey and Documents, 1974-75.* New York: Africana Publishing, 1975

Legum, Colin, and John Drysdale (eds.). *Africa Contemporary Record: Annual Survey and Documents, 1969-70.* Exeter: Africa Research, 1970.

Legum, Colin, and Anthony Hughes (eds.). *Africa Contemporary Record: Annual Survey and Documents, 1970-71.* London: Rex Collings, 1971.

————. *Africa Contemporary Record: Annual Survey and Documents, 1971-72.* New York: Africana Publishing, 1972.

Legum, Colin, Elizabeth Clements, and Richard Synge (eds.). *Africa Contemporary Record: Annual Survey and Documents, 1972-73.* New York: Africana Publishing, 1973.

————. *Africa Contemporary Record: Annual Survey and Documents, 1973-74.* New York: Africana Publishing, 1974.

Lewis, I.M. *The Modern History of Somaliland: From Nation to State.* New York: Praeger, 1965.

————. "The Politics of the 1969 Somali Coup," *Journal of Modern African Studies* [London], X, No. 3, October 1972, 383-408.

————. "Somalia." Pages 739-753 in *Africa South of the Sahara, 1975.* London: Europa Publications, 1975.

Lewis, I.M. (ed.) *Abaar: The Somali Drought.* London: International African Institute, February 1975.

Lydgate, Charles. "Kenya Sets Off on the African Arms Race," *African Development* [London], X, No. 6, June 1976, 569.

The Military Balance, 1975-1976. London: International Institute for Strategic Studies, 1975.

Noor Muhammad, Haji N.A. "The Legal Systems of the Somali Democratic Republic." In Kenneth R. Redden (ed.), *The Legal Systems of African Series.* Charlottesville, Virginia: Michie, 1972.

Pestalozza, Luigi. *The Somalian Revolution.* (Trans., Peter Glendening.) Paris: Editions Afrique, Asie, Amérique Latine, 1974.

Pothholm, Christian P. *Four African Political Systems.* Englewood Cliffs: Prentice-Hall, 1970.

Puzo, William Daniel. *Mogadishu, Somalia: Geographic Aspects of Its Evolution, Population, Functions, and Morphology.* Ph.D. dissertation. University of California at Los Angeles, 1972. Ann Arbor: Xerox University Microfilms. 73-10465.

Robbs, Peter. "Africa and the Indian Ocean," *Africa Report,* XXI, No. 3, May-June 1976, 41-45.

Roucek, Joseph S. "Somalia in Geopolitics," *New Africa* [London], VII, No. 5, May 1965, 9-10, 22.

Siad Barre, Mohamed. *My Country and My People: Collected Speeches.* Mogadishu: Ministry of Information and National Guidance, October 1970.

————. *My Country and My People: Collected Speeches, 1970-1971,* II. Mogadishu: Ministry of Information and National Guidance, October 1971.

————. *My Country and My People: Collected Speeches, 1971-1972,* III. Mogadishu: Ministry of Information and National Guidance, October 1973.

Sivard, Ruth Leger. *World Military and Social Expenditures, 1976.* Leesburg, Virginia:WMSE Publications, 1976.

Smaldone, Joseph P. "Materials for the Study of African Military

History," *A Current Bibliography on African Affairs*, IV, No. 3, May 1971, 177-190.

Smolansky, Oles M. "Soviet Entry into the Indian Ocean: An Analysis." Pages 337-356 in Alvin J. Cottrell and R.M. Burrell (eds.), *The Indian Ocean: Its Political, Economic, and Military Importance.* New York: Praeger, 1972.

Somalia Laws, Statutes, etc.

"Decree of the President of the Supreme Revolutionary Council of January 4, 1973, No. 14: Police Regulations," *Bollettino Ufficiale* (Mogadishu), IV, No. 1, Supplement No. 3, January 17, 1973, 121-247.

"Law No. 2 of December 23, 1972: Organization of the Police Force," *Bollettino Ufficiale* (Mogadishu), IV, No. 1, Supplement No. 3, January 17, 1973, 98-109.

"Law No. 37 of September 10, 1972: Law on the Somali Territorial Sea and Ports," *Bollettino Ufficiale* (Mogadishu), IV, No. 1, Supplement No. 7, July 21, 1973, 244-249.

Somalia. Ministry of Information and National Guidance. *Beautiful Somalia.* Mogadishu: 1972.

―――. *Somalia's Socialist Revolutionary Construction, 1969-73.* Mogadishu: October 1973.

―――. *Somalia Today: General Information.* (Rev. ed.) Mogadishu: 1970.

―――. *Somalia under the Revolution: Two Years of Progress.* Mogadishu: 1971.

Somalia. Ministry of Planning and Coordination. *Draft Development Programme, 1974-1978.* Mogadishu: January 1974.

Somalia. Ministry of Planning and Coordination. Central Statistical Department. *Statistical Abstract, 1971,* VIII. Mogadishu: August 1972.

Somalia. Presidency of the Supreme Revolutionary Council. General Directorate of Planning and Coordination. Central Statistical Department. *Statistical Abstract, 1973.* (No. 10.) Mogadishu: September 1975.

"Somalia," *The Times* [London], Special Supplement, March 9, 1971, I-IV.

Thurston, Raymond. "Détente in the Horn," *Africa Report*, XIV, No. 2, February 1969, 6-13.

U.S. Arms Control and Disarmament Agency. *World Military Expenditure and Arms Trade, 1963-1973.* (ACDA Publication, No. 74.) Washington: GPO, 1975.

U.S. Department of Commerce. Office of Technical Services. Joint Publications Research Service—JPRS (Washington). The following items are from the JPRS Series:

Translations on Africa.

"Afriscope Interviews Somali Head of State," *Afriscope*, Lagos, June 1974. (JPRS: 62365, No. 1487, July 1, 1974.)

"Anti-Tribal Law," October 1973. (JPRS: 60278, No. 1381, October 15, 1973.)

"Arab-Somali Relations Seen Improving," *Al-'Arabi*, Kuwait, January 1975. (JPRS: 64245, No. 1569, March 5, 1975.)

"Controversy over Soviet Military Base in Berbera Resolved," by Bakr al-Shargawi, *Al-Usbu' Al-'Arabi*, Beirut, July 7, 1975. (JPRS: 65629 No. 1613, September 8, 1975.)

"FRG Reviews Police Aid Program," *Stella d'Ottobre*, Mogadishu, April 11, 1972. (JPRS: 56062, No. 1160, May 22, 1972.)

"Government's Ruling Techniques Revealed, Discussed," *L'Unita*, Rome, October 7, 1971, 3. (JPRS: 54466, No. 1081, November 11, 1971.)

"Legislation to Curb Drunkenness Promulgated," August 8, 1973. (JPRS: 59838, No. 1355, August 17, 1973.)

"Measures Taken to Curb Smuggling by Officials," *Al-Taliah*, Mogadishu, October 10, 1975. (JPRS: 66184, No. 1627, November 20, 1975.)

"Multifaceted Evolution under Revolutionary Regime," Philippe Decraene, *Le Monde*, Paris, March 26, 1975, 7. (JPRS: 64548, No. 1580, April 15, 1975.)

"No Soviet Base in Berbera, President Asserts," by 'Ali Hashim, *Al-Nahar*, Beirut, July 6, 1975. (JPRS: 65372, No. 1606, August 1, 1975.)

"Police Servants of the People," by Ahmed Zaki Gulaid, *Dawn*, Mogadishu, December 31, 1971. (JPRS: 55071, No. 1111, February 1, 1972.)

"Progress Achieved by Somali Government Described," by Philippe Decraene, *La Revue Française d'Etudes Politiques Africaines*, Paris, July 1975, 29-40. (JPRS: 65586, No. 1611, September 2, 1975.)

"Soviet Assistance Helps Somalia on Independent Path," by Vasiliy Andrianos, *Za Rubezhom*, Moscow, September 1975. (JPRS: 66138, No. 1625, November 12, 1975.)

"Soviet-Somali Cooperation Reported by Somali Official," *Za Rubezhom*, Moscow, September 1975. (JPRS: 65929, No. 1620, October 15, 975.)

"Success of Socialist Mobilization Program Described," by Christian Hoche, *Le Figaro*, Paris, May 16, 1973. (JPRS: 59601, No. 1341, July 24, 1973.)

U.S. Department of State. Bureau of Public Affairs. Office of Media Services. *Background Notes: Somalia*. (Department of State publication, No. 7881.) Washington: GPO, April 1974.

United States Information Service. *Somali Democratic Republic: Country Data*. Mogadishu: January 1, 1976.

World Armaments and Disarmament SIPRI Yearbook, 1975. Cambridge: MIT Press, 1975.

(Various issues of the following periodicals were also used in the preparation of this section: *Africa Research Bulletin* [Exeter], January 1969-May 1976; *Arab Report and Record* [London], January 1975-May 1976; *New Era* [Mogadishu], February 1970-November 1974; *New York Times*, May-July 1976; and *Washington Post*, May-July 1976.)

GLOSSARY

abbaan—Patron, in a relationship between a member of a dominant and a member of a servile group; also used to refer to a host who bears some responsibility for a guest in his camp, village, or territory and to a man who acts as the protector of a merchant traveling through an area.

baraka—Blessing. To have *baraka* is to be in a state of special blessedness and therefore to have special power.

challe—See *jalle.*

clan—A large group of people believed to be descendants through males of a common ancestor whose name is also the name of the clan. Several clans constitute a clan-family *(q.v.),* and each clan is divided into a number of lineages *(q.v.).*

clan-family—A group of clans *(q.v.)* believed to be ultimately linked by descent from a common ancestor. The six clan-families are Darod, Hawiya, Isaq, Dir, Digil, and Rahanwein.

contract *(heer)*—An agreement, often written, among members of an existing group (lineage, *q.v.*) or of more than one such group explicitly setting out their rights and duties in specified circumstances. A contract is the basis of a *dia*-paying group *(q.v.).*

dia-paying group—A group bound by contract either to pay blood compensation *(dia)* or to collect it if one of its members is the perpetrator or victim of homicide or other damage. Members of the group may also be bound by other rules agreed to by contract.

fiscal year—Corresponds to calendar year.

GDP—Gross domestic product. The sum of value added in domestic activities. Value added in any activity is equivalent to the difference between material inputs and gross output and comprises compensation of employees, profits, and depreciation (consumption of capital). In the case of subsistence production these are imputed returns to the labor and investment of the farm family.

GNP—Gross national product. GDP *(q.v.)* less net factor payments (compensation of employees, profits, and depreciation) remitted abroad. A more accurate measure than GDP of income accruing to nationals from domestic activities.

Haud—Wet season grazing area, lying partly in southern part of northern Somalia, partly in Ethiopia.

heer—Contract *(q.v.),* compact, or treaty.

holding grounds—Area to which livestock, especially cattle, are brought to be fattened before sale.

jalle—(Sometimes *challe*); Somali term translated as comrade and widely used in public and official contexts. Precedes other titles, e.g., comrade general.

jamaha—An agricultural community established by an Islamic brotherhood.

jiffo-paying group—A narrow group of kin responsible for paying or receiving that portion of the bloodwealth *(dia)* that goes to the close kin of the victim of a homicide. *See dia*-paying group.

lineage—A group of persons tracing descent from a common ancestor; in Somalia the ancestor is male, and descent is traced through males. The group carries his name. A lineage may be part of a larger one and consist of several smaller ones.

Northern Region—Sometimes used in official documents before the coup of October 1969 to refer to that part of Somalia formerly under British rule (British Somaliland).

qadi—A magistrate applying the sharia *(q.v.)* usually in subordinate courts.

rer—Meaning descendants of; applied to the members of a lineage *(q.v.)* of any size and genealogical depth; *rer* is followed by the name of the ancestor; the term is sometimes applied to a group even if its members are not necessarily descended from a common ancestor; *rer* is then followed by the name of the group.

Saab—Applied to the sedentary, agricultural Somali living between the Juba and Shabelle rivers and comprising the members of the Digil and Rahanwein clan-families. Contrasted to Samaal *(q.v.)*.

sab—Meaning low. Term used by the Somali to refer to groups having low occupational and social status. To be distinguished from Saab *(q.v.)*.

Samaal—Those Somali of pastoral nomadic tradition, principally of four clan-families (Darod, Dir, Isaq, and Hawiya), in contrast to the Saab *(q.v.)*.

sharia—Islamic law. In Somalia the Shafii school of Islamic law.

sheikh—A term sometimes used for a *wadad (q.v.)*.

shir—Council of elders (all adult males) of a clan *(q.v.)* or lineage *(q.v.)*.

Somali shilling (Sh)—Currency since independence in 1960, divided into 100 Somali cents. The par value of the Somali shilling corresponded to that of the British shilling until the British devaluation of November 1967. Through 1970 the value was US$0.139; since then it has fluctuated but averaged US$0.144 in 1971, US$0.143 in 1972, and US$0.159 from 1973 through June 1976.

Southern Region—Sometimes used in official documents before October 1969 to refer to that part of Somalia formerly under Italian rule (Italian Somalia or Trust Territory of Somaliland under Italian Administration).

sultan—A term used for the head of a clan *(q.v.)* or lineage *(q.v.)* where such an office exists; a sultan did not have substantial secular authority.

SYL—Somali Youth League. Dominant political party before independence and through 1969.

tariqa—In Islam an order of religious devotees; a religious brotherhood.

tribe—A term sometimes applied to a clan-family *(q.v.)*.

wadad (pl., *waddado*)—A religious figure or functionary; member of a *tariqa (q.v.)* or of a hereditary lineage of religious figures; the Arabic term *sheikh* is sometimes used for *wadad*.

waranle—Spear carrier (warrior). Applied to adult males, particularly those of the pastoral tradition; excluded from this category are religious figures. *See wadad.*

World Bank—International Bank for Reconstruction and Development (IBRD). Leading multilateral lending and advisory agency.

World Bank Group—Consists of the International Bank for Reconstruction and Development (IBRD) and its two financial affiliates, the International Finance Corporation (IFC), which became operational in 1956, and the International Development Association (IDA), which became operational in 1960. IFC works specifically with the private sector in developing countries; IDA operates in the same sectors and with the same policies as the World Bank but provides credits only to the poorer developing countries and on easier terms than conventional World Bank loans.

SOMALIA

INDEX

380

executive functions (see also cabinet; Council of Ministers; government, national; ministries; president; prime minister): 32, 141-142, 143 exports (see also foreign trade): x, 26, 31, 189, 213, 275, 276, 284, 287, 289, 292; charcoal, 272, 284; farm, 266; livestock, 290, 299; to socialist countries, 290-291; spices, 288-289; and the world recession, 215

family life (see also clan-family; descent groups; kinship; men; nomads; rural society; social system; women): 67, in camps, 96-97; and welfare, 110

Fanole (place): 238; irrigation project, 229, 295; sugar complex, 225, 240, 261, 279, 288

Farah, Nuruddin: 134

farming (see also camels; cultivators; droughts; irrigation; jamahayo): x, 6-7, 8-9, 19, 212, 213, 249, 253-258, 261-267; dryland, 244-245, 249, 254-258; collectives, 7, 206, 211, 220, 236, 260, 262; cooperatives, 7, 77, 210-211, 218, 232, 236, 245, 266; machinery, 211, 235, 244, 266; sedentary, 97, 99, 103, 104; state, 7, 203-204, 206, 210, 236, 239, 260, 261, 263; tenant, 246

films: 136, 200-201

firearms: 331-332

fishing (see also occupational groups): x, 8, 54, 56, 99, 270-271, 275; communities, 71, 99; and employment, 204, 243; and industry, 284, 291; prejudice against, 270, 271; tuna, 260, 270-271, 278

floods: 50, 295

Food and Agriculture Organization (FAO) (see also United Nations): 103, 246, 250, 251, 253, 268, 271, 280, 296; Lockwood Survey, 254-255; Rangeland Conservation and Development Project, 247

food supply (see also World Food Program): 102-104, 213, 216, 237, 241-242; and the Arab League, 185; from Asia, 295; black market, 216; famine, 8, 219, 242; fluctuations, 253-254; and land use, 247-248; milk, 98, 102, 265, 267-268; rationing, 103, 126, 261

foreign aid (see also Arab Fund for Economic and Social Development; China, People's Republic of; European Development Fund (EDF); European Economic Community (EEC); Internation-al Bank for Reconstruction and Development (IBRD); International Development Association (IDA); International Finance Corporation; International Monetary Fund (IMF); Soviet Union; United Arab Emirates; United Nations Development Program (UNDP); United States; World Food Program (WFP): x-xi, 5, 6, 186, 205-206, 208, 209, 214, 216, 217, 219, 220, 221-230, 288; Arab, 110, 185, 220, 221, 223, 224, 225-226, 228; grants, 229-230 Italian, 189, 207, 224, 259; technical assistance, 209

foreign debts: 213, 214, 229

foreign exchange: 207, 213, 216

foreign relations (see also Arabs; Egypt; Ethiopia; France; Great Britain; Italy; Kenya; Ogaden Region; Soviet Union; treaties; United States): ix-x, 171, 191; improving relations, 177-180; irredentism, 27, 171, 172, 174-176, 177, 178, 179, 180; proposed plebiscites, 174; and the West, 185-186, 188-191

foreign trade (see also exports; imports): x, 276, 283-297; deficit, 275, 287, 288; government control of, 276, 289

forests: 50, 51, 271-272; mangroves, 51

Four Power Commission: 29-30

France (see also French Somaliland; French Territory of Afars and Issas (FTAI): 159, 171, 189; in colonial period, 20, 21, 22-23, 24, 29, 157, 181-182

freedom of assembly: 331

freedom of expression (see also communication): ix, 130, 153, 154, 158, 337; censorship, 193, 200-201; films, 200-201; government control of, 193-194, 195, 198-199; and intellectuals, 129; and public criticism, ix, 6, 330, 349; and rumor mongering, 166; and the United Nations, 31

freedom of religion: 94

French Somaliland: 13, 27, 34, 181

French Territory of Afars and Issas (FTAI): v, 1, 45, 54, 160, 171, 181-183; school bus capture, 312; Somali in, 174, 306, 312

Front for the Liberation of the Somali Coast (FLSC): 182, 312

futa: 102

Galaday (place): 291

Galgduud Region: xvi, 52

Galla people: 15, 16, 18, 19, 86, 175, 306

gas, natural: 52, 180, 311

Gaveire Kedie, Salah: 167
Gelib (town): xvi, 239
German Democratic Republic (East Germany): 186, 276
Germany, Federal Republic of (West Germany): 11, 122, 198, 214, 258, 263, 265, 278, 294-295, 297; and police force, 189, 325, 334, 338
Ghalib, Jama Muhammad: 340, 345
Ghalib, Omar Arteh: 173
Golweyn: 297
government, local (*see also* administrative divisions; *dia*-paying; *shir* meetings): ix, 77, 150-151; and the military, 309; in the preindependence period, 36; and socialist indoctrination, 151
government, national (*see also* cabinet, executive functions; judicial system; legislative functions; Supreme Council; Supreme Revolutionary Council): viii-x, 141-152; opposition to, 330, 349; structure of, 143-149, 160
grains (*see also* crops): 236, 239, 244, 266, 276; corn, 98, 235, 263; imports, 284-285, 287; industry, 281; sorghum, 98, 235, 257, 258, 263, 268
Great Britain (*see also* British Somaliland): ix, 13-14, 54, 55, 147, 186, 188-189; and banking, 207; and the colonial period, 20, 21-29, 31, 143, 157-158, 175, 176; Imperial British East Africa Company, 21; and industry, 279
Grechko, Andrei: 325
gross domestic product (GDP): x, 5, 203, 213, 219, 275
gross national product (GNP): 233, 313
Guban (plain): 48, 238
guerrillas: 24, 25, 176, 179, 307, 308, 312, 336
guilds: 74
Gulf of Aden: xvi, 11, 20, 21, 46, 50, 55

Hafun (place): 99
Halane Revolutionary Training School: 152
Hargeysa (place): xvi, 28, 50, 57, 100, 101, 126, 128, 198, 254, 281, 298, 301, 302
Hassan, Abdullahi Mahmud: 338
Hatrawi, Mohamed Ibrahim: 134
Haud Region: 36, 49, 50, 96, 173, 176, 177, 238
Hawiya clan-family: 19, 33, 34, 37, 38, 61, 98, 137, 162, 241
health (*see also* diet and nutrition, disease): 104-109; exorcism, 135; folk

medicine, 108; spending for, 222
Hersi, Daud Abdullah: 307
Hiiraan Region: xvi, 105
Home Guard: 321
Horn of Africa: 20, 45, 159, 171, 181, 189, 310, 311, 312
hospitals (*see also* health): 106-107, 245
housing: 100-102; furnishings, 101-102; nomad, 100, 101, 255; rural, 101, 255; shanty town, 101; urban, 100, 101
human rights (*see also* civil liberties; freedom of expression): 147-150
Humphrey, Hubert H.: 190
Hussein, Abdirazak Haji: 38-39
Hussein, Ali: 134
Hussein, Haji Mohamed: 30, 34, 35, 38

Ibrahim Hassan Jebro, Sheikh: 86
Ifat (state): 18
imports (*see also* foreign trade): x, 216, 275, 284-286, 288, 289, 292, 294, 301; and aid, 276; food, 213, 236, 287-288; taxes, 233
income: distribution of, 210, 212, 221; per capita, 95
independence (*see also* nationalism): 30, 31, 33, 35, 37-42, 142, 143; north-south disputes, 37-38
Indian Ocean: xvi, 55, 172, 303, 325
indoctrination. *See* scientific socialism
industry (*see also* bananas; fishing; livestock; mineral resources; nationalization; sugar): x, 207, 210, 213, 274, 276-283; clothing and textiles, 275, 277, 278, 279, 280, 288; food processing, 275, 277-280; iron, 281; and private investment, 210
intellectual expression (*see also* languages): 129-130
International Bank for Reconstruction and Development (IBRD): x, 11, 224, 233, 256-257, 300
International Development Association (IDA): 126, 129, 220, 224, 229, 243, 245, 252, 255, 262-263, 273, 297, 298, 300; Highway Development Program, 299
International Finance Corporation: 278
International Labor Office: 120
International Labor Organization (ILO): 107, 110, 250, 267, 269
International Monetary Fund (IMF): 208, 296
international relations. *See* foreign relations
investments: foreign, 205, 229, 275; pri-

land allocation: 7, 245-247, 257; and brotherhoods, 87; and clans, 245; concessions, 246; and private ownership, 148

Land Tenure Law of 1975: 211, 245, 246

land use: 247-258; cultivation and grazing potential, 247-248, 249; dune stabilization, 252, 257, 298, 314

languages: viii, 9, 72-73, 125, 143, 162; Arabic, 9, 125; Arabic script, vi, 114, 116; and the art of negotiation, 72-73; English, viii, 9, 118, 123, 27, 133, 134; Italian, viii, 9, 127, 189; Osmanya alphabet, 115; and the press, 195, 196; skill in, 2, 72, 73; Somali, viii, 72, 125, 126; Swahili, 15, 71; Wadad Writing, 114; written, vi, viii, 9, 29, 34, 72, 88, 114-116, 124, 126, 133, 141, 163, 189, 195, 197

Las Koreh: 238, 278, 279, 280

League of Arab States (Arab League) (see also Arabs): x, 11, 185, 225, 230, 245; Maritime Academy, 294

League of Nations: 27

Least Developed Country (LDC): 203, 214, 225, 230

legal system. See judicial system

legislative functions: 1, 4-5, 7, 32, 37, 143; abolition of, 5, 42; Legislative Assembly, 32, 36, 41; Legislative Council, 36; National Assembly, 15, 35, 38, 39, 42, 141, 142, 162, 174; parliamentary period, 156, 158, 161-162

Lewis, I. M.: 41-42

Libya: 184, 225-226, 228

lineages. See descent groups

literacy (see also education): viii, 9, 72, 116-117, 124, 141, 165; classes, 76; and the media, 193; and military training, 319, 321

literature (see also drama; poetry): 130-134; oral, 114-115, 130-134, 136

livestock (see also camels; exports; nomads; Trans-Juba Livestock Project): x, 7, 52, 56, 97, 98, 99, 240-241, 242, 250, 251, 259; breeding, 268-269; cattle, 56, 96, 97-98, 99, 267; development programs, 264-265; diseases, 265, 266; erosion, 257-258; goats, 96, 97, 98, 241, 267, 269; herding, 66, 96-97, 236, 243, 245, 252, 255, 264; industry, 210, 211, 213, 216, 218, 219, 275, 284, 286, 287, 294, 299; meat industry, 278, 279-280, 290-291; meat yield, 269; overgrazing, 236, 237, 243, 248-251, 257;

overstocking, 236, 267; ownership of, 168; pastoralism, 63, 66, 235, 240; payments, 66, 67, 97, 306; range deterioration, 250, 252; sheep, 96, 97, 98, 241, 267, 269; stockraising, 203, 235-236, 245, 264-265, 267-270; theft of, 332; trading, 268-269; and tribal conflict, 341

Livestock Development Agency: 264, 266, 280

living conditions (see also diet and nutrition; health; housing): 95-111

lower class (see also social stratification): 9

Manila Declaration of February 1976: 213

manufacturing (see also industry): 213, 274, 275, 276-281; development spending, 222

Mariano, Michael: 36, 93

Marka (place): xvi, 299

markets: nomad, 97; small shops, 168; urban, 100

marriage (see also divorce): 67, 68; exogamous, 67; intermarriage, 74; modern wedding ceremonies, 78; polygamy, 77-78

Marxism (see also communism; scientific socialism): viii, ix, 1, 6, 9, 75, 168, 213; Marxism-Leninism, 163, 168, 172, 211-212; and the military, 319; and religion, 93

meat supply. See livestock

media (see also books; communication; films; newspapers and periodicals; radio): broadcasting, 197-200; printed, 194-197

men (see also Muslims; nomads; social stratification—warriors): 2, 65, 99; elders, 65, 67, 69, 78; equality, 9; and ideals, 156-157; nomad, 96; paternal authority, 344

Menelik II, Emperor: 21, 305

Middle East: 13, 19, 184, 185, 290; exports and imports to, 292, 296; and livestock, 291, 294

migration (see also nomads): internal, 56; urban, 99-100, 236

military. See armed forces

mineral resources (see also gas, natural; petroleum): 45, 51-52, 281-283; gypsum, 282-283; iron, 281, 282; meerschaum, 282; uranium, 282

ministries (see also cabinet; Council of Ministers; executive functions): 37, 38,

ices, 8, 63-64, 69, 91; nomad views, 8, 23

Ogaden: 96, 160, 173, 180, 238, 307, 308, 311

Ogo: 48-49, 50, 238

oil. *See* petroleum

Organization for Economic Cooperation and Development (OECD): x

Organization of African Unity (OAU): x, 171, 172, 176, 177, 178, 180, 185, 308; African Liberation Committee, 180

Organization of Petroleum Exporting Countries (OPEC): 213; aid from, x, 215, 225, 226, 229

Osman, Aden Abdullah: 34, 35, 38-39, 40

pan-Somalism (*see also* foreign relations, irredentism; nationalism): 39, 159-160, 171, 172, 173-183

Panza, Bruno: 115

parliament. *See* legislative functions

pastoralism. *See* livestock

Persian Gulf: 303

petroleum: 52, 174, 180, 185, 213, 229, 281, 311; imports, 285, 295

poetry: classical, 131-132; modern, 133; oral, 114-115, 130-134; themes, 131-132

Police Custodial Corps: 339

police force: 303, 314, 318, 325, 334-341; air wing, 337, 339; British, 28, 306, 307, 334, 335-337; camel constabulary, 334, 336; Darawishta, 315, 337, 338, 340; equipment, 338-339; Italian, 306, 334, 335-336; local, 330-331; and the public attitude, 340; quarters, 341; ranks, 339; secret, 145, 152; specialized units, 338; Somalia Gendarmerie, 28, 334, 336; women, 337

Politburo: 145, 154, 164, 165, 315

political parties (*see also* Somali Socialist Revolutionary Party; Somali Youth League; Supreme Revolutionary Council): 3, 4, 14, 29, 37, 40-41, 61, 73, 141, 142, 145, 153, 156, 160, 164, 165; abolition of, 5, 42, 330; exile parties, 182; Greater Somali League (GSL), 35, 37, 38; Liberal Party, 35; Merehan Union, 32; National United Front (NUF), 36, 37; and socialist indoctrination, 145; Somali Democratic Party, 32; Somali Democratic Union (SDU), 38; Somali Digil Clan Party (Hizbia Digil-Mirifle Somali—HDMS or HDM), 29, 30, 32, 33, 34, 35; Somali Independent Constitutional Party (Hizbia Dustur Mustaquil Somali), 33; Somali National Congress (SNC), 38, 41; Somali Youth Club (SYC), 29; Somaliland National League (SNL), 29, 36, 37, 38; Somaliland National Society (SNS), 28, 29; United Somali Party (USP), 29, 36, 37

political system (*see also* government, local; government, national; social values): 153-169; values, 154-160, 304

population (*see also* ethnic groups; nomads): viii, 45-46, 57-59; age-groups, 58; density, 58; ethnicity, 58; growth rate, 59; homogeneity of, 1, 58, 157; origins of, 15-17; sedentary, 3, 56, 57, 134, 137

ports (*see also* Berbera; Djibouti; shipping): xi, 57, 188, 220, 273, 274, 299-301; and the United States, 273

Portugal: 18

poverty: 93, 95; urban, 100

president (*see also* executive functions; Siad Barre, Mohamed): 4, 6, 35, 37, 38, 39, 141-142, 154, 168

prices: food, 103; and government policy, 206, 216; international price stabilization, 214, 216; world, 215

prime minister (*see also* executive functions): 4, 33, 38, 39-40, 142

prisons: 346-347; juvenile, 346; rehabilitation of, 347

public corporations: 146-147; control over employees, 152

Public Ministry (*see also* courts; judicial system): 149

radio: 131, 133, 158, 193, 197-200, 302; BBC, 199; and border clashes, 177; foreign broadcasts, 130, 199-200; listening centers, 197-198; Voice of America, 199; Voice of Somalia, 176

Radio Hargeysa: 136, 199

Radio Mogadishu: 128, 198, 199

Rahanwein clan-family: 17, 19, 33, 35, 61, 68, 69, 98, 137, 155, 162, 198, 240

railroads: 181

rainfall (*see also* droughts; floods): 45, 46-48, 49, 50, 51, 98, 237, 241-242, 254, 256; and cultivators, 98; monsoons, 46, 300

recession: world, 215

regions. *See* administrative divisions

religion (*see also* Christianity; Islam; schools): viii, 65, 81-94; evil eye, 90, 108; freedom of, 94; rainmaking, 71, 88; rites and ceremonies, 10, 71, 78, 135; and socialism, 168

resources. *See* livestock; mineral re-

sources
Revolution of 1969 (see also Supreme Revolutionary Council): 42, 75-79; and religion, 81; Second Charter, 75
rights. See civil liberties; freedom of expression; human rights; voting
riots: 29, 31, 118, 182
rivers: 45, 49, 55
roads: xi, 11, 40, 104, 186, 187, 220, 273-275, 297-299; Italian, 26; roads, 298-299
Rodd, Rennell: 21
rural society (see also nomads; villages): 63, 74, 95-99, and the economy, 219

Saab group: viii, 2, 13, 19, 61, 63-64, 66, 68-69, 74, 155, 162
Sablale (place): 244
salaries. See wages and salaries
Samaal group: viii, 13, 61, 63, 64-68, 74, 99
Samantar, Mohamed Ali: 144, 145, 163, 314, 315
sanitation: 108-109
Saudi Arabia: 172, 184-185, 225, 240, 275, 290, 294, 302
scholarships (see also education): 121, 128, 129; Italian, 120; and military training, 317; Soviet, 128, 186; United States, 189
School of Islamic Studies: 120
School of Politics and Administration: 120
School of Public Finance and Commerce: 120
schools (see also education): and art work, 139; British, 117-118, Christian, 113, 117-118; colonial, 28; and drama, 136; intermediate, 122, 124-126; Italian, 117; and language, 123-124; nomadic, 113, 119; primary, 118-119, 120-121, 122, 123, 124-126, 128; private, 94; Quranic, 113, 117, 118, 120; 123; secondary, 118, 119-120, 122, 126-127
scientific socialism (see also communism; Marxism): v, ix, 6, 75-76, 81-82, 92, 93, 152, 154, 163, 164, 167-169, 194, 199, 212, 309-310, 348, 349; and the armed forces, 315, 319; and the economy, 205, 232; indoctrination, 6, 76, 93, 145, 151, 152, 164-165; and Islam, 10, 81, 91-92, 93
script. See languages, written
security, internal (see also coups; firearms; judicial system; National Securi-

ty Court; National Security Service): 329-350
security, national. See armed forces; National Security Service
Selassie, Emperor Haile: 178, 179, 307
self-help projects. See employment
Shabelle Dhexe Region: xvi, 105
Shabelle Hoose Region: xvi, 105
Shabelle River: 1, 7, 15, 49-50, 51, 56 239
sharia (see also courts): 83, 147, 343
sheikhs: 85, 86
Shermarke, Abderashid Ali: 35, 38-39, 42, 161, 178, 242, 308; assassination of, 148
shipping (see also ports): 299-301, 316-317; dhows, 273, 288, 289, 299; problems, 294
shir meetings (see also government, local; sultans): 36, 40, 65, 155, 156, 162
Siad Barre, Mohamed: ix, 6, 10, 11, 18, 25, 42, 92-93, 111, 127, 129, 141, 142, 143, 145, 153, 164, 166, 168; and agriculture, 260; and the armed forces, 143, 145, 309, 315, 320; and corruption, 206; and the economy, 205, 207, 208, 209, 210, 211-212, 215, 217-218, 221; and foreign affairs, 172, 180, 185, 188, 191; and internal security, 330, 333, 338, 339, 348, 350
slavery: 2, 13, 15-16, 19, 25, 71, 84
smuggling: 206, 216, 279, 288, 311, 332, 333
social security: 110
social stratification (see also egalitarianism; elite; ethnic groups; occupational groups): 72, 75, 155; bourgeoisie, 9, 75, 304, 348; lower class, 9; military, 308, 319; nomad, 154-155; patrons and clients, 9; status, 9, 63; warriors, 2-3, 66, 81, 157, 303, 304, 305
social system (see also clan-family; descent groups; ethnic groups; nomads; social stratification; tribalism): 16, 61-79; post revolutionary, 75-78; after World War II, 73-75
social values (see also clan-family loyalty; political system, values): 153, 154, 156-157, 158, 160; leadership, 156-157, 160; military virtues, 304, 305
socialism. See communism; Marxism; scientific socialism
soils: 50-51
Somali Airlines: 301-302
Somali Army Officers' Academy: 318

tribalism (*see also* clan-family; ethnic groups; kinship; nomads): 42, 61, 205, 305, 341, 348, 349; antitribalism, 78, 131, 163, 320, 329, 341; military tradition, 304, 305, 319-320; Quraysh of Arabia, 16, 61

Trust Territory of Somaliland: 1, 30, 35, 36, 37, 73, 118, 142, 147, 160, 259, 306-307, 336

Tug Wajaleh (place): 238, 239, 254, 255, 261, 307-308

Ugas, Raage: 133-134

underemployment: 100

unemployment: 76, 100, 126, 203, 204, 205

United Arab Emirates: 225; and roads, 298; and sugar, 279

United Arab Republic: 34

United Brands: 296

United Nations (UN) (*see also* Food and Agriculture Organization (FAO); World Food Program): x, 14, 31, 36, 37, 52, 174, 185, 203, 225; and agriculture, 263; grain prices, 216; industrial aid, 278; prison inspection, 346

United Nations Advisory Council: 30, 31, 32

United Nations Children's Fund (UNICEF): 105, 108

United Nations Conference on Trade and Development (UNCTAD): at Nairobi in 1976, 214

United Nations Declaration of Human Rights: 147-148

United Nations Development Program (UNDP) (*see also* Food and Agriculture Organization): 240, 270, 280, 281, 282

United Nations Educational, Scientific and Cultural Organization (UNESCO): 119

United Nations Emergency Operation: 215, 225

United Nations General Assembly: 14, 30

United Nations Industrial Development Organization (UNIDO): 278

United Nations Special Fund for Most Seriously Affected (MSA): 215, 225, 230

United Nations Trust Territory: 4, 11, 120, 158, 160, 306

United Nations Trusteeship Agreement, 30, 118

United Nations Trusteeship Council, 31

United States: ix, 5, 29, 122, 207-208, 210, 215, 334; Agency for International Development, 990; agricultural aid, 210, 239, 248, 250-251, 255-256, 257, 260; economic and technical assistance, 178, 189-191, 207-208, 214, 222, 224, 226, 271, 273, 278; films, 200; industrial aid, 278, 279; Peace Corps, 190; and price stabilization, 214; police and military aid, 311-312, 313, 316, 323, 325, 326, 334, 338; and Soviet naval base, 188; and trade, 292, 294

United States International Cooperation Administration, 31

universities and colleges (*see also* Somali National University): 127, 129, 265; abroad, 119, 120, 129; military, 318

urban society (*see also* towns): 99-100, 154

urbanization: 58-59, 159

values. *See* political system; social values

vegetation: 50-51

Victory Pioneers (*see also* police force; Young Pioneers): 77, 109, 165, 166, 322, 323, 330; duties, 341; and security surveillance, 330, 341, 350

Vietnam, Democratic Republic of (North Vietnam): 190, 208

villages (*see also* towns): ix, 56-57, 98; councils, 150, 151, 193-194; and the new order, 166

vocational training. *See* technical and vocational training

Vocational Training School: 120

voting: 37, 38, 39; male suffrage, 33; in 1954, 32; in 1969, 40-42; for women, 34, 77

wadaddo (*see also* Islam): 85, 89, 108, 156

wages and salaries: 6, 95, 233; in colonial period, 26; government, 100, 208; military, 322; required pay cuts, 208

Waqooyi Galbeed Region (*see also* North West Region Development Project): xvi, 248, 257, 258

warriors. *See* social stratification

Wasuge, Abdulle: 111

water supply (*see also* irrigation): 49, 55, 66, 96, 108-109, 252, 253; contamination of, 108-109; and livestock, 96, 97, 251; spending for, 222; tank reservoirs, 247, 251; United States project, 191; water law, 251-252; wells, 49, 55, 66, 69, 85, 96, 97, 109 welfare: 109

wells. *See* water supply

Western countries: 185-186, 188-191, 215, 222, 223, 224, 228-229

wildlife: 52-54; birds, 53-54; endangered species, 52-53; insects, 53; reserves, 52-53; snakes, 53

women: clothing, 102; cultivators, 99; and drama, 136; and education, 122, 123, 125; and equality, 9, 66, 77-78, 93, 158, 166, 184, 349; and Islam, 83-84, 90, 122, 184-185, 349; and lineage, 68; maternity leave, 110; nomad, 97; and poetry, 132; policewomen, 337; in sports, 111; and voting, 34

Women's Auxiliary Corps: 321, 323

World Bank. *See* International Bank for Reconstruction and Development

World Food Program (WFP): 107, 110, 208, 218, 224, 225, 252, 261, 274-275, 298

World Health Organization (WHO): 105, 107, 108

World War II: 27, 29

Yassin Nur Hassan: 337

Yemen, People's Democratic Republic of: 184

Young Pioneers (*see also* Victory Pioneers): 258, 261, 321-322

youth. *See* Victory Pioneers; Young Pioneers

Zeila (town): 56

PUBLISHED AREA HANDBOOKS

550-65	Afghanistan	550-39	Indonesia
550-98	Albania	550-68	Iran
550-44	Algeria	550-31	Iraq
550-59	Angola	550-25	Israel
550-73	Argentina	550-69	Ivory Coast
550-169	Australia	550-177	Jamaica
550-176	Austria	550-30	Japan
550-175	Bangladesh	550-34	Jordan
550-170	Belgium	550-56	Kenya
550-66	Bolivia	550-50	Khmer Republic (Cambodia)
550-20	Brazil	550-81	Korea, North
550-168	Bulgaria	550-41	Korea, Republic of
550-61	Burma	550-58	Laos
550-83	Burundi	550-24	Lebanon
550-166	Cameroon	550-38	Liberia
550-96	Ceylon	550-85	Libya
550-159	Chad	550-163	Malagasy Republic
550-77	Chile	550-172	Malawi
550-60	China, People's Republic of	550-45	Malaysia
550-63	China, Republic of	550-161	Mauritania
550-26	Colombia	550-79	Mexico
550-67	Congo, Democratic Republic of (Zaire)	550-76	Mongolia
		550-49	Morocco
550-91	Congo, People's Republic of	550-64	Mozambique
550-90	Costa Rica	550-35	Nepal, Bhutan and Sikkim
550-152	Cuba	550-88	Nicaragua
550-22	Cyprus	550-157	Nigeria
550-158	Czechoslovakia	550-94	Oceania
550-54	Dominican Republic	550-48	Pakistan
550-52	Ecuador	550-46	Panama
550-43	Egypt	550-156	Paraguay
550-150	El Salvador	550-92	Peripheral States of the Arabian Peninsula
550-28	Ethiopia		
550-167	Finland	550-42	Peru
550-29	Germany	550-72	Philippines
550-155	Germany, East	550-162	Poland
550-173	Germany, Federal Republic of	550-181	Portugal
550-153	Ghana	550-160	Romania
550-87	Greece	550-84	Rwanda
550-78	Guatemala	550-51	Saudi Arabia
550-174	Guinea	550-70	Senegal
550-82	Guyana	550-180	Sierra Leone
550-164	Haiti	550-86	Somalia
550-151	Honduras	550-93	South Africa, Republic of
550-165	Hungary	550-171	Southern Rhodesia
550-21	India	550-95	Soviet Union
550-154	Indian Ocean Territories	550-179	Spain

550-27	Sudan, Democratic Republic of	550-74	Uganda
550-47	Syria	550-97	Uruguay
550-62	Tanzania	550-71	Venezuela
550-53	Thailand	550-57	Vietnam, North
550-178	Trinidad and Tobago	550-55	Vietnam, South
550-89	Tunisia, Republic of	550-99	Yugoslavia
550-80	Turkey	550-75	Zambia

☆ U.S. GOVERNMENT PRINTING OFFICE : 1978 O—272-038